Software Development for SAP R/3®

Springer-Verlag Berlin Heidelberg GmbH

Ulrich Mende

Software Development for SAP R/3®

Data Dictionary, ABAP/4®, Interfaces

With Diskette
With 124 Figures and Many Example Programs

Springer

Dr. Ulrich Mende
EDP Consultancy
Senefelder Str. 7
15370 Fredersdorf/ Berlin, Germany
u.mende.edv@t-online.de

Additional material to this book can be downloaded from http://extras.springer.com.

ISBN 978-3-642-62971-6

ACM Computing Classification (1998): D.2

Library of Congress Cataloging-in-Publication Data
Mende, Ulrich.
(Softwareentwicklung für R/3. Englisch)
Software development for SAP R/3®: data dictionary, ABAP/4®, interfaces/
Ulrich Mende.
p. cm. Includes bibliographical references and index.
ISBN 978-3-642-62971-6 ISBN 978-3-642-57225-8 (eBook)
DOI 10.1007/978-3-642-57225-8
1. SAP R/3®. 2. ABAP/4® (Computer program language)
3. Client/server computing. I. Title
HF5548.4.R2M4613 2000
650`.0285`53769--dc21 99-32064 CIP

Originally published by Springer-Verlag Berlin Heidelberg New York in 2000
Softcover reprint of the hardcover 1st edition 2000

Cover design: Künkel + Lopka, Heidelberg
SPIN 10685064 - 45/3142PS - 5 4 3 2 1 0

For my wife Ingrid and my daugther Julia

Preface

The use of commercial standard software is increasing in importance throughout the world. With its R/3 product, SAP AG has brought the package on the market that provides the most comprehensive functionality. When standard solutions are used, there is, a priori, a conflict of aims between what the standard offers and the company-specific requirements. SAP counters this in the R/3 System by building a modular software that can be customized to meet the customer requirements. However, many users still see themselves forced to make in-house developments, to various degrees, to fit the R/3 System. Here they can use the ABAP Workbench that SAP supplies with every system.

The present book targets those persons who need to perform these customer-oriented supplementary developments. It leads the reader through the fundamentals of software development within the R/3 System using the ABAP Workbench. These principles differ from other development environments, in particular, through their complexity and the close integration with the R/3 System. Because an installation for testing and training purposes on the PC at home is not an option, I considered a structured, understandable introduction to the material in the form of a book to be more important. If you initially read the book "offline" from an R/3 System, you will have it much easier later when you use the system directly. You will be familiar with new terms and their interrelationships. You can then concentrate on their form in the system-user interface and the operation of the system.

I am grateful to the Mummert + Partner Consultancy AG, who provided me with generous background and technical support for this book project.

In particular, I would like to thank my colleague, Rainer Illmann, who read the manuscript and provided important comments; Frank Wachtel, who wrote the programs and text parts in Chapter 6; Bernd Jastrow, who developed the transaction manager in Chapter 9; Jens Schötzig and Carola Rensen, who as administrators supported me and provided information for Chapter 2.

My thanks also go to Anthony Rudd, who translated the text into English, and Axel Fräßdorf, who adapted the data and sample programs into English.

I would also like to thank Springer-Verlag, especially Hans Wössner, for the excellent cooperation.

Berlin, January 2000 Ulrich Mende

Table of Contents

1 Introduction

SAP AG, in a spectacular development history, has developed the worldwide largest business DP system: R/3. The reference list of R/3 users covers thousands of companies. SAP is on the way to create a similar market-dominating position in the sector of business standard software that Microsoft has in the area of standard PC software. R/3 thanks its dominant position to the following properties:

- a modern computer and system architecture
- a comprehensive business functionality
- a modern software development environment

R/3 is realized as a multi-level client-server system with the following components:

- a database server (MVS, UNIX, Windows NT)
- multiple application servers (UNIX, Windows NT)
- several presentation servers (Windows 3.1, Windows NT, UNIX)

Support is provided for heterogeneous computer systems (IBM, DEC, SUN, HP, Siemens, PCs), and various operating systems and networks (TCP/IP, LU 6.2, Novell).

The division of the business functionality into modules permits an incremental expansion to the system. All modules are integrated within the company-wide data model. The following factors and capabilities characterize the business functionality:

- client capability
- scalability and parameterability by customizing
- integrated authorization system
- integrated partner system
- complete separation of the user-view from the DP-view
- SAP workflow between modules to handle business processes
- process modeling with the ARIS toolkit
- secure mass data import (migration) using batch input
- executive information systems
- coupling of external systems (archive, CAD)
- R/3 industry solutions, such as for
  - banks
  - insurance companies
  - hospitals
  - energy supply utilities

The development environment plays a central role in the R/3 system by providing the following important characteristics:

- Central data dictionary
- ABAP/4 4GL language (4GL = 4th generation language) with
  - Open SQL
  - Event control
  - Software modularization techniques
    (forms, function modules, reports, transactions, LUWs)
  - Object orientation
- Support for software development in large, distributed teams
- Structuring of development tasks into development classes
- Integration of all tools (navigation, usage references)
- Correction and transport system
- Versioning
- Integrated documentation
- Multilingual capability
- Secure administration of large data files
- Queries
- Matchcodes
- Change log
- Openness and standard interfaces
- Remote Function Call (RFC) from and to external systems
  (R/2, R/3, UNIX, frond-end PC)
- Object Linking and Embedding (OLE)
- Application Link Enabling (ALE)
- Change concept

It is important for the R/3 developer that the complete business functionality of the system is available as source code. This is initially a guarantee that there is no clash between system software and application software (disregarding the quality of the programs). With increasing level of knowledge, the developer will find new ways of using existing software components. There are R/3 users that use the system exclusively for their own development and do not use any additional modules.

1.1 Content and Aim of the Book

Because even the most comprehensive standard software can never satisfy all requirements of a user, even the wide module offering of R/3 will require development effort from the user. This book is aimed at all those persons confronted, either directly or indirectly, with the software development for R/3. These include:

- Computer scientists, business computer specialists, economists and DP managers in the DP departments of R/3 users
- Computer consultants in the DP sector
- Students and university lecturers in computer science, business data processing and economics.

This book arose from many years of developer and consultancy activity with R/3 users in the financial services sector. It covers those problems that frequently confront consultants and application developers.

The first chapters of the book are introductory. Those readers who are (initially) interested only in writing simple reports should read Chapters 5, 6 and 7.

Chapters 8 and 9 are recommended to those readers who want to start with advanced programming techniques and in the dialog programming.

The last chapters discuss the background processing, the data import using batch input and the coupling to external system (file interfaces, RFC, OLE). In contrast to other books about ABAP/4 that largely ignore these questions, this book provides a detailed discussion of these topics. Experience has shown that these problems occur in almost all development tasks for R/3 users.

An introductory chapter on data modeling and a final chapter on development aids (debuggers, runtime analysis) completes this book.

All program examples in the book are based on a data model of a service provider introduced at the start of the book. This data model contains products, partners, contracts, accounts and documents with document positions. The table definitions, relationships and contents are printed in the appendix. Readers can use the table data in the appendix to verify the results of the sample programs specified in the text and so continually check their own level of understanding. Readers can also load the table data from the diskette into the system and then set and solve their own problems using the data.

1.2 Limitations

This book does not replace the R/3 documentation for the development environment or the ABAP/4 language manual. However, whereas the short program examples there only explain a keyword or an instruction in isolation, the aim of this book is to use more complex examples to show solutions for practical problems. In order to concentrate on more important topics, this book is deliberately not intended to be complete.

The operation of the R/3 system and that of the ABAP/4 workbench are also not a central topic of this book, which in this case is restricted to specific references.

2 R/3 Computer and Software Architecture

2.1 Three-level Client-Server Architecture

R/3 can be realized as a three-level client-server system (Figure 2.1). This system configuration provides both simple scalability and a calculatable load distribution. It contains in the general case:

- a database server with a central DBMS
- multiple application servers
- many presentation servers (= front-ends = PCs).

The central DBMS runs on the database server that manages all the R/3 user data and repository data (metadata and software). The application servers process the R/3 system programs and the application programs of the users logged onto these servers. The application servers process and buffer the entered data, or use SQL for access to the database and so load data selections into main storage. The application servers further process these data or pass them to the presentation server for display.

Because many users with large data volumes each operate concurrently on an application server, high transmission rates in the order of MB per second are required to the database server. Consequently, database servers and application servers are normally connected with each other using a fast local network (normally in the immediate vicinity).

The presentation servers represent the user interface of the R/3 system. The dialogs for the data acquisition and the online report outputs are presented here. The presentation servers and the application servers are characterized by only requiring low transmission rates in the order of KB per second. A list displayed with 15 lines each with 70 characters on the dialog requires approximately 1 KB. However, it must be mentioned in this context that the R/3 architecture does not make full use of the graphic capability of the windowing systems used on the presentation servers. The presentation servers, the actual workstations of an R/3 system, can be distributed in some arbitrary manner. The low transmission rates permit them to be linked with an application server in various ways:

- using a local network
- using a leased line
- using the Internet, such as with TCP/IP (Transmission Control Protocol / Internet Protocol)
- using a modem.

This three-level architecture can adapt itself according to the requirements for data volumes, program complexity and number of users. The low demands made on the transfer rates between the front-end and application servers make it particularly suitable for decentral data acquisition and data presentation for decentralized data storage.

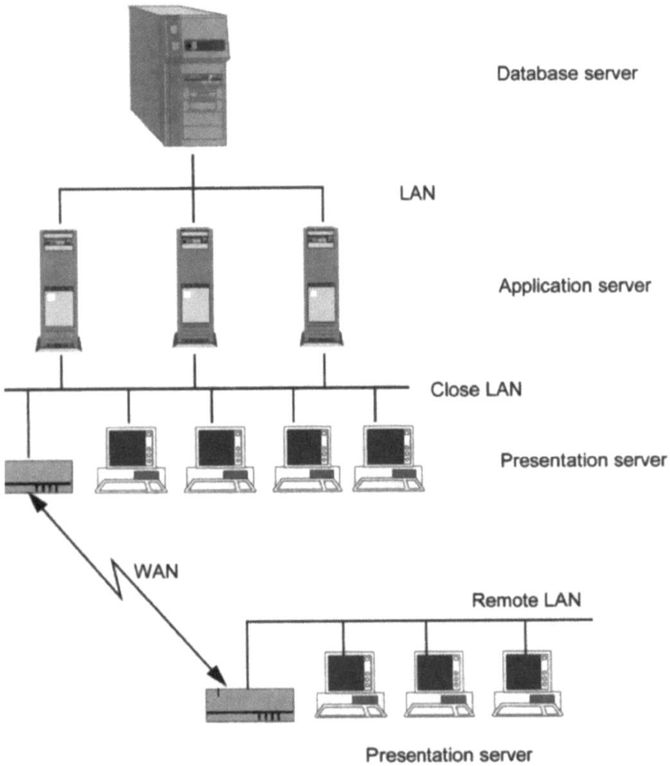

Figure 2.1: Three-level client-server architecture for R/3

The designation of the computers on the second and third level as application and presentation *servers* provide only a single viewpoint. The application server in this regard represents a server for the application programs. At the same time, it adopts a client role at the DB server. The presentation server is a graphics server in the sense of Windows or Motif, the client of which is the associated application server. From the function viewpoint, the presentation server itself is a client of the connected application server.

R/3 supports a wide combination of hardware, operating system software, DBMS and windowing systems for the presentation. Although currently the UNIX operating system is most widely used for the application and DB servers, the integrated solution with Windows NT shows a large growth. The Windows NT solution is particularly appropriate for mid-sized systems with up to approximately 100 front-ends.

Systems are often used for development tasks that realize a two-level special case of the above architecture. The database and application servers run on a few connected front-ends for these systems.

2.1.1 Database Server and DBMS

The relational DBMS (Data Base Management System) selected for R/3 runs on the database server. All metadata and all user data of the associated R/3 installation are stored as tables in a single user's database with the name SAPR3.

The workbench is provided to interactively maintain the table and field definitions, together with other metadata. The Open SQL operations repertoire from ABAP/4 is used to manipulate the user data. The use of Open SQL provides the user with full independence from the associated DBMS. Programs produced in this manner can be freely ported between different databases.

Native SQL also permits access to non-R/3 databases and tables. Similarly, external applications (e.g. SQL, ODBC) have read access to all R/3 tables.

2.1.2 Application Server

The ABAP/4 programs processed on the application servers represent the true functionality of the R/3 system. The application servers provide here a number of services in the form of parallel operating tasks. The single dispatcher process that runs on each application server also controls several different work processes. The following specializations are available for work processes:

- *Dialog work process* is used for the execution of ABAP/4 dialog programs or reports. It alternately assigns the control to the dynpro interpreter or the ABAP/4 interpreter.
- *Batch work process* is required for the processing of reports in background.
- *Spool work process* controls the buffered printing of report lists.
- *Booking work process* is used for the automatic asynchronous booking of logged booking records.
- *Lock work process* controls the SAP-internal lock management.

2.1.3 Presentation Server

The so-called SAPGUI (SAP Graphical User Interface) runs on each presentation server. This terminal program (SAPGUI.EXE) realizes the complete graphical user interface of the R/3 system. It has been written for each window environment (Windows 3.1, Windows NT, OS/2 Presentation Manager, OSF/Motif) and uses the CPI/C protocol to communicate with the dispatcher (or with one of its dialog processes) of the assigned application server. The exchanged data are independent of the associated user interface and are highly compressed. For example, if a dialog is to be displayed on a PC, the application server sends layout and data information, from which the SAPGUI dynamically creates and displays the dialog at run-time.

2.2 Software Architecture

2.2.1 Layer Model

The R/3 software is built using a layer concept (see Figure 2.2). The operating system and network software form the lowest layer. The software of the associated DBMS is based on this layer. The system-dependent parts of the R/3 software are contained in an intermediate layer (middleware) that is written in the C language. The functions provided by this layer are used to process ABAP/4 code from the ABAP/4 interpreter or indirectly from the ABAP/4. They directly access the C kernel or the application server's system.

2.2.2 Application Software

The application layer that forms the upper layer contains the programs written in ABAP/4. These include:

- Basic modules
  - Data Dictionary
  - Data Modeler
  - workbench
  - batch management
  - batch input
  - administration
- Base modules
  - CA Cross-Application Functions
  - WF Workflow
  - OSS Online Service System
  - FI Financial Accounting
  - TR Treasury
  - CO Controlling
  - IM Investment Management
  - EC Enterprise Controlling
  - LO Logistics General
  - SD Sales & Distribution
  - MM Materials Management
  - QM Quality Management
  - PM Plant Maintenance
  - PP Production Planning and Control
  - PS Project System
  - PD Personnel Planning and Development
  - PA Personnel Administration and Payroll Accounting

- Industry modules (IS = Industrial Solution)
  - IS-H — Health
  - IS-B — Banking
  - IS-IS — Insurance Systems
  - IS-IS/PP — Mass encashment and payment for insurance companies
- User developments.

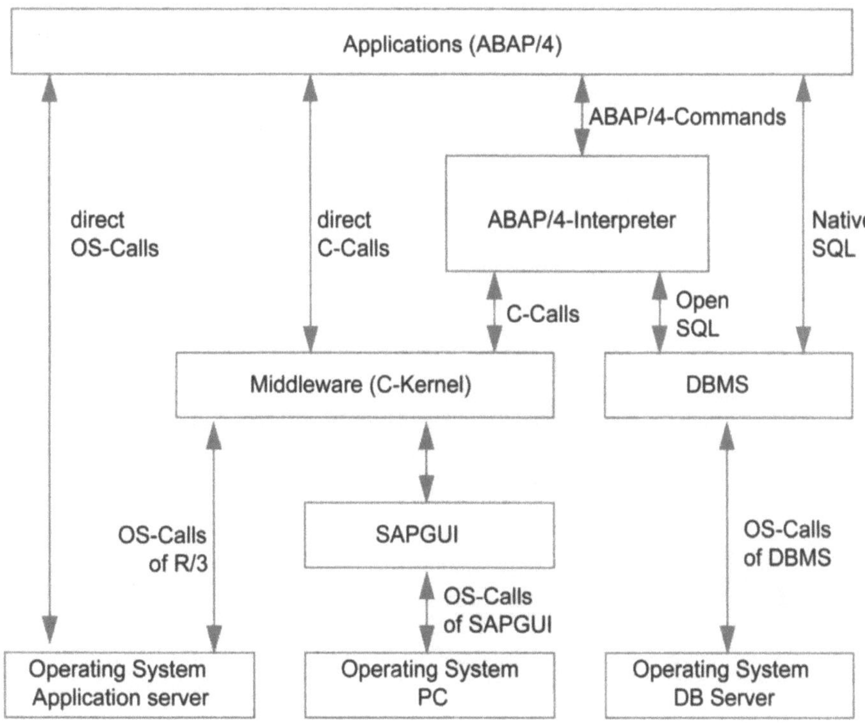

Figure 2.2: R/3 software layer structure

2.3 Operational Modes for Developers

2.3.1 Logon

From Release 3.0 onwards, SAPLOGON.EXE is used to connect to an R/3 system (see Figure 2.3). The user is assigned an application server in the other case of the group selection. This server is explicitly named only in those cases in which a specific application server is to be used (e.g. for file imports from the file system of a specific server).

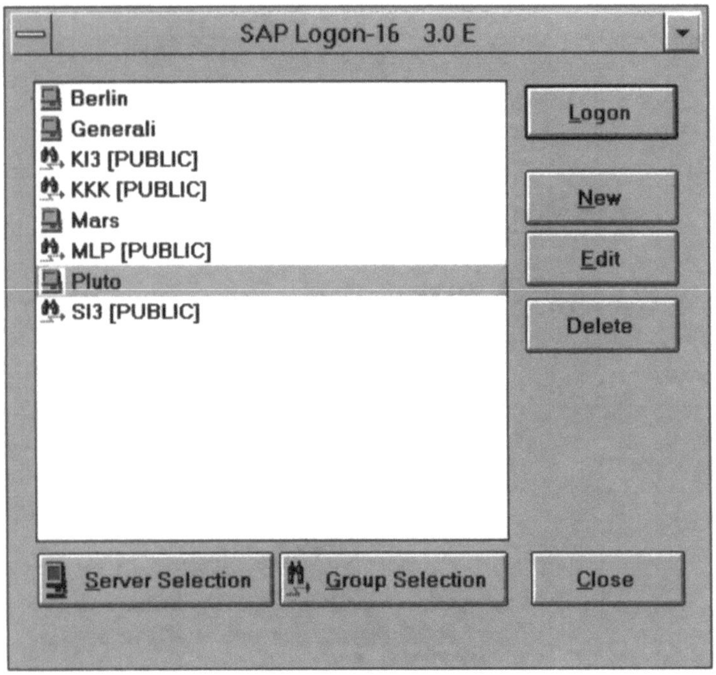

Figure 2.3: SAPLOGON.EXE

The screen from Figure 2.4 is shown once the connection has been established. The inputs requested here have a significant effect on the function of the complete system, in particular, also on the development environment. The clients separate themselves from the user data files for the duration of the complete session. Each user can only work with the data of the connected client. This avoids the client from needing to be specified in a dialog or in an ABAP/4 program. The logon is rejected if the user does not have the required authorization for the specified clients.

In contrast, metadata in the data dictionary and programs in the repository are always client-independent. Every program, every table or field definition is immediately visible for every other developer on the system once it has been stored or is usable after it has been activated.

The system uses the user name for reports, change logs, etc. The logon language controls the selection of language-dependent texts and menus. The developer can use the named inputs with the system variables contained in parentheses.

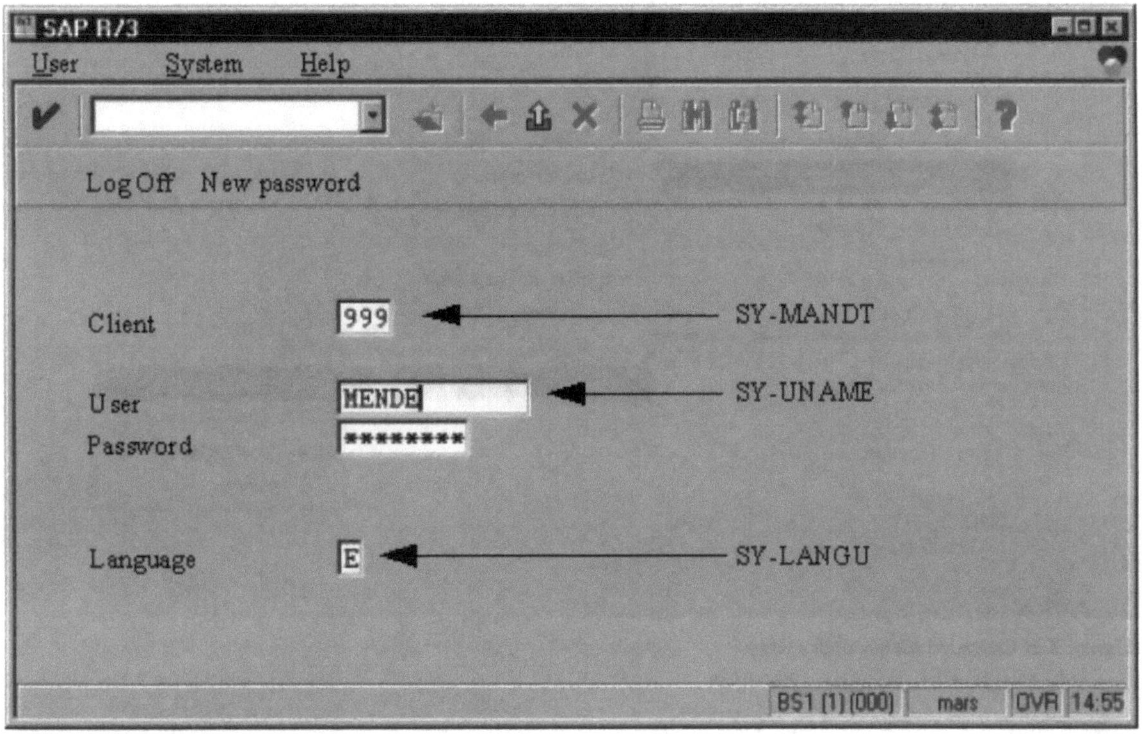

Figure 2.4: R/3 system logon screen

2.3.2 Mouse Operation, Menus, Function Keys, Transaction Codes

Although the SAPGUI is written in the style of the associated user interface, there are only small differences in the operation between Motif, OS/2 and Windows.

The SAPGUI uses Windows in following example. Its user interface behaves like a normal Windows program. Menus, symbol bars, key bars, and status line are arranged and operated as usual. It is not necessarily clear for the user whether a menu item starts a new transaction (area menu) or only invokes a new dialog in a transaction (program menu).

The menus are cascaded in the usual Windows manner. Function keys (see Figure 2.5) are provided in addition to the commands. Because the same tools were used for the development, the operator cannot distinguish SAP menus from self-developed menus. The standardized menu items *System* and *Help* are provided in every menu. The *System* menu item can be used to access various system services, such as list processing, spool monitor, lock monitor, and batch control.

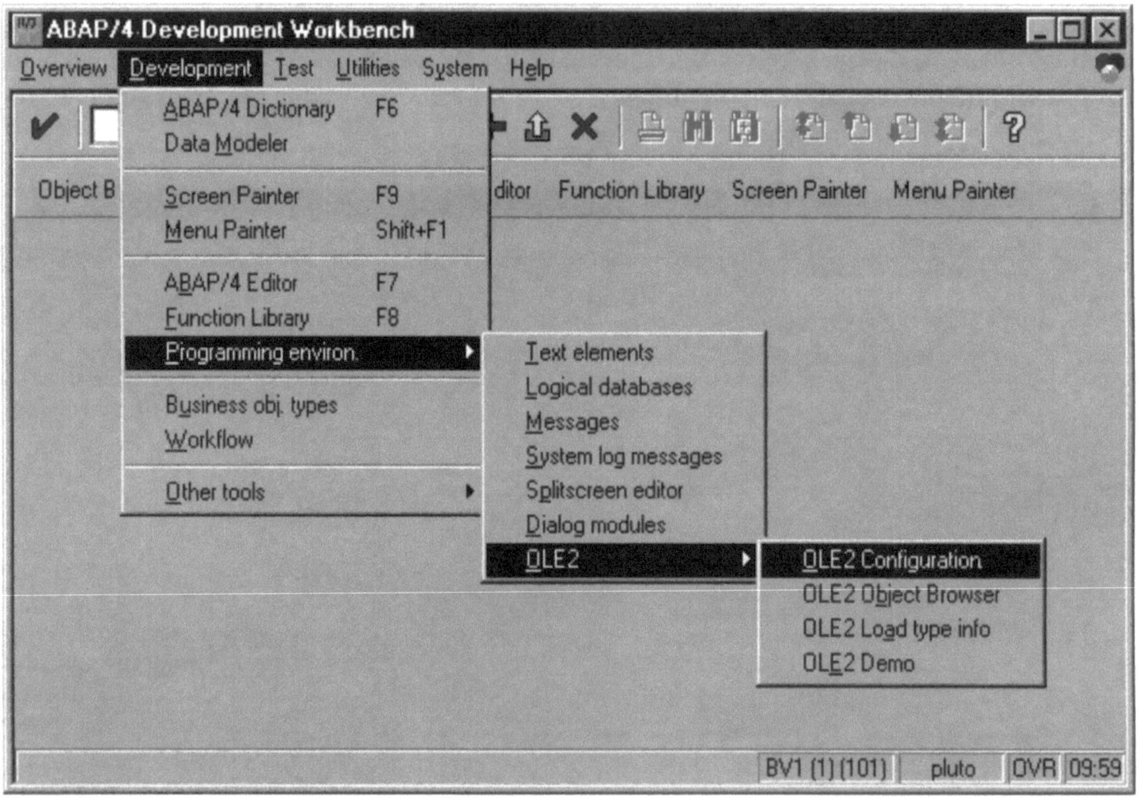

Figure 2.5: Cascaded menus under R/3

The dialog programs invoked from the menu can also be started using so-called transaction codes from the command field of the system bar (see Figure 2.6). A /n (start in the same mode) or a /o (start in a new mode) switch must be prefixed to the code. The appendix contains a list of the most important transaction codes. The symbol bar always contains the same symbols.

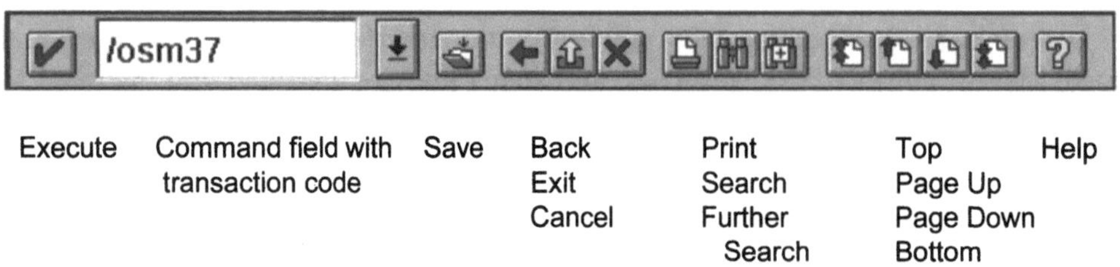

Figure 2.6: Symbol bar with command field for transaction input

The function key bar provides important program functions as pushbuttons.
From Release 3.0, keys that contain only icons without additional text are increasingly used as shortcuts. Figure 2.7 shows the most important icons with their standardized meaning.

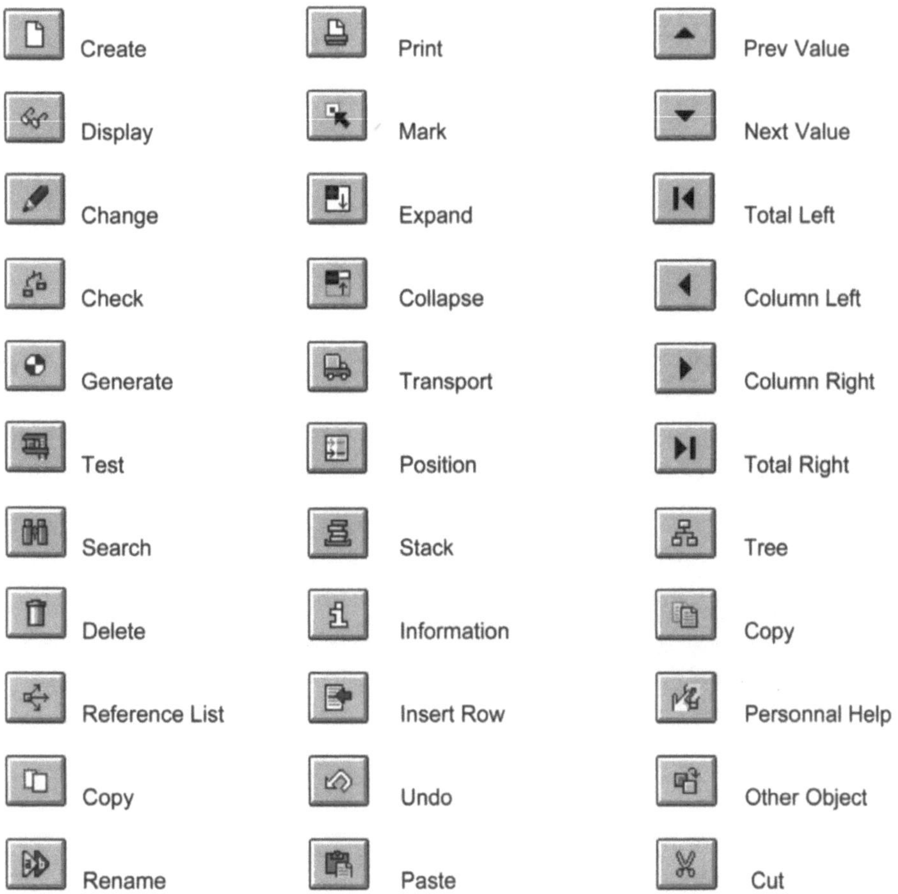

Figure 2.7: Frequently used icons and their meaning

The palette at the upper right-hand diagram edge is used to make the various SAPGUI settings (see Figure 2.8). These settings are made in SAPGUI.INI and apply for all subsequent logons.

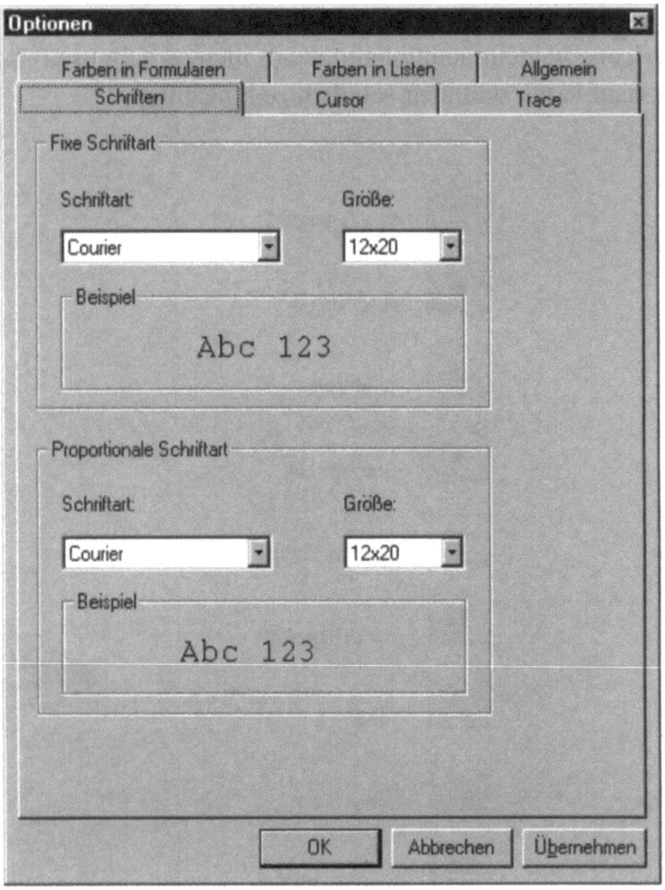

Figure 2.8: SAPGUI settings

2.3.3 Working with Several Modes

Although the SAPGUI itself is not an MDI program (Multi-Document Interface) with regard to Windows, the *System / Create Mode* command can be used to open several SAPGUI instances (so-called modes) for an existing connection.

The modes 2, 3, etc., inherit the logon data from the first mode. Although all modes are connected to the same server, they are not attached to the same work process. Many developers work with two or three modes that they arrange in a cascaded form (see Figure 2.9). This makes it easy to change between frequently used tools (for example, Screen Painter, ABAP/4 editor, table display).

A second mode has proved to be useful when the first mode "locks" (endless loop in the program, lock entry for program after a short dump).

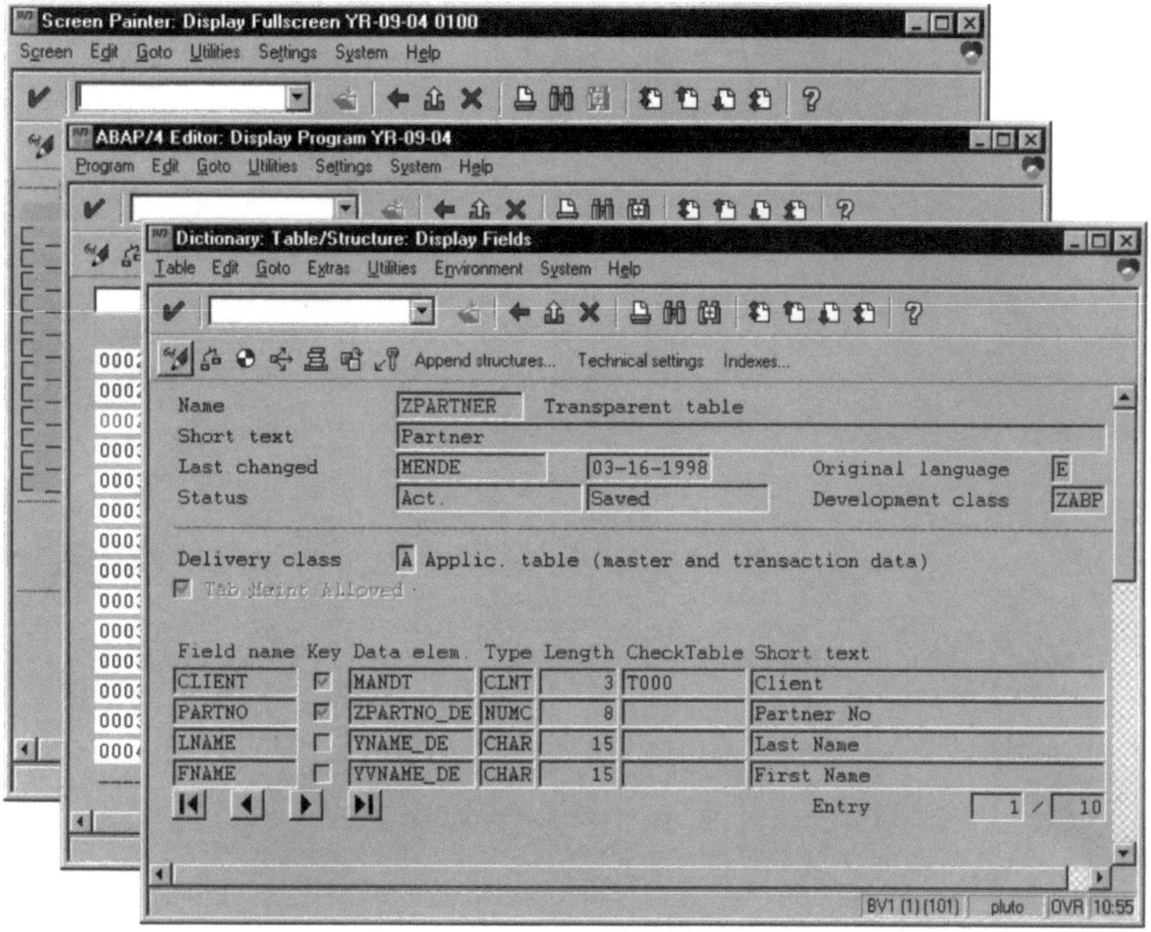

Figure 2.9: Working with several modes

3 The Example – A Service System

All following chapters of this book refer to the example of a greatly simplified inventory and booking system for a service provider. Although the field and table definitions and the designations in the data records are taken from the insurance business, they are also appropriate for banks, energy or water utility companies, or telecommunication enterprises. The service provider manages products, partners and contracts as part of an inventory system. A product number identifies the various products that are divided into product groups. The products are sold to partners in the form of signed contracts.

A contract number identifies a contract that has a start date, a policy term, an amount (premium, etc.) and an associated currency unit. The contract contains details of the associated product and the business partner.

Accounts in the booking system are maintained for all signed contracts. The accounts manage credits (benefits, repayments, etc.) in the form of records. Accounting transactions, payments and reimbursements, etc., are made to the account. Such an accounting system represents a subledger accounting department.

Table 3.1: Logical data model components

System	Object	Attribute
Contract		
Administration	**Products**	
System		Product Number
		Product Group
		Description
	Partner	
		Partner Number
		Last Name
		First Name
		Title
		Sex of Partner
		Street
		Town
		Postal Code
	Contracts	
		Contract Number
		Partner Number
		Product Number
		Account Number

System	Object	Attribute
		Amount and Currency
		Starting and End Date
		Sign of the Offer
Accounting System		
	Accounts	
		Account Number
		Account Type
		Block Indicator
	Documents	
		Document Number
		Company Code
		Contract Number
		Account Number
		Document Type and Posting Key Text
		Amount and Posting Key
		Posting Date
		Document Text

3.1 Logical Data Model

Figure 3.1 shows the logical data model of the highly simplified service provider system. The partner, product, etc., objects that are connected with each other using association arrows have a predicate as designation.

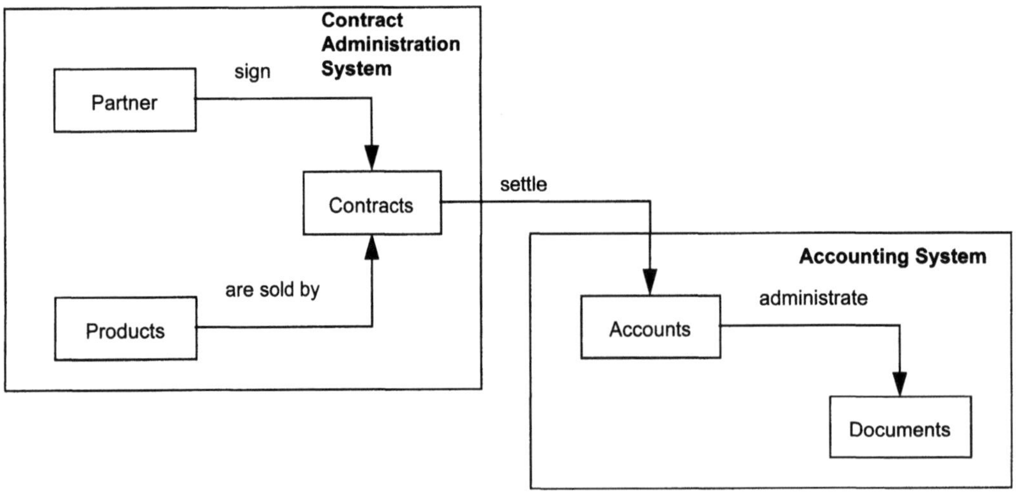

Figure 3.1: Data model of a service system

Reading in the direction of the arrow yields meaningful sentences such as "Partners sign contracts", "Account manages records", etc. In practice, the inventory (contract management) and the account (sub-ledger accounting) systems normally together form a separate and very complex system. Normally, these systems are supplemented by additional special systems, for example, systems for claims/reimbursement, commissions and reinsurance for the insurance industry.

This book is not concerned with representing this reality, but rather provide a highly simplified data model that can be used to learn the development environment.

3.2 Use of the Example

Chapter 4 shows how to represent the logical data model from Figure 3.1 in the Data Modeler. R/3 supports the transition from the logical to the physical data model in the Data Dictionary (tables, fields and foreign keys). A report described in the appendix and provided on the diskette populates the tables with sample data. The report programming for database access with Open SQL is demonstrated using these data (the data are also fully described in the appendix). The examples show the solution to simple questions, such as "show all contracts of a partner", but also complex queries with multiple joins such as "show all partners who have signed the contracts for all products". A booking dialog is used to provide an introduction to the dialog programming. The use of matchcodes, logical databases and batch programming can also be illustrated with this example. The data import using batch input and the file interfaces is also discussed. The reader can use the sample system to immediately verify all programs with database access.

The advanced reader is urged to solve the formulated questions using his/her own outlined program before confirming this with the solution provided in the text. The novice can follow the solution step-by-step. The fact that all examples use the same tables and data is a large help here. It is easier to concentrate on the program content when the tables with their contained data are known.

4 Data Dictionary and Data Modeler

4.1 Data Dictionary

4.1.1 Concept

The Data Dictionary (DDIC) contains all information about the structure, designations and references of R/3 system data. The Data Dictionary does not manage any user data but rather the so-called metadata. As with the user data, the metadata are stored in the R/3 database.

Commands such as CREATE TABLE, DROP TABLE, CREATE VIEW and GRANT are used to maintain the system tables for the direct operation with an DBMS. These system tables constitute a type of data dictionary for the DBMS.

The system tables of the associated DBMS are stored in the R/3 Data Dictionary; the system tables are exclusively maintained in this data dictionary. However, the Data Dictionary contains far more data than just the contents of the system tables.

4.1.2 Initial Screen, Objects

The Data Dictionary is maintained interactively using the SE11 transaction. Developers normally invoke the dictionary using the ABAP/4 workbench pushbutton. The initial screen shows all object types that are managed in the Data Dictionary. The operation is standardized for all object types; the name is entered, and then the action selected (create, change or display). The following details are entered for all elements in the heading of the subsequent maintenance masks:

- Short description
- Last change, name, date
- Status
  - new, not saved
  - revised, not saved
  - revised, saved
  - active, saved
- Development class

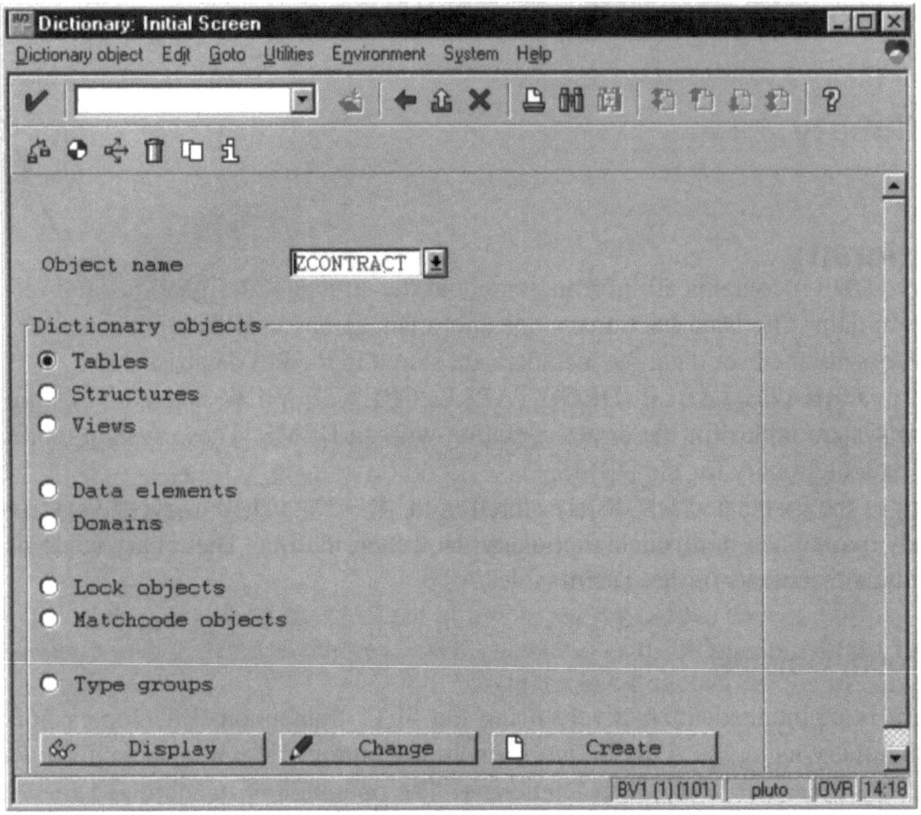

Figure 4.1: Initial screen for the Data Dictionary

Tables, structures and views are handled uniformly as *table-like* items. Data elements and domains describe the properties of those fields that only occur within the *table-like* items.

Lock objects and matchcode objects are aggregated, complex objects that are based on existing table definitions. Matchcodes are used to search for information in tables when the primary key is not known. Lock objects are used for the SAP-specific, logical locking method.

Type groups are persistent, user-specific type definitions. They are included in ABAP/4 programs and describe arbitrary complex data types, such as nested structures or structures with embedded tables. Multiple programs can use them to access central type definitions. Type groups are comparable to C header files and are currently also realized as Includes.

4.1.3 Tables in the Data Dictionary

Without doubt, the tables are the Data Dictionary's most important data types. The dictionary of the sample installation contains 10644 tables. The following characteristics must be saved in the Data Dictionary for all tables used in R/3 (customizing tables, tables for master data, tables for detail data):

- Name
- Fields with semantic and physical characteristics
- Primary key
- Technical characteristics

Optionally, it is possible to maintain

- Foreign key relationships
- Secondary indexes

A significant differentiation must be made between DDIC tables and database tables. A DDIC table represents a table description as part of a table declaration or table definition. User data can be stored only when a database table has been created using a DDIC table. The database table here represents the data definitions or the specific data object.

In previous R/3 release levels, the user had to explicitly create a database table after defining the DDIC table. From release 3.0A, this is performed automatically during the activation of the DDIC table, which relieves the user of the work involved, but hides the mentioned difference.

Creation and Activation

The initial screen for the table maintenance is shown in Figure 4.2. The following details must be input or displayed for the table:

- Delivery class
  - "A" = application table
  - "C" = customizing table, etc.
- Flag whether maintenance allowed

The table fields are also entered in table form. The following entries are made for each field in the columns:

- Field name
- Primary key flag
- Data element
- Check table

It is assumed that the specified data elements have already been created. If they are missing, the user will be requested to create them. In many cases you can use existing data elements that exist in the SAP tables.

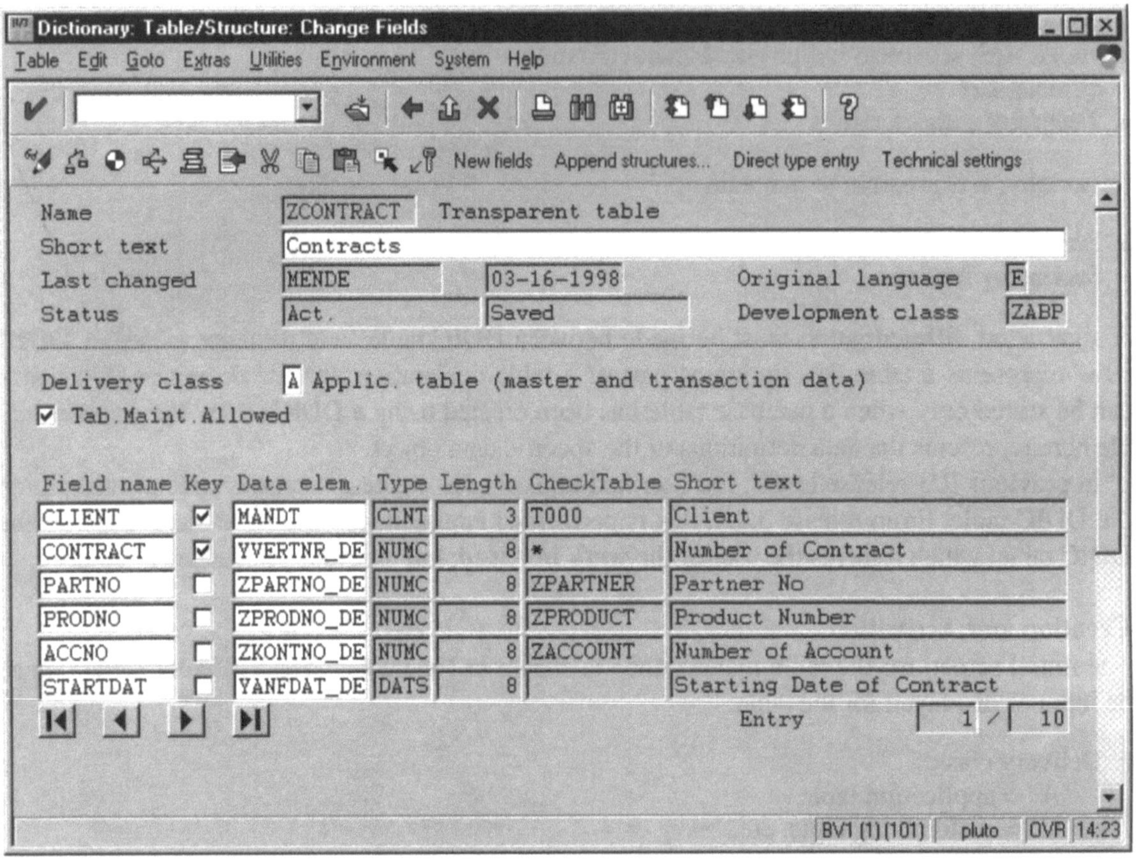

Figure 4.2: Table fields

The CLIENT field must be entered in the first line for client-specific tables. It is always a primary key field. Normally, the other primary keys and then the attribute fields follow.

The table's technical characteristics must have been determined and the expected table size determined before a table is activated. It is also possible to specify whether the table is to be buffered, and, if yes, how it is to be buffered.

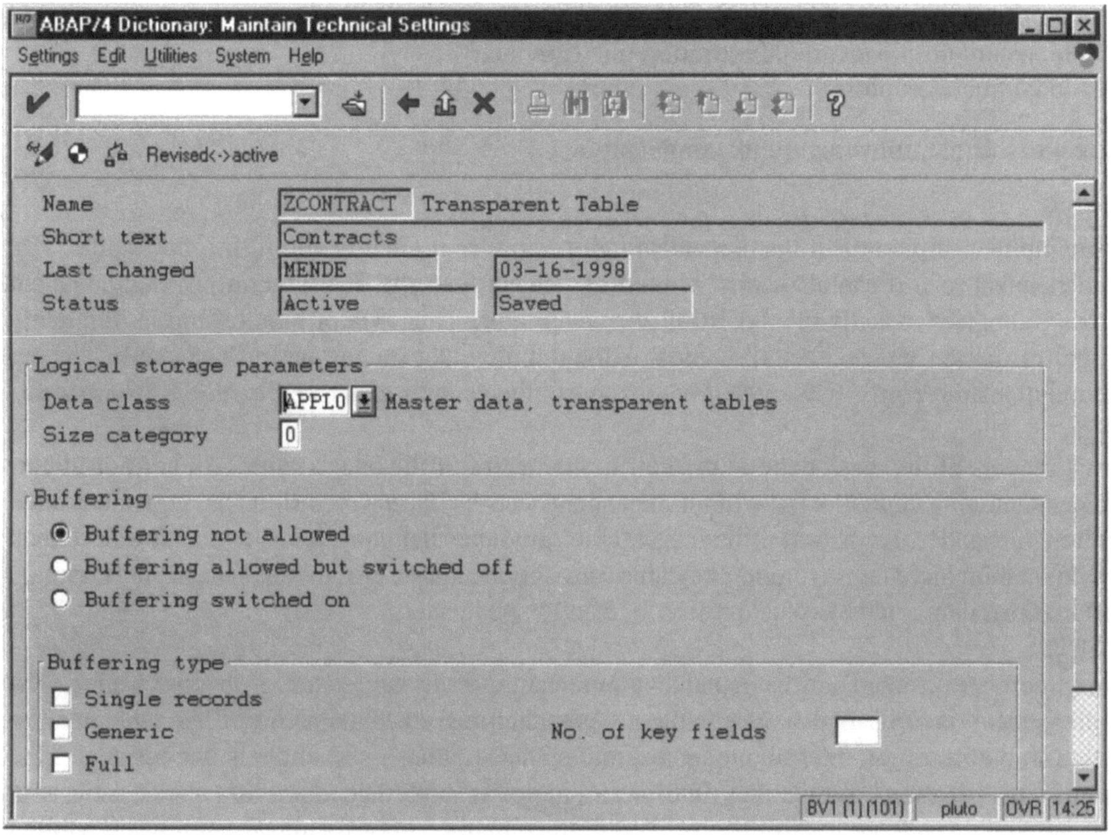

Figure 4.3: Technical characteristics of a table

Foreign Key

A so-called check table can be entered for every table field. Those fields that contain this entry are called foreign key fields. They reference a record in the specified check table. For example, the PRODNO field in the ZCONTRACT table points to exactly one record in the ZPRODUCT check table. Although PRODNO is not a primary key field in ZCONTRACT (even though it could be), PRODNO must be a primary key field in ZPRODUCT.

The cardinality of the following form can be maintained for every foreign key relationship:

- U : A
- U = Number of records in the independent check table, {1,C}
- A = Number of records in the dependent foreign key table, {C,N}

The details should be read as follows. A records from the dependent table can reference a record of the independent table. One record of the dependent table can reference U records of the independent table.

A can assume any positive value. U can assume values between 0 and 1. The following abbreviations are used:

- 1: exactly one record
- C: no record or one record (abbreviation for "can have")
- N: one or more records.

These provide the following useful combinations:

- 1:CN
  Any number of records of the dependent table can refer to one record of the check table. The independent record can also exist without dependent records. Every record of the dependent table references exactly one record of the check table. This type of relationship is frequently used for master data and detail records. Although the independent master data can be created without detail records (CN), detail records must always refer to a specific master data record.
- 1:N
  1..N records of the dependent table refer to one record of the check table. A record of the independent table cannot exist without dependent records. Every record of the dependent table refers to exactly one record of the check table. Invoices that consist of invoice header (check table) and invoice items (foreign key table) are a typical case. An invoice header must contain at least one item, and every item refers to exactly one header.
- C:CN
  Any number of records of the dependent table can refer to one record of the check table. The independent record can also exist without dependent records. One record of the dependent table can, but need not, refer to one record in the check table. An example is the optional "academic qualification" foreign key field in an employee table that refers to a check table with the possible academic qualifications. The field remains empty for those employees without academic qualifications.
- C:N
  1..N records of the dependent table refer to one record of the check table. One record of the independent table cannot exist without dependent records. One record of the dependent table can, but need not, refer to one record of the check table.

The definition of foreign key relations provides the only non-redundant method of storing large interrelated data.

If frequent table accesses using non-key fields are to be expected, so-called secondary indexes can be maintained in addition to the primary index. For example, because a typical booking task requires finding all invoices for an account, it is desirable to provide a secondary index to the account for tables that contain booking material.

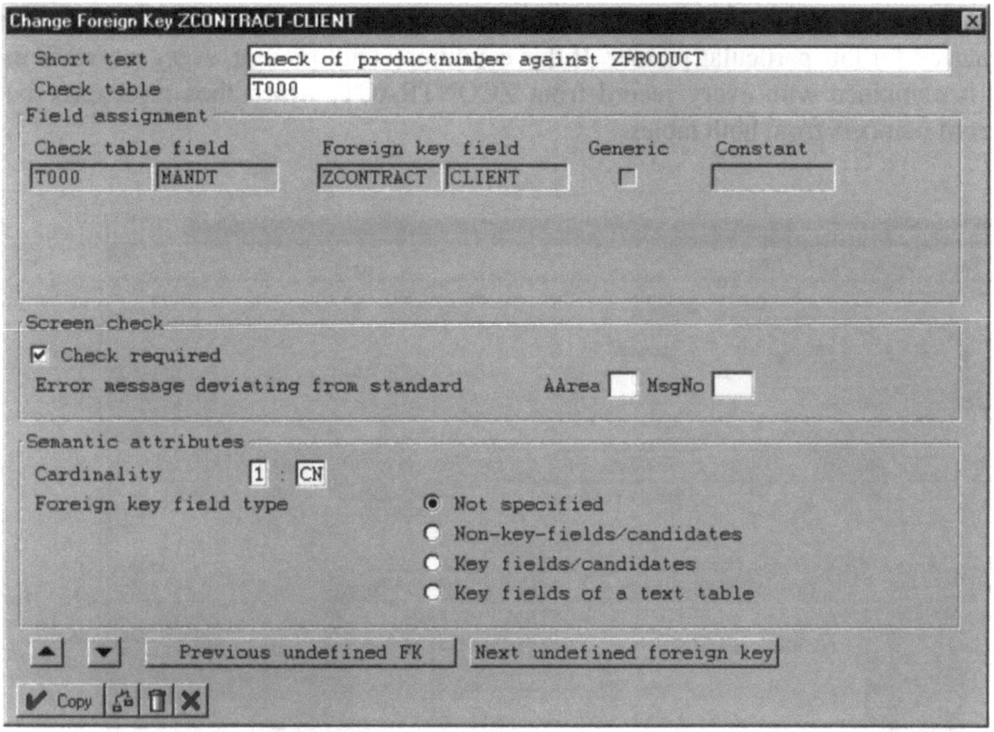

Figure 4.4: Foreign key relationships for table fields

4.1.4 Structures

As with tables, structures are stored in the Data Dictionary. The main difference between the two is that no database tables are assigned to structures. Structures cannot be used to store any data in the database. Consequently, the term key or index has no significance for structures. Structures are typically used to define parameter types or records for file interfaces. The SYST structure is used in almost every program. The system provides every user with a field structure with the name SY of type SYST. The structure contains 176 system fields, which, depending on the program context, can be set by either the system or the application program. The appendix lists a selection of the most important SYST fields.

4.1.5 Views

Views represent a form of virtual table that can be based on one or more table definitions. Views permit apparent access to information using a single table, a view, that for database reasons is actually maintained in several tables.

Figure 4.5 shows an example of the definition of a view using the ZPARTNER and ZCONTRACT tables. Both tables of the view are joined using a foreign key relationship. This relationship is entered in the join conditions, which then ensure that only the associated contracts are displayed for this particular partner. If this condition is not present, every record from ZPARTNER is combined with every record from ZCONTRACT, which then represents the product of record numbers from both tables.

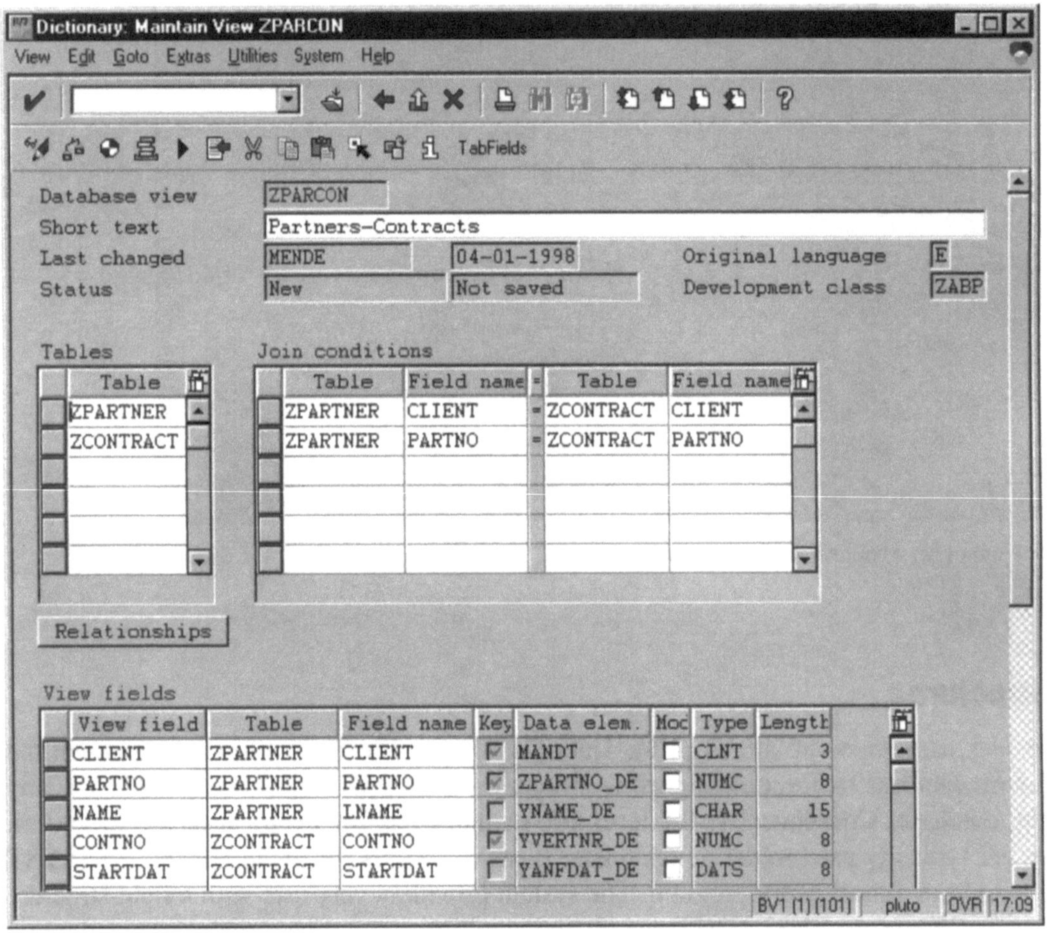

Figure 4.5: View definition

Fields from both tables are passed to the view table. A view does not have any database tables of its own. It provides a new, combined view of existing database tables.

Section 6.9.4 shows how easy it is to use this view to create a partner contract list, which otherwise could only be realized using nested selects.

4.1.6 Field Definitions in the Data Dictionary

A two-level concept is used in R/3 to define the properties of table fields. In addition to other properties, every table field has exactly one data element that describes the semantic field characteristics. Similarly, every data element has exactly one domain that contains the semantic field characteristics (field type, length, value range or value table, conversions). This concept has the advantage that it permits the multiple use of data elements in different fields or domains in different data elements. If a foreign key relationship exists between different tables, these fields typically have the same data element, and, thus implicitly the same domain. Subsequent changes, such as the change of a field length at a domain, affect all associated tables. This avoids inconsistencies. Figure 4.6 shows the relationships between domains, data elements and table fields of the type 1:CN.

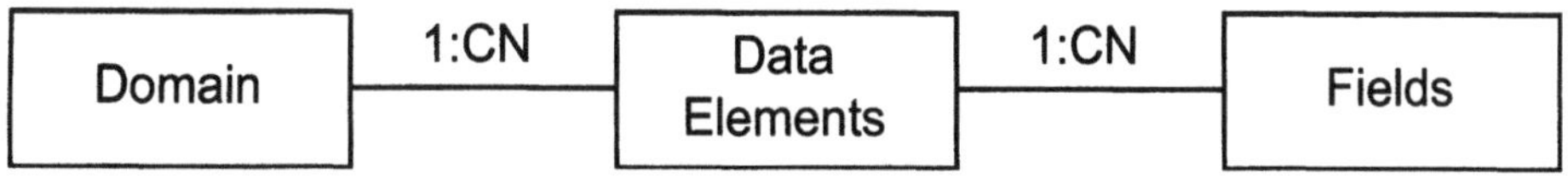

Figure 4.6: Relationships between domains, data elements and table fields

4.1.7 Data Elements

Data elements can be created directly from the Data Dictionary or during the table updating. In addition to the reference to an existing domain, various texts are updated. These can later be used as input texts or column headings in dialog masks. Because the updating can be performed in several languages, different headings can appear depending on the language used for the logon.

A parameter ID can be used to automatically assign default values to all dialog fields associated with this data element. The default values can be either fixed values from the user master record or values set by other programs.

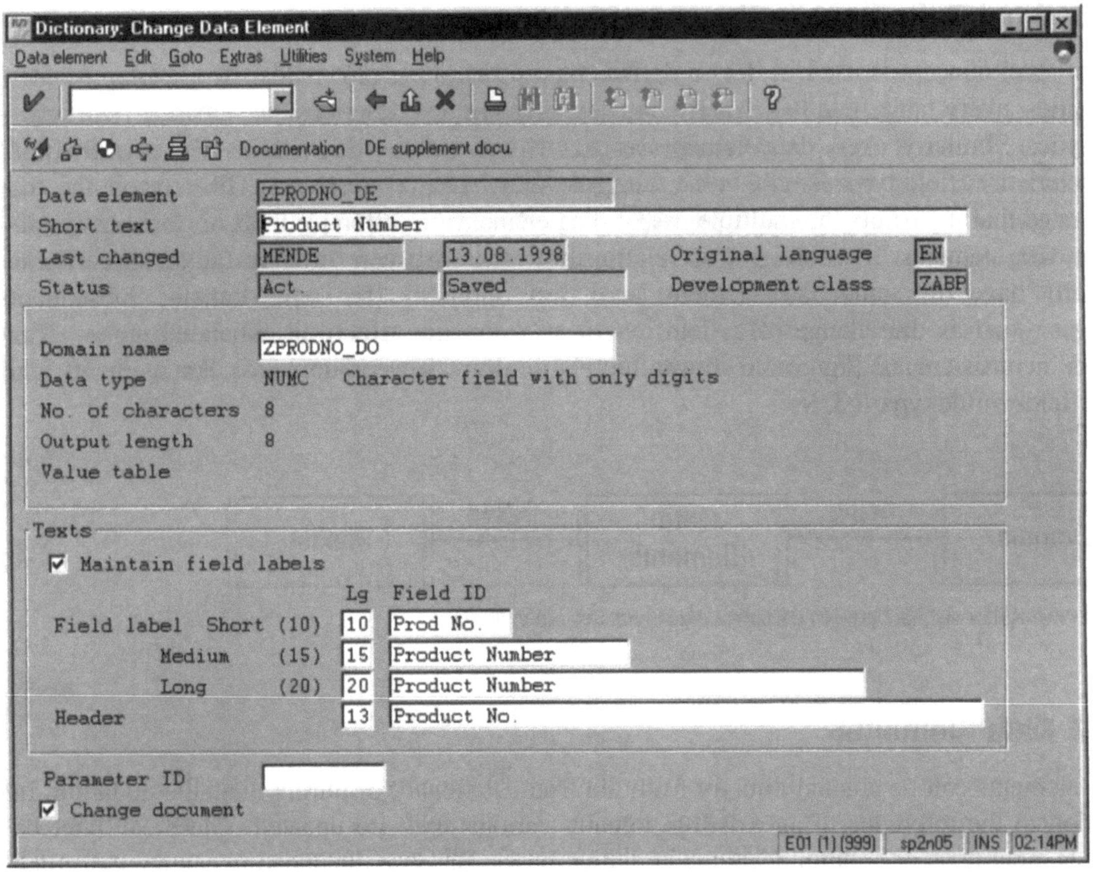

Figure 4.7: Creation of a data element

4.1.8 Domains

Domains are created either directly from the initial display of the Data Dictionary or from a data element. The format details refer to a special intermediate data type, also known as external data type. This represents the connection layer between the database data types and the ABAP/4 data types.

It is not possible to convert in both directions. The conversion into ABAP/4 data types is shown in the last column. You can see that the field length in most cases corresponds to the internal ABAP/4 field length. An external length and the flag for two conversion functions (Chapter 8) can be specified for special output processing.

Table 4.1: Data types in domains

Type	Description	Field Length	Output Length	ABAP/4 Data Type
ACCP	Accounting period YYYYMM	6 (fixed)	6	N(6)
CHAR(n)	Character strings	n < 255	N	C(n)
CLNT	Client	3 (fixed)	3	C(3)
CUKY	Currency field, referenced by CURR-fields	5 (fixed)	5	C(5)
CURR (n, m, s)	Amount field, points to a CUKY-field	n = 17		P((n+2)/2) DECIMAL m (NO-SIGN)
DATS	Date YYYYMMDD	8 (fixed)	10	D(8)
DEC (n, m, s)	Computational or amount field with colon and algebraic sign	n = 17		P((n+2)/2) DECIMAL m (NO-SIGN)
FLTP	Floating-point number	8	22 + arithmetic sign	F(8)
INT1	1-byte integer up to 254, decimal number	1 (fixed)	3	I
INT2	2-byte integer up to 65 535	2 (fixed)	5	I
INT4	4-byte integer up to 536 870 991, decimal number with arithmetic sign	3 (fixed)	10	I
LANG	Language key	1 (fixed)	1	C(1)
LCHR(n)	Long character string , needs leading INT2-field	n > 255		C(n)
LRAW(n)	Long byte string, needs leading INT2-field	n > 255		X(n)
NUMC	Arbitrary long field, which is only able to contain numeric data			N(n)
PREC	Precision of a QUAN-field			
QUAN (n, m, s)	Quantity field, is related to UNIT-field	n = 17		P((n+2)/2) DECIMAL m (NO-SIGN)
RAW(n)	Uninterpreted byte string	n		X(n)
TIMS	Time, HHMMSS	6	8	T(6)
UNIT	Quantity units	3	3	C(3)

The associated domain can restrict value range of a field in two ways: using fixed values or using a value table. Fixed values are assigned to the domain in the Data Dictionary and are usually of limited number. Fixed values are used for programming, i.e., they appear as constants in the program text and cannot be changed by customizing without making program changes. A new fixed value requires new source text. In contrast, value tables represent a value range that can be changed externally. They do not have any immediate control effect. Many customizing tables are used as value tables in domains.

If fixed values or a value table have been assigned to a domain, F4 can be used to request a value help for every dialog field that uses this domain.

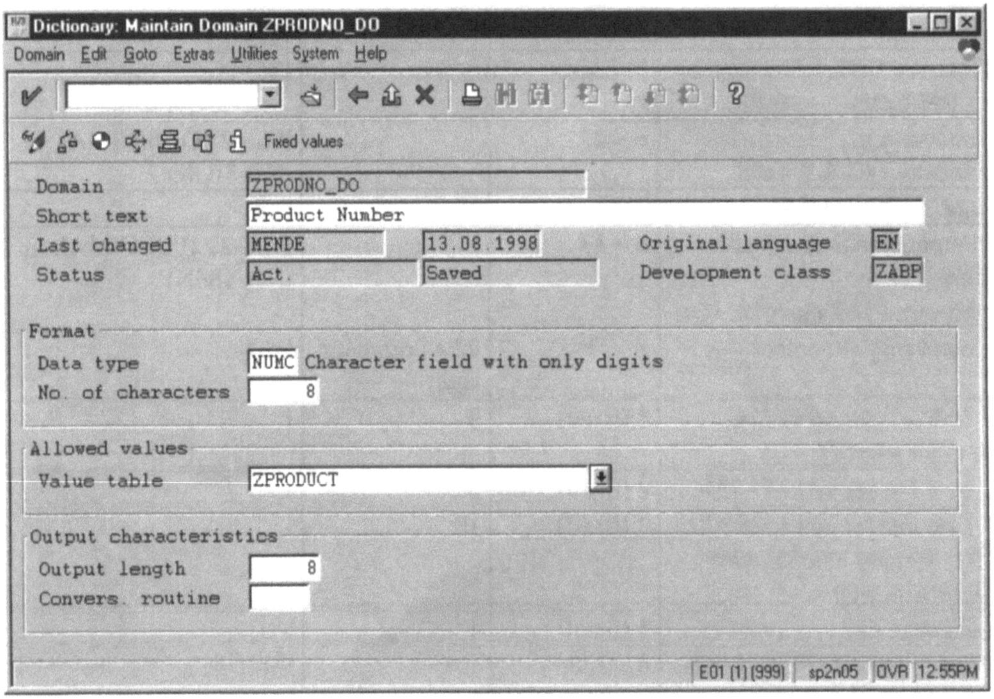

Figure 4.8: Create a domain

4.1.9 Lock Objects

Lock objects are created to implement the SAP-internal locking logic. In contrast to database locks, the SAP locking mechanism can lock single table records or also inter-related records from several tables. Locking means that an entry is set in a lock table for a lock object stored in the dictionary; the object key must be specified in this case. In contrast to database locks, the SAP locks are not associated with Open SQL commands. The SAP locks must be set, validated and deleted using separate function modules. They can be ignored either knowingly or unknowingly, at any time.

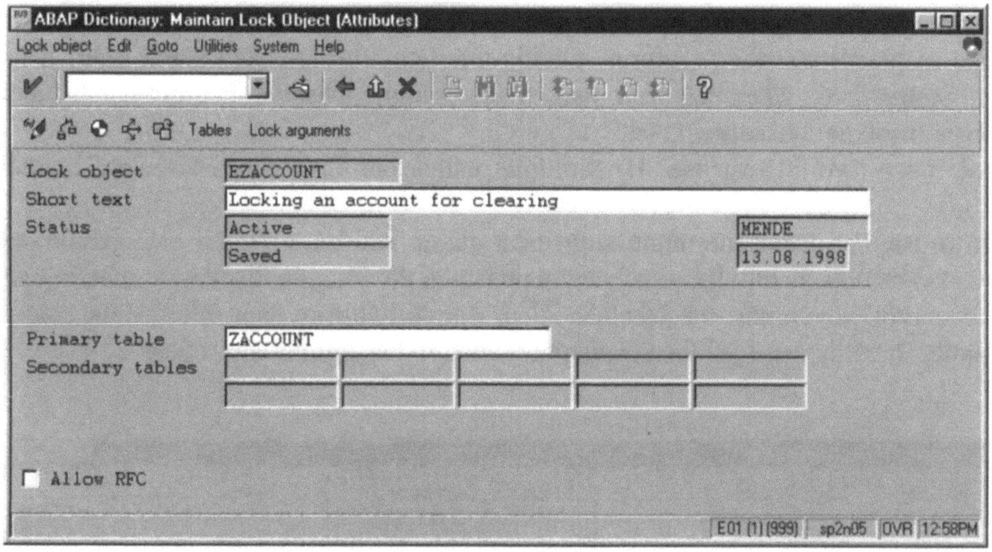

Figure 4.9: Updating a lock object

Figure 4.9 illustrates updating a lock object EZACCOUNT that is required to lock an account during the compensation. All programs that want to book records to an account must first test whether a lock has been set. In the shown case, the lock object represents a single record in the ZACCOUNT table. Accordingly, the keys for this table are also the lock arguments. The system generates the following function modules when the EZACCOUNT lock object is activated:

ENQUEUE_EZACCOUNT (set and query lock entries for an account)
DEQUEUE_EZACCOUNT (delete lock entries for an account)

Chapter 8 describes the parameters and the use of lock modules.

4.1.10 Matchcodes

Normally coded keys (numbers) are used to identify objects in large data files. The system itself normally assigns these keys, which then do not have any relationship to the object's contents. Account numbers, personnel numbers or form numbers are typical examples. An object can be most easily identified using the key number(s). This is the reason for frequent requests of the form "Please always enter your account number / invoice number / contract number". It is more difficult to locate an object if the number is not known, not readable or incorrect. The input help (F4) does not normally provide much help for large data files, because, in the extreme case when you have no idea of the number, all key numbers of the object class in the system must be shown without any comments. It is more important to locate the key on the base of other, incomplete or imprecise, information. Matchcodes support such a search. The information on the partner who signed the contract (name, first name and postcode) should be used to determine a contract number. The associated matchcode object ZPAV is created (Figure 4.10).

The object contains ZPARTNER as primary table (independent table) and ZCONTRACT as secondary table. A matchcode always returns exactly one field, the so-called search field. This is the contract number here, which has been marked accordingly. Observe that the search field in this case comes from the secondary table.

A matchcode must have at least one ID. Multiple matchcode-IDs represent several search variants.

If you want to use the matchcode input help for a dialog field on a dynpro or a parameter field, the field must be linked with the associated matchcode. Pressing F4 displays a selection of matchcode-IDs, one of which must be selected. Their search fields are then filled, either completely or partially. Pressing the ENTER key displays a list of the appropriate values.

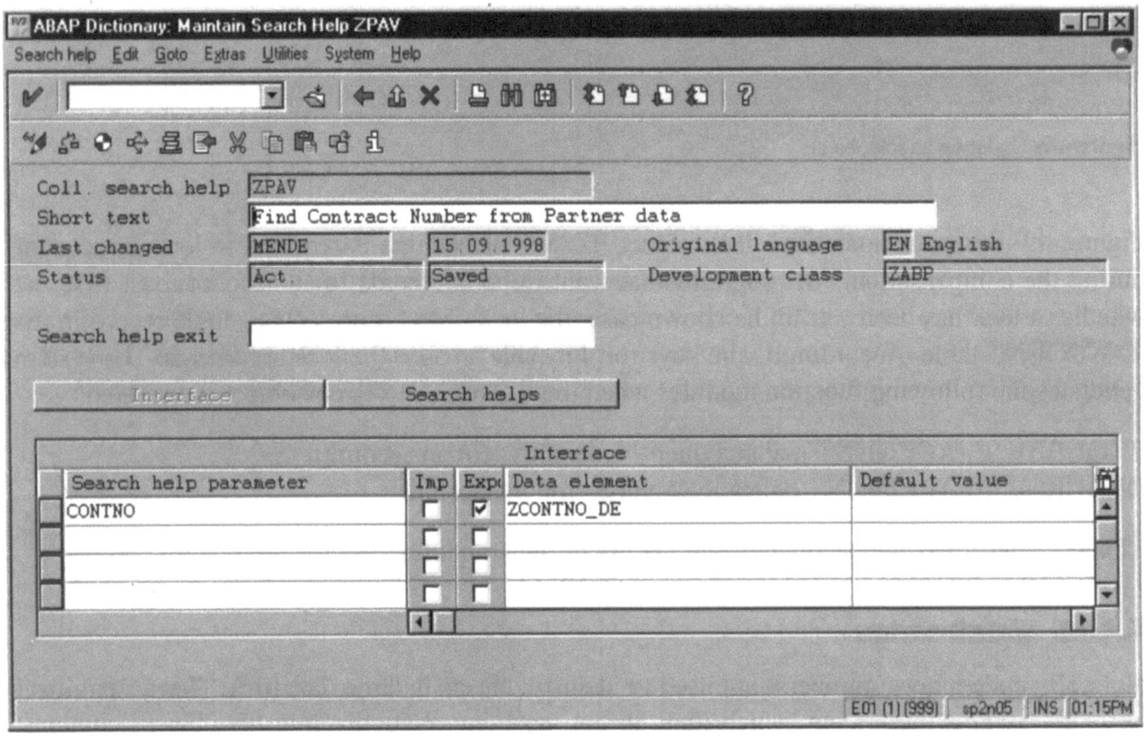

Figure 4.10: Create a matchcode object

Figure 4.12 illustrates the ZM-09-03 service program whose contract field has been assigned the matchcode ZPAV.

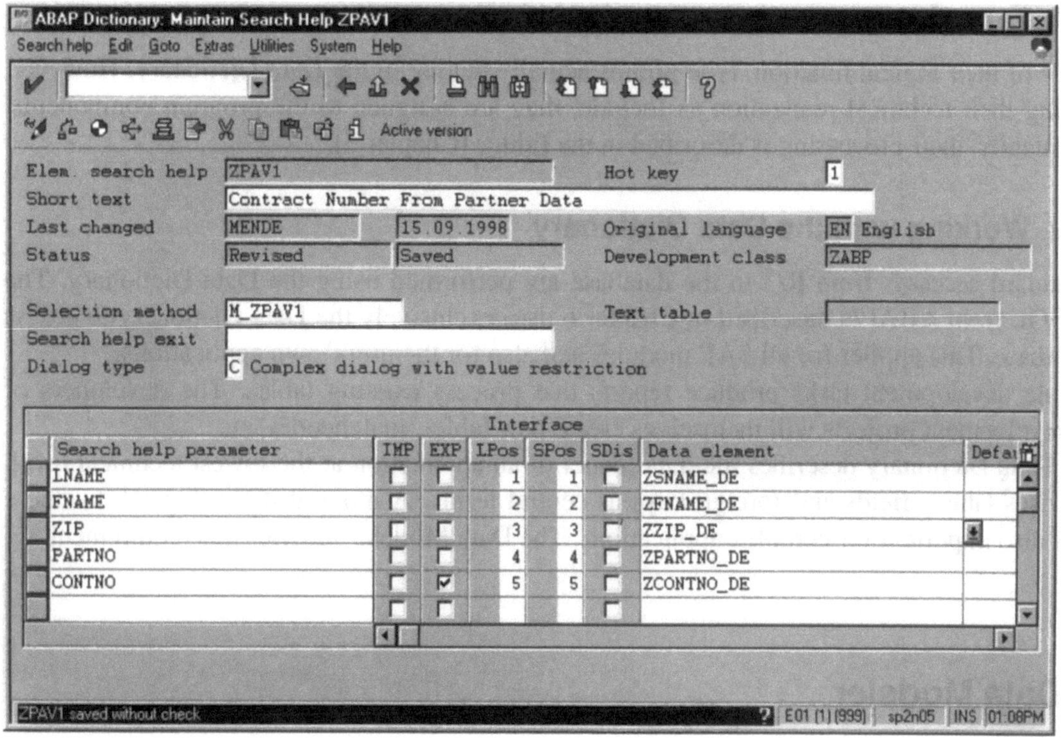

Figure 4.11: Update matchcode-ID

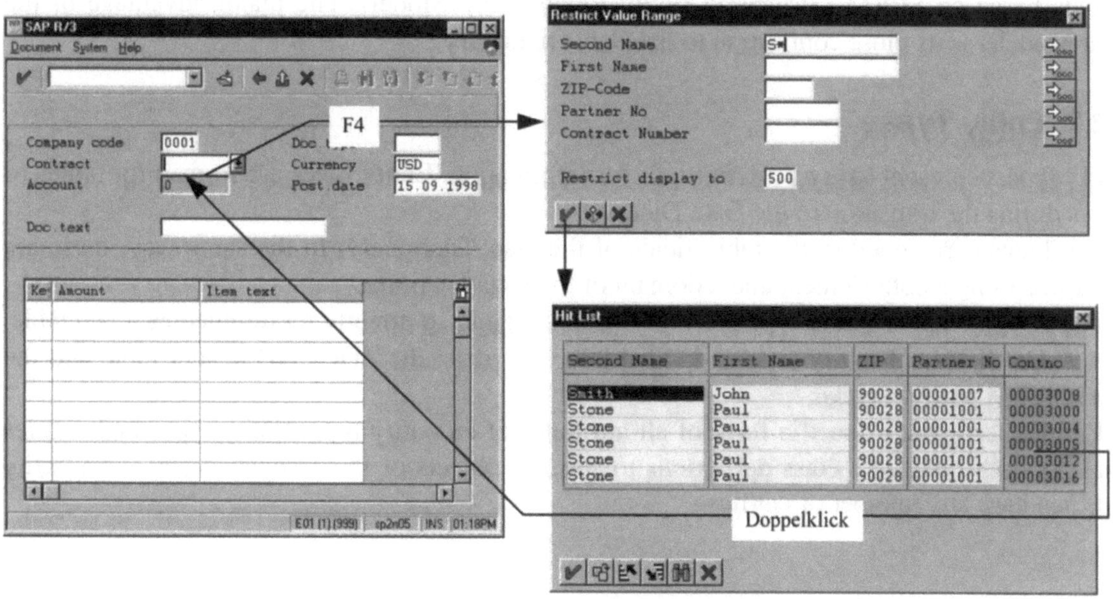

Figure 4.12: Matchcode ZPAV at a field for the input of a contract number

4.1.11 Type Groups

Because of their logical function, type groups actually belong in the Data Dictionary. However, following their technical realization as Include, they are assigned to the program components. Consequently, their processing is described in the Editor (Chapter 5).

4.1.12 Working with the Data Dictionary

All standard accesses from R/3 to the database are performed using the Data Dictionary. The Open SQL from ABAP/4 described in Chapter 6 uses exclusively the Data Dictionary to access the database. This applies for all SAP modules and also for the users' own applications.

Simple development tasks produce reports that process existing tables. The developers of large development projects will themselves create new tables, matchcodes, etc.

The Data Dictionary describes the data model of an application at the lowest technical level, which uses tables, fields and foreign keys as central terms. A more abstract, logical, business view is also important for complex applications. The Data Modeler satisfies this requirement.

4.2 Data Modeler

4.2.1 Concept

The Data Modeler makes it possible to create and verify complex, hierarchically structured data models based on SERM (Structured Entity Relationship Model). The major advantage of the Data Modeler is its close connection to the Data Dictionary.

4.2.2 Entity Types

Entity types represent structure definitions for information. Entity types are formed for tables or views during the transition to the Data Dictionary.

Attributes correspond to the table fields of the Data Dictionary. In the same way, these are described using a data element and a domain of the Data Dictionary.

The Z_ACCOUNT entity type is simply structured and so directly represented as a DD table. The Z_DOCUMENT entity type is divided into two parts: the ZDOCHD header table and the ZDOCITEM position table.

Entities represent a specific form of all attributes of an entity type. Entity types and entities relate to each other like class definitions to specific objects of the associated class. An entity type can have any number of entities.

Table 4.2: The Z_Account and Z_Receipt entity types

Entity Type	Attributes	DD View	DD Table1	DD Table2
Z_ACCOUNT	Client		ZACCOUNT	
	Account Number			
	Account Type			
	Block			
Z_RECEIPT	Client	Z_DOCUMENT	ZDOCHD	ZDOCITEM
	Document Number			
	Document Item			
	Amount			
	Currency			
	...			

4.2.3 Relationships

Different types of relationships can exist between the entity types. A relationship is represented as a directed arrow from the independent to the dependent entity type. For example, a relationship exists between the entity type Z_PARTNER (partner) and the entity type Z_CONTRACT (contracts), where Z_PARTNER is the independent and Z_CONTRACT is the dependent entity type.

Foreign key attributes record the relationships between entity types. The value forms of such attributes identify a specific independent entity.

The direction of the relationship arrow is often troublesome, in particular for developers. They interpret the foreign key in Z_CONTRACT as pointer to the Z_PARTNER entity and would consequently orient the relationship arrow exactly reversed.

- *Referential relationship type:*
  In a relation of this type, a key attribute of a dependent entity refers to a key attribute of an independent entity. The example mentioned above, partner-contract, is of this type. A contract always has a partner, which, however, is not a key attribute in the contract entity. It is at anytime possible to reattach a contract to another partner.
- *Hierarchical relationship type:*
  The dependent entity is existent-dependent on the independent entity. This means that the foreign key attribute is part of the key. Consequently, its value cannot be changed during the lifetime of the dependent entity. The attribute values of the independent entity distinguish the dependent entity.

- *Aggregating relationship type:*
  Although this relationship type is also hierarchical, it has the additional characteristic that an independent object has at least two dependent objects associated with it.

Relationships between entity types are realized as specific relationships between specific entities of the associated entity types. Because both entity types can process an arbitrary number of entities, the question of the cardinality of a relationship arises. The cardinality specifies how many dependent entities can exist for an independent entity or whether a dependent entity must always refer to an independent entity. The characteristics correspond to those for the foreign key cardinalities in the Data Dictionary.

4.2.4 Specializations and Generalizations

Specializations represent inheritances between entity types. The derived entity type is the specialization and the base type represents the generalization.

A specialized entity references the attributes of the general entity. This reference is best described using the words "is a ...". The specialization entity type defines additional, specific attributes.

The inheritance described here does not correspond to inheritance in the object-oriented sense (C++). There, no distinction is made between base object and derived object when an object of a derived class is created. Because both are created as a unit; they always have a 1:1 relationship.

Generally, several specialized entities for a base entity can exist in the Data Modeler. At the same time, base entities can normally exist without specializations.

In special cases, it is possible to request that a specialization is complete and/or disjunctive.

Complete Specialization

At least one specialized entity is assigned to every base entity. In other words: there are no isolated base entities. Such classes in C++ that cannot be used to form objects are called abstract base classes.

Disjunctive Specialization

A base entity can only be specialized in a single way. This specialization corresponds to the inheritance in the object-oriented sense. It has the advantage of avoiding redundancy in the data definition. The generalization entity type is described only once and used in all specialization types.

4.2.5 Data Models

Data models combine entity types and the associated relationships. The entities linked through many relationships are combined in a common data model. The example of the service provider in Chapter 3 has two data models, Z_CAS (Contract Administration System) and Z_ACCSYS (Accounting System). These two data models are not independent of each other but are linked using the relationships between the Contract and Account entity types.

Z_FS (Financial Service) is created as a complete, comprehensive data model, which does not itself contain any entity types but only those of the two previously mentioned sub-data models.

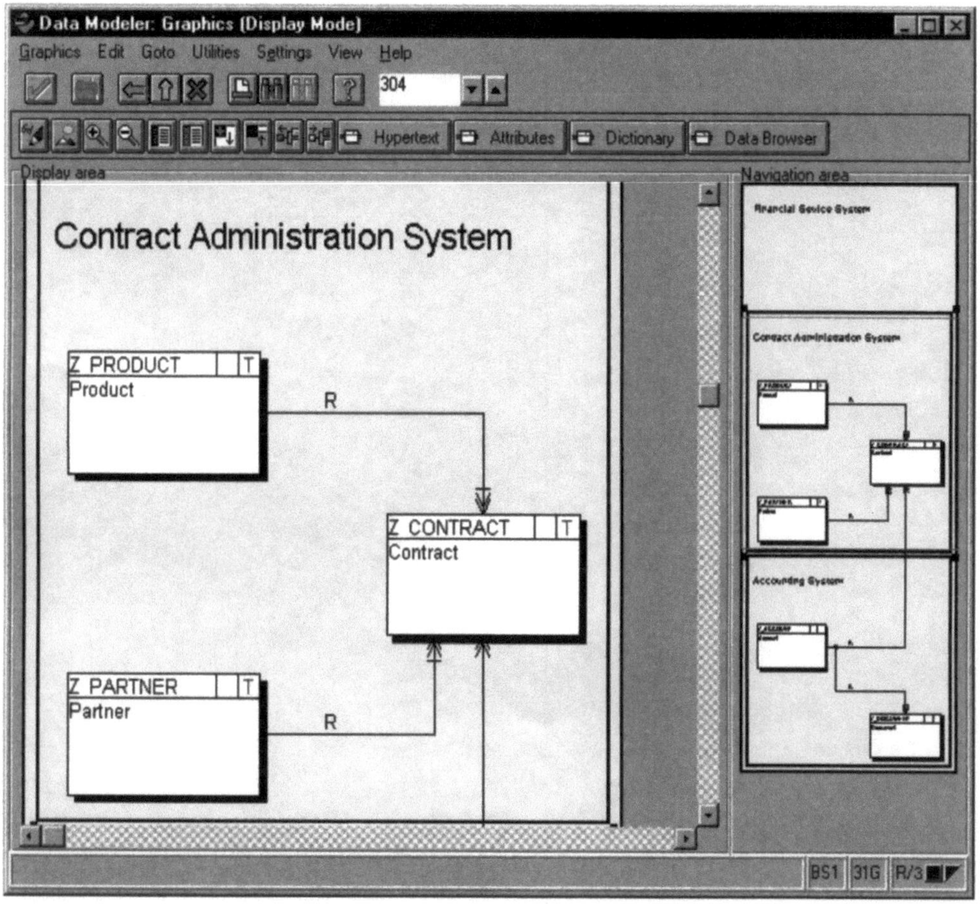

Figure 4.13: Graphical display of the Data Modeler

4.2.6 The Connection to the Data Dictionary

The entity types of the Data Modeler are represented as tables or views of the Data Dictionary. The data model can be designed first. The tables then can be derived. Similarly, existing table or view definitions can be used as starting point for new entity types.

The relationships of the Data Modeler are converted to foreign key relationships between the associated tables.

5 Workbench

The ABAP/4 Workbench is used for all software development work in R/3. The Workbench is designed to reliably process comprehensive software projects in large distributed teams. The aim of this chapter is not to provide a detailed introduction to the operation of the Workbench and its comprehensive tools. Rather, it explains the principles of the structuring and the interaction of the various development objects and development tools. Once these principles are understood, an intuitive operation of the Workbench is possible without requiring the study of extensive user guides. The Workbench can be started from the Tools/ABAP4-Workbench menu item or directly using the S001 transaction.

Figure 5.1: Workbench initial screen

The program development objects are stored in the Data Dictionary and in the Repository. Although the literature does not consistently differentiate between the two, the following general differentiation is often made:

- Data Dictionary
  contains the metadata of the system, i.e., the tables, field and key descriptions. These apply between programs.
- Repository
  includes the Data Dictionary and also contains all software development objects, such as programs, function modules, logical databases and message classes.

The Object Browser displays the contents of the Repository. The Object Browser can be invoked using the object lists shown in Figure 5.2 or using single objects. If single objects are used, the input of a name immediately starts the associated processing tool. Related development objects can be better represented in various list forms. Whereas the so-called development class represents the most general list form, program lists are specialized lists. Lists cannot be directly processed, but only selected and displayed.

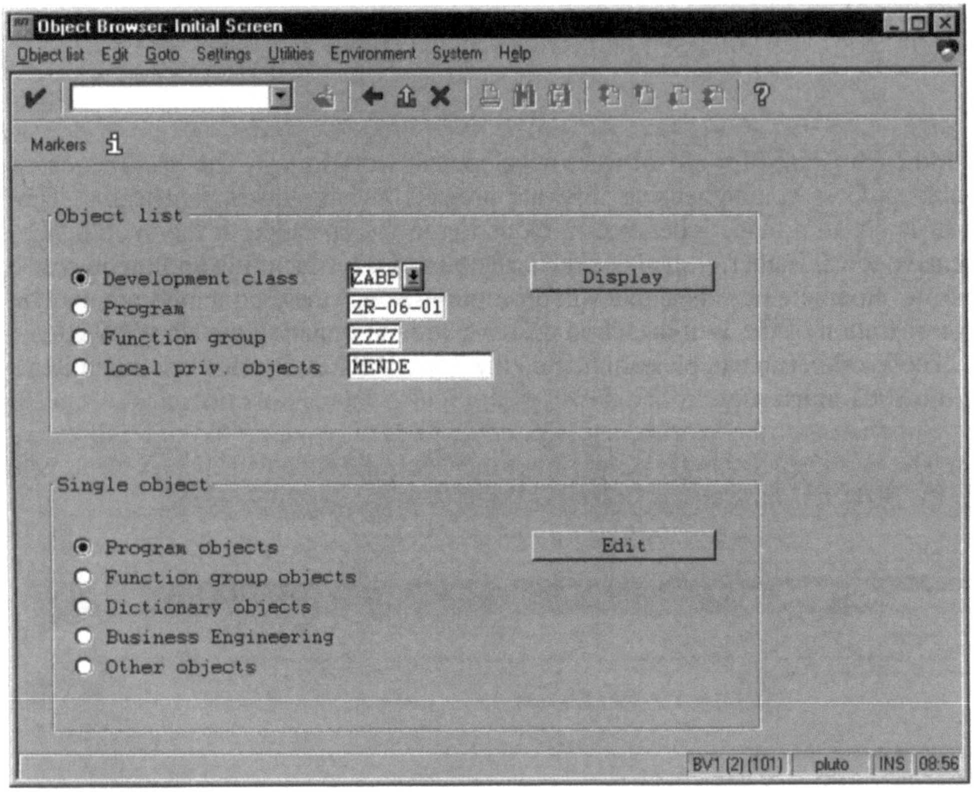

Figure 5.2: Workbench Object Browser

5.1 Program Development Objects

5.1.1 Development Classes

A development class represents a container for all development objects of a development task. It is organized hierarchically and can contain all types of development objects.

All data definitions and programs described in this book have been processed in the ZABP development class (see Figure 5.3).

The Workbench Organizer can transport a closed development class into another R/3 system.

The special development class $TMP is assigned to every developer. You can create development objects in this class that are not initially assigned to any development task. Such objects are called local, private objects.

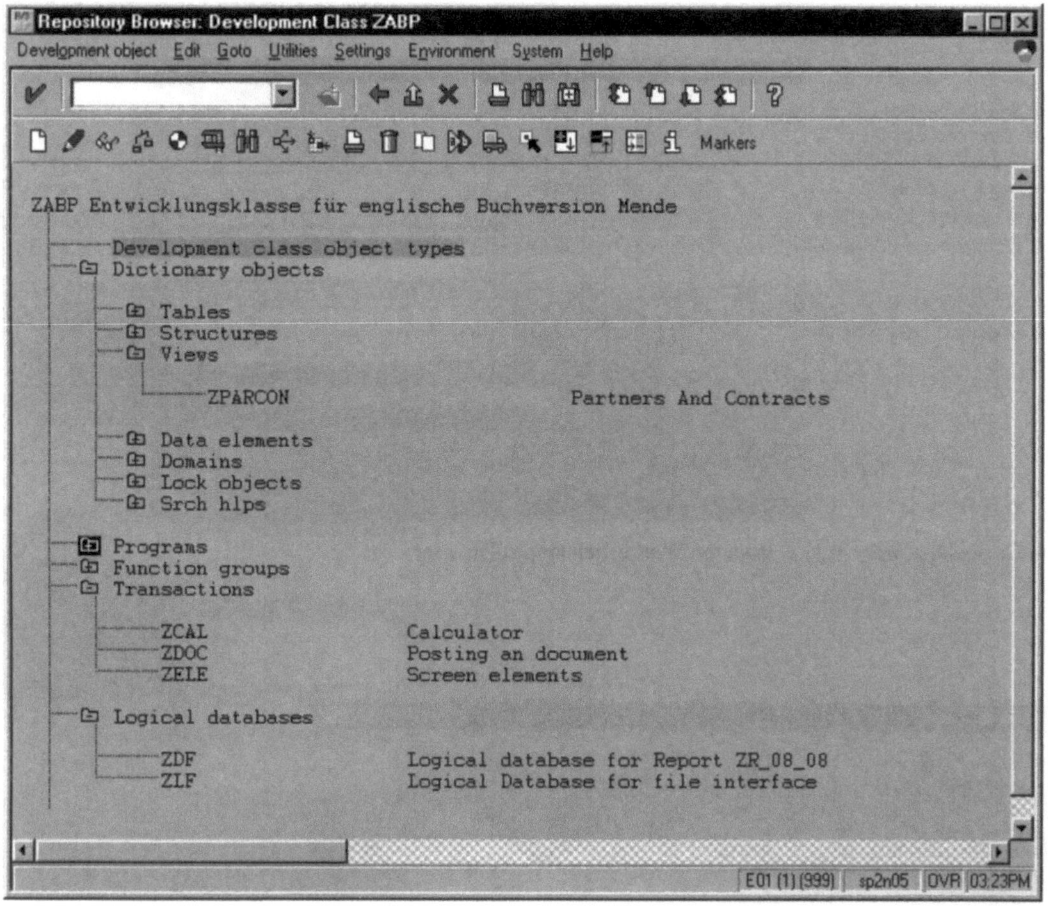

Figure 5.3: ZABP development class

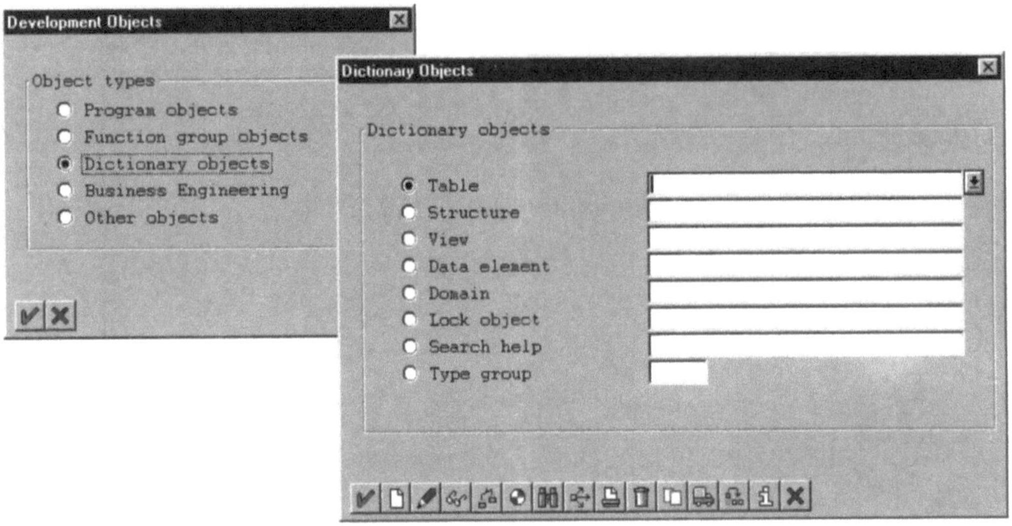

Figure 5.4: Create Dictionary objects from the Workbench Object Browser

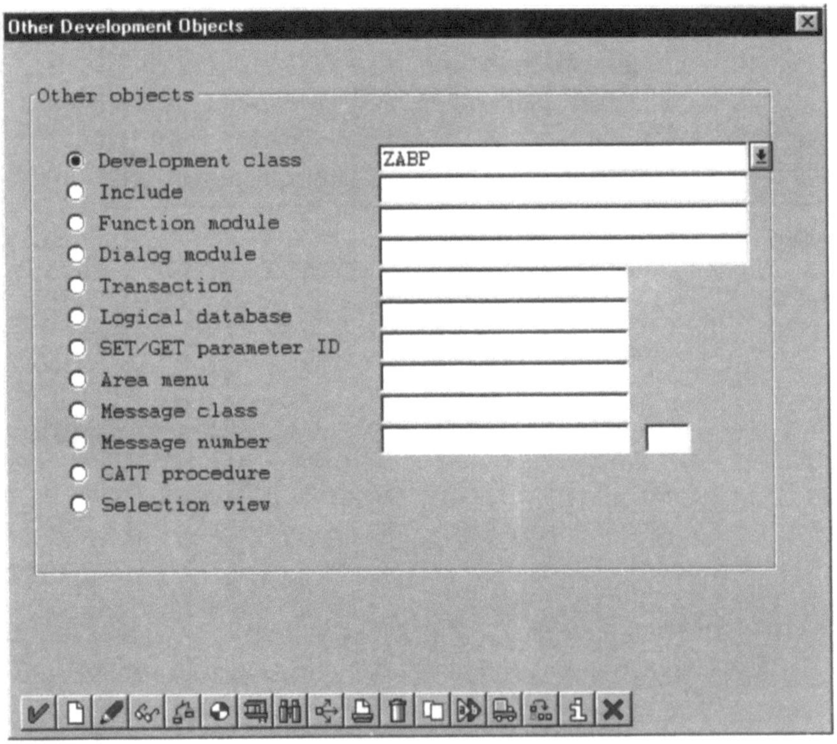

Figure 5.5: Create further objects using the Object Browser

The program lists and function group lists group all objects of a program or function group. In contrast to the independent, inter-program objects, such as message classes and logical databases, these are objects that only exist within a specific program.

Objects for all object types are processed in a similar manner. Once the object type has been selected, the name is entered and the object created or processed.

A double-click on a list of the Object Browser shows all available elements of the class. A double-click on an element opens the corresponding processing tool. The following example illustrates the creation of a new program.

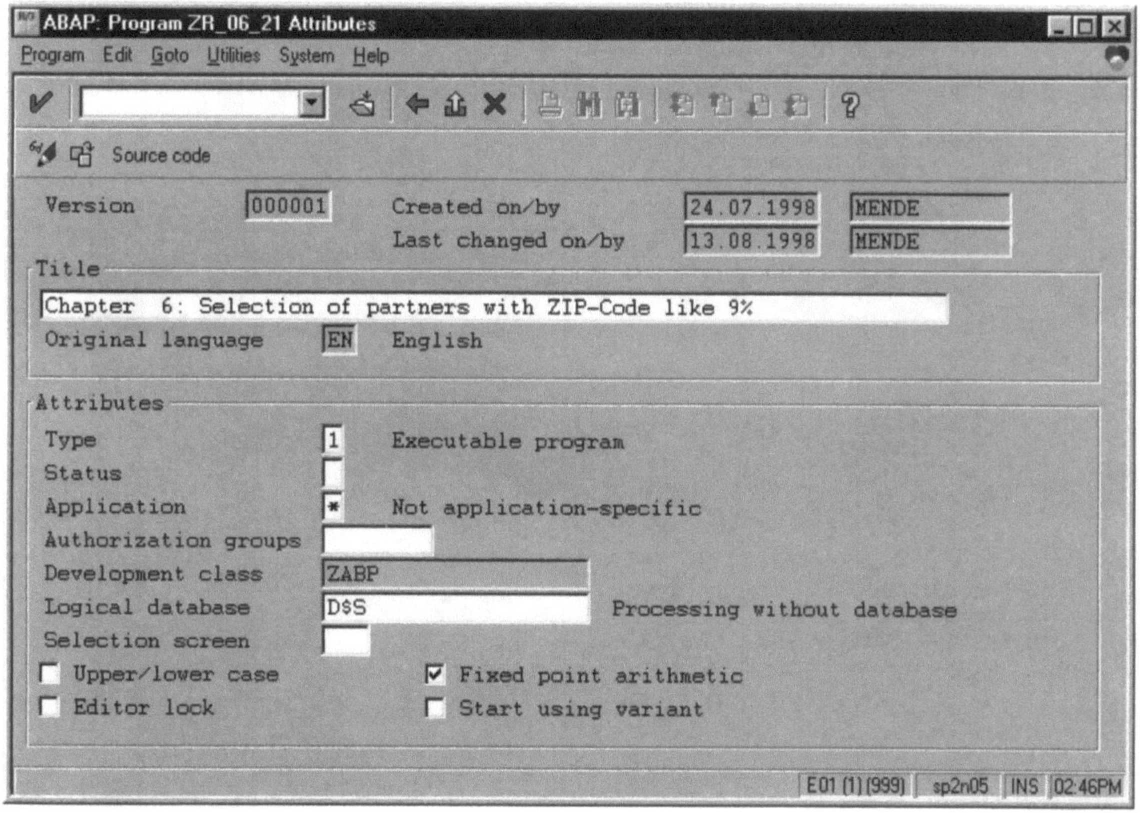

Figure 5.6: Create a new program

5.1.2 Program Lists

The program list of a specific program manages all objects and classifications that are assigned to the program. True program objects and references are intermixed. Figure 5.7 shows the program list for the program ZM-09-03. The telegram names contained in the DDIC structures item show that the corresponding TABLES declarations are contained in the program. The same applies for the global data, the PBO modules, etc. This part of the list is derived from the source code. Screens (dialog masks with processing) and menus differ. These are explicitly created from the program list and are processed with the Screen Painter or Menu Painter.

A double-click on an element opens the corresponding processing tool. Positioning is performed to the appropriate location for the source code editor.

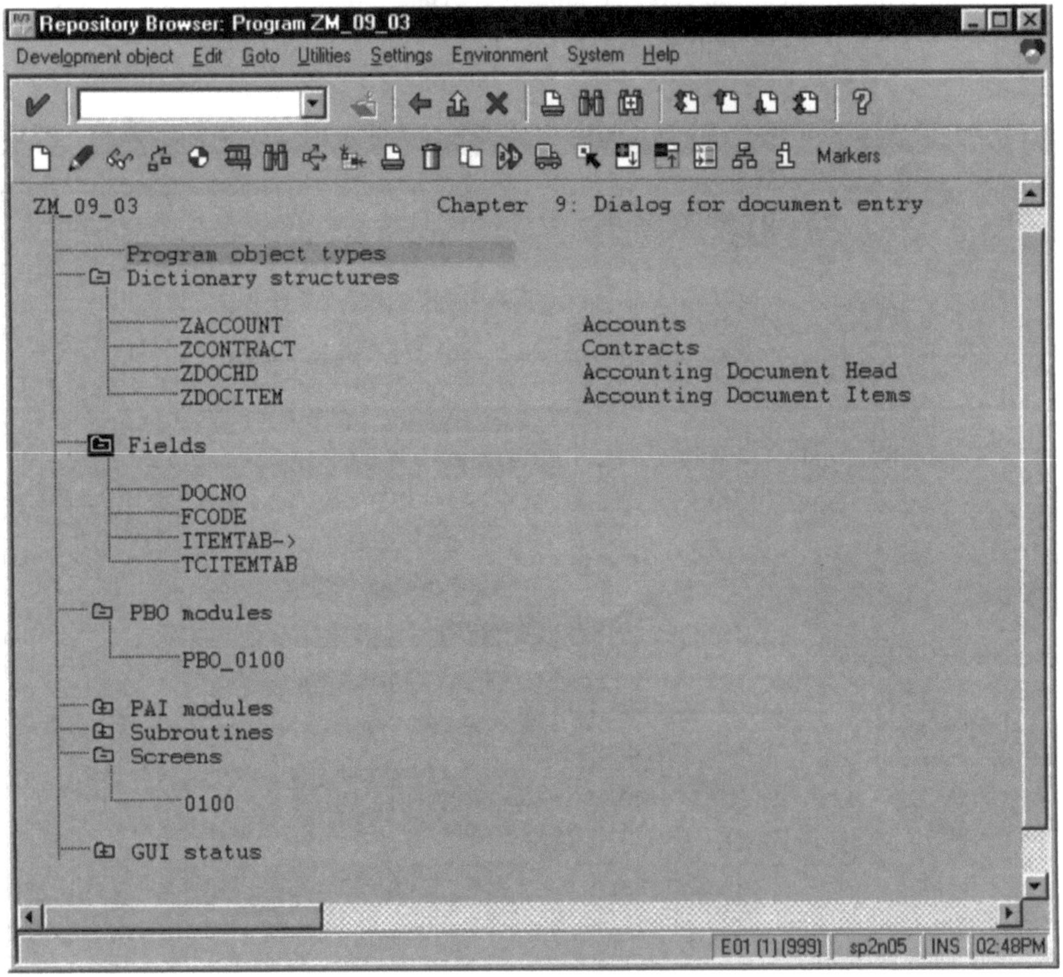

Figure 5.7: Program list with true program objects and source references

5.1.3 Includes

Includes represent reusable source code components that the appropriate command can incorporate in a program. SAP supports the automatic name assignment for Includes. The Editor is used for the processing.

5.1.4 Message Classes

A message class encapsulates the content of the associated messages. The message number can be used to invoke the messages in a program. Message numbers have the following advantages compared with text literals when used in the program:

- Programs do not contain any language-dependent texts
- Messages can be modified without requiring program changes
- Messages can be used by several programs.

The message text can contain up to 4 placeholders (&) that are replaced with specific values when the message is invoked.

The following system variables can be used in the program to query component parts of requested messages:

SY-MSGGR	Message group
SY-MSGNR	Running number in the group
SY-MSGTY	Invocation type of the message
SY-MSGV1	Value of the 1st placeholder variable
SY-MSGV2	Value of the 2nd placeholder variable
SY-MSGV3	Value of the 3rd placeholder variable
SY-MSGV4	Value of the 4th placeholder variable.

5.1.5 Logical Databases

Logical databases group several associated tables. The aim is to allow the uniform, automated data acquisition from these tables. Chapter 7 discusses logical databases. Chapter 13 extends the concept of logical databases to include the automated development of file interfaces.

5.1.6 Transactions

Transactions as development objects are four-character codes for programs. These can be entered in the command field together with the /o or /h switch. Various types of transactions can be created:

- *Dialog transaction*: Start a dialog program with the specified start screen
- *Report transaction*: Start the specified report
- *Variant transaction*: Start a (client-dependent) transaction variant
- *Area menu*: Start the specified area menu
- *Parameter transaction*: Start a transaction with parameters (e.g., SM30 table maintenance; the table name and the update flag serve as parameters).

5.1.7 Area Menus

In contrast to program menus, area menus represent interfaces between programs. The individual menu items here are programs that are specified by their transaction number.

A four-character code identifies area menus. In general, area menus can be used at all places where transaction codes are permitted. This means that area menus can be started in the same manner as transactions. In addition, area menus can also invoke other area menus. No program code is required for an area menu itself. All standard SAP transactions can be easily included in user-specific area menus. An area menu represents a very simple means of creating an appropriate frame for a current development.

The entry diagrams in the R/3 modules such as FI, CO, etc., usually exist as area menus.

5.2 Primary Objects

5.2.1 Number Ranges

The key values for entries in master tables and transaction tables are normally created automatically. Partner numbers, account numbers and document numbers are typical examples. Number range objects (see Figure 5.8) are used in R/3 for the assignment and validation of numbers.

In addition to names and descriptive texts, a reference domain is also specified for all numbers of the object. It determines the length and type of the numbers. Although several number range intervals can be assigned to every number range object, the intervals cannot overlap. An interval can operate with internal or external number assignment. The number range object can be used for external number assignment to validate an external number. Numbers in the associated intervals can be generated for internal assignment (creation of master data, books of documents, etc.).

Figure 5.9 shows two intervals of the ZDOCNO number range object. The upper interval is used for the acceptance of externally input documents that already have document numbers. The lower interval is provided for the creation of internal document numbers. Chapter 9 introduces the ZDOC booking transaction that invokes the NUMBER_GET_NEXT function module to obtain new document numbers in the internal number range for ZDOCNO.

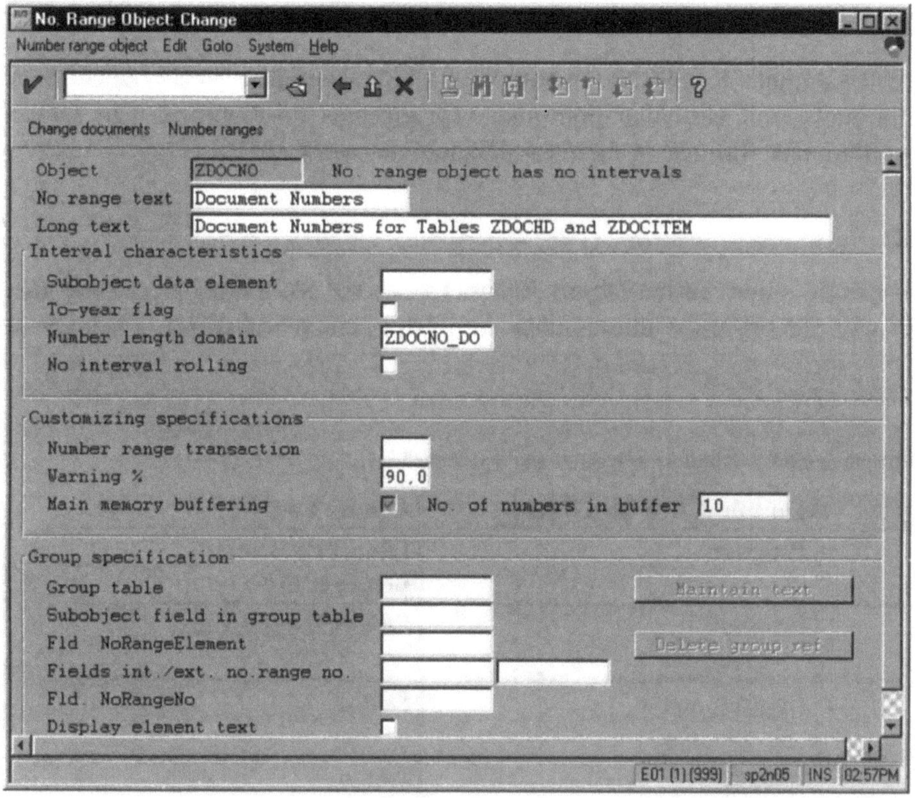

Figure 5.8: Create a number range object

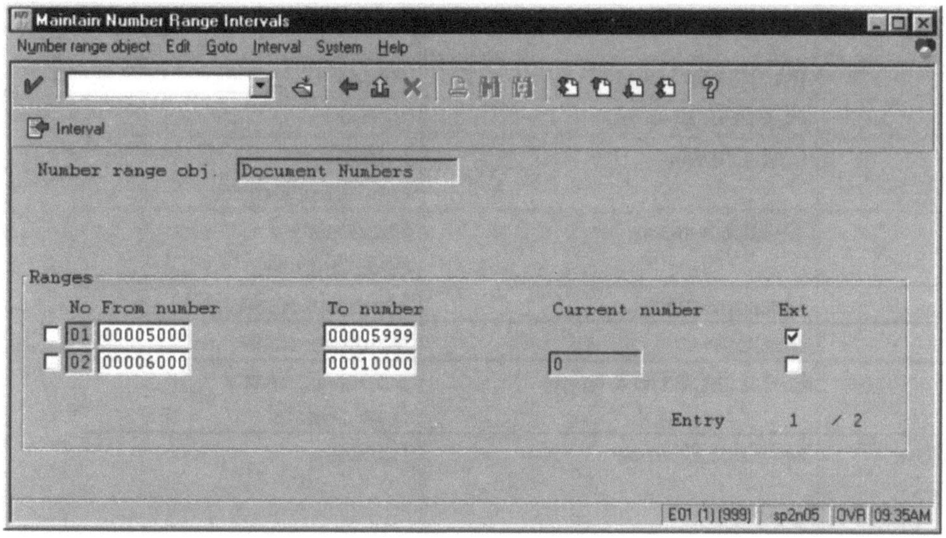

Figure 5.9: Number range interval of the ZDOCNO number range object

5.3 Use of the Workbench

The Workbench provides a range of tools, the operation of which is not described in detail here. The integration of the tools is of particular importance for efficient development. The Object Browser should be used to make full use of them for development work.

5.3.1 Navigation

A double-click on a specific object in the Object Browser starts the associated processing tool and loads it together with the object. A double-click on a list opens it and displays sublists or specific objects.

Table 5.1: Examples of the navigation capabilities offered in the Workbench

Tool	Double-Click on Object	Opens Tool
Object Browser / development class	Programs	Object Browser/ program list
Object Browser/ program list	Program	Object list program
Object Browser/ object list program	Program name	Editor
	Include	Editor
	Global data	Editor
	GUI status	Menu Painter
	Screen	Screen Painter / flow control
Editor	INCLUDE *name*	Editor
	PERFORM *name*	Editor
	CALL *name*	Editor / function element
	TABLES *name*	Dictionary / table display
	Message class	Maintain message class
	Message	Maintain class
	CALL SCREEN *name*	Screen Painter / flow control
Screen Painter/ flow control	MODULE *name*	Editor

If an object contains other objects or references to other objects, a double-click can also be used to process this new object. The Return key returns to the original tool.

Not only the Workbench tools, but also the Data Dictionary with its maintenance dialogs is included in this navigation. Table 5.1 shows the examples for the navigation within the Workbench tools and the Data Dictionary.

In many cases a new object can be created directly during the processing of another object. For example, assume you have determined that a new subprogram (FORM) is required while working with an ABAP/4 source code. It is not necessary to leave the Editor. Rather, you simply enter the call to the subprogram (PERFORM name) at the appropriate location. You must confirm in the dialog that appears after a double-click that a new FORM object is to be created. You can make the assignment to an existing or new source code. This source code is opened automatically and then the code for the subprogram can be entered. The original program reappears once the program has been stored. Another example is the creation of data elements directly from the table field maintenance.

All tools provide their own menus. The menus are standardized and contain the following submenus:

- <object>
  This contains the associated object type, namely "program" for the Editor, "screen" for the Screen Painter, etc. Commands are provided that relate to the complete object:
  - test
  - generate
  - print
  - exit
- Process
  - copy
  - insert
  - search
- Go to
  normally provides different views. The "Attribute" command is often available.
- Help
  permits the branching to related applications or tools, to version management or where-used lists

5.3.2 Where-Used List

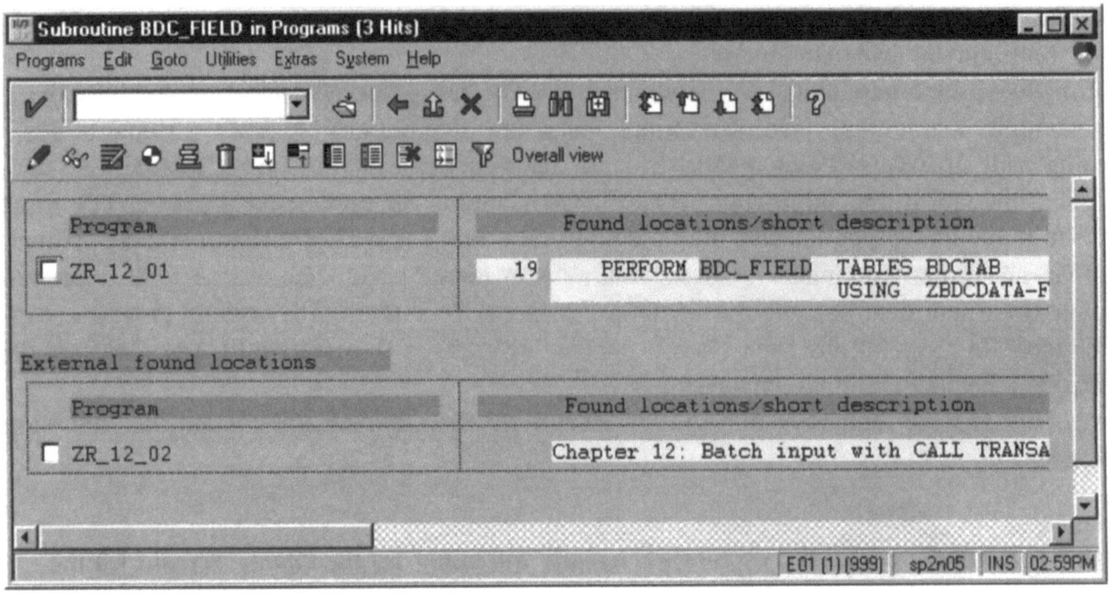

Figure 5.10: Where-used list for a subprogram

Starting with a definition location or an entry in an object list, so-called where-used lists can be created for almost all development objects.

Such lists in other development systems are commonly called reference lists or cross-reference lists for functions. Where-used lists provide the users with the essential support for large applications. For example, they can use them to provide an overview of the other affected objects before he changes an object. Figure 5.10 shows the where-used list of the BDC_FIELD subprogram that is defined in the ZR-12-01 program. The report shows that the subprogram is not only invoked in this program but also in the ZR-12-02 program (externally found locations).

Other objects, e.g., tables, can be used in various ways. In this case, the where-used list can be restricted to specific usage types (see Figure 5.11).

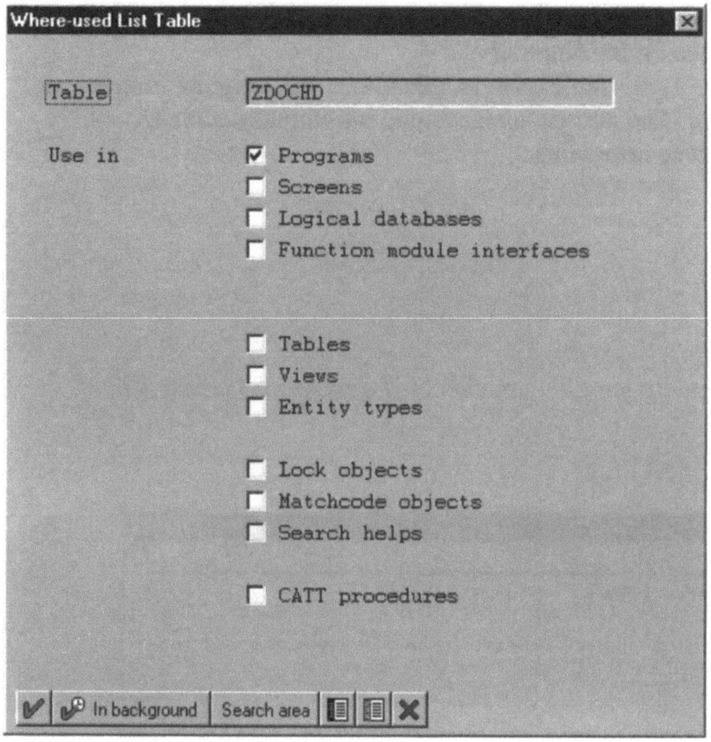

Figure 5.11: Selection of the usage type before the display of the where-used list

5.4 Important Workbench Tools

5.4.1 Source Code Editor

The source code editor is used to process all ABAP/4 texts. The Settings/Editor Mode menu item can be used to select three different modes. The older command mode provides a five-character command column in which the commands can be entered from the keyboard. The block commands (CC, DD, MM), in particular, are very efficient. However, the fact that the Enter key does not produce a new line but merely transfers data (display refresh) is often found to be non-intuitive.

The PC modes were developed for these reasons. Figure 5.12 shows the Editor in PC mode with line numbering. Enter produces a new line in this mode. The commands are selected with the mouse from the menu or directly input using pushbuttons. The following characteristics and commands are of particular importance:

- Block commands
  - Mark blocks through the double use of the Mark key (F9)
  - Three system-wide block buffers (X, Y, and Z storage areas) that the program components can transfer between various modes. The storage areas can be individually edited.
  - Assign comments to blocks or delete comments
  - Move blocks horizontally
- General assistance
  - Upload and download editor text
  - Help for ABAP/4
  - Switch ruler on/off
- Search and replace
  - Search and replace can be performed over all source code of a program framework.

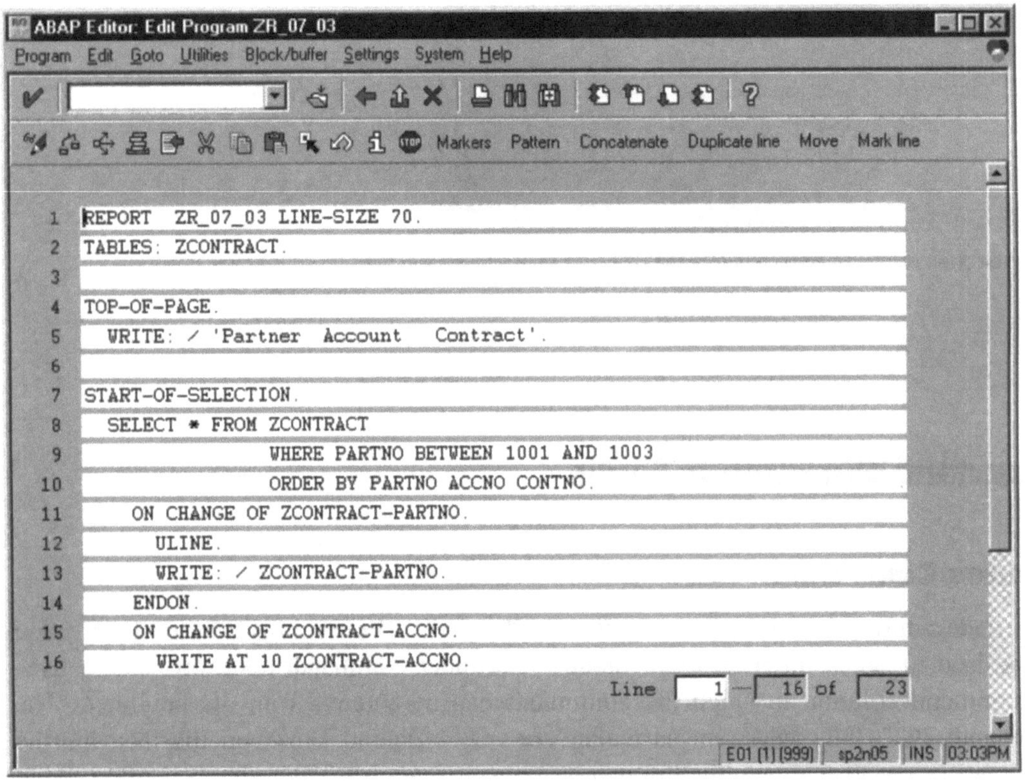

Figure 5.12: Source code editor in PC mode with line numbering

The Editor is itself written in ABAP/4 (SAPMEDIT program). A study of the sources can be very interesting for advanced ABAP/4 developers. Such developers can learn a great deal about string processing, DDIC access, menu processing, program calls and authorization validation from the function of well-known and understandable programs. The Editor offers many useful navigation capabilities and can be used as model for the complete development environment.

5.4.2 Menu Painter

The Menu Painter is used to design program menus and area menus. Program menus are assigned to programs and stored as GUI status in the associated program list. Chapters 7 and 9 show how the SET PF-STATUS command can be used to include them in reports and dialog programs. Area menus can be used across program boundaries. The four-character function code that must be assigned to all menu components forms the connection element between the user interface (menu) and a program (menu evaluation). This function code is sent to the program and evaluated there when a menu element is activated.

The following components can be maintained in the Menu Painter:

- *Menu*: Multi-cascaded menu trees can be created. The function codes are assigned only to the lowest level commands of the tree. Transaction codes are used in place of the function codes for area menus.
- *Symbolbar*: Small buttons immediately below the menu bar that usually have standard assignments (Return, Exit, Cancel. Print, Find, Scroll, Help).
- *Print key bar*: Important, frequently-used menu commands in icon, text or mixed form.
- *Function key assignment*: Assignment of the menu command to function keys. Standard assignments of the function keys are used for standard commands (Print, Help, etc.).

Figure 5.13 shows the program menu of the ABAP/4 editor from Figure 5.12.

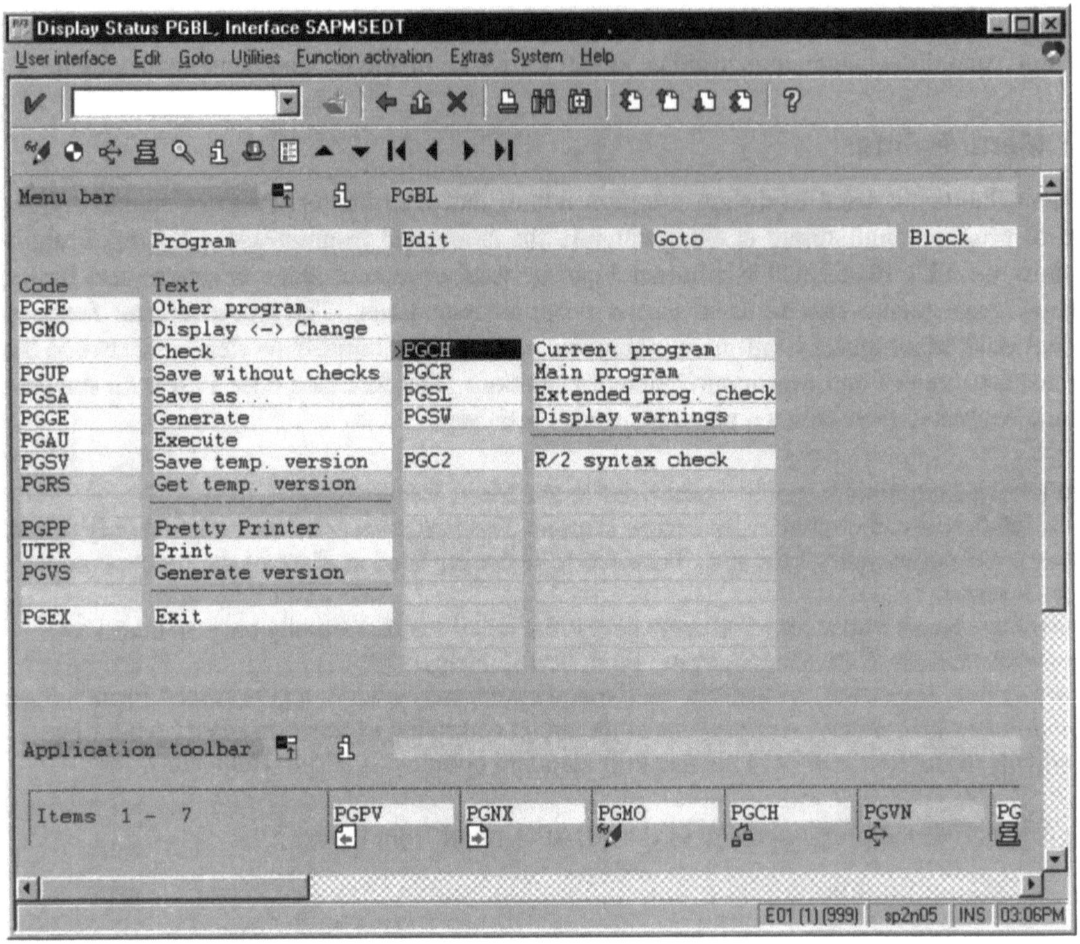

Figure 5.13: Menu Painter

6 ABAP/4 Fundamentals

ABAP/4 is the acronym for **A**dvanced **B**usiness **A**pplication **P**rogramming / **4**th Generation. Based on the widely used COBOL language, ABAP/4 has become a true 4GL. This chapter provides an introduction to the significant characteristics of ABAP/4. The subsequent chapters provide a detailed description.

In contrast with other languages, it is not practical to separate ABAP/4 from the associated development environment. Its comprehensive capabilities for the development of modern client-server software systems in a team forms an important success factor for ABAP/4.

On the other hand, the close integration of ABAP/4 in the R/3 system means that programs are written exclusively for the R/3 system or its successor. Porting to other systems is not practicable. However, we can largely disregard this characteristic, often criticized as being proprietary. Other large development systems also demand a decision to be made for *a* language and *an* environment. Furthermore, the call for portability has a rather academic character. For development times lasting several years, data volumes involving terabytes of information, and investments running into many millions of dollars, one is more interested in long-term stability of the software system than in easy porting.

A truly practice-oriented demand made of a modern software system and its development environment is openness. In this regard, great efforts have been made in R/3 in general and ABAP/4 in particular. The RPC and OLE components of the ABAP/4 language that provide efficient program coupling to a wide range of external system are representatives of this openness.

6.1 ABAP/4 Characteristics

6.1.1 User-Defined Data Types of Various Complexity

ABAP/4 can use fundamental data types to define its own structured data types of various degrees of complexity. An internal field is a storage area for exactly one value of a specific data type. Field strings are groupings of various internal fields; they are also designated as structures. Identical structures can be combined as internal tables (Figure 6.1). These are generally assigned a dynamic memory management in ABAP/4.

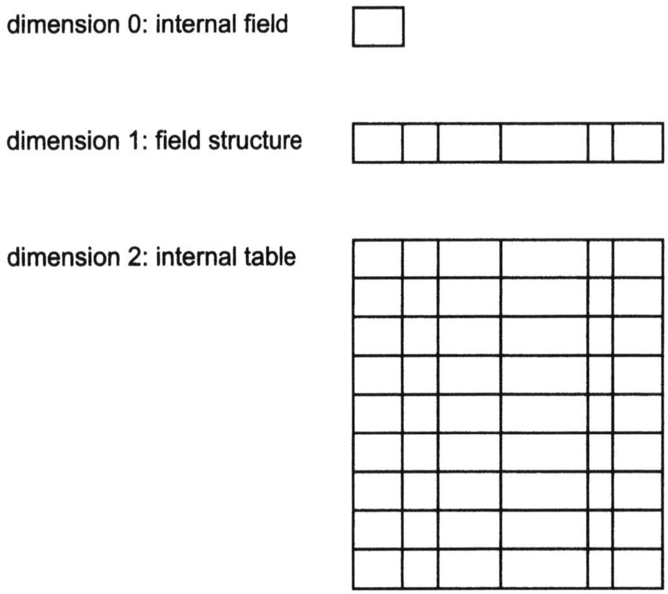

Figure 6.1: Data types of various complexities in ABAP/4

Combinations of various complexities are also possible, for example

- Structures whose fields are also structures
- Structures whose fields are tables
- Tables whose fields are structures
- Tables whose fields are also tables.

ABAP/4 generally differentiates between data types and data objects. Data types can be grouped as so-called TYPE-POOLS and are stored in the Dictionary. All modularization techniques can use typed symbolic parameters. Powerful functions not known from other programming languages exist, in particular for complex data objects.

If you make assignments between fields of different data types in other programming languages, these normally cause errors such as type conflict if you have forgotten to explicitly convert the data contents before the assignment. In ABAP/4, the appropriate type conversions are automatically performed during the assignment between fields having different data types.

6.1.2 Access to the Data Dictionary and Repository

In ABAP/4, you can access all metadata of the R/3 system in the Data Dictionary. The information stored here greatly exceeds that normally stored in the system tables of a database.

ABAP/4 possesses commands for the manipulation of the programs in the Repository (add, delete).

6.1.3 Database Access Using Open SQL

The Open SQL commands of ABAP/4 provide access to the database data.

Those commands that relate directly to complex ABAP/4 data types, for example a SELECT that immediately creates an internal table from all records read from the database, are particularly efficient.

In addition to the database-independent Open SQL, direct access to the R/3 database is also possible using native SQL (see Section 6.9).

6.1.4 Windows and Event-Oriented Dialog Programming

ABAP/4 is an event-oriented language. Several keywords identify events that can be initiated in various ways. If an event occurs, all instructions up to the next event keyword are processed.

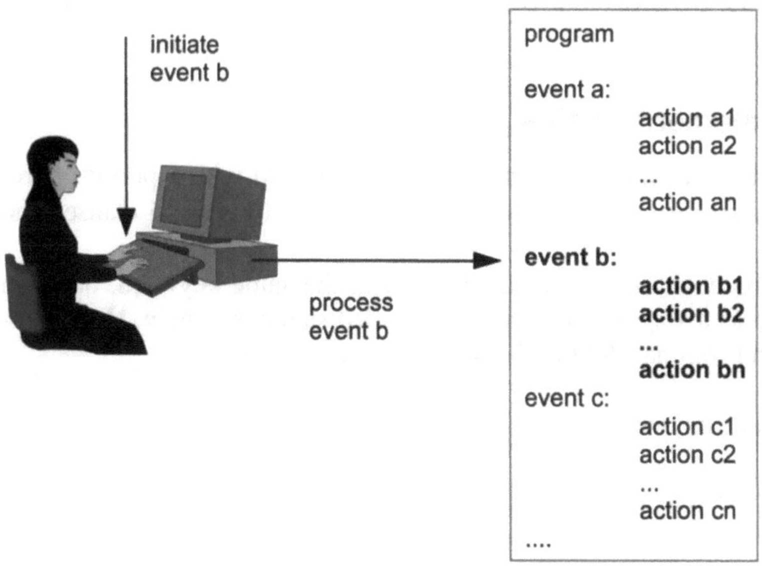

Figure 6.2: Event control

6.1.5 Code Generation and Interpreter Operation

A generation operation converts the ABAP/4 source code into a macro code that is then interpreted. The Workbench automatically performs the generation operation and so permits the developer to execute his source code without having to perform practically any intermediate steps. The interpretative processing permits access at run-time to the field names, which the appropriate dynamic variants provide support for many commands.

Every program can be started immediately in debug mode without requiring any special generation.

6.1.6 Modularization

ABAP/4 provides various techniques to support the modularization of programs. Whereas reports are normally grouped into events, subroutines and function modules, dialog programs are grouped as events, modules, subroutines and function modules. The individual modularization techniques are described at those places in the book where the required basis for the program example is available.

6.1.7 System Fields

System fields are the fields of the SY structure that serve as interface between a program and the system. Depending on specific executed program steps, the R/3 system sets values in these fields. The program can query the contents of these fields without requiring that the SY structure has been declared explicitly. The program can also manipulate some system fields. Chapter 6 describes the SY-DATUM, SY-SUBRC, SY-DBCNT, SY-TABIX, SY-INDEX and SY-FDPOS system fields.

6.1.8 Instructions and Statement Chains

A program in ABAP/4 is comprised of individual instructions terminated with a period. A reserved word or a keyword starts an instruction, which can be followed by several clauses and data objects.

If two or more identical instructions, namely instructions with the same keyword, occur in sequence, they can be combined as a *single* instruction, a so-called statement chain. Here a colon is suffixed to the keyword and commas delimit the following data objects.

Series of instructions with the same keyword:

```
 Keyword   Dataobject 1.
 Keyword   Dataobject 2.
...
 Keyword   Dataobject n.
```

Statement chain:

```
 Keyword:  Dataobject 2, Dataobject 2, ... , Dataobject n.
```

6.1.9 Assignments with Offset and Length Details

The assignment of values to fields can specify an offset and a length to address an individual byte of the target field that is to contain a value. The first byte of the target field has the offset 0, the second byte has the offset 1, etc. The length specifies the number of bytes to be assigned starting at the offset.

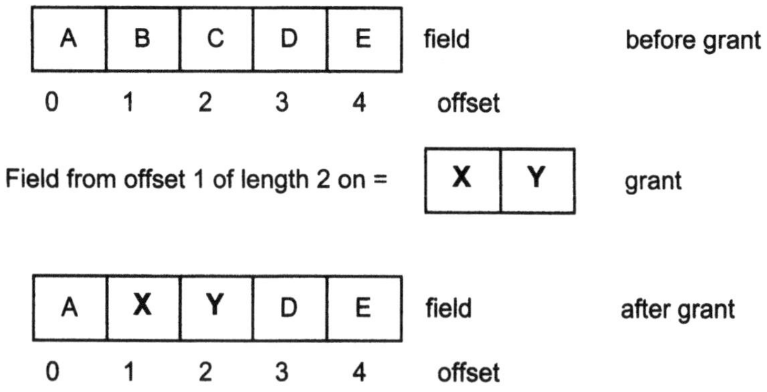

Figure 6.3: Assignment with offset and length details

6.1.10 Comments in the Source Code

An asterisk character (*) in the first column of a source code line indicates that the complete line is a comment line. The Editor highlights the complete line in color. Any asterisk not present in the first column produces a syntax error. The quotation mark character (") is used to introduce an embedded comment in an ABAP/4 instruction. The following text is not highlighted.

Comments:

```
* complete comment line
 instruction. " comment started after instruction (task)
```

6.2 Internal Fields

6.2.1 Declaration – DATA

An internal field is a storage area for a single word of a specific data type and is declared in the following general form:

DATA *field name*
[(*field length*)]
[**TYPE** *data type*]
[**DECIMALS** *digits*]
[**VALUE** *start value*].

The field name can have a maximum length of 30 characters and can contain alphabetic characters, digits and underscores. Names with certain special characters and names that only contain digits are not permitted.

The type specification with TYPE is optional. A field of type C is assumed if the data type is omitted. ABAP/4 recognizes the C; N, D, T, X, I, P and F basic data types.

Table 6.1: ABAP/4 basic data types

Type	Significance of Type	Standard Length	Initial Value	Internal Format
C	Character string	1	Blank	
N	Numeric string	1	'0'	
D	Date	8	'00000000'	YYYYMMDD
T	Time	6	'000000'	HHMMSS
X	Hexadecimal number	1	X'00'	
I	Integer	4	0	
P	Packed number	8	0	
F	Float	8	'0.0'	

The optional field length can be specified in parentheses after the field name for the C, N, P and X data types. This length overrides the standard data length for the associated data type.

The field is initialized appropriately for its type if no default value is specified with VALUE. Although it is not necessary to set the initialization value in apostrophes for some data types, apostrophes are always permitted.

The DECIMALS clause can be used for the P data type. DECIMALS specifies the number of numeric digits that follow the decimal point. This value is used for the field output and for rounding operations.

Examples of possible declarations follow:

```
Field of type C, 20 byte, standard setting Michael Smith
DATA NAME(20) VALUE 'Michael Smith'.

* Field of type C, 1 byte, start value A
DATA LETTER VALUE 'A'.
* Field of type N, 5 byte, initial value 00000
DATA ZIP CODE(5) TYPE N.

* Field of type N, 1 byte, start value 2
DATA DIGIT 1 TYPE N VALUE '2'.

* Field of type I, 4 byte, start value  5
DATA NUMBER TYPE I VALUE 5.

* Field of type P, 8 byte, 2 decimals, start value 7,00
DATA AMOUNT EURO TYPE P DECIMALS 2 VALUE 7

* Field of type P, 8 byte, 4 decimals, start value 3,514
DATA MULTIPLICATOR TYPE P DECIMALS 4 VALUE '3.514'.

* Field of type D, 8 byte, start value 31.01.1999
DATA DATE TYPE D VALUE '19990131'.
```

The LIKE clause can be used instead of the detailed notation with length and data type to assign an internal field the same properties as a table field from the Data Dictionary or a previously defined internal program field. The field contents can be initialized with VALUE.

DATA *fieldname* **LIKE** *field* [**VALUE** *startvalue*].

```
* Field like DDIC table field, initial value
DATA PRODNO LIKE ZPRODCT-PRODNO.

* Field like system field, initial value
DATA DATE1 LIKE SY-DATUM.

* Field definition like the field defined previously in the program,
    initial setting
DATA DATE2 LIKE DATE1 VALUE '19991231'.
```

6.2.2 Processing – CLEAR, MOVE, COMPUTE

Values can be assigned to internal fields in the program using

- the = assignment operator
- the MOVE keyword.

An arithmetic expression using the basic computation operators can be assigned using

- the = assignment operator and the +, -, * and / operators
- the COMPUTE keyword and the +, -, * and / operators
- the ADD, SUBTRACT, MULTIPLY and DIVIDE keywords.

CLEAR can be used in the program processing to initialize a field to its type-appropriate value.

```
REPORT ZR 06 01 LINE-SIZE 70.
DATA: NUMBER1 TYPE P DECIMALS 2 VALUE '5.9',
      NUMBER2 TYPE P DECIMALS 2 VALUE '7.2'.
DATA RESULT TYPE P DECIMALS 2.

RESULT = NUMBER1 + NUMBER2.
WRITE / RESULT.                     " Output
CLEAR RESULT.                       " initialize result depending on type
RESULT = NUMBER2 - NUMBER1.
WRITE / RESULT.
CLEAR RESULT.
COMPUTE RESULT = NUMBER1 * NUMBER2.  " RESULT = NUMBER1 * NUMBER2.
WRITE / RESULT.
CLEAR RESULT.
COMPUTE RESULT = NUMBER2 / NUMBER1.
WRITE / RESULT.
* an alternative way to program:
SKIP 2.                               " 2 blank lines
MOVE NUMBER1 TO RESULT.
ADD NUMBER2 TO RESULT.
WRITE / RESULT.
MOVE NUMBER2 TO RESULT.
SUBTRACT NUMBER1 FROM RESULT.
WRITE / RESULT.
MOVE NUMBER1 TO RESULT.
MULTIPLY RESULT BY NUMBER2.
WRITE / RESULT.
MOVE NUMBER2 TO RESULT.
DIVIDE RESULT BY NUMBER1.
WRITE / RESULT.
```

```
22.09.1998 Chapter  6: Internal fields and basic calculations       1
----------------------------------------------------------------------
           13,10
            1,30
           42,48
            1,22


           13,10
            1,30
           42,48
            1,22
```

In addition to the basic computation operators, ABAP/4 also provides various functions in its language repertoire.

Table 6.2: Functions for all numeric argument types x

Function	Significance
ABS(x)	Amount (absolute value) of x
SIGN(x)	Sign (arithmetic sign) of x, y = 1, 0, -1
TRUNC(x)	Integer part of x
FRAC(x)	Fractional part of x

```
REPORT  ZR-06-02 LINE-SIZE 70.
CONSTANTS: PI TYPE P DECIMALS 2 VALUE '3.14'.
DATA: NUMBER LIKE PI.

NUMBER = TRUNC( PI ).
WRITE / NUMBER.
NUMBER = FRAC( PI ).
WRITE / NUMBER.
NUMBER = NUMBER * ( -1 ).
NUMBER = ABS( NUMBER ).
WRITE / NUMBER.
NUMBER = NUMBER * ( -1 ).
NUMBER = SIGN( NUMBER ). " NUMBER = -1, if algebraic sign is neg.
WRITE / NUMBER.
```

```
22.09.1998      Chapter  6: Internal Fields and Functions          1
---------------------------------------------------------------------
                3,00
                0,14
                0,14
                1,00-
```

Table 6.3: Real-value functions for real-value arguments x

Function	Significance
y = COS(x)	Cosine of an angle specified as radians
y = SIN(x)	Sine of an angle specified as radians
y = TAN(x)	Tangent of an angle specified as radians
y = EXP(x)	Exponential function to Euler number base
y = LOG(x)	Natural logarithm of a positive number
y = SQRT(x)	Square root of a non-negative number

Table 6.4: Character string functions

Function	Significance
CONCATENATE	Concatenate character strings
SPLIT	Split character strings
SHIFT	Shift character strings to the left or to the right
CONDENSE	Condense character strings (delete blanks)
TRANSLATE	Translate characters into character strings
OVERLAY	Overlay two character strings
REPLACE	Replace substrings in a character string
SEARCH	Search for substrings in a character string

Internal functions of type D can be manipulated in ABAP/4 using the offset, because the data type D is stored internally like a 8-digit field of type N. Addition and subtraction, namely date arithmetic, are also defined for the type D. If you add one day to February 28, the result is either February 29 or March 1, depending whether the year is a leap year.

```
REPORT  ZR 06 03 LINE-SIZE 70.
DATA: DATE LIKE SY-DATUM.

DATE = SY-DATUM.          " current date
WRITE / DATE.
DATE+6(2) = '01'.        " first day of the month
WRITE / DATE.
DATE = DATE - 1.         " subtract day -> last day of the previous month
WRITE / DATE.
DATE+4(4) = '1231'.  " last day of the year
```

```
WRITE / DATE.
DATE = DATE + 1.     " add day -> first day of the following year.
WRITE / DATE.
DATE = '00000001'.
WRITE / DATE.
DATE = 1.
WRITE / DATE.
```

```
22.09.1998            Chapter  6: Date arithmetics              1
-----------------------------------------------------------------
22.09.1998
01.09.1998
31.08.1998
31.12.1998
01.01.1999
01.00.0000
02.01.0001
```

6.2.3 Constants

An internal field that has been declared with the DATA keyword can be changed during the program processing. The CONSTANTS keyword and the mandatory VALUE clause are used if a constant is to be defined. Because the value of a constant cannot be changed, a constant can only be used on the right side of an assignment in a program.

CONSTANTS *fieldname* [**TYPE** *datatype*] [**DECIMALS** *digit*] **VALUE** *value.*

The use of constants improves the readability and maintainability of source code.

```
DATA: NET TYPE P DECIMALS 2,
      GROSS TYPE P DECIMALS 2.
CONSTANTS TAX TYPE P DECIMALS 2 VALUE '1.15'.
* ...
GROSS = NET * TAX.
```

6.3 Output Instructions – WRITE, SKIP, ULINE, NEW-PAGE

The WRITE output instruction creates an output on the standard output diagram of a report. This diagram is comparable with continuous paper that can be written, displayed, stored and printed. The command cannot be used on the dialog programming diagrams, the screens. The dialog programming screens are screen masks with input/output fields, the content of which is directly manipulated using data transport.

The WRITE instruction can act on an internal field not only as output. This type of WRTITE is not described here. The simplest form of a WRITE instruction outputs a value.

```
WRITE 'ABAP/4'. " output literal
WRITE fieldname.      " output Field
```

Several successive WRITE instructions are output in a single line to the extent permitted by the defined width of the report. The field contents are set in the next line if insufficient space is available in the line. Unless an explicit definition has been made, the report has a standard width of 120 characters.

An output line consisting of literals and field contents can be produced not only multiple WRITE instructions but also using a WRITE with chained record.

Example without statement chain:

```
WRITE 'With the customer'.
WRITE NAME OF CUSTOMER.
WRITE AMOUNT.
WRITE 'a turnover of'.
WRITE 'EURO has been realized'.
```

Example with statement chain:

```
WRITE: 'With the customer', NAME, 'a turnover of EURO',AMOUNT,'has
         been realized'.
```

Observant readers will have noticed that no space characters are produced for the succession of outputs as is usual with other programming languages. The previous instruction in PASCAL would produce the following output on the screen:

```
With the customerSMITHaturnoverof100EURO has been realized
```

ABAP/4 automatically produces space characters between fields and literals. The NO-GAP clause after WRITE is used if no space characters are to be produced. The WRITE instruction has the following complete syntax:

WRITE [formatting] *value* [clauses].

Formatting is specified in the form /c[l), where / produces a line feed before the output, c specifies the output column and l the output length. The term value refers to fields and literals. A clause is NO-GAP, etc.

SKIP, ULINE and NEW-PAGE are other output instructions. SKIP produces a empty line. ULINE produces a line of underscores. NEW-PAGE produces a new page only on printer output but not for screen output.

```
REPORT  ZR_06_04 LINE-SIZE 70.

WRITE / '2'.           " new row, output
WRITE '2'.             " output
WRITE / '3'.           " new row, output
WRITE '3'.             " output
SKIP.                  " empty row
WRITE '5'.             " output
SKIP 2.                " 2 empty rows
ULINE.                 " dotted line

* complete formatting follows by /s(l)
WRITE /10(12) 'Outputlength: this is not viewable'.

* a new row is not displayed on the screen,
* but is typed out as new page on the printer
NEW-PAGE NO-TITLE.
WRITE 10 'new page'.
```

```
22.09.1998          Chapter  6: Output statements                1
--------------------------------------------------------------------
2 2
3 3

5


--------------------------------------------------------------------
         Outputlength
         new page
```

6.4 Control Instructions

The control instructions in ABAP/4 can be divided into three groups:

- Condition differentiation, e.g. IF and CASE
- Loop instructions e.g. DO and WHILE
- Other control instructions, e.g. CHECK, EXIT, CONTINUE

ABAP/4 does not provide the GOTO branch instruction and the FOR loop, two commonly known control instructions from other programming languages.

6.4.1 Conditional Instructions – IF, CASE

Branches are required in the program if specific program logic only applies for certain cases, but not for all. IF and CASE permit a branching of the program logic.

```
IF logical expression.
*       program logic
ENDIF.
```

The ELSE clause is required if an alternative program branch is to be produced depending on the logical expression.

```
IF logical expression.
*       program logic1
ELSE.
*       program logic2
ENDIF.
```

The IF branch is processed if the logical expression evaluates true. The ELSE clause of the ELSE branch is processed if the logical expression evaluates false.

```
IF logical expression 1.
*       program logic 1
ELSE.
        IF logical expression2.
*               program logic2
        ELSE.
*               program logic3
        ENDIF.
ENDIF.
```

IF instructions can be nested. A direct IF after an ELSE can be alternatively programmed with the ELSEIF keyword. The simplest logical expression comprises of the following components:

<fieldname><OP><value>

The left side of the expression , the contents of the <fieldname> field, is compared at run-time with the value of the right side, a literal or another field's contents. The comparison operator <OP> symbolizes a possible operator, which in ABAP/4 can be specified in either verbal or mathematical terminology.

IF *logical expression1.*
*   program logic1
ELSEIF *logical expression2.*
*   program logic2
ELSE.
*   program logic3
ENDIF.

Table 6.5: Relational operators

Mathematical Term	Verbal Term	Meaning
=	EQ	Equal
<>	NE	Not equal
>	GT	Greater than
>=	GE	Greater than or equal
<	LT	Less than
<=	LE	Less than or equal

```
REPORT  ZR 06 05 LINE-SIZE 70.
DATA: VAL1 TYPE I VALUE '4',
      VAL2 TYPE I VALUE '2'.

IF VAL1 EQ VAL2.                                " or: VAL1 = VAL2
  WRITE: 5(1) VAL1, '=', 9(1) VAL2.
ELSEIF VAL1 GT VAL2.                            " or: VAL1 > VAL2
  WRITE: 5(1) VAL1, '>', 9(1) VAL2.
ELSE.
  WRITE: 5(1) VAL1, '<', 9(1) VAL2.
ENDIF.
```

```
22.09.1998              Chapter  6: IF-Statement              1
-------------------------------------------------------------------
    4 > 2
```

ABAP/4 provides powerful string operators to support comparisons with literal or field contents that consist not just of one character but of character strings.

Table 6.6: String operators

Logical Expression	Significance	Description
"field" **CO** *"value"*	Contains only:	*field* contains only *value*
"field" **CA** *"value"*	Contains any:	*field* contains at least one character from *value*
"field" **CS** *"value"*	Contains string:	*field* contains character string from *value*
"field" **CP** *"value"*	Contains pattern:	*field* contains pattern from *value*

Additional operators are provided for the logical negation of the four specified operators. It is also possible to use the NOT operator. Please note that the logical inverse of "*field* contains only characters from *value*" is not "*field* contains no characters from *value*" but "*field* contains at least one character that does not come from *value*".

```
REPORT  ZR_06_06 LINE-SIZE 70.
DATA: STR1(5) VALUE 'ABCDE'.

IF STR1 CO 'CDE'.
  WRITE: / '''ABCD'' CO ''CDE'' = true ', SY-FDPOS.
ELSE.
  WRITE: / '''ABCD'' CO ''CDE'' = false', SY-FDPOS.
ENDIF.
IF STR1 CA 'D'.
  WRITE: / '''ABCD'' CA ''D'' = true ', SY-FDPOS.
ELSE.
  WRITE: / '''ABCD'' CA ''D'' = false', SY-FDPOS.
ENDIF.
IF STR1 CS 'CD'.
  WRITE: / '''ABCD'' CS ''CD'' = true ', SY-FDPOS.
ELSE.
  WRITE: / '''ABCD'' CS ''CD'' = false', SY-FDPOS.
ENDIF.
IF STR1 CP '+B*'.
  WRITE: / '''ABCD'' CP ''+B*'' = true ', SY-FDPOS.
ELSE.
  WRITE: / '''ABCD'' CP ''+B*'' = false', SY-FDPOS.
ENDIF.
```

```
22.09.1998              Chapter  6: String operators                    1
--------------------------------------------------------------------------
'ABCD' CO 'CDE' = false      0
'ABCD' CA 'D' = true       3
'ABCD' CS 'CD' = true       2
'ABCD' CP '+B*' = true       0
```

Other programming languages usually require a loop over all characters of a string to duplicate the comparison logic that can be formed with these operators. The power of these operators means that it does not suffice to return true or false as comparison result. Because the programmer is normally interested in the offset of the character string at which the comparison was successful or not, the SY-FDPOS system field contains the required information immediately after the comparison.

The AND, OR and NOT logical operators can be used to form an expression from several subexpressions that as a *whole* is evaluated using Boolean logic as true or false.

Table 6.7: Logical operators

Operator	Significance
expression1 AND *expression2*	AND operation on two expressions
expression1 OR *expression2*	OR operation on two expressions
NOT *expression*	Negation of an expression

All operators have an implicit priority that is used to evaluate the complete expression.

Priorities:

1. EQ, NE, CO, CA, ... highest priority
2. NOT
3. AND
4. OR lowest priority

Parentheses can be used to control the priority for the processing of the expression.

The following De Morgan rules have proved to be useful for the conversion of an expression in complex logical expressions:

- **NOT** (*expression1* **AND** *expression2*) = **NOT** *expression1* **OR NOT** *expression2*
- **NOT** (*expression1* **OR** *expression2*) = **NOT** *expression1* **AND NOT** *expression2*

```
REPORT ZR_06_07 LINE-SIZE 70.
DATA: F1 VALUE '1', F2 VALUE '2', F3 VALUE '3',
      F4 VALUE '4', F5 VALUE '5', F6 VALUE '6'.
IF NOT F1 = F2 OR F3 = F4 AND F5 = F6.
* same as IF ( NOT ( F1 = F2 ) ) OR ( F3 = F4 AND F5 = F6 ).
  WRITE / 'true'.
ELSE.
  WRITE / 'false'.
ENDIF.
IF ( NOT F1 = F2 OR F3 = F4 ) AND F5 = F6.
  WRITE / 'true'.
ELSE.
  WRITE / 'false'.
ENDIF.
```

```
22.09.1998           Chapter  6: Logical operators              1
------------------------------------------------------------------
true
false
```

In contrast with other programming languages, care must be taken whether spaces must be placed before or after a parenthesis. A space must *always* be set before and after the parenthesis for logical expressions, unless the instruction delimiting period follows. An elegant means of testing whether a field contains its appropriate initialization value is to use IS INITIAL rather than EQ.

```
IF DATE EQ '00000000'.
IF NAME EQ ' '.
```

```
IF DATE IS INITIAL.
IF NAME IS INITIAL.
```

The BETWEEN ... AND rather than GE ... LE can be programmed to test whether a field contents lies within a specific value range.

```
IF NUMBER GE 2 AND NUMBER LE 5.
```

```
IF NUMBER BETWEEN 2 AND 5.
IF NUMBER BT 2 AND 5.
```

As with the IF instruction, the CASE instruction also permits a branching of the program logic. Different logic can react to the various value settings of a field.

CASE *fieldname*
    WHEN *value1*
*   program logic1
    WHEN *value2*
*   program logic2
*   ...
    WHEN *valuen*
*   program logicn
  [**WHEN OTHERS.**
*   program logicx
  ]
ENDCASE.

The corresponding CASE branch is processed depending on the setting of the field. Thus, CASE corresponds to a multiple IF-nesting with test for equality.

```
IF fieldname EQ value1.
*   program logic 1
ELSEIF fieldname EQ value2.
*         program logic 2
*   ...
ELSEIF fieldname EQ valuen.
*         program logic n
ELSE.
*   program logic o
ENDIF.
```

A field name can follow WHEN instead of a value. Originally the CASE could not use any logical and relational operators, such as AND, OR, GT and LT. From Release 3.0E, multiple comparison values or fields can be joined with OR in an WHEN expression.

```
REPORT ZR 06 08 LINE-SIZE 70.
DATA CONTROL VALUE '1'.
DATA STATUS1 VALUE '1'.
DATA STATUS2 VALUE '2'.
DATA STATUS3 VALUE '3'.
```

```
WRITE: / 'executed CASE branch:'.
CASE CONTROL.
  WHEN STATUS1 OR STATUS2 OR '7'.
    WRITE '1 OR 2 OR 7'.
  WHEN '3'.
    WRITE '3'.
  WHEN OTHERS.
    WRITE 'others'.
ENDCASE.
```

```
22.09.1998            Chapter  6: CASE statement                  1
-------------------------------------------------------------------
executed CASE branch: 1 OR 2 OR 7
```

6.4.2 General Loop Instructions – DO, WHILE

Loops such as DO, WHILE or LOOP are used for the repeated execution of program logic.

DO *number* **TIMES**.
*   program logic
ENDDO.

DO is programmed with the TIMES keyword if you know how often a logic is to be repeated.

The following program determines the repayment schedule for an installment credit with specified term. The installment is computed from the credit amount, interest rate and term using the equation:

$$\text{rate} = \text{credit} * q * \frac{(1+q)^n}{(1+q)^n - 1} \quad ; q = \text{ interest per annum } [\%] / 1200$$

The CREDIT, MONTHS and INTEREST_RATE input variables are defined as constants. EXP and LOG express the exponential. The number of installments (MONTHS) is used directly in the DO loop.

```
REPORT  ZR_06_09 LINE-SIZE 70.

DATA: MONTHS            TYPE I VALUE '12'.
DATA: INTRATE(7)        TYPE P DECIMALS 2 VALUE '7.0'.
DATA: LOAN(7)           TYPE P DECIMALS 2 VALUE '10000.00'.
```

```
DATA: INSTALLMENT(7)   TYPE P DECIMALS 2.
DATA: INTEREST(7)      TYPE P DECIMALS 2.
DATA: REPAYMENT(7)     TYPE P DECIMALS 2.
DATA: REST(7)          TYPE P DECIMALS 2.
DATA: Q                TYPE F,
      F                TYPE F.

Q    = INTRATE / 1200.                  " interest factor per month
F    = EXP( MONTHS * LOG( 1 + Q ) ).    " calc. factor
INSTALLMENT = LOAN * Q * F / ( F - 1 ).

WRITE: /'Repayment list for a rate loan for a given runtime'.
SKIP.
WRITE: /'Loan                         =', (9)LOAN.
WRITE: /'Run time in months           =', (3)MONTHS.
WRITE: /'Interest rate                =', (5)INTRATE, '% p.a.'.
SKIP.
WRITE: /'Calculated installment    =', (9)INSTALLMENT.
SKIP.
WRITE: /' ', 'Nr', 8'Interest', 20'Repayment', 35'Rest'.
REST = LOAN.
DO MONTHS TIMES.
  INTEREST  = REST * INTRATE / 100  / 12 ." interest in curr. month
  REPAYMENT = INSTALLMENT - INTEREST.      " repayment in curr. month
  REST      = REST - REPAYMENT.            " new rest
  WRITE:  /' ', (2)SY-INDEX, (10)INTEREST, (10)REPAYMENT, (15)REST.
ENDDO.
```

```
22.09.1998              Chapter  6: DO loop                        1
--------------------------------------------------------------------
Repayment list for a rate loan for a given run time

Loan                       = 10000,00
Run time in months         = 12
Interest rate              = 7,00  % p.a.

Calculated installment     =   865,27

  Nr   Interest    Repayment       Rest
  1      58,33     806,94         9.193,06
  2      53,63     811,64         8.381,42
  3      48,89     816,38         7.565,04
  4      44,13     821,14         6.743,90
  5      39,34     825,93         5.917,97
  6      34,52     830,75         5.087,22
  7      29,68     835,59         4.251,63
  8      24,80     840,47         3.411,16
  9      19,90     845,37         2.565,79
  10     14,97     850,30         1.715,49
  11     10,01     855,26           860,23
  12      5,02     860,25             0,02-
```

The number of loop passes is frequently not known in advance. In this case WHILE or DO is used without the TIMES keyword. DO without the TIMES keyword requires that a logical expression and EXIT is provided to end the loop. An endless loop can result if the logical expression is not chosen correctly.

```
DO.
*    program logic
     IF logical expression.
          EXIT.
     ENDIF.
*    program logic
ENDDO.
```

WHILE is a loop that already contains the logical expression for termination.

WHILE *logical expression.*
*   program logic
ENDWHILE.

A loop of this type is also called a loop with entry condition. Whereas the loop entry is not tested for DO, i.e. the loop is performed at least once, the logical expression after the WHILE stops an initial execution if the expression evaluates false. The following program uses a WHILE loop to determine the repayment schedule for an installment credit for which some arbitrary installment is specified.

```
REPORT  ZR_06_10 LINE-SIZE 70.

CONSTANTS: LOAN(7)          TYPE P DECIMALS 2 VALUE '10000.00'.
CONSTANTS: INSTALLMENT(7)   TYPE P DECIMALS 2 VALUE '1200.00'.
CONSTANTS: INTRATE(5)       TYPE P DECIMALS 3 VALUE '7.0'.

DATA: INTEREST(7)           TYPE P DECIMALS 2.
DATA: REPAYMENT(7)          TYPE P DECIMALS 2.
DATA: REST(7)               TYPE P DECIMALS 2.
DATA: MONTHS                TYPE I.

WRITE: /'Repayment list for a rate loan at given installment'.
SKIP.
WRITE: /'Loan                 =', (9)LOAN.
WRITE: /'Monthly intallment   =', (9)INSTALLMENT.
WRITE: /'Interest rate        =', (5)INTRATE, '% p.a.'.
SKIP.
WRITE: /' ', 'Nr', 8'Interest', 20'Repayment', 35'Rest'.
SKIP.
REST = LOAN.
WHILE REST > 0.
  INTEREST  = REST * INTRATE / 100  / 12 ." Interest in curr. month
  REPAYMENT = INSTALLMENT - INTEREST.      " Repayment in curr. month
```

```
  IF REPAYMENT > REST.
    REPAYMENT = REST.
  ENDIF.
  REST = REST - REPAYMENT.                          " new Rest
  WRITE:  /' ', (2)SY-INDEX, (8)INTEREST, (14)REPAYMENT, (14)REST.
  MONTHS = SY-INDEX.
ENDWHILE.
SKIP.
WRITE: /'Run time in months =', (2)MONTHS.

22.09.1998            Chapter  6: WHILE loop                     1
----------------------------------------------------------------------
Repayment list for a rate loan at given installment

Loan                  = 10000,00
Monthly intallment    = 1.200,00
Interest rate         = 7,000 % p.a.

  Nr    Interest     Repayment       Rest

  1     58,33        1.141,67        8.858,33
  2     51,67        1.148,33        7.710,00
  3     44,98        1.155,02        6.554,98
  4     38,24        1.161,76        5.393,22
  5     31,46        1.168,54        4.224,68
  6     24,64        1.175,36        3.049,32
  7     17,79        1.182,21        1.867,11
  8     10,89        1.189,11          678,00
  9      3,96          678,00            0,00

Run time in months = 9
```

The CREDIT, RATE (monthly payment) and INTEREST_RATE input variables are defined as constants. The loop is terminated when there is no remaining debt. Note that the last installment is smaller than all others.

If the ZR_06_09 and ZR_06_10 reports are combined with the capabilities of interactive reporting described in Chapter 7 (parameter input, Drill Down), these are well suited for use by R/3 specialists to check mortgage loans.

6.4.3 Other Control Instructions – EXIT, CONTINUE, CHECK

EXIT is the keyword used to terminate a current modularization unit or a current loop. In the current situation, EXIT in an inner loop ends only the *inner* loop but not the outer loop.

The SY-INDEX system field is set for the DO and WHILE instructions. SY-INDEX contains the current loop index. Multiple instances of SY-INDEX exist if several loops are nested.

IF and CONTINUE or CHECK as short form are used if a loop is not to be ended but just started at the next pass. This permits specific data records or values to be excluded from further processing.

If the logical expression after CHECK evaluates false, the loop continues with the next pass provided this exists. CHECK behaves like EXIT for modularization units; the unit is terminated if the check evaluates false.

```
DO.
*    program logic
     IF logical expression . true -> next loop
          CONTINUE.
     ENDIF.
*    program logic
ENDDO.
```

```
DO.
*    program logic
     CHECK logical expression.    false -> next loop
*    program logic
ENDDO.
```

6.5 Field Strings

The "field string" data object combines internal fields as a unit. A field string is also commonly called a structure. When used with an internal table, field strings occur as header lines and as table work areas in database tables.

Irrespective whether used as field string, header line or table work area: the technique is the same in all cases.

6.5.1 Declaration – DATA, LIKE

The BEGIN OF and END OF keywords indicate the start and end of the field string declaration. The internal fields that are the elements of the field string are declared in the usual manner. It is important for chain records to be understood to permit colons, commas to be set correctly for field string declarations after the DATA keyword.

DATA: BEGIN OF *structure*
field1,
field2,
* ...
fieldn,
END OF *structure*.

If a field string has been declared in the program, INCLUDE STRUCTURE can be used to refer to this in other declarations.

DATA: BEGIN OF *structure.*
INCLUDE STRUCTURE *structure.*
DATA: BEGIN OF *structure.*

```
DATA:      BEGIN OF ADDRESS,
           SECOND NAME LIKE zpartner_name,
           FIRST NAME(30),
           STREET(50),
           ZIP(5) TYPE N,
           TOWN(30) VALUE 'Hamburg',
    END OF ADDRESS.

DATA: BEGIN OF ADDRESS_OLD.                   " Caution: point in front of
           INCLUDE
           INCLUDE STRUCTURE ADDRESS.
DATA: END OF ADDRESS_OLD.
```

If the structure of the field string is already available in the Data Dictionary, it can also be referenced. Observe that INCLUDE STRUCTURE is *not* part of a DATA chain record but is framed by two DATA instructions.

Thus every field string can be specified using a reference with INCLUDE STRUCTURE rather than requiring the detailed declaration when the structure exists in the Data Dictionary or previously as structure or table in the program.

The declaration using INCLUDE STRUCTURE is ugly when a field string builds on an existing structure, i.e., when additional fields are required in the field string to be declared.

```
DATA:      BEGIN OF structure, F
           fielda,
           ...
           fieldn.
           INCLUDE STRUCTURE <DDIC-structure>.
DATA:             field z,
    END OF structure.
```

6.5.2 Processing – CLEAR, WRITE, MOVE, MOVE-CORRESPONDING

The program can use field string – fieldname to refer to specific fields or field string to refer to all fields of a field string. In other words, an instruction can access a single field of the field string or the complete field string.

CLEAR *structure.* Initialize *all* fields of the type string appropriate for the type.
CLEAR *structure–fieldname.* Initialize the specified field of the type string.
WRITE *structure.* Output the complete type string as character string.
WRITE *structure–fieldname.* Output a single field of the type string appropriate for its type.

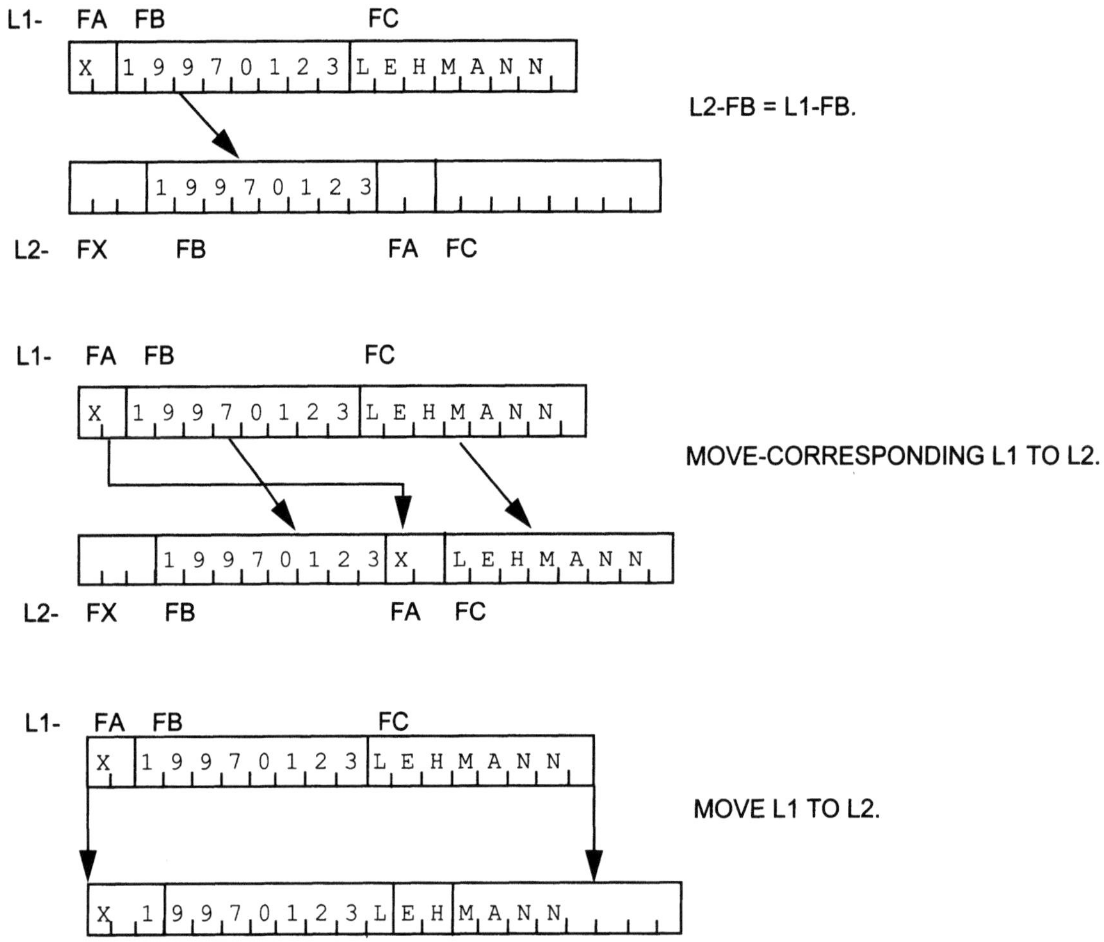

Figure 6.4: Field string assignments

Three alternatives are provided to transfer the contents of the fields of a field string to another field string:

1. **MOVE** *structure-fieldname* TO ... or ... = structure-fieldname
2. **MOVE-CORRESPONDING** *structure1* TO *structure2.*
3. **MOVE** *structure1* **TO** *structure2.* or structure2 = structure1

MOVE-CORRESPONDING transfers all fields of the source field string to *identically named* fields of the target field string. MOVE-CORRESPONDING is expanded into single MOVE instructions.

If a MOVE of a field string is programmed, the target field string must be at least as long as the source field string.

```
REPORT  ZR 06 11 LINE-SIZE 70.

DATA: BEGIN OF LDAT,
        START LIKE SY-DATUM VALUE '19000101',
        ENDE  LIKE SY-DATUM VALUE '19993112'.
DATA: END OF LDAT.

DATA: BEGIN OF LPART1.                " Reference to a table
        INCLUDE STRUCTURE ZPARTNER.   " in the data Dictionary
DATA:   RCODE  LIKE SY-SUBRC,
      END OF LPART1.

DATA: BEGIN OF LPART2.                " Reference to a structure
        INCLUDE STRUCTURE LPART1.     " defined in this program
DATA: END OF LPART2.

WRITE / LDAT.
WRITE: / LDAT-START, LDAT-ENDE.
CLEAR LDAT.
WRITE: / LDAT-START, LDAT-ENDE.
LDAT-START = SY-DATUM.
MOVE LDAT-START TO LDAT-ENDE.
CLEAR LDAT-START.
WRITE: / LDAT-START, LDAT-ENDE.

SKIP.
LPART1-PARTNO = '1'.
LPART1-LNAME    = 'Petersen'.
WRITE: / LPART1-PARTNO, LPART1-LNAME.

SKIP.
LPART2-RCODE = 5.
MOVE-CORRESPONDING LPART1 TO LPART2.  " RCODE is overwritten by 0!
WRITE: / LPART2-PARTNO, LPART2-LNAME, LPART2-RCODE.

22.09.98 Chapter  6: Structures defined with INCLUDE STRUCTURE      1
----------------------------------------------------------------------
1900010119993112
01.01.1900 12.31.1999
00.00.0000 00.00.0000
00.00.0000 22.09.1998
```

```
00000001 Petersen

00000001 Petersen          0
```

If WRITE is used to output a complete field string, it is interpreted as being a *single* field of type C. Because no type conversion is performed, WRITE on a field string does not produce any readable output for packed fields.

6.5.3 Declaration and Processing – LIKE

As with INCLUDE STRUCTURE, LIKE permits a declaration with reference to an existing structure.

DATA *structure* **LIKE** *structure.*

Which of the two declarations – LIKE or INCLUDE STRUCTURE – is chosen has no effect in the program if a field string has been declared *exactly* like an existing structure. The simpler declaration with LIKE is normally used.

If *additional* fields are required in a structure, there is a difference whether LIKE or INCLUDE STRUCTURE is used for the declaration.

```
DATA:     BEGIN OF structure,
          fielda,
*         ...
          fieldn,
          substructure LIKE structure,
          fieldz,
          END OF structure.
```

Field string – substring – fieldname can be used to refer to a field as *substructure.* Thus, when a substructure is included, whereas the association of the fields to the original structure are resolved for INCLUDE STRUCTURE it is retained for LIKE.

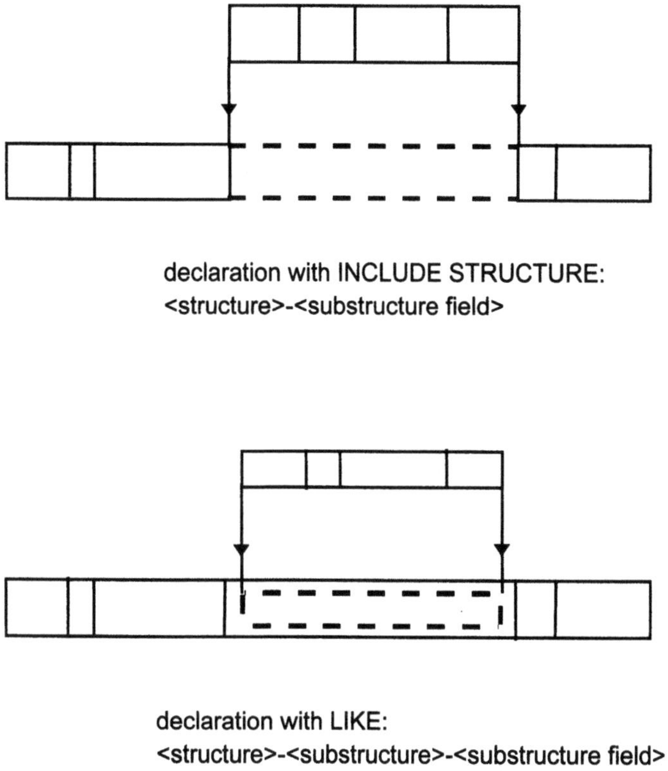

Figure 6.5: LIKE and INCLUDE STRUCTURE

```
REPORT ZR_06_12 LINE-SIZE 70.

DATA: LPART1 LIKE ZPARTNER.      " Reference to DDIC table

DATA: BEGIN OF LPART2,           " Reference to a structure
        PARTNER LIKE LPART1,     " defined in this program
        RCODE LIKE SY-SUBRC,
      END OF LPART2.

LPART1-PARTNO = '1'.
LPART1-LNAME  = 'Petersen'.
WRITE: / LPART1-PARTNO, LPART1-LNAME.

SKIP.
LPART2-RCODE = 5.
MOVE LPART1 TO LPART2-PARTNER.
WRITE: / LPART2-PARTNER-PARTNO, LPART2-PARTNER-LNAME, LPART2-RCODE.
```

```
22.09.1998       Chapter  6: Structures defined with LIKE            1
----------------------------------------------------------------------
00000001 Petersen

00000001 Petersen               5
```

6.6 Internal Tables

Internal tables are a feature of ABAP/4. On the one hand, they represent the main storage in an analog form to database tables. They can be processed similarly to these. Efficient ABAP/4 commands exist to load data from database tables into internal tables or to output internal tables to database tables. A key defined from fields does not exist for internal tables.

On the other hand, internal tables replace the ARRAY type that otherwise does not exist in ABAP/4. Internal tables in this sense are a dynamic array of structures. The advantage of the internal tables compared with static arrays of other programming languages is the dynamic memory management. The disadvantage is the ineffective access to single table lines.

The table body of an internal table can only be accessed using a header line or another work area – a field string.

A header line can be optionally assigned to an internal table when it is defined. It has the same name as the table itself.

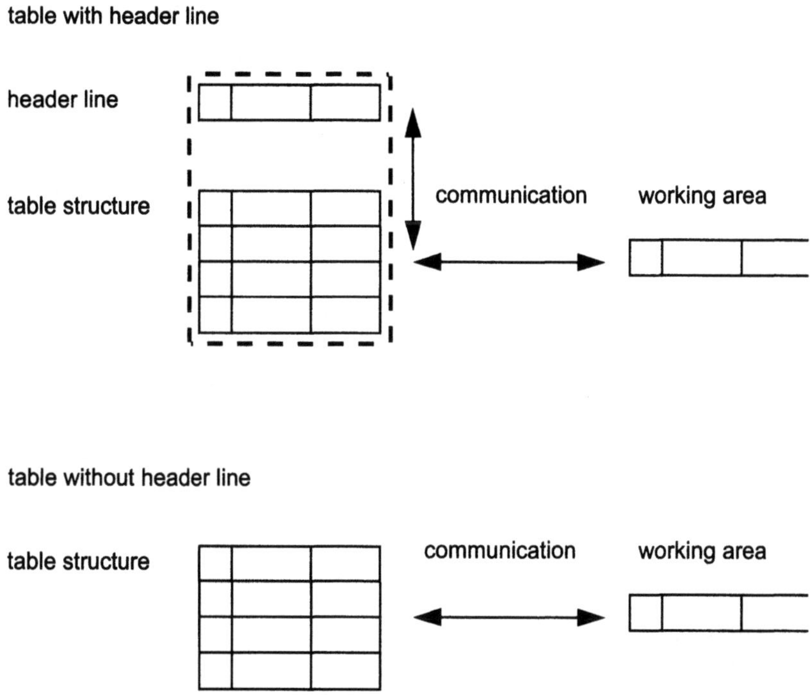

Figure 6.6: Communication for internal tables with and without header line

6.6.1 Declaration – DATA, INCLUDE STRUCTURE, LIKE

The declaration of an internal table with header line is analog to that of a field string, with however the addition of the OCCURS parameter. OCCURS specifies the number of table lines for the initialization.

DATA:BEGIN OF *itab* **OCCURS** *rows*,
field1,
* ...
fieldn,
END OF *itab*.

```
DATA:  BEGIN OF address OCCURS 100,
          second name like dbtab name,
          first name like dbtab name,
          street (30),
          zip(5) type n,
          town(30),
       END OF address.
```

OCCURS is no static limit but defines the quantity of main memory to be initially allocated for the table. If the program processing requires more lines than specified as the OCCURS parameter, the table can dynamically grow up to a limit defined in the system.

DESCRIBE TABLE is used to obtain the current number of lines of an internal table as LINES or the initially allocated lines as OCCURS. *One* of these keywords *must* be specified. The line count after executing the instruction is contained in the field that follows LINES or OCCURS.

DESCRIBE TABLE *itab* **LINES** *currentrows* | **OCCURS** *occursrows.*

However, the DESCRIBE instruction with the LINES keyword can be replaced by access to the SY-TFILL system field, because SY-TFILL contains the current line count after a LOOP.

Internal tables can also use INCLUDE STRUCTURE or LIKE to reference structures or tables or the Data Dictionary.

Syntax with INCLUDE STRUCTURE:

```
DATA: BEGIN OF itab OCCURS rows.
                  INCLUDE STRUCTURE structure.
      END OF itab.
```

Syntax with LIKE:

DATA: *itab* **LIKE** *structure* **OCCURS** *n* **[WITH HEADER LINE].**

The detailed declaration and the declaration with INCLUDE STRUCTURE specifies an internal table *with* header line. LIKE can be used to specify tables both with and without header line. An internal table *without* header line is specified when the WITH HEADER LINE keyword is omitted.

6.6.2 Selection of Table Lines– LOOP, READ

Whereas DO and WHILE are used for general loops, the LOOP instruction specifies a special loop for the processing of internal tables..

```
LOOP AT itab
      [ INTO workarea ]
      [ WHERE condition | FROM index TO index ].
*           processing
ENDLOOP.
```

The syntax of the LOOP instruction corresponds to some extent to the SELECT instruction of Open SQL for database tables. Each LOOP selects either the next table entry in the header line of the internal table or the explicitly specified work area. The selected entry of the header line can be processed between LOOP and ENDLOOP, e.g., an address with WRITE.

The WHERE, FROM or TO keyword can be used to specify that only specific table lines are to be fetched into the header line or the work area. Whereas FROM or TO uses indexes to reference a continuous area of the internal table, WHERE can be used to filter out specific individual lines which satisfy the logical expression that follows the WHERE keyword. All explanations described for IF apply for the logical expression.

In exactly the same way that the SY-INDEX system field contains the current loop index for DO and WHILE, the system supplies in the SY-TABIX field the number of the current LOOP line.

Whereas the LOOP instruction is a repetitive instruction, namely selects successive table lines for processing, READ TABLE is an instruction that copies exactly one line for processing in the header line or in an explicitly specified work area. The index or the unique key of the table entry to be read must be specified.

READ TABLE *itab* [**INTO** *workarea*] [**WITH KEY** key] [**INDEX** *index*].

```
READ TABLE PARTTAB INDEX '5'.

READ TABLE PARTTAB WITH KEY PARTNO = '2'.

PARTTAB PARTNO = '2'.
READ TABLE PARTTAB.
```

A WHILE or DO loop must enclose the READ TABLE instruction if several consecutive table lines are to be are to be copied into a work area for processing. The following example illustrates the functionality and compactness of LOOP instead of READ TABLE:

```
REPORT ZR 06 13 LINE-SIZE 70.
DATA: BEGIN OF PARTTAB OCCURS 20.        " internal table of partners
        INCLUDE STRUCTURE ZPARTNER.
DATA: END OF PARTTAB.
DATA: LIN LIKE SY-INDEX.

* The following 2 statements fill the internal table PARTTAB
* with values. They will be explained in chapter 6.4. .
TABLES: ZPARTNER.
SELECT * FROM ZPARTNER INTO TABLE PARTTAB.

WRITE 'Processing table with LOOP AT'.
LOOP AT PARTTAB WHERE LNAME GE 'L'.
  WRITE: / SY-TABIX, PARTTAB-FNAME, PARTTAB-LNAME.
ENDLOOP.
```

```
SKIP.
DESCRIBE TABLE PARTTAB LINES LIN.
WRITE / 'Processing table with WHILE'.
WHILE SY-INDEX LE LIN.
  READ TABLE PARTTAB INDEX SY-INDEX.
  CHECK PARTTAB-LNAME GE 'L'.
  WRITE: / SY-INDEX, PARTTAB-FNAME, PARTTAB-LNAME.
ENDWHILE.
```

```
22.09.1998    Chapter  6: Internal tables: LOOP and WHILE        1
-------------------------------------------------------------------
Processing table with LOOP AT
         1  Sharon          Stone
         2  Paul            Stone
         6  Peter           Wolf
         7  Mary-Ann        Wolf
         8  John            Smith
        11  Anh             Li

Processing table with WHILE
         1  Sharon          Stone
         2  Paul            Stone
         6  Peter           Wolf
         7  Mary-Ann        Wolf
         8  John            Smith
        11  Anh             Li
```

Once a table line has been selected with LOOP or a specific line has been selected with READ, the appropriate instructions can be used to copy, delete, modify or otherwise process the table lines.

The technique of the communication with the table body using header line or work area emphasizes a weakness of ABAP/4: to process *one* field of a line, the complete line must be copied into a work area, the field changed there, and then the complete line copied back. This is significantly slower than accessing the field directly in the table body. Unfortunately, ABAP/4 does not permit the referencing of a field of a line, such as in the form *itab[index]-field*. Figure 6.7 uses the example of a table with header line to graphically illustrate the effect of the READ and LOOP instructions and also the DELETE, MODIFY, INSERT and APPEND that have not yet been described.

6.6.3 Addition of Lines to an Internal Table – APPEND

The APPEND instruction adds table lines to the table body. The line to be appended can come from the header line or optionally from another work area. Generally the fields of the work area cleared with CLEAR and then supplied with the required values, e.g., using MOVE. The APPEND instruction is then used to append the contents of the work area to the table body. If the table has already attained the number of lines specified with OCCURS, the table grows dynamically with additional initialized entries.

APPEND [*workarea* **TO**] *itab* [**SORTED BY** *field*]

The SORTED BY keyword does not add the line but only sorts the table in accordance with the *field* criteria; this is appropriate only if the table was previously presorted using this criteria.

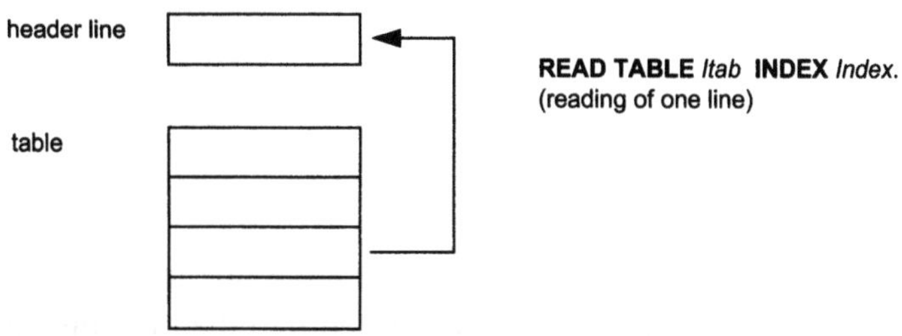

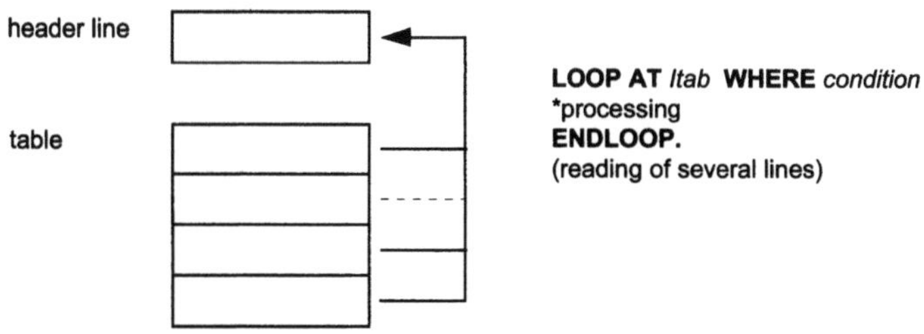

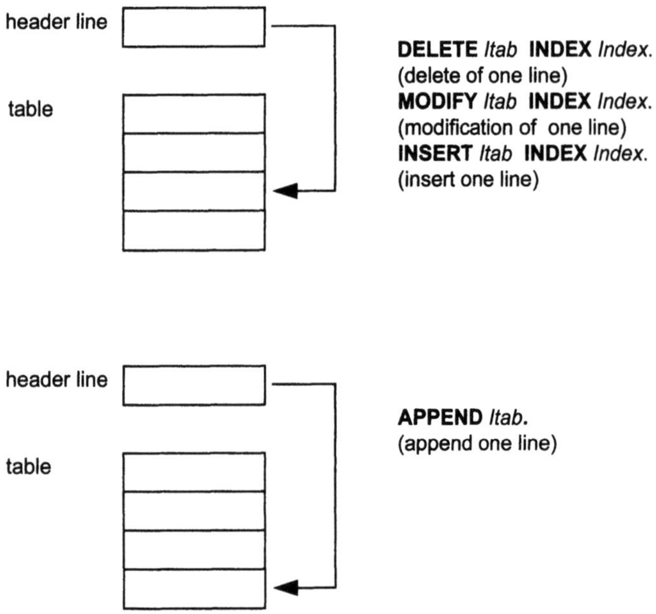

Figure 6.7: Effect of instructions for internal tables

The clause is particularly suitable for ranking lists, because every further table line that exceeds the OCCURS value removes the last table line if the new line can be sorted into the ranking list. If the table has already been dynamically extended above the OCCURS value defined in the program, the currently valid value in SY-TFILL is used to delete the last table line.

```
REPORT ZR_06_14 LINE-SIZE 70.

DATA: BEGIN OF RANCLIST OCCURS 3,
        ELEM(10),
        VALUE LIKE SY-INDEX,
      END OF RANCLIST.

DATA: DIGIT(1) TYPE N.

DO 4 TIMES.
  ZIFFER = SY-INDEX.
  CONCATENATE 'old' DIGIT INTO RANCLIST-ELEM SEPARATED BY SPACE.
  RANCLIST-VALUE = 10 - ( 2 * SY-INDEX ).
  APPEND RANCLIST.
ENDDO.

LOOP AT RANCLIST.
  WRITE: / RANCLIST-ELEM, RANCLIST-VALUE.
ENDLOOP.
WRITE: / SY-TFILL, 'Tabelleneinträge'.
```

```
CLEAR RANCLIST.
DIGIT = SY-TFILL + 1.
CONCATENATE 'new' DIGIT INTO RANCLIST-ELEM SEPARATED BY SPACE.
MOVE DIGIT TO RANCLIST-VALUE.
APPEND RANCLIST SORTED BY VALUE.

SKIP.
LOOP AT RANCLIST.
  WRITE: / RANCLIST-ELEM, RANCLIST-VALUE.
ENDLOOP.
WRITE: / (2)SY-TFILL, 'Lines in table'.
```

```
22.09.1998        Chapter  6: Internal tables: APPEND              1
--------------------------------------------------------------------
old 1                8
old 2                6
old 3                4
old 4                2
4  Lines in table

old 1                8
old 2                6
new 5                5
old 3                4
4  Lines in table
```

6.6.4 Sorting an Internal Table – SORT

An internal table can be sorted using various criteria as often as required:

SORT *itab* [**BY** *field1 field2 ... fieldn*]
[**ASCENDING | DESCENDING**] **.**

If no supplementary keywords are specified, the table is sorted using the fields of the type C, N and D that form the table structure. Fields of the type I, P or F are omitted from the standard sorting. The sorting is frequently performed using specifically specified fields. Counter fields can also be used here. Default setting for the sort sequence is ASCENDING: Only the descending sort sequence needs to be specified explicitly.

6.6.5 Insertion of Lines in an Internal Table – INSERT

INSERT adds a line in the table at the position specified by INDEX. The table line is appended if the index is larger than the current number of table lines.

The INDEX keyword is required when INSERT is used *outside* a LOOP instruction. The specification of an index is optional when an INSERT is used *within* a LOOP instruction, because the line is inserted before the currently selected table line.

INSERT [*workarea* **TO**] *itab* [**INDEX** *index* **].**

The line to be inserted can originate from work area other than the header line.

6.6.6 Deletion of Lines from an Internal Table – DELETE

The DELETE instruction can be used to delete internal table lines.

DELETE *itab* [**INDEX** *index* | **WHERE** *condition*].

If DELETE is used within a LOOP instruction, the INDEX keyword does not need to be specified if the currently selected entry is to be deleted.

If a WHERE-clause is specified, DELETE operates like a loop. All table records that satisfy the logical expression following the WHERE keyword will be deleted. Consequently, the following two examples yield the same result.

```
LOOP AT itab.
    CHECK condition.
    DELETE itab.
ENDLOOP.
```

```
DELETE itab WHERE condition.
```

6.6.7 Modification of Lines of an Internal Table – MODIFY

The MODIFY instruction also required an index if the instruction is used without a LOOP instruction. MODIFY changes the table line based on the values of the header line or the explicitly specified work area.
MODIFY *itab* [**FROM** *workarea*] [**INDEX** *index*].

A frequent ABAP/4 error occurs when the programmer changes the fields of the header line of an internal in a loop and forgets to use MODIFY to transfer these changes to the table. The following program example illustrates the use of APPEND, MODIFY and DELETE.

```
REPORT ZR 06 15 LINE-SIZE 70.
DATA: BEGIN OF PARTTAB OCCURS 20.         " internal table of partners
        INCLUDE STRUCTURE ZPARTNER.
DATA: END OF PARTTAB.

* Append lines
PARTTAB-LNAME = 'Smith'.
PARTTAB-FNAME = 'Joe'.
APPEND PARTTAB.
PARTTAB-LNAME = 'Smith'.
PARTTAB-FNAME = 'Jane'.
APPEND PARTTAB.
* Output
WRITE: / 'Contents after APPEND'.
LOOP AT PARTTAB.
  WRITE: / PARTTAB-PARTNO, PARTTAB-FNAME, PARTTAB-LNAME.
ENDLOOP.
* Change values
LOOP AT PARTTAB.
  PARTTAB-PARTNO = SY-TABIX.
  MODIFY PARTTAB.
ENDLOOP.
* Delete a line
DELETE PARTTAB WHERE PARTNO = '1'.
* Output
SKIP.
WRITE: / 'Contents after MODIFY and DELETE'.
LOOP AT PARTTAB.
  WRITE: / PARTTAB-PARTNO, PARTTAB-FNAME, PARTTAB-LNAME.
ENDLOOP.
```

```
22.09.1998  Chapter  6: Internal tables: MODIFY and DELETE          1
----------------------------------------------------------------------
Contents after APPEND
00000000 Joe                Smith
00000000 Jane               Smith

Contents after MODIFY and DELETE
00000002 Jane               Smith
```

6.7 User-Defined Data Types – TYPES

TYPES can be used to create user-defined data types without also requiring the definition of variables of this type. TYPES is only used when the data types are suitably complex. If they are also to be used in several programs, all type definitions can be grouped in an Include (see Chapter 7). The use of special TYPE-POOLs (described in Chapter 9) have the same effect. Figure 6.8 shows how the continuation of a substructure in a field string can produce an embedded table. Several lines of such a structure with embedded table produce a table with one or more embedded tables.

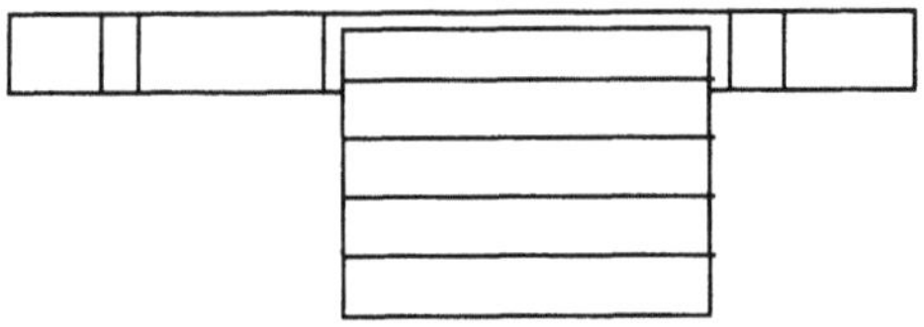

table inside a structure

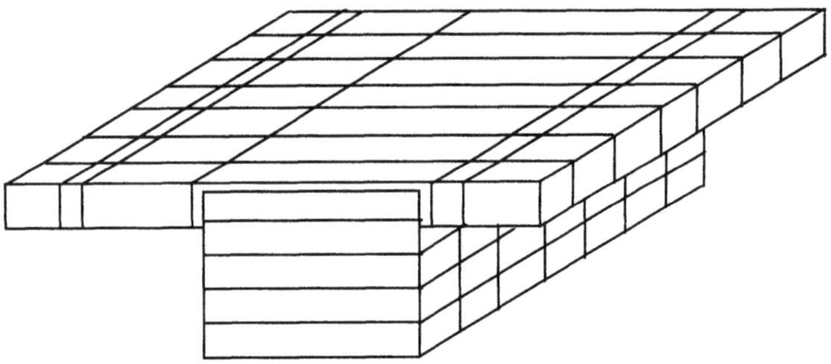

table inside a table

Figure 6.8: Tables in structures and tables in tables

Report ZR_06_24 shows several interrelated type definitions. POSTABTYPE describes an internal table without header line. It records document positions. The DOCTYPE type defines a document type a field string type that initially contains a HEAD substructure. This is derived using LIKE from the ZDOCHD database table. The use of LIKE permits the subsequent use of a document header as an entity. The second DOCTYPE field is a POSTAB positions table of the above defined type POSTABTYPE. The use of such a declared document type DOCTYPE is used to define a document table type DOCTABTYPE. This describes a table of documents. The three TYPES declarations do not define any data objects. A document list as data object is only defined using the DATA DOCTAB. DOCTAB is an internal table of type DOCTABTYPE with header line.

```
REPORT ZR_06_16 LINE-SIZE 70.
TYPES: ITEMTABTYPE LIKE ZDOCITEM OCCURS 10.
TYPES: BEGIN OF DOCTYPE,
         HEADER  LIKE ZDOCHD,
         ITEMTAB TYPE ITEMTABTYPE,
       END OF DOCTYPE.
TYPES: DOCTABTYPE TYPE DOCTYPE OCCURS 100.

DATA DOCTAB TYPE DOCTABTYPE WITH HEADER LINE.
DATA ITEM LIKE ZDOCITEM.

DO 5 TIMES.
  DOCTAB-HEADER-DOCNO = 1000 * SY-INDEX.
  CLEAR DOCTAB-ITEMTAB. REFRESH DOCTAB-ITEMTAB.
  DO SY-INDEX TIMES.
    ITEM-DOCNO = DOCTAB-HEADER-DOCNO.
    ITEM-ITEMNO = SY-INDEX.
    APPEND ITEM TO DOCTAB-ITEMTAB.
  ENDDO.
  APPEND DOCTAB.
ENDDO.

LOOP AT DOCTAB.
  WRITE: / DOCTAB-HEADER-DOCNO.
  LOOP AT DOCTAB-ITEMTAB INTO ITEM.
    WRITE: ITEM-ITEMNO.
  ENDLOOP.
  ULINE.
ENDLOOP.
```

```
22.09.1998       Chapter  6: Complex data types                    1
----------------------------------------------------------------------
00001000 001
----------------------------------------------------------------------
00002000 001 002
----------------------------------------------------------------------
00003000 001 002 003
----------------------------------------------------------------------
00004000 001 002 003 004
----------------------------------------------------------------------
00005000 001 002 003 004 005
----------------------------------------------------------------------
```

The program stores five documents in DOCTAB, where SY-INDEX is used to place only the document number in the DOCTAB-HEAD header. The corresponding positions are set in the associated position table. The document number is taken from the header and the position number formed from SY-INDEX of the inner loop. Observe that the DOCTAB-POSTAB position table being an embedded table of a document cannot have any header line. Consequently, a POS temporary work area is used for operations on this table.

Although the shown construction may at first appear complicated, it is appropriate, because it permits individual substructures and embedded tables of a complex data object to be accessed as a unit. In particular, this proves to be desirable for the use of forms and function modules with the appropriately structured parameters.

6.8 Field Symbols – FIELD-SYMBOLS, ASSIGN

There are problem situations in which the name of a field is to be accessed is only known during the program run-time. However, a storage area must still be declared and an appropriate program logic developed without the name, data type and the length of the field being known in advance.

Field symbols in ABAP/4 can be compared to references in C++. They provide alias names for other data objects, such as fields or field strings. Internally, field symbols as with references are realized using const pointers.

The principal difference field symbols have to C++ references is that they can exist without requiring a referenced data object. The specification of a field symbol in ABAP/4 provides a data object for a reference to be created at run-time:

FIELD-SYMBOLS *fieldsymbol.*

A field symbol always occupies the same 4-byte memory space, irrespective of the size of the data object to which it later points. The reference to a field or a field string is created at run-time as follows:

ASSIGN *field* **TO** *fieldsymbol.*
ASSIGN *(field)* **TO** *fieldsymbol.*

Internally, the address of the field is assigned to the field symbol. This creation of the reference with ASSIGN should be differentiated from assignments of field symbols using MOVE or '='. These are forwarded using the created reference to the referenced variable.

```
REPORT ZR_06_17 LINE-SIZE 70.
DATA: TEXTFIELD(10) VALUE 'ABAP/4',
      FIELDNAME(10) VALUE 'textfield'.   " points to field textfield
FIELD-SYMBOLS <FS>.

WRITE: / 'Textfield=', TEXTFIELD.
WRITE: / 'Fieldname=', FIELDNAME.
SKIP.
```

```
ASSIGN TEXTFIELD TO <FS>.
WRITE:   / 'ASSIGN textfield TO <FS>   : <FS>        =', <FS>.
<FS> = 'R/3'.
WRITE:   / 'Move <FS> = R/3            : textfield = ', TEXTFIELD.
SKIP.

ASSIGN (FIELDNAME) TO <FS>.
WRITE:   / 'ASSIGN (fieldname) TO <FS>: <FS>        =', <FS>.
<FS> = 'ABAP/4'.
WRITE:   / 'Move <FS> = ABAP/4         : textfield = ', TEXTFIELD.
```

```
22.09.1998           Chapter  6: Field Symbols                   1
-------------------------------------------------------------------
Textfield= ABAP/4
Fieldname= textfield
ASSIGN textfield TO <FS>  : <FS>        = ABAP/4
Move <FS> = R/3           : textfield =  R/3
ASSIGN (fieldname) TO <FS>: <FS>        = R/3
Move <FS> = ABAP/4        : textfield =  ABAP/4
```

Figure 6.9 shows the inter-relationships for the direct and indirect assignment of field symbols. A run-time error occurs if a value is to be assigned to a null reference or if the value to be assigned does not match the referenced data object.

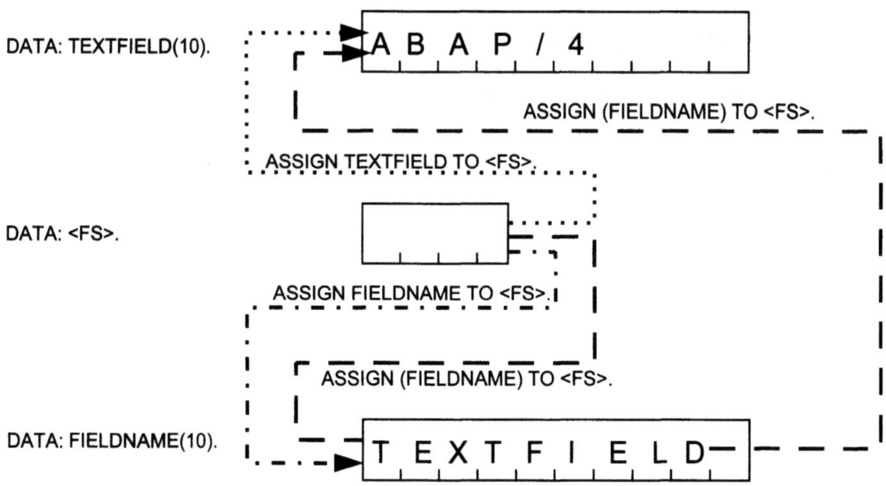

Figure 6.9: Various assignments of field symbols

The conversion of settings while customizing SAP applications is a typical practical use of field symbols. It is conceivable that the user is provided with the capability only to display specific fields of a database table in a specific sequence. Depending on the setting in the customizing, the program must place the associated field names and contents on the screen.

Chapter 12 introduces an interface program that reads data and structure information from a file. Field symbols are also used here.

6.9 Database Access Using Open SQL

Open SQL are the database commands contained in the ABAP/4 repertoire. It is oriented on the SQL Standard without consistently adhering to it. Large parts of Standard SQL are not offered in ABAP/4 because they are not required. In particular, these are all commands for the maintenance of database system tables, such as CREATE TABLE, DROP TABLE, GRANT, etc. The dialog-oriented maintenance of the Data Dictionary implements these functions. However, complex SELECTs with joins also cannot be directly programmed in ABAP/4. One reason for these restrictions is that programs in ABAP/4 should be able to run without change on all R/3 database types. This complicates the adherence of the SQL Standard compared with other 4GLs that normally use just a single database type (e.g., Ingres4GL for Windows, Informix, Visual BASIC). On the other hand, ABAP/4 provides a number of specific, powerful Open SQL commands that greatly simplify the work with the database compared with conventional 4GLs.

6.9.1 Table Definitions in the Program

The Open SQL commands can only access the R/3 database of the system in which the program in running. Only those tables that have been specified in the Data Dictionary can be processed. The following command makes the tables available for use by the program:

TABLES *table.*

or

TABLES: *table1, table2, ...tablen.*

The TABLES command performs two tasks: Firstly, it indicates the program that is to access the specified tables. This permits a check at compile time whether the tables are defined as active tables in the Data Dictionary. Names and properties of the table fields can be used after this declaration.

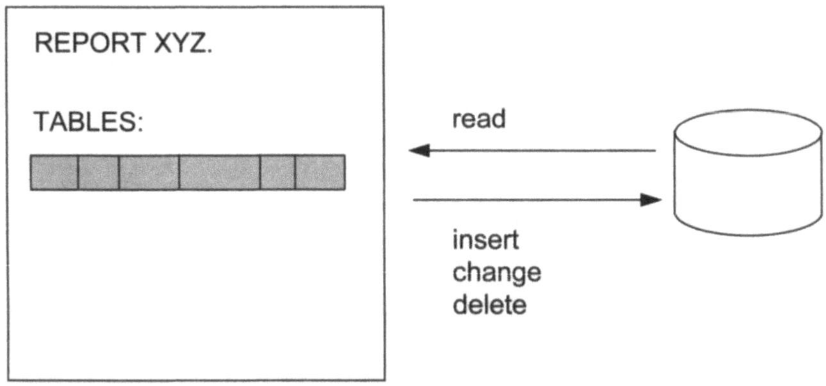

Figure 6.10: Table work area as transfer buffer between ABAP/4 and database

Secondly, the TABLES command also provides a data definition of a field address with the structure of the associated table. This field string is also called a table work area. This provides a transfer area for a record from the corresponding table. This has the advantage that no special host variables need to be defined for the database access.

6.9.2 Open SQL Commands

The list of the most frequently used Open SQL command follows:

SELECT	Read one or more records from a table
INSERT	Insert one or more records into a table
UPDATE	Change one or more records of a table
MODIFY	Insert or change one or more records in a table
DELETE	Delete one or more records from a table
ROLLBACK WORK	Discard the database commands performed since the last COMMIT WORK
COMMIT WORK	Commit the database commands performed since the last COMMIT WORK
SY-SUBRC	Provide information on the success of an Open SQL command.
SY-SUBRC = 0:	At least one record was processed.
SY-SUBRC = 4:	No records were processed.
SY-DBCNT	Specifies the number of processed records in the case SY-SUBRC = 0.

A further characteristic of all Open SQL commands is the handling of client-dependent tables. The client (MANDT) is specified at logon and stored in SY-MANDT. All database tables automatically refer only to records with this client. Consequently, the user sees only the data for his client. The CLIENT SPECIFIED keyword is used in the Open SQL commands in the few cases where inter-client work using client-dependent tables is necessary.

6.9.3 Read Records from One Table – SELECT

SELECT is by far the most powerful, and probably also the most widely used, Open SQL command. SELECT reads a number of data records from the specified dbtable table. The result can be considered as being a table whose line format is specified in field string. INTO indicates one or more target fields, although internal tables can also be used as target areas. The WHERE-condition specifies which records are to be read. The ORDER BY-clause is used to sort the read records according to the field contents. The GROUP BY-clause permits the combining of read records into groups, where aggregations are also possible.

SELECT [**SINGLE** [**FOR UPDATE**]] | **DISTINCT** *field list*
[**INTO** (*field1, field2, ...*) |
structure |
TABLE *itab* [**PACKAGE SIZE** *recordnumber*]] |
[**APPENDING TABLE** *itab* [**PACKAGE SIZE** *recordnumber*]]
FROM *dbtable* | (*namevariable*)
[**CLIENT SPECIFIED**] [**BYPASSING BUFFER**] [**UP TO** *n* **ROWS**]
[**WHERE** *condition*]
[**GROUP BY** *field1 field2* ...]
[**ORDER BY** *field1 field2* ...| **PRIMARY KEY**].

* process records

ENDSELECT.

The following section describes the WHERE-condition in further detail. Several important special cases of SELECT are then discussed using examples. The condition following the WHERE can be a complex logical expression that combines subexpressions using AND, OR and NOT as described in Section 6.4.1. The WHERE-clause recognizes the following special formats for logical subexpressions:

Table 6.8: Logical expressions of the WHERE-clause

Format of the WHERE-Condition	Example (SELECT * FROM ZPARTNER)
tabfield OP field OP: =, >, <, >=, <=	...WHERE NAME = 'Black'
tabfield [NOT] BETWEEN field1 AND field2	...WHERE PARTNO BETWEEN 1000 AND 2000
tabfield LIKE string '%': arbitrary character string '_': precisely one string	...WHERE NAME LIKE 'Mei%' (WHERE ROLLNAME LIKE '#_VK' ESCAPE '#') (ESCAPE switches of role of placeholder)
tabfield [NOT] IN (field1,..., fieldn)	...WHERE PARTNO NOT IN (1002, 1004, 1009)
tabfield [NOT] IN itab	DATA PARTNO LIKE ZPARTNER-PARTNO. RANGES: selopt FOR PARTNO. ....WHERE PARTNO IN SelOpt (see Chapter 7)
tabfield IS [NOT] NULL	...WHERE ZIP IS NOT NULL
(itab)	... WHERE (itab) (see Section 6.9.11)

Refer to the SAP documentation for the complete description of the SELECT command. The most frequently used variants are shown here.

SELECT * **FROM** *table* **WHERE** *condition* **.**

* process records

ENDSELECT.

All fields of the specified table are read in this variant. Because the target area is not explicitly specified, the table work area from the TABLES declaration is used. The new record that is available in the work area after every SELECT can be processed with the program logic specified between SELECT and ENDSELECT. Program ZR_06_21 shows an example. It selects all customers that have a zipcode starting with 1.

```
REPORT  ZR 06 21 LINE-SIZE 70.
TABLES: ZPARTNER.

SELECT * FROM ZPARTNER WHERE ZIP LIKE '9%'
                       ORDER BY LNAME FNAME.
  WRITE:  / ' ',  (1)SY-DBCNT,
          ZPARTNER-TITLE, (10) ZPARTNER-FNAME, (10)ZPARTNER-LNAME,
          (5)ZPARTNER-ZIP, (18)ZPARTNER-TOWN,
          ZPARTNER-PARTNO.
ENDSELECT.
SKIP.
WRITE: / '  Count of selected partners:', (2)SY-DBCNT.
PERFORM LISTE TO JOBLOG USING 'Z0' '021'.
```

```
22.09.98 Chapter  6: Selection of partners with ZIP-Code like    1
----------------------------------------------------------------------
  1 Mr         Frank      Black      92407 San Bernadino      00001002
  2 Mrs Dr.    Jane       Black      92407 San Bernadino      00001003
  3 Mrs        Wanda      Huesing    93013 Carpenteria        00001004
  4 Mr         John       Smith      90028 Santa Barbara      00001007
  5 Mr Dr.     Paul       Stone      90028 Hollywood          00001001
  6 Mrs        Sharon     Stone      90028 Hollywood          00001000

  Count of selected partners: 6
```

The SY-DBCNT system variable specifies within the SELECT-loop the running number of the data record in the SELECT. SY-DBCNT after the ENDSELECT contains the total number of records that have been read.

Complex algorithms often require repeated access to the same data record. Because a multiple database access would cost too much time, the records to be processed can be read with a single SELECT command into an internal table. The mentioned algorithm then only accesses this table contained in main memory. This buffered table must have the same structure as the database table.

SELECT * INTO TABLE *itab* **FROM** *table* **WHERE** *condition.*

This variant does not have any ENDSELECT. It acts like a single command. Processing is not possible while the reading is being performed. The records are available in the internal *itab* table after the command has been processed. A frequent error is to forget the TABLE keyword. *Itab* in this case is interpreted as being a simple field string that naturally can only accept a single record. As consequence, the syntax checker then searches for an ENDSELECT that encloses the required processing commands.

```
REPORT ZR_06_22 LINE-SIZE 70.
TABLES: ZACCOUNT.
DATA   : ITAB LIKE ZACCOUNT OCCURS 30 WITH HEADER LINE.

WRITE: / 'Without PACKAGE SIZE and without ENDSELECT:'.
WRITE: / 'Curr.No.', 10 'Acc.No.', 20 'Blocked'.
SELECT * INTO TABLE ITAB FROM ZACCOUNT.
LOOP AT ITAB.
  WRITE:  / ' ',  (5)SY-TABIX     UNDER 'Curr.No.',
                     ITAB-ACCNO   UNDER 'Acc.No.',
                  (4)ITAB-BLOCKED UNDER 'Blocked' RIGHT-JUSTIFIED.
ENDLOOP.
SKIP 2.
WRITE: / 'With PACKAGE SIZE and with ENDSELECT:'.
WRITE: / 'Curr.No.', 10 'Acc.No.', 20 'Blocked'.
SELECT * INTO TABLE ITAB PACKAGE SIZE 4 FROM ZACCOUNT.
  LOOP AT ITAB.
    WRITE:  / ' ',  (5)SY-TABIX     UNDER 'Curr.No.',
                       ITAB-ACCNO   UNDER 'Acc.No.',
                    (4)ITAB-BLOCKED UNDER 'Blocked' RIGHT-JUSTIFIED.
  ENDLOOP.
  SKIP.
ENDSELECT.
```

```
22.09.98 Chapter  6: Select all accounts into an internal tabl     1
--------------------------------------------------------------------
Without PACKAGE SIZE and without ENDSELECT:
Curr.No. Acc.No.   Blocked
   1     00004000
   2     00004001
   3     00004002
   4     00004003
   5     00004004
   6     00004005
   7     00004006
   8     00004007
   9     00004008
  10     00004009
  11     00004010
  12     00004011
  13     00004012
```

```
With PACKAGE SIZE and with ENDSELECT:
Curr.No. Acc.No.   Blocked
    1     00004000
    2     00004001
    3     00004002
    4     00004003

    1     00004004
    2     00004005
    3     00004006
    4     00004007

    1     00004008
    2     00004009
    3     00004010
    4     00004011

    1     00004012
```

If the number of records to be read is very large, the reading into the internal table can be portioned using the PACKAGE SIZE keyword. An ENDSELECT is required again in this case. Each SELECT with INTO TABLE overwrites the contents of the specified internal table. The APPENDING TABLE keyword rather than INTO TABLE is specified if the new records are to be added to the existing table.

SELECT * INTO TABLE *itab* **PACKAGE SIZE** *itabrows*
FROM *table* **WHERE** *condition.*

* internal table processing, typically with LOOP

ENDSELECT.

6.9.4 Read Records from Linked Tables – SELECT

Standard SQL can read concurrently from several tables. Tables are normally processed using so-called joins that are linked with external keys. The external key relationship must be specified in the WHERE-condition. Nested SELECTs can be used in Open SQL instead of joins. Program ZR_06_23 reads partner and contract data for the partner numbers 1005 to 1007.

```
REPORT ZR 06 23 LINE-SIZE 70.
TABLES: ZPARTNER, ZCONTRACT, ZPARCON.

WRITE: / 'Combined selects'.
WRITE: / 'Partner', 10'Name', 30'Contract', 40 'Start', 52'End'.
SELECT * FROM ZPARTNER WHERE PARTNO BETWEEN 1003 AND 1005.
  WRITE: / ZPARTNER-PARTNO UNDER 'Partner',
           ZPARTNER-LNAME  UNDER 'Name'.
  SELECT * FROM ZCONTRACT WHERE PARTNO = ZPARTNER-PARTNO
                          AND OFFER NE 'X'.
    WRITE: / ZCONTRACT-CONTNO   UNDER 'Contract',
             ZCONTRACT-STARTDAT UNDER 'Start',
             ZCONTRACT-ENDDAT   UNDER 'End'.
  ENDSELECT.
ENDSELECT.
ULINE.
WRITE: / 'Select with View ZPARCON'.
WRITE: / 'Partner', 10'Name', 30'Contract', 40 'Start', 52'End'.
SELECT * FROM ZPARCON WHERE PARTNO BETWEEN 1003 AND 1005
                        AND OFFER NE 'X'.
  WRITE: / ZPARCON-PARTNO   UNDER 'Partner',
           ZPARCON-LNAME    UNDER 'Name',
           ZPARCON-CONTNO   UNDER 'Contract',
           ZPARCON-STARTDAT UNDER 'Start',
           ZPARCON-ENDDAT   UNDER 'End'.
ENDSELECT.
```

```
22.09.98 Chapter  6: Combined SELECTs and View            1
-----------------------------------------------------------------
Combined selects
Partner  Name                Contract Start      End
00001003 Black
                             00003002 23.07.1996 12.07.2006
00001004 Huesing
                             00003003 23.07.1996 12.07.2006
00001005 Wolf
                             00003006 23.07.1996 12.07.2006
                             00003014 23.07.1996 12.07.2006
-----------------------------------------------------------------
Select with View ZPARCON
Partner  Name                Contract Start      End
00001003 Black               00003002 23.07.1996 12.07.2006
00001004 Huesing             00003003 23.07.1996 12.07.2006
00001005 Wolf                00003006 23.07.1996 12.07.2006
00001005 Wolf                00003014 23.07.1996 12.07.2006
```

The sought information for the contracts is contained in the ZCONTRACT table, which also contains the information on the partner who closed the contract (PARTNO) as external key. The ZPARTNER table that provides the relationship to the partner has PARTNO as external key.

Thus, the outer SELECT loop selects all partners of interest. The inner SELECT loop reads the contracts for each found ZPARTNER. Whereas the first part of the inner WHERE-condition represents the external key relationship between the tables, the second part excludes the offerings from the display. The result shows that it is possible for a partner to have several contracts.

If the external key relationship for PARTNO is forgotten in the inner SELECT, the data quantity can be very large, because *all* contracts of the *complete* data are read for *every* partner. The complete number of read records is the product of the number of records of the individual SELECTs. Although this would not be critical in the shown example, 135 billion records would result if the system had 300 000 partners with 450 000 contracts.

Although nested SELECTs can also represent so-called auto-joins, namely external key relationships of a table with itself, SAP recommends the use of the CURSOR.

The use of views (see Section 4.1.5) is preferable if the number of read records is very large or several programs access linked tables. The same list is created in the second part of the ZR_06_23 report using the ZPARTNER view. Here only a single SELECT command is required. However, the data are return in a different sequence. The ORDER BY PARTNO clause suffices to provide the correct sequence.

6.9.5 Insert Records into a Table – INSERT

The most important forms of the command are:

INSERT *table.*	One record from the table work area
INSERT *table* **FROM TABLE** *itab.*	Several records from an internal table
INSERT INTO *table* **FROM** *WA.*	One record from some work area

All commands can be combined with a WHERE-condition.

6.9.6 Change Records in a Table – UPDATE

The most important forms of the command are:

UPDATE *table.*	One record from the table work area
UPDATE *table* **FROM TABLE** *itab.*	Several records from an internal table

Whereas

UPDATE *table* **SET** *f1=value1 ... fn = valuen .*

can be used to set the values of individual fields. All commands can be combined with a WHERE-condition.

6.9.7 Delete Records from a Table – DELETE

The most important forms of the command are:

DELETE *table.*	One record from the table work area
DELETE *table* **FROM TABLE** *itab.*	Several records from an internal table

All commands can be combined with a WHERE-condition.

6.9.8 Change Records in a Table or Insert Records into a Table – MODIFY

This Open SQL command is SAP-specific. It combines the INSERT and UPDATE commands. An attempt is made to insert the record (or records) into the table. The attribute is changed (to UPDATE) if records with the specified keywords are already present. Otherwise a normal INSERT is performed. The command saves the developer the tedious checking of duplicate keys.

6.9.9 Commit or Discard Database Changes

All database changes of a program are initially made in a buffer. This permits the changes to be revoked if necessary. Other programs do not have any access to these buffered data in normal database operation. However, for performance reasons, access within R/3 is permitted as standard (Section 6.9.10). The

COMMIT WORK.

command makes permanent the changes made to the database since the last COMMIT WORK. The ROLLBACK WORK can no longer be used to revoke the changes. All database locks are released. COMMIT WORK also has additional effects with regard to bundled or asynchronous booking in dialog transactions (Chapter 9).

ROLLBACK WORK.

revokes all changes made to the database since the last COMMIT WORK.

The following example uses SELECT SINGLE to read a personnel record from the database which is then changed with UPDATE. A repeated SELECT to this record shows the changed record without COMMIT WORK having being performed. A SELECT issued after ROLLBACK WORK shows again the initial situation. If a COMMIT WORK had been performed instead of ROLLBACK WORK, the change of address of partner 10002006 to Hofweg 9 would be written in the database.

```
REPORT  ZR 06 24 LINE-SIZE 70.
TABLES: ZPARTNER.
CONSTANTS: PARTNO LIKE ZPARTNER-PARTNO VALUE '1006'.

SELECT SINGLE * FROM ZPARTNER WHERE PARTNO = PARTNO.
WRITE: / 'Data Base       :',  ZPARTNER-PARTNO, ZPARTNER-STREET.
UPDATE ZPARTNER SET STREET = 'Mainstreet 9'.
SELECT SINGLE * FROM ZPARTNER WHERE PARTNO = PARTNO.
WRITE: / 'After UPDATE    :',  ZPARTNER-PARTNO, ZPARTNER-STREET.
ROLLBACK WORK.
SELECT SINGLE * FROM ZPARTNER WHERE PARTNO = PARTNO.
WRITE: / 'After ROLLBACK :',  ZPARTNER-PARTNO, ZPARTNER-STREET.

22.09.98 Chapter  6: COMMIT WORK and ROLLBACK WORK                1
----------------------------------------------------------------------
Data Base      : 00001006 2229 East University Drive
After UPDATE   : 00001006 Mainstreet 9
After ROLLBACK : 00001006 2229 East University Drive
```

The COMMIT-ROLLBACK procedure permits complex data objects to be stored consistently in the database even though such objects may be stored in several tables. The documents that consist of a record in ZDOCHD and several associated records in ZITEMNO are a typical example. A COMMIT WORK is performed for booking a document only when all records of the document have been stored without error in the associated tables.

6.9.10 Locking Mechanisms

In a database in which many users work in parallel, competing data accesses can occur when several programs make write access to the same data. This can result in loss of data in an extreme situation. So-called locking mechanisms can be used to avoid this.

All database systems provide capabilities to set and release such locks. The SELECT, UPDATE, INSERT and DELETE database commands set locks; COMMIT or ROLLBACK release the locks. Although the most reliable and simplest method would be to use SQL commands to set exclusive locks of all read data and for the data to be written, this would cause continuous blocking of the database during heavy parallel work and long processing times. For this reason different types of locks have been introduced:

- Read lock (shared lock)
- Write lock (exclusive lock)

SELECT sets the read lock. It assumes that the read data are not going to be changed. Such a lock can be set several times for a data object. Several users in this case access the same data concurrently. Because a concurrent write access is not permitted, no write lock can be set for objects that have an active read lock. The object is then released for writing when the last read lock has been cleared by COMMIT or ROLLBACK.

The write lock is exclusive. The UPDATE, INSERT, DELETE and MODIFY write commands set the write lock. It locks the data object for personal use of the initiating program until its COMMIT or ROLLBACK.

The read lock has the advantage that parallel read accesses can be made to the data. It has the disadvantage that every read access through setting a read lock stops write processing of the data. To avoid this problem, database systems provide the capability to choose between Uncommitted Read and Committed Read. This option us known as the Isolation Level of the database. A SELECT with Isolation Level Uncommitted Read reads a data object independent of any locks that may have been set. It does not set any locks itself. Figure 6.11 shows an example. Program A adds a record with INSERT. Program B reads this record with Uncommitted Read before a COMMIT or ROLLBACK has been performed in program A. If program A discards the record, program B has read a so-called phantom record, because soon the record will no longer exist in the database. An UPDATE for this record will fail. A SELECT with Isolation Level Committed Read makes a short-term setting of the read lock to test whether a program envisages changing the affected object, namely a check is made whether an corresponding write lock exists. If this is not the case, the read lock is cleared and the object becomes free again.

The choice of an Isolation Levels involves making a compromise between the contradicting demands for data reliability and database performance. A frequently used method involves using fast Uncommitted Reads. Before an UPDATE is made to such a read data object, the object must be re-read to ensure that it still exists in the database and it has not been changed by some other user in the meantime.

R/3 uses Isolation Level Uncommitted Read as standard setting. A change to Committed Read can be made with the DB_SET_ISOLATION_LEVEL function module. In the default setting, SELECT does not set any locks, INSERT, UPDATE, MODIFY and DELETE set write locks in the database. Note that the lock units for most databases are not individual records but are larger units (pages). This further degrades the performance for Committed Read.

Parallel to the lock mechanisms of the database system, R/3 provides the capability to lock and unlock individual table records by calling special function modules (Chapter 9). These function modules have the form

ENQUEUE_<lock_object> to set locks
DEQUEUE_<lock_object> to release locks.

Lock objects can be individual records of a table. However, lock objects can also consist of several records from joined tables. An example for a complex lock object is a document that consists of a line from ZDOCHD and several lines from ZITEMNO. The keys used to locate the records to be locked serve as arguments for the lock modules.

These SAP locks are independent of COMMIT or ROLLBACK and can be retained over long transactions that involve several different screen displays.

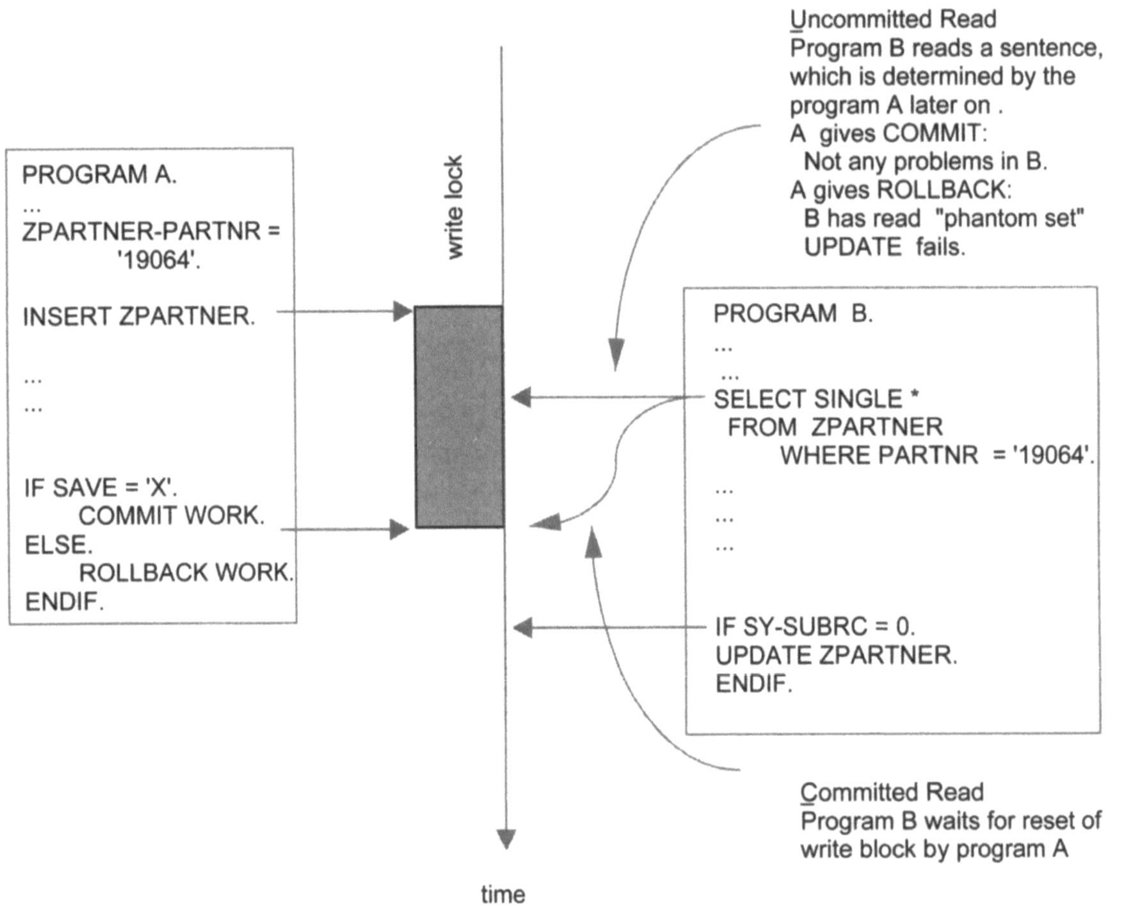

Figure 6.11: Competing access of two programs on a single data record

6.9.11 Dynamic Open SQL

All Open SQL commands can also be performed in dynamic form. This means that the WHERE-condition and also possibly the fields to be processed are only known at the program run-time. In particular, this means that the tables to be processed do not occur in the program's TABLES declaration. An ABAP field that must contain at run-time the name of the table is set instead of the table in the Open SQL commands. The field name is specified within parentheses to distinguish it from the static case.

The following report permits at run-time the input of a table name and two conditions. It can be executed with the indicated default values and provides the results shown below.

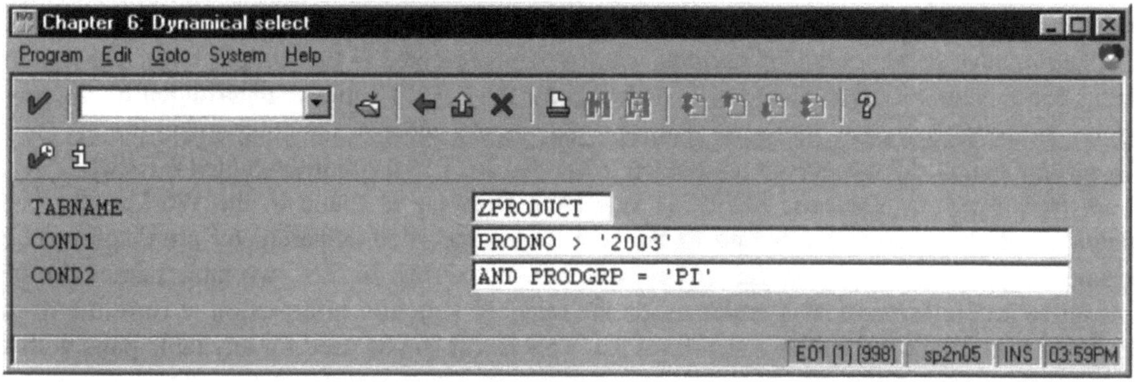

Figure 6.12: Selection figure for dynamic Open SQL

The input fields are defined with the PARAMETERS keyword and are used after input like an input field defined with DATA. Any table names can be specified at run-time. The conditions naturally must be specified for fields of *this* table. The program produces a short dump if incorrect field names or incorrectly written constants are specified.

```
REPORT ZR 06 25 LINE-SIZE 70.
PARAMETERS:  TABNAME(10) DEFAULT 'ZPRODUCT',
             COND1(60)  DEFAULT 'PRODNO > ''2003''',
             COND2(60)  DEFAULT 'AND PRODGRP = ''PI'''.
DATA:    BEGIN OF WHERETAB OCCURS 2,
           COND(60),
         END OF WHERETAB.
DATA:    WA(200).

WHERETAB-COND = COND1. APPEND WHERETAB.
WHERETAB-COND = COND2. APPEND WHERETAB.

SELECT * INTO WA FROM (TABNAME) WHERE (WHERETAB).
  WRITE: / WA(100).
ENDSELECT.
```

```
22.09.98 Chapter  6: Dynamical select                              1
--------------------------------------------------------------------
99800002004PIcar fully comprehensive insurance
99800002005PIcar fully comprehensive insurance
99800002006PIcar fully comprehensive insurance
99800002007PIpassenger insurance
```

Note that the report does not have any TABLES area. Consequently, a target area WA must be specified for the read data. Because the report does not know the structure of the read table, this work area can only be defined as a CHAR area. It must have at least the length of a record from the read table. Similarly, the output of a work area can also only be made in CHAR format. Packed number or binary-coded numbers cannot be represented in this simple form. The conditions can be entered interactively or – as shown for the default values – determined by the program. In the second case, the string delimiter that should occur in the comparison literals must be written paired. All conditions are passed to the SELECT as a condition table (WHERETAB).

A typical use for dynamic SELECTs is a Data Browser as found in the Workbench. The fields of all the records that belong to the table name specified as parameter are displayed by group. The YXXXX report in the appendix demonstrates this. In fact, two table names can be passed to it. Furthermore, this report reads the required structure information at run-time from the Data Dictionary and builds a two-level list. This report can be used for any table pairs with a foreign key relationship 1:n and permits field-oriented horizontal scrolling for long record lengths.

6.9.12 Generally Applicable Notes for the Performance of Open SQL

Independent of the associated database system, SAP provides the following notes for the efficient use of Open SQL:

- Keep the quantity of selected records as small as possible
  It is better to tune the WHERE-condition than to unnecessarily read records that are later rejected
- Keep the number of transferred fields as small as possible
  - Rather than "*", specify only those fields actually needed
  - Use aggregate functions (MAX, MIN, SUM ...)
  - UPDATE only those fields actually changed rather than the complete record
  - Where possible, use SELECT DISTINCT to avoid duplicates
- Restrict the number of Open SQL calls
  - It is better to use views rather than nested SELECTs
  - SELECT ... INTO TABLE is better than many single selects
  - Use SELECT ... FOR ALL ENTRIES
- Optimize the search algorithms
  - Where possible combine complex WHERE-condition with AND and EQ.
    Indexes are not supported for the OR, NOT and IN operators.
  - Use indexes with few fields; specify the most selective fields first.
- Relieve load on the database
  - Use table buffer
  - No multiple reads, buffer in internal tables
  - No repeated starts of extensive SELECTs, use PACKAGE SIZE instead
  - If possible replace ORDER BY with SORT of the read internal table
  - If possible replace SELECT DISTINCT with DELETE ADJACENT of the internal table.

6.10 Database Access with Native SQL

In addition to the capabilities provided by the Open SQL integrated in ABAP/4 described in Section 6.9, it is also possible to initiate so-called native SQL commands. They are specified in an EXEC SQL-ENDEXEC block of the following form:

EXEC SQL [PERFORMING *form* **].**

SQL statements

ENDEXEC.

Other programming languages (COBOL, C) know this form of SQL as "Embedded SQL".

No ABAP/4 commands can be placed within the EXEC-ENDEXEC block, but just SQL statements of the associated database. In particular, no ABAP period can be used to terminate the SQL statement.

A SELECT command normally returns several records. In Open SQL, ABAP/4 commands that process these records can be coded within the SELECT-ENDSELECT block. This is not the case within the EXEC-ENDEXEC block. However, the processing can take place in a special non-parameterized form (see Chapter 7). The processing is specified after the PERFORMING keyword.

6.10.1 Native SQL on the R/3 Database

The R/3 system is connected with the R/3 database during the start. All Open SQL commands refer automatically to this database. Native SQL also uses this database by default.

The ZR_06_26 report uses a Native SQL instruction to determine all partners that have signed at least two contracts.

```
REPORT ZR_06_26 LINE-SIZE 70.
DATA TABNAME(70).
DATA CREATOR(70).
DATA: BEGIN OF WA,
        PARTNO(8), LNAME(15), FNAME(15),
      END OF WA.

EXEC SQL PERFORMING ANZEIGEN.
  SELECT PARTNO, LNAME, FNAME INTO :WA FROM ZPARTNER P
    WHERE CLIENT = '999'
          AND 1 <
         ( SELECT COUNT(*) FROM ZCONTRACT V
             WHERE V.CLIENT  = P.CLIENT
               AND V.PARTNO  = P.PARTNO  )
    ORDER BY LNAME, FNAME
ENDEXEC.
*-----------------------------------------------------------
```

```
FORM ANZEIGEN.
  WRITE:  / ' ', (15)WA-FNAME, (15) WA-LNAME, (8)WA-PARTNO.
ENDFORM.
```

```
22.09.98 Chapter  6: Native SQL with subselect                          1
-------------------------------------------------------------------------
  Maria               Hernandez           00001009
  Miguel              Hernandez           00001008
  Anh                 Li                  00001010
  Paul                Stone               00001001
  Peter               Wolf                00001005
```

The main select determines all partners from ZPARTNER. P represents the alias name for ZPARTNER. A subselect returns the number of contracts from ZCONTRACT for the associated partner. The WHERE-condition in the subselect joins ZPARTNER and ZCONTRACT using the foreign key relationship. Note that the client in Native SQL is not subjected to any special processing. The selected data are set into the WA work area. This appears in the INTO-clause of the main select as so-called host variable with a colon as prefix. The ANZEIGEN form is invoked for every record of the main select.

6.10.2 Native SQL on Non-R/3 Databases

The real need for Native SQL only occurs when an ABAP/4 program simultaneously accesses both Data Dictionary tables and non-R/3 tables.

The following examples result from the development of an R/3-external procedure control (VGS) that contains R/3 transactions.

The source code fragment shows a Native SQL on an Oracle DBMS. The SAPR3 database that has been created as usual does not need to be explicitly specified for the tables. These are all tables that start with “Z”. The non-R/3 tables of the EINTRAG procedure control and OB belong to the VGS database being non-R/3 database must be explicitly specified in SQL.

```
* EXEC-SQL-Statements for DB-System Oracle.
*
EXEC SQL PERFORMING TK_FUELLEN_01.
     SELECT  E.EINTRAG_KEY_U, E.EINTRAG_KEY_N, ' ', ART,
             VORGANG_KEY_U, VORGANG_KEY_N, ' ', TERMIN, FRIST,
             NAME, OB_TYPE, OB_WERT, STATUS, BENUTZER, E.POSTFACH,
             E.AENDERUNG_KEY, START_DATE, 0, ' ',
             YLFACHDAT.INFO_1, YLFACHDAT.INFO_2, YLFACHDAT.INFO_3,
             P1.PART_TITEL, P1.PART_VORS, P1.PART_NAME, P1.PART_ZUS,
             P1.PART_VNAME, P1.PART_GEB, P2.PLZ, P2.ORT, P2.STRASSE,
             P2.HAUS_NO, E.PRIORITAET, E.DIALOG_TYPE, VORGANG_TYPE,
             VORGANG_NAME, E.MANDANT, P1.MA_KZ
             TYPE, GUELTIG_AB, AUFRUF_LFD, ' ', ' ', ' ', ' ', ' '
       FROM  VGS.EINTRAG E, VGS.OB O, YLFACHDAT,
             YYPPAR P1, YYPANS P2
       WHERE E.EINTRAG_KEY_U  = O.EINTRAG_KEY_U               AND
             E.EINTRAG_KEY_N  = O.EINTRAG_KEY_N               AND
             E.EINTRAG_KEY_U  = YLFACHDAT.EKEY_U              AND
             E.EINTRAG_KEY_N  = YLFACHDAT.EKEY_N              AND
*          ( O.BELEGT_KZ     >= '0' AND O.BELEGT_KZ <= '2' ) AND
             E.MANDANT        = :SY-MANDT                     AND
             P1.PART_KEY      = YLFACHDAT.INFO_SPEZ           AND
             P1.PART_KEY      = P2.PART_KEY                   AND
             P2.DEFAULT_KZ    = 'X'                           AND
             P1.MANDANT       = :SY-MANDT                     AND
             P2.MANDANT       = :SY-MANDT                     AND
             ART              = 'K'                           AND
           ( STATUS           = 'A'        OR
             STATUS           = 'L'        OR
             STATUS           = 'W'                         ) AND
             OB_WERT          = :YLTERMFIL-OBWERT_1           AND
             E.POSTFACH       = :YLTERMFIL-POSTFACH           AND
             TERMIN           < :FT_VON_01
       ORDER BY 11, 12 DESC, 5 DESC, 6 DESC, 4 DESC, 33, 34, 1, 2
       INTO  :TK_01
   ENDEXEC.
```

The same example has been realized for an Informix DBMS, where although the procedure control tables have been created within the SAPR3 R/3 database, they are not contained in the Data Dictionary. These tables can also be used as DD tables without requiring the SAPR3 prefix.

```
* EXEC-SQL-Statements for DB-System Informix.
*
EXEC SQL PERFORMING TK_FUELLEN_01.
    SELECT  E.EINTRAG_KEY_U, E.EINTRAG_KEY_N, ' ', ART,
            VORGANG_KEY_U, VORGANG_KEY_N, ' ', TERMIN, FRIST,
            NAME, OB_TYPE, OB_WERT, STATUS, BENUTZER, E.POSTFACH,
            E.AENDERUNG_KEY, START_DATE, 0, ' ',
            YLFACHDAT.INFO_1, YLFACHDAT.INFO_2, YLFACHDAT.INFO_3,
            P1.PART_TITEL, P1.PART_VORS, P1.PART_NAME, P1.PART_ZUS,
*           P1.PART_VNAME, P1.PART_GEB, P2.PLZ, P2.ORT, P2.STRASSE,
*           P2.HAUS_NO, E.PRIORITAET, E.DIALOG_TYPE, P1.MA_KZ,
            P1.PART_VNAME, P1.PART_GEB, ' ', ' ', ' ',
            ' ', E.PRIORITAET, E.DIALOG_TYPE, P1.MA_KZ,
            VORGANG_NAME, VORGANG_TYPE, E.MANDANT, TYPE, GUELTIG_AB,
            AUFRUF_LFD, START_ZEIT, ' ', ' ', ' ', ' ', ' '
*     FROM  EINTRAG E, OB O, YLFACHDAT, YYPPAR P1, YYPANS P2
      FROM  EINTRAG E, OB O, YLFACHDAT, YYPPAR P1
      WHERE E.EINTRAG_KEY_U  = O.EINTRAG_KEY_U               AND
            E.EINTRAG_KEY_N  = O.EINTRAG_KEY_N               AND
            E.EINTRAG_KEY_U  = YLFACHDAT.EKEY_U              AND
            E.EINTRAG_KEY_N  = YLFACHDAT.EKEY_N              AND
            E.MANDANT        = :SY-MANDT                     AND
            P1.PART_KEY      = YLFACHDAT.INFO_SPEZ           AND
*           P1.PART_KEY      = P2.PART_KEY                   AND
*           P2.DEFAULT_KZ    = 'X'                           AND
            P1.MANDANT       = :SY-MANDT                     AND
*           P2.MANDANT       = :SY-MANDT                     AND
            ART              = 'K'                           AND
          ( STATUS           = 'A'        OR
            STATUS           = 'L'        OR
            STATUS           = 'W'                         ) AND
            OB_WERT          = :YLTERMFIL-OBWERT_1           AND
            E.POSTFACH       = :YLTERMFIL-POSTFACH           AND
            TERMIN           < :FT_VON_01
      ORDER BY 11, 12 DESC, 5 DESC, 6 DESC, 4 DESC, 33, 34, 1, 2
      INTO  :TK_01
 ENDEXEC.
```

7 Interactive Reports

Reports in the conventional sense are programs that extract data from the database that they then present in list form. Reports often run in batch and directly output the required lists to a printer without involving any dialog.

R/3 provides an important and very powerful extension to the report technology – interactive reports. The realized extensions to the simple report programming have the following aims:

- Increase of the variability of a report through various input capabilities (parameters, buttons, function keys)
- Increase of the degree of interaction of a report (drill down)
- Improved program structuring (results, macros, includes, forms)

The interactive reports are one of the strengths of the ABAP/4 Workbench that should be particularly emphasized. It would be difficult to find another development tool that provides a comparable report technology with the same low programming effort.

The event concept is a significant concept to achieve these above aims of the interactive report technology. This concept defines internal and external events to which the report program must or can respond.

7.1 Event Control

Event control is used by all modern programming systems (such as Visual Basic, Visual C++, Visual Age COBOL, Delphi, Ingres-Windows 4GL) that create program development objects. The principle behind the event control is that you write code fragments (CALLBACK routines) and assign them defined events. The actual program processing is not coded, but results from the occurrence of various events. The processing control is not part of the user program, but is contained in a runtime environment.

Interactive reports under ABAP/4 are dialog programs for online database access. The creation and interactive processing (drill down) of lists assume priority.

The interactive reports have an important feature compared to a *real* dialog program (Chapter 8). The dialog reports (selection reports for the input of parameters, list reports) are not created with the dialog editor (Screen Painter) but produced using program commands in the report program itself. The interactive reports can be produced much more easily by the programmer compared with true dialog programs.

Interactive reports are event controlled. ABAP/4 recognizes only the few events defined as ABAP keywords. They are listed in the program as a record with a delimiting period. The associated code forms the processing block that is assigned to this event. A processing block is terminated when a new key word begins, i.e., at the end of a form (Section 8.2) or the end of the source code.

The ABAP processor controls the program flow by triggering the corresponding events and by processing the assigned processing blocks.

7.1.1 General Report Processing

Figure 7.1 shows the flow chart for an interactive report. The ABAP/4 processor initially processes the INITIALIZATION event code. The report is then in the *selection report* status and awaits user inputs to limit the database access (parameter inputs) and for the program control.

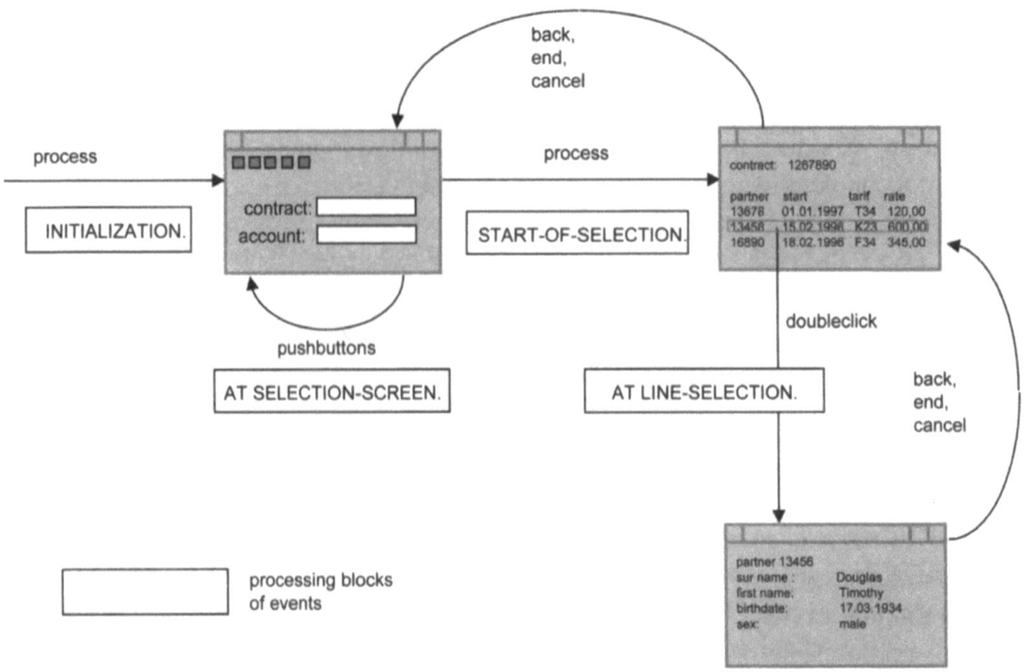

Figure 7.1: Flow chart for an interactive report

The following events trigger the AT SELECTION-SCREEN event:

- Menu actions
- Pushbuttons
- PF keys

They cause the ABAP/4 processor to execute the associated processing block. Pressing the execution key returns the control to the ABAP/4 processor. This processes the START-OF-SELECTION block, which usually processes the data records it has read using the specified limits. The WRITE command outputs the results in a list. The basic list appears at the end of the processing block and the report is in the "List 0" status. The user has now assumed control again. He can scroll through the displayed list, perform special USER commands or double-click on specific lines. The later is designated as drill down. The processing block following the AT-LINE-SELECTION is performed in the result. The result appears in a so-called details list. The report is now in the "List 1" status. User inputs are possible again. The "Return" key can be used to jump from the details list into the controlling list. The source code of an interactive report has the following appearance:

```
* global data definitions
TABLES:
DATA:
SELECTION-SCREEN:
SELECT-OPTIONS:
PARAMETERS:
*------------------------------------------ standard events ------
INITIALIZATION
* This is the code that is necessary to prepare the initial
   screen
* Typical: preassignment of input parameters

AT SELECTION-SCREEN OUTPUT.
* Dynamic changes inside MODIFY SCREEN)
* Afterwards, the changed MODIFY SCREEN appears

AT SELECTION-SCREEN INPUT.
* Response to user entries during use of the MODIFY SCREEN
* - pushbuttons
* - function keys
* - menus

START-OF-SELECTION.
* Import of data records SELECT
* Manipulation of data records by UPDATE, INSERT, DELETE
* Output of data records by WRITE

*----------------------------------------- Preparation of lists-----
TOP-OF-PAGE.
* Header on every page during printout,
* fixed header on report output
```

```
END-OF-PAGE.
* Page footing on each printout

*---------------------------------------- Interactions----------
AT LINE-SELECTION.
* Responses to double-click in list
* Typical: generation of details list

AT USER-COMMAND.
* Responses to function keys and entries in instruction fields

AT FK-<nn>.
* Responses to function keys

*---------------------------------------- Logical database-----
GET <table>.
* New record from tables is provided by the reading program

GET <table> LATE.
* Last subordinate record of tables is read

END-OF-SELECTION.
* All records have been read by the reading program
```

If a logical database is used, the read program triggers additional events. These are discussed in Section 8.4.

A report typically defines only a few of the above mentioned events as processing blocks. No event keywords are specified in the extreme case. The found code lines in this case are assigned automatically to the START-OF-SELECTION event and performed when the processing the selection report has been completed.

7.1.2 Selection Screen for a Report

Figure 7.2 shows a selection screen for a report. This appears before the start of the actual work. The selection screen is produced using ABAP/4 commands. The following key words are available with various options:

- SELECTION–SCREEN
- SELECT–OPTIONS
- PARAMETERS

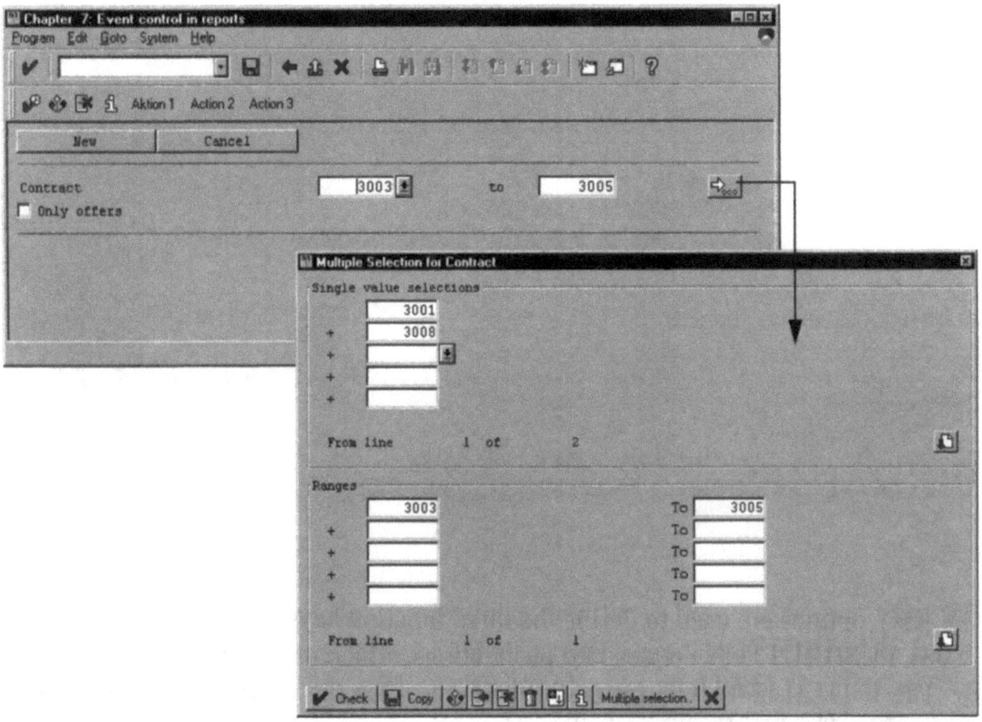

Figure 7.2: Selection screen of the ZR_07_01 report

The ZR_07_01 report demonstrates how the shown selection screen is produced. To avoid over-complication, the actual data selection and list output have been kept short.

```
REPORT ZR_07_01 LINE-SIZE 70.
TABLES: SSCRFIELDS, ZCONTRACT.
DATA: LUCOMM LIKE SSCRFIELDS-UCOMM.
DATA: CONTNO LIKE ZCONTRACT-CONTNO.
*-----------------------------------------------------------------
SELECTION-SCREEN:
  FUNCTION KEY 1,
  FUNCTION KEY 2,
  FUNCTION KEY 3,
  PUSHBUTTON /1(15) PSH1 USER-COMMAND PSH1,
  PUSHBUTTON 17(15) PSH2 USER-COMMAND PSH2,
  ULINE.
SELECT-OPTIONS: SO_CNO FOR CONTNO DEFAULT '3003' TO '3005'.
PARAMETERS    : OFFER LIKE ZCONTRACT-OFFER DEFAULT SPACE.
SELECTION-SCREEN ULINE.
SELECTION-SCREEN SKIP 2.
*-----------------------------------------------------------------
INITIALIZATION.
  SSCRFIELDS-FUNCTXT_01 = 'Aktion 1'.
  SSCRFIELDS-FUNCTXT_02 = 'Action 2'.
```

```
  SSCRFIELDS-FUNCTXT 03 = 'Action 3'.
  PSH1 = 'New'.
  PSH2 = 'Cancel'.
*------------------------------------------------------------------
AT SELECTION-SCREEN.
  LUCOMM = SSCRFIELDS-UCOMM.
  IF LUCOMM = 'PSH1' OR LUCOMM = 'PSH2' OR
     LUCOMM = 'FC01' OR LUCOMM = 'FC02' OR LUCOMM = 'FC03'.
    SSCRFIELDS-UCOMM = 'ONLI'.
  ELSEIF LUCOMM = 'ONLI'.
    SSCRFIELDS-UCOMM = SPACE.
  ENDIF.
*------------------------------------------------------------------
START-OF-SELECTION.
SELECT * FROM ZCONTRACT
     WHERE CONTNO IN SO_CNO AND OFFER = OFFER.
  WRITE: / ZCONTRACT-CONTNO, ZCONTRACT-STARTDAT, ZCONTRACT-OFFER.
ENDSELECT.
```

The FUNCTION KEY options are used to define the three function keys after the SELECTION-SCREEN key word. PUSHBUTTON creates two pushbuttons, which are assigned the PSH1 and PSH2 variables. The INITIALIZATION program block specifies the designations for the key buttons and pushbuttons. The SELECTION-SCREEN event is triggered when the user presses a key button or pushbutton. The initiating user code is then passed in the SSCRFIELDS-UCOMM field to the program. UCOMM has the form FC<nm> for function keys, where nn is the two-digit number of the function key. The definition of the pushbuttons explicitly specifies UCOMM. Note that no literals appear here. The statement

SELECT-OPTIONS *selopt* **FOR** *field* [*options*].

places input fields of value ranges of the program's database selections on the selection screen. An internal selopt table with the following structure is also created for each selection option:

```
DATA: BEGIN OF SELOPT OCCURS ...
            SIGN,
            OPTION(2),
            LOW LIKE FIELD,
            HIGH LIKE FIELD,
      END OF SELOPT.
```

The reference variable *field* passes its type to the lower and upper limits of the selection table. This can accept several areas joined with a logical OR on its rows. The dialog can add individual rows to the internal table (key next to the selection options in Figure 7.2). The

INITIALIZATION can specify an initialization in the program. Report ZR_07_10 shows an example. The statement

PARAMETERS *field* [*options*].

can be used to create both an input field and a program variable.

Normally the report can only be started using the Execute key. This sets SSCRFIELDS-UCOMM to the value "ONLI" (online) and starts processing the START-OF-SELECTION block. Consequently, the defined key buttons and pushbuttons cannot be used to start the program logic. A small trick can be used to avoid this restriction. You can save SSCRFIELDS-UCOMM in user field LUCOMM. If this contains the value of a key button or a pushbutton, set to SSCRFIELDS-UCOMM to ONLI. The following START-OF-SELECTION processing block uses LUCOMM to determine the actions to be performed. The selection screen is closed immediately after the *Action 1* key is pressed and the following output appears on the screen:

```
08.06.1998         Chapter  7: Event control in reports              1
--------------------------------------------------------------------------
00003003 23.07.1996
00003004 23.07.1996
00003005 23.07.1996
```

7.1.3 Variants

A specific value assignment of all parameters and selection options for a report can be stored with a common name as a so-called variant in the database. Every report can have any number of such variants. A variant can be loaded instead of individual inputs when a report is started online. A variant *must* be specified when a report with parameters or selection options executes in batch. If the batch job is started from a program using SUBMIT ... VIA JOB, the specified parameter is automatically stored as variant. The names of such variants start with an "&".

Time-dependent parameters are a feature of variants. To avoid storing new variants for each of these parameters, date variables can be used in variants. Variants can also reference user-specific fixed values. This permits different users to work with the same variants.

7.2 Texts and Menus

7.2.1 Texts

Observant readers will ask themselves where the *Contract* and *Only Offers* texts that appear on the selection screen occur in the ZR_07_01 program. These language-dependent components are not integrated in the program as text constants, rather they are assigned to the variable names in the PARAMETERS definition using the *Jump/Text Elements/Selection Texts* menu item:

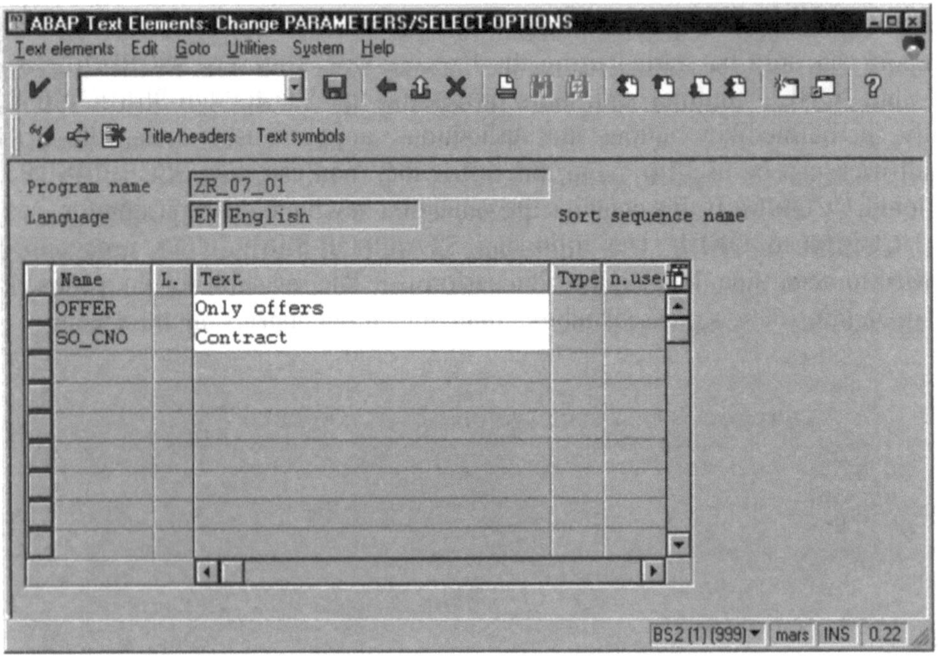

Figure 7.3: Input of selection texts

7.2.2 Menus

A report can contain its own menu. The Menu Painter is used to process menus, which are set with the

SET PF-STATUS *status*.

statement before the list output. The Menu Painter is described in Chapter 5. The function code of the keys and menu commands are passed to the report in SY-UCOMM and can be evaluated at the time of AT SELECTION-SCREEN INPUT.

7.3 List Processing

The START-OF-SELECTION block is processed if the *Execute* key has been used to exit from the selection screen. This contains the required SELECTs with the associated processing. Most reports produce lists, which WRITE outputs on the program window. The interactive list processing has a feature that the lists can be changed interactively (scroll, sort, display and suppression of columns). A double-click on list lines permits so-called details lists to be opened with the detail information for the associated line. This procedure is designated as drill down. It can also be used in multi-levels.

7.3.1 Creation of Basic Lists and Details Lists with WRITE

WRITE commands in the START-OF-SELECTION processing block create the basic lists. The fundamentals of WRITE have already been discussed in Section 6.3. The list appears in the basic list screen only when this processing block has been completely executed. The automatically generated basic list is built row and column-oriented. Very large data volumes can take several minutes before the basic list appears. The scrollbar present on the basic list can be used for vertical scrolling. A horizontal scrollbar is added automatically if the output width of the report exceeds the visible number of columns.

The delayed output behavior of the list has the following cause: WRITE outputs all data after the appropriate conversion into the external, namely readable, format in an internal table. These data are output to the basic list screen only at the END-OF-SELECTION. This has the advantage that not only the ABAP/4 processor, but also the program, can always access the list data. Consequently, the output lists cannot only be viewed but also easily processed in the program. Not surprisingly, it is possible to store or scroll through the displayed lists.

A double-click on a line of the basic list initiates the LINE-SELECTION event and executes the assigned processing block. If this block is present in the report, the contained WRITE commands produce a details list of Level 1. The SY-LSIND (list index) system variable contains the list level. SY-LSIND = 0 in the basic list. The details list writes in the same internal table as the basic list. To permit the assignment of the lines to the individual lists, the table also contains the list index. You can consider that the internal list table has the following structure:

```
TYPES:    BEGIN OF LISTTAB,
                INDEX LIKE SY-LSIND,
                ROW(255),
          END OF LISTTAB.
```

In the normal case, the output overlays the details list of the basic list. *Return* restores the basic list that is output immediately using the currently available internal table. The START-OF-SELECTION block is not executed again when the return is made to the basic list. However, the data for the details list are discarded. They are deleted from the internal table.

A double-click can be performed again on a details list. The AT LINE-SELECTION block is then performed once again. The developer has the task to make a test of SY-LSIND within AT LINE-SELECTION to determine in which details level the program is located. A CASE SY-LSIND should be programmed for multi-level details lists.

7.3.2 Add Hidden Additional Information to List Lines – HIDE

The programming of multi-level details lists requires that the program knows the key information of the line for which a drill down is required. The contents of the clicked line are contained in SY-LISEL. These system variables can be used to reconstruct all output information of the line. However, the line itself is present in external format and does not need to contain all keys of the record. The

HIDE ***field*.**

command permits any information to be added without being visible to the line. HIDE is normally invoked immediately after WRITE. HIDE can be invoked several times for different fields for each line. A double-click on the line writes to the program data all those fields stored with HIDE. Thus, the above LISTTAB output list can be considered as being an internal table whose rows contain a small internal table HIDETAB in addition to the actual row information. HIDE fills this table with the names and values of the appropriate variables. A double-click on the line causes the HIDETAB to be reread.

```
TYPES:    BEGIN OF HIDETABTYPE,
                NAME(32),
                VALUE(50),
          END OF HIDETAB.

TYPES:    BEGIN OF LISTTAB,
                INDEX LIKE SY-LSIND,
                ROW(255),
                HIDETAB TYPE HIDETABTYPE OCCURS 5,
          END OF LISTTAB.
```

Observe the following when the WRITE, and thus also the HIDE, outputs are made in a subprogram (FORM, Section 8.2): no local fields of the FORM can be used as HIDE parameters because they exist only while the form is being processed. The LINE-SELECTION event, before whose processing the HIDE areas are rewritten, can only be processed when all subprograms have completed.

The ZR_07_02 report outputs a basic list of account numbers. The SO_ANO selection options performs the limitation. Drill down should be used on the basic list to display the details list 1 of all document headers for an account. Details list 2 contains all items for the selected document.

The START-OF-SELECTION block reads the requested accounts and writes the basic list. HIDE ZACCOUNT-ACCNO saves the key (i.e., the account number) used to create details list 1. This is created in AT LINE-SELECTION using SY-LSIND = 1. To read the account's documents, the previously saved ZACCOUNT-ACCNO is used in the selection condition for the document headers. If the HIDE command was omitted from the basic list, the details list would reference the *last account* of the basic list. After WRITE to the document list, HIDE saves the ZDOCHD-DOCNO document number. It is required in the details list 2 for the SELECT to ZDOCITEM:

```
REPORT ZR_07_02 LINE-SIZE 70.
TABLES: SSCRFIELDS, ZACCOUNT, ZDOCHD, ZDOCITEM.
DATA:   ACCNO LIKE ZACCOUNT-ACCNO.
DATA:   LIN1 TYPE I, COL1 TYPE I.
DATA:   LIN2 TYPE I, COL2 TYPE I.
*-----------------------------------------------------------------
SELECT-OPTIONS: SO_ANO FOR ACCNO DEFAULT '4000' TO '4010'.
*-----------------------------------------------------------------
START-OF-SELECTION.
SELECT * FROM ZACCOUNT
     WHERE ACCNO IN SO_ANO.
  WRITE: / ZACCOUNT-ACCNO.
  HIDE ZACCOUNT-ACCNO.
ENDSELECT.

*-----------------------------------------------------------------
AT LINE-SELECTION.
LIN1 = 2 * SY-LSIND. COL1 = 4 * SY-LSIND.
LIN2 = 10 + LIN1. COL2 = 50 + COL1.
WINDOW STARTING AT COL1 LIN1 ENDING AT COL2 LIN2.
CASE SY-LSIND.
  WHEN 1.
    WRITE: / 'Account: ', ZACCOUNT-ACCNO.
    ULINE.
    SELECT * FROM ZDOCHD WHERE ACCNO = ZACCOUNT-ACCNO.
      WRITE: / ZDOCHD-DOCNO, ZDOCHD-CURRKY.
      HIDE ZDOCHD-DOCNO.
    ENDSELECT.
  WHEN 2.
    WRITE: / 'Account ', ZDOCHD-DOCNO, 'Currency:', ZDOCHD-CURRKY.
    ULINE.
    SELECT * FROM ZDOCITEM WHERE DOCNO = ZDOCHD-DOCNO.
      WRITE: / ZDOCITEM-DOCNO, ZDOCITEM-ITEMNO, ZDOCITEM-AMOUNT.
      HIDE ZDOCHD-DOCNO.
    ENDSELECT.
ENDCASE.
```

```
08.06.1998      Chapter  7: Details lists                              1
--------------------------------------------------------------------------
00004000
00004001
00004002
00004003
00004004
00004005
00004006
00004007
00004008
00004009
00004010
-------------------------------SY-LSIND= 01
Account:   00004001
--------------------------------------------------------------------------
00005000 USD
00005001 USD
00005002 USD
00005015 USD
-------------------------------SY-LSIND= 02
Account  00005001 Currency: USD
--------------------------------------------------------------------------
00005001 001            1.450,00
00005001 002              100,00
00005001 003               45,00
```

The report displays the basic list and the details lists of Levels 1 and 2. Only one of these three lists is visible on the output screen. A double-click creates the appropriate higher list level, Return restores the next higher list. The details list with the highest index is always at the top.

7.3.3 Details Lists in Their Own Windows – WINDOW

In some circumstances, it is desirable that each details list appears in its own window (see Figure 7.4).

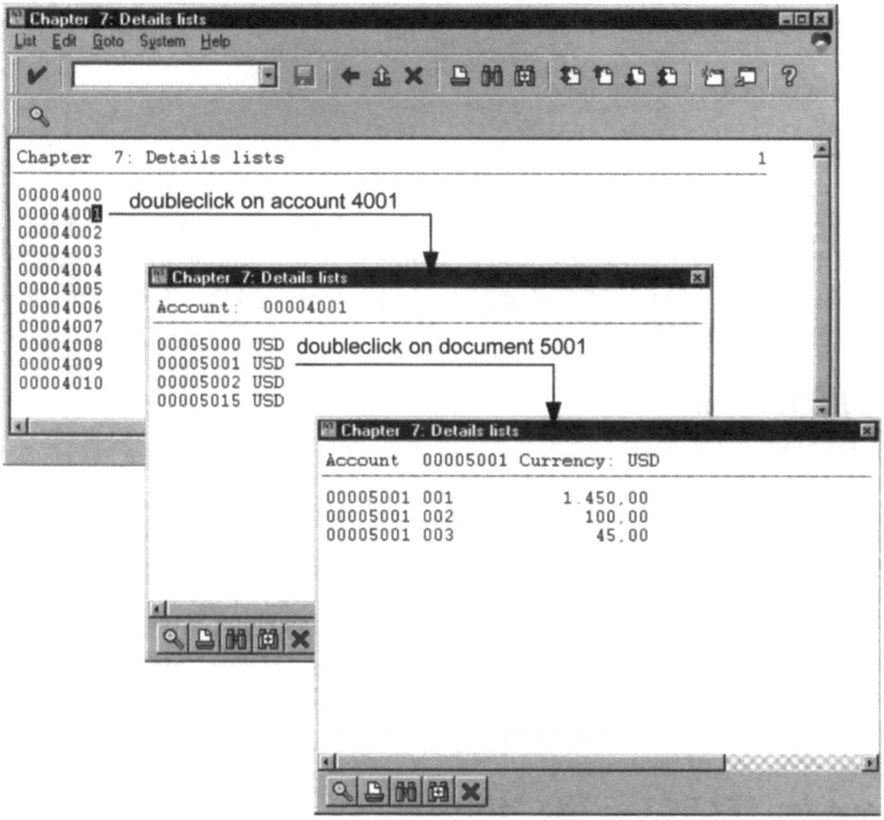

Figure 7.4: Basic list with details list with separate windows

The following command should be issued before the output of the details list to achieve this.

WINDOW STARTING AT *line column* **[ENDING AT** *line column*]**.**
Such a window is modal. Inputs can only be made in each upper window. Only this window can be moved.

7.3.4 Manipulating Lists

The program that created an internal list table can use various ABAP/4 commands to process it. Several variants of the SCROLL command permit program-controlled horizontal and vertical scrolling in the list:

SCROLL LIST [TO FIRST PAGE | TO LAST PAGE | FORWARD | BACKWARD | LEFT | RIGHT].
SCROLL LIST TO PAGE *page.*

SCROLL LIST TO COLUMN *column.*

A frequently used command form to read list lines:

READ LINE *lineno* **INDEX** *level.*

As usual, SY-SUBRC indicates the success of the command. In this case, the contents of the associated line are set in SY-LISEL (LIne SELection). The command is well-suited to pass lists or list hierarchies for purposes of file output (download) into an internal table. The following commands can be used to change list lines:

MODIFY LINE *lineno* **INDEX** *level*
MODIFY CURRENT LINE.

7.4 Group Change

Grouping data is a standard report technique. The ABAP/4 language provides various constructions to support this so-called group processing. As example, the ZCONTRACT class should be used to create a list with partner, account and contract numbers. The partner number constitutes the highest grouping term, with the account number being the second. The group number should only be output once for all elements of the group.

7.4.1 Group Change for SELECT – ON CHANGE

The following construction can be used in a SELECT loop:

ON CHANGE OF *field* **[OR** *field2* **OR** *field3* **...].**

ENDON.
A comparison variable to test for group change is created for each field listed in a CHANGE clause. The ZR_07_11 program shows how the required is created. A list heading is output at the TOP-OP-PAGE condition. This always remains visible during the vertical scrolling of a long list. The ZCONTRACT-PARTNO field is output whenever it changes. The same applies for ZCONTRACT-ACCNO. The contract number is always output and then the line ended.

ORDER BY *must* be set to the sequence of the grouping for sorting to avoid the individual partners appearing more than once.

```
REPORT  ZR_07_03 LINE-SIZE 70.
TABLES: ZCONTRACT.

TOP-OF-PAGE.
  WRITE: / 'Partner   Account   Contract'.
```

```
START-OF-SELECTION.
  SELECT * FROM ZCONTRACT
                WHERE PARTNO BETWEEN 1001 AND 1003
                ORDER BY PARTNO ACCNO CONTNO.
    ON CHANGE OF ZCONTRACT-PARTNO.
      ULINE.
      WRITE: / ZCONTRACT-PARTNO.
    ENDON.
    ON CHANGE OF ZCONTRACT-ACCNO.
      WRITE AT 10 ZCONTRACT-ACCNO.
    ENDON.
    WRITE AT 20 ZCONTRACT-CONTNO.
    WRITE: / '  '.
  ENDSELECT.
```

```
Partner  Account   Contract
--------------------------------------------------------------------
00001001 00004001  00003000
                   00003005
         00004004  00003016
         00004005  00003004
         00004014  00003012
--------------------------------------------------------------------
00001002 00004002  00003001
--------------------------------------------------------------------
00001003 00004003  00003002
```

7.4.2 Group Change for Internal Tables – AT NEW

The following commands are used for group change processing in loops over internal tables:

AT FIRST.
AT LAST.
AT NEW *table_field.*
AT END OF *table_field.*

They are all terminated with ENDAT. Header and footer information of the complete table are output for AT FIRST and AT LAST. The grouping fields of the internal table are specified as fields in AT NEW and AT END. The header information of the associated group (here only the PARTNO and ACCNO numbers) is normally output after AT NEW. End information of the group (new line, underscores) can be output after AT END. SUM can also be used to accumulate numeric fields within a group.

You might assume that SELECT INTO TABLE could be used to read all lines from ZCONTRACT into an internal table and then AT NEW used to create the same list as in the ZR_07_11 program. However, this is not possible. The use of AT NEW requires that the sequence of the fields in the internal table must correspond to the grouping sequence. For this reason, the internal CONTRACTTAB table was created in the ZR_07_24 program that only contains the PARTNO, ACCNO, CONTNO and AMOUNT fields. CONTRACTTAB cannot be read with SELECT ... INTO CONTRACTTAB from ZCONTRACT. MOVE-CORRESPONDING with a subsequent APPEND brings the fields into the required sequence. The internal table must be sorted with SORT in accordance with the grouping hierarchy, otherwise lines with the same group number will be separated.

```
REPORT  ZR 07 04 LINE-SIZE 70.
TABLES: ZCONTRACT.
DATA:   BEGIN OF CONTRACTTAB OCCURS 15,
          PARTNO LIKE ZCONTRACT-PARTNO,
          ACCNO LIKE ZCONTRACT-ACCNO,
          CONTNO LIKE ZCONTRACT-CONTNO,
          BASAM LIKE ZCONTRACT-BASAM,
        END OF CONTRACTTAB.

START-OF-SELECTION.
  SELECT * FROM ZCONTRACT
              WHERE PARTNO BETWEEN 1001 AND 1003.
    MOVE-CORRESPONDING ZCONTRACT TO CONTRACTTAB.
    APPEND CONTRACTTAB.
  ENDSELECT.

  SORT CONTRACTTAB BY PARTNO ACCNO CONTNO.

  LOOP AT CONTRACTTAB.
    AT FIRST.
      WRITE: / 'Partner  Account  Contract      Amount'.
    ENDAT.
    AT NEW PARTNO.
      WRITE: / CONTRACTTAB-PARTNO.
    ENDAT.
    AT NEW ACCNO.
      WRITE AT 10 CONTRACTTAB-ACCNO.
    ENDAT.
    WRITE AT 19 CONTRACTTAB-CONTNO.
    WRITE AT 30(11) CONTRACTTAB-BASAM.
    WRITE: / '  '.
    AT END OF ACCNO.
      WRITE: / '  '.
    ENDAT.
    AT END OF PARTNO.
      SUM. ULINE AT 30(11).
      WRITE AT 30(11) CONTRACTTAB-BASAM.
      ULINE.
    ENDAT.
  ENDLOOP.
```

```
08.06.1998   Chapter  7: Control break with AT NEW                  1
---------------------------------------------------------------------
Partner  Account  Contract          Amount
00001001 00004001 00003000        1.200,00
                  00003005        2.450,00
         00004004 00003016        5.200,00
         00004005 00003004        2.200,00
         00004014 00003012        4.200,00
                                 15.250,00
---------------------------------------------------------------------
00001002 00004002 00003001        1.450,00
                                  1.450,00
---------------------------------------------------------------------
00001003 00004003 00003002        1.700,00
                                  1.700,00
---------------------------------------------------------------------
```

8 Advanced Programming Techniques

8.1 Macros and Includes

8.1.1 Macros as Source Code Modules

Macros are source code modules that can be used as short source code items in various places in the source code. ABAP/4 macros are defined in a similar way as C macros:

DEFINE *macroname***.**
* source code using &1, &2, &3,... placeholders
END-OF-DEFINITION.

The invoked macros are expanded during the generation of the source code, i.e., the source code lines from the macro definition are inserted at the point of invocation. The actual parameters replace the placeholders &1, &2, etc. Blanks are used to separate the actual parameters for a macro call. This means that null parameters cannot be specified. The following example defines the ONERROR macro that has two placeholders.

```
DEFINE ONERROR.
  IF SY-SUBRC = &1.
    &2.
  ENDIF.
END-OF-DEFINITION
```

The macro can be used, for example, to handle errors in a loop. The loop is terminated for the ERR_NO_VALUE error; ERR_IS_EMPTY starts a new loop iteration.

```
CONSTANTS: ERR_NO_VALUE TYPE I VALUE 77.
CONSTANTS: ERR_IS_EMPTY TYPE I VALUE 9.
DO.
* program logic , sets SY-SUBRC
  ONERROR ERR_NO_VALUES EXIT.
  ONERROR ERR_IS_EMPTY CONTINUE.
* program logic
ENDDO.
```

The first parameter is a program constant, the second parameter is the EXIT or CONTINUE key word. These key words are used for the macro expansion without being changed or interpreted. Parameters cannot be specified as key words for subprograms (forms).

In general, macros should only be used when the required functionality cannot be obtained with an appropriate FORM (see Section 8.2). This is the case in the above example. If you replace the macro call with a suitable PERFORM, the corresponding EXIT or CONTINUE in this FORM applies and not that in the DO loop.

The number of actual parameters for a macro must be the same as the number of placeholders in the macro definition. Macros can themselves use other macros. The sequence of the macro definitions has no significance. The syntax checking rejects a recursive or mutual call of macros.

The ZR_08_01 program shows how the A1 and A3 macros (A represents APPEND, the number represents the number of parameters) can be used to fill an internal table with program code. This method can be used for automatic source code generation.

```
REPORT ZR 08 01 LINE-SIZE 70.
DATA: BEGIN OF PROGTAB OCCURS 20,
        ROW(72),
      END OF PROGTAB.

DEFINE A1.
  PROGTAB-ROW = &1. APPEND PROGTAB.
END-OF-DEFINITION.
DEFINE A3.
  CONCATENATE &1 &2 &3 INTO PROGTAB-ROW. APPEND PROGTAB.
END-OF-DEFINITION.

CLEAR PROGTAB. REFRESH PROGTAB.
A1 'REPORT ZTEST.'.
A1 'WRITE: / ''Here is report       :'', SY-REPID.'.
A3 'WRITE: / ''Generated by report:' SY-REPID '''.'.

LOOP AT PROGTAB.
  WRITE: / PROGTAB-ROW.
ENDLOOP.

*INSERT REPORT 'ZTEST' FROM PROGTAB.
*SUBMIT ZTEST AND RETURN.

REPORT ZTEST.
WRITE: / 'Here is report       :', SY-REPID.
WRITE: / 'Generated by report:ZR 08 01'.
```

The first call of A1 generates the REPORT instruction. The second call of A1 lists the SY-REPID program name in the target program. Note that the name "SY-REPID" for the produced report ZR_08_01 is part of a constant string and is *not* evaluated in ZR_08_01. Two consecutive apostrophes ('') produce a single apostrophe in PROGTAB-ZEILE.

The call to A3 evaluates SY-REPID of the generating report ZR_08_01 and writes "ZR_08_03" in the string. The last two lines can be used to write the YTEST report in the Repository and then immediately start it.

8.1.2 Division of Source Code Using INCLUDE

The INCLUDE method can be used to divide extensive ABAP/4 source code into several smaller source code units. This method is also known from other programming languages, in particular C. INCLUDE sources are managed as type "I" programs in the Data Dictionary. An include is placed in the source code using the command

INCLUDE *programname.*

Multi-level includes are permitted, i.e., an include can itself contain other include instructions. Recursive includes are, of course, prohibited.

8.2 Subprogram Technique Using Forms

Forms are one of the most important structuring capabilities in ABAP/4. Forms are similar to sections in COBOL, void functions in C, subroutines in FORTRAN or BASIC, and procedures in Pascal.

Forms are parameterizable subprograms. They are defined at a position in the program and can be invoked where required. In contrast to macros, the invocation of a FORM causes the processing of the program lines of the definition and the subsequent return to the point of invocation.

8.2.1 Definition

A FORM is defined using the following scheme:

FORM *form_name*
    TABLES *tabparam1* [*type1*] *tabparam2* [*type2*] ...
    USING *refparam1* [*type1*] *refparam2* [*type2*] ...
    USING VALUE(*valueparam1*) [*type1*] **VALUE**(*valueparam2*)] [*type2*] ...
    CHANGING *changeparam1* [*type1*] *changeparam2* [*type2*] ...
* Declaration of local data FORM
* Program logic of FORM
ENDFORM.

Because most declaration, definition and execution statements of an ABAP/4 program are permitted within the FORM – ENDFORM block, the designation as subprogram is appropriate. The event key words that are useful only at the highest program level form an important exception. Section 8.2.3 describes the lifetime and the scope of the data defined in a form.

The TABLES, USING and VALUE key words define the list of the symbolic parameters. These parameters are tables, fields, and structures that describe the structure of the interface for the form to the called program. The symbolic parameters are used as "normal" program variables within the form. The symbolic parameter list can be empty.

Tables with or without header records can be passed to a form by reference using the TABLES option. If the typing of a table parameter is omitted, only operations on complete table rows can be executed in forms. Field accesses are not possible in this case. The typing of tables can make reference to both tables or structures in the Data Dictionary and also to internal tables. The ZR_08_02 report illustrates this capability.

Field or structure parameters are always passed by reference with the USING field. This means that the form actually uses field symbols. Although these have the name of the symbolic parameters, they address the actual parameters. A read access to such a parameter obtains a variable that lies outside the form. A write access changes these variables immediately. Even though constants or literals can be used as current values for a reference parameter, a write access in the form causes the program to fail with the MOVE_TO_LIT_NOTALLOWED runtime error.

USING parameters are used either for information export from the form or for bi-directional information transfer. The typing of USING parameters is performed in the same manner as for normal data. For performance reasons, you should also declare large structures as USINGs if they are only to be read in the form. The form then assumes responsibility that the original is not changed.

If a parameter is only to be used to import information into the form, it can be specified with USING VALUE (parameter). Local copies (Section 8.2.3) are created in the form from such parameters. These can be read and written without changes being made to the original data. Thus, the VALUE parameters provide protection for such original data that is not allowed to be changed in the form.

CHANGING combines the properties of USING with those of USING VALUE. Although the parameter is passed as reference, processing is performed using a local copy created for the duration of the form. The changed values from the local copy replace the original data only when the form completes successfully. This avoids inconsistency of the original data.

8.2.2 Invocation and Actual Parameters

The following instruction is used to invoke a form defined with FORM:

PERFORM *form_name*
  TABLES *tabparam1 tabparam2 ...*
  USING *param1 param2 ....*

The field names or literals specified after USING and TABLES are called the actual parameter list. This must have the same number of USING parameters as the symbolic parameters in the definition. The same applies for the TABLES parameters.

The actual parameters are assigned in the sequence of the symbolic parameters. A syntax error results if the parameters are not type-compatible with the corresponding symbolic parameters.

The ZR_08_02 report defines the internal table PTAB with the structure of ZDOCITEM in the main program. The READ_ITEMS form reads into this table all items for a specified document number.

```
REPORT ZR 08 02 LINE-SIZE 70.
TABLES: ZDOCITEM.
DATA  : ITAB LIKE ZDOCITEM OCCURS 10 WITH HEADER LINE.
DATA  : ITEMCOUNT LIKE SY-DBCNT.

PERFORM READ_ITEMS TABLES ITAB USING '5001' ITEMCOUNT.

LOOP AT ITAB.
WRITE: / ITAB-DOCNO, ITAB-ITEMNO, ITAB-AMOUNT.
ENDLOOP.
WRITE: / 'ITEMS:', ITEMCOUNT.
*---------------------------------------------------------------------
FORM READ_ITEMS
         TABLES ITEMTAB STRUCTURE PTAB
         USING VALUE(DOCNO) LIKE ZDOCHD-DOCNO
         ITEMCOUNT.
SELECT * INTO TABLE ITEMTAB FROM ZDOCITEM WHERE DOCNO = DOCNO.
ITEMCOUNT = SY-DBCNT.
ENDFORM.

15.09.1998       Chapter  8: Form with table parameters        1
---------------------------------------------------------------------
00005001 001          1.450,00
00005001 002            100,00
00005001 003             45,00
ITEMS:          3
```

The internal table POSTAB of the symbolic parameters takes the structure from PTAB with STRUCTURE PTAB. This functions only because PTAB has been defined in the main program as an internal table with header area (WITH HEADER LINE). There are four ways of typing the parameter table:

Table 8.1: Typing of table parameters

Variant	Reference Table	With Header?	Typing in FORM ... TABLES :
1	ZDOCITEM	yes (always)	ITEMTAB STRUCTURE ZDOCITEM
2 a, b	ITAB	yes	ITEMTAB STRUCTURE ITAB or ITEMTAB LIKE ITAB[ ]
3	ITAB	no	ITEMTAB LIKE ITAB

In general, STRUCTURE references tables with a header area. These can be either internal or external tables. LIKE can only be used in conjunction with internal tables; the empty angular brackets indicate a reference table with header area. All the above variants return the same result. Note, however, a target field must be specified in the LOOP if PTAB is used without header line.

The DOCNO parameter is a typed value parameter. It cannot be changed in the form. ITEMCOUNT is a reference parameter without type that returns the number of read items in the invoked program.

Symbolic and actual parameters can have the same names, which is often the case. Parameter prefixes, such as "P_" or "I_" for import and "E_" for export, are often used to improve the identification of the symbolic parameters.

8.2.3 Local and Global Variables

Program data in ABAP/4 are differentiated with regard to:

- *Visibility*
  – *global*: can be used everywhere in programs, and also in forms
  – *local*: can only be used in forms.
- *Lifetime*
  – *static*: duration of the complete program
  – *temporary*: duration of the individual forms

The data defined in the main program are global. Both the main program and all forms have read and write access to this data. Forms have access without requiring that the data be defined in the parameter lists. The lifetime of such data corresponds to that of the program. The data are stored in the program's working storage when it starts and released only when it ends. Global data in this sense are static data.

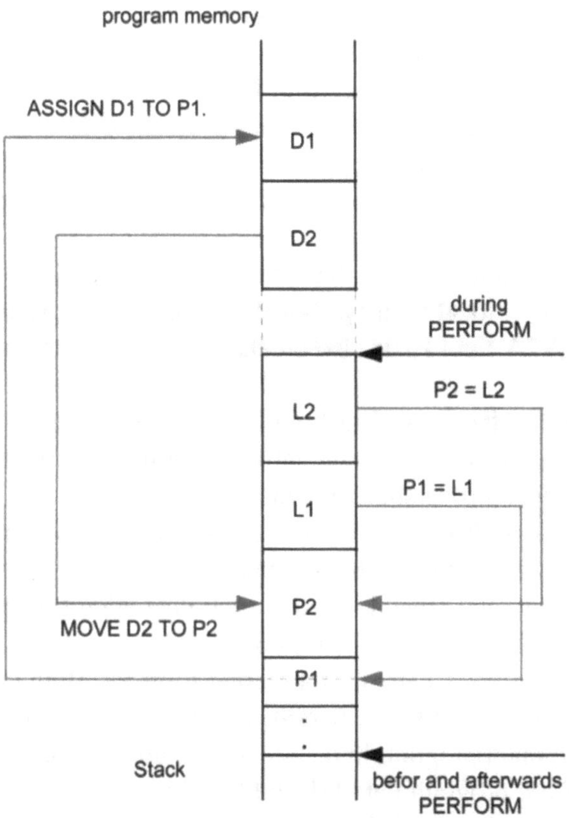


```
REPORT XYZ.
DATA:  D1(8), D2(12).

PERFORM F USING D1 D2.


FORM F USING P1 LIKE D1
       USING VALUE(P2) LIKE D2.

DATA L1 LIKE D1, L2 LIKE D2.

P1 = L1.
P2 = L2.

ENDFORM.
```

Figure 8.1: Local and global variables

Those fields, field strings and tables defined in a form without further options are designated as being local data. They are visible and usable only within the associated form. Local data have only a temporary life. They are stored in a stack that is created on entry to the form. The data exist only when the program is being executed and are subsequently overwritten by other invoked forms.

The term "dynamic data" in this context can cause confusion. Dynamic data are those data items that obtain the required memory at runtime on request to the system and then release it immediately after use. These are the *malloc* or *calloc* functions in the C language. Although ABAP/4 does not provide such commands, the memory for internal tables is always managed dynamically. However, the internal tables are designated as being static for the main program and temporary for forms.

The stack itself is not dynamic storage. Its maximum size has been predefined. The stack pointer indicates its current size. A PERFORM places data and the return address on the stack and changes the stack pointer appropriately. The stack pointer is reset on leaving the form.

It is important for the understanding of the interaction of symbolic and actual parameters to appreciate that all parameters on entry to a form are stored as local data in the stack. The value parameters (USING VALUE) are specified like normal data with DATA. The invocation of PERFORM copies the contents of the actual parameter into this local variable.

Reference parameters are stored as field symbols. The invocation of PERFORM executes an ASSIGN of the local field symbol to the specified parameter. The main program defines two global fields: D1 and D2. The form F has a reference parameter of the same type as D1 and a value parameter of the same type as D2. Two local fields L1 and L2 of the corresponding type are also defined in the form.

Whereas the global fields D1 and D2 lie in program memory, the local fields L1 and L2 lie in the stack. On entry to the form, the system creates a local field symbol P1 in addition to L1, and L2 and points this to D1 using ASSIGN. A DATA field P2 is also created into which the contents of D2 are copied.

The assignment P2=L2 in the form then defines the local data field P2. A back reference to D2 is not possible. In contrast, consider the assignment P1 = L1: the information in effect passes from L1 through P1 into the field D1. The specified arrows illustrate this.

The use of global data hides the information flow. It is always better to use parameters to explicitly show which information flow into and out of the form. In general, you should try to avoid the use of global data. If you use such data, you should identify such data appropriately (e.g., with the "GBL_" prefix) and then consistently never pass them as parameters.

Naturally, forms can call other forms. Assume form F1 invokes a second form F2. Both can exchange information either using global variables or using the parameter list for F2. With the transfer of parameters, F1 adopts the role of the main program in the above example. Local data of the invoked form F1 would exist instead of the program data D1 and D2. Consequently, the reference parameters from F2 would address the stack area of F1.

Local static data have a special feature. These are defined in forms with the STATICS key word. The following examples for recursive forms contain such STATICS definitions.

8.2.4 Forms with Complex Parameters

The ZR_08_03 report demonstrates how complex structures can be appropriately used as parameters for forms. Here a DOCUMENT structure of the type DOCTYPE is defined as shown in Section 6.7. The report defines the READ_DOCUMENT form that has a reference parameter of the type DOCTYPE. It is assumed that the DOCHD-DOCNO key as been set by the caller. The form should read from the database all details for the document header and the document items.

```
REPORT ZR_08_03 LINE-SIZE 70.
TABLES: ZDOCHD, ZDOCITEM.

TYPES   : BEGIN OF DOCTYPE,
            HEAD LIKE ZDOCHD,
            ITAB LIKE ZDOCITEM OCCURS 10,
          END OF DOCTYPE.
```

```
DATA:     DOCUMENT TYPE DOCTYPE.
DATA:     ITEM LIKE ZDOCITEM.
DOCUMENT-HEAD-DOCNO = '5001'.
PERFORM READ_DOCUMENT USING DOCUMENT.
WRITE: / 'DOCUMENT:', DOCUMENT-HEAD-DOCNO.
WRITE: / 'ITEMS:'.
LOOP AT DOCUMENT-ITAB INTO ITEM.
  WRITE: / ITEM-DOCNO, ITEM-DOCNO, ITEM-AMOUNT,
           DOCUMENT-HEAD-CURRKY.
ENDLOOP.
*------------------------------------------------------------------
FORM READ_DOCUMENT USING DOCUMENT TYPE DOCTYPE.
DATA: ITEMCOUNT LIKE SY-DBCNT.
PERFORM READ_HEAD USING DOCUMENT-HEAD.
PERFORM READ_ITEM TABLES DOCUMENT-ITAB
                        USING DOCUMENT-HEAD-DOCNO ITEMCOUNT.
ENDFORM.
*------------------------------------------------------------------
FORM READ_HEAD USING HEAD LIKE DOCUMENT-HEAD.
SELECT SINGLE * INTO HEAD FROM ZDOCHD
   WHERE DOCNO = HEAD-DOCNO.
ENDFORM.
*------------------------------------------------------------------
FORM READ_ITEMS
         TABLES ITAB LIKE DOCUMENT-ITAB
         USING VALUE(DOCNO) LIKE ZDOCHD-DOCNO ITEMCOUNT.
SELECT * INTO TABLE ITAB FROM ZDOCITEM WHERE DOCNO = DOCNO.
ITEMCOUNT = SY-DBCNT.
ENDFORM.
```

The form itself invokes two further forms. DOCHD-DOCNO is a form that has a structure of the table header type as reference parameter. This shows an important advantage provided by the use of the HEADER substructure in the DOCTYPE type: the header data can be passed to the form as a *single* parameter. This would not have been possible with an INCLUDE STRUCTURE declaration. Consequently, the embedded table DOCUMENT-ITAB is passed as TABLES parameter to the READ_ITEMS form. The form fills the table with the found items. Note that the table parameters in this case describe a table without header line.

```
11.09.1998     Chapter  8: Forms with complex parameters           1
--------------------------------------------------------------------
DOCUMENT: 00005001
ITEMS:
00005001 00005001          1.450,00  USD
00005001 00005001            100,00  USD
00005001 00005001             45,00  USD
```

8.2.5 Recursion

Recursive forms invoke themselves. The parameters are normally changed from call to call until some termination criterion ends the recursion. An example is a form for the recursive computation of factorial N! for a natural number N. It codes the following recursive factorial formula:

$$N! = 1 \quad \text{for } N = 1$$
$$ = N * (N-1)! \quad \text{for } N > 1.$$

```
REPORT ZR 08 04 LINE-SIZE 70.
DATA N TYPE I VALUE 7.
DATA FACT TYPE I.
PERFORM CALC_FACT USING  N FACT.
ULINE.
WRITE: / 'Factorial of', (2) N, '=', FACT.
*---------------------------------------------------------------------
FORM CALC_FACT USING VALUE(N) TYPE I    FACT TYPE I.
STATICS: LEVEL TYPE I VALUE 0.
DATA N1 TYPE I.
DATA COLUMN TYPE I.
LEVEL = LEVEL + 1.
COLUMN = LEVEL * 3.
WRITE: /COLUMN 'Start level', (2)LEVEL.
IF N = 1.
  FACT = 1.
ELSE.
  N1 = N - 1.
  PERFORM CALC_FACT USING N1 FACT.
  FACT = N * FACT.
ENDIF.
WRITE: / '  '.
WRITE: AT /COLUMN 'N=', (2) N, 'Factorial=', FACT.
WRITE: AT /COLUMN 'End level',(2) LEVEL.
LEVEL = LEVEL - 1.
ENDFORM.

11.09.1998   Chapter  8: Recursive calculation of faculties        1
---------------------------------------------------------------------
   Start level 1
      Start level 2
         Start level 3
            Start level 4
               Start level 5
                  Start level 6
                     Start level 7
                     N= 1  Factorial=           1
                     End level 7
                  N= 2  Factorial=           2
                  End level 6
               N= 3  Factorial=           6
               End level 5
            N= 4  Factorial=          24
```

```
          End level 4
        N= 5  Factorial=           120
        End level 3
      N= 6  Factorial=           720
      End level 2
    N= 7  Factorial=      5.040
    End level 1
-----------------------------------------------------------------
  Factorial of 7  =      5.040
```

CALC_FACT is initially tested for the value parameter N. If the parameter is greater than 1, CALC_FACT invokes itself with the parameter N1 = N–1. The local variable N1 is required only because ABAP/4 does not permit the use of expressions in actual parameter lists. A nesting level of 7 produces N = 1 that sets the FACT reference parameter to 1. The actual computation of the factorial is now performed by successively multiplying FACT with the local values of N. Although the same code is executed in this seven-level nested call, up to seven different values of N and N1 exist concurrently in the stack. The recursive calls consequently place a heavy load on the stack. The static variable *level* specifies the current nesting level of the form. The report uses the appropriate indentation to indicate the level. This simple example is only demonstrative. The following code would be better to compute the factorial:

```
FACT = 1.
DO N TIMES.
 FACT = FACT * SY-INDEX.
ENDDO.
```

The computations of graphs are examples of useful and elegant applications for recursive forms. Figure 8.2 shows such a directed graph that is described by its nodes and a node connection list.

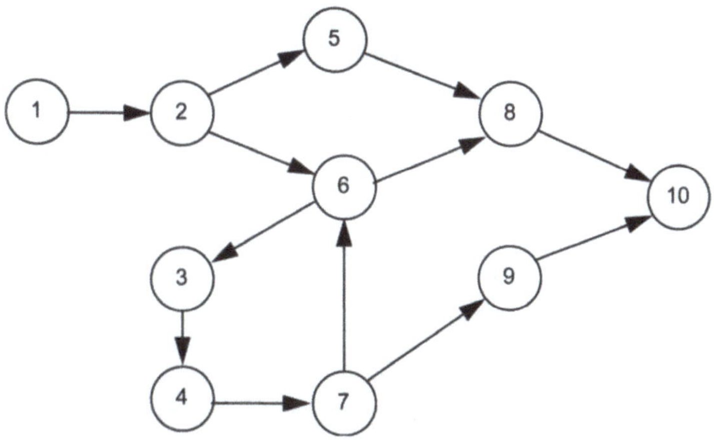

node connections

predecessor	successor
1	2
2	5
5	8
8	10
2	8
6	3
3	4
4	7
7	6
7	9
9	10

Figure 8.2: Directed graph with node connection list

ZR_08_05 defines the node connection list as internal table NCLTAB. The C macro (connection) is used to enter the connections shown in the figure. The recursive form FINDPATH searches in the graphs for a path from the START node to the FINISH node. Two tables are passed to the form: the NCLTAB node connection list and the PATHTAB table, in which the nodes on the found path are stored.

```
REPORT ZR_08_05 LINE-SIZE 70.

DATA: BEGIN OF NCLTAB OCCURS 20,
        PRED TYPE I,
        SUC TYPE I,
      END OF NCLTAB.
DATA  PATHTAB TYPE I OCCURS 20 WITH HEADER LINE.

DATA: START  TYPE I VALUE 1.
DATA: FINISH TYPE I VALUE 9.

DEFINE C.
NCLTAB-PRED = &1. NCLTAB-SUC = &2. APPEND NCLTAB.
END-OF-DEFINITION.

C 1 2.  C 2 5.  C 5 8.  C 8 10.
C 2 6.  C 6 8.  C 6 3.  C 3 4.  C 4 7.  C 7 6.  C 7 9.  C 9 10.
CLEAR PATHTAB. REFRESH PATHTAB.

PERFORM FINDPATH TABLES NCLTAB PATHTAB
                USING  START FINISH.
WRITE: / 'Path from', (2) START, 'to',(2)FINISH,'  ='.
WRITE: (2) START, '-->'.
LOOP AT PATHTAB. WRITE: (2) PATHTAB, '-->'. ENDLOOP.
WRITE: (2)FINISH.
*---------------------------------------------------------------------
FORM FINDPATH TABLES NCL LIKE NCLTAB[]
                     PATH LIKE PATHTAB[]
              USING  VALUE(START)
                     VALUE(FINISH).
STATICS: MARK TYPE I OCCURS 20 WITH HEADER LINE.
STATICS: FOUND  VALUE SPACE.
DATA   : LONG TYPE I.

LOOP AT NCL WHERE PRED = START.
  IF NCL-SUC = FINISH.
    FOUND = 'X'.
    EXIT.
  ENDIF.
  READ TABLE MARK WITH KEY NCL-SUC.
  IF SY-SUBRC = 0.    " already in MARK
     CONTINUE.
  ENDIF.
  APPEND NCL-SUC TO MARK .
  APPEND NCL-SUC TO PATH.
```

```
   PERFORM FINDPATH TABLES NCL PATH USING NCL-SUC FINISH.
   IF FOUND = 'X'. EXIT. ENDIF.
   DESCRIBE TABLE PATH LINES LONG.
   DELETE PATH INDEX LONG.
ENDLOOP.
ENDFORM.
```

```
15.09.1998   Chapter  8: Recursive path search inside a net        1
--------------------------------------------------------------------
Path from 1  to 9    = 1  --> 2  --> 6  --> 3  --> 4  --> 7  --> 9
```

The general principle of the recursive path search can be explained as follows: If there is a path from the START node to the FINISH node, this path must lead to a successor of the start node. This statement also applies for each of the successors. Thus, the algorithm searches for all successor nodes beginning at the start node and begins the search for each new successor by using this as the new start node. The process completes when one of the successor nodes is the required destination node or when all the reachable nodes have been tested for starting nodes.

The FINDPATH form searches in a loop all successor nodes of the passed initial node START. A path has been found when the successor node is the same as the specified FINISH node. If not, a test is made whether the successor node has been reached in earlier steps of the algorithm. The form defines the local static table MARK for this purpose. If a node has been marked, i.e., has been entered in the MARK table, then it does not need to be tested again and the LOOP is iterated with CONTINUE. If the node is new, it is marked for following steps. The form now invokes itself with START = NCL-SUC as actual parameter.

The static variable FOUND is initialized with SPACE in the first call. It is set to 'X' when the destination node has been reached. This permits the depth of the recursion to show the completion of the search.

The MARK table ensures that any loops contained in the graph do not cause an endless loop in the program. This would be the case for the determined path $1 \rightarrow 2 \rightarrow 6 \rightarrow 3 \rightarrow 4 \rightarrow 7$ from node 1 to node 9. When node 7 is reached, node 6 would be tested as first successor node if there was no marking. The result would be an endless recursion that would cause program failure.

Each new successor node is provisionally entered in the PATHTAB table. If the recursive invocation of FINDPATH does not find the destination using this node as starting node, the node does not lie on a path. It is then removed from the PATHTAB table.

The algorithm uses the DEPTH FIRST method, i.e., the recursive invocation is performed in the LOOP over all successors before the loop has been completely processed. The "vertical" search for successors of additional generations has precedence over the "horizontal" search, i.e., for immediate successors.

8.2.6 Invocation of External Forms

In the course of time, the processing of large projects will produce forms that can (and should) be used in other programs. Forms for conversions and for string processing are such examples. There are two ways to use such forms in a range of programs.

The first possibility is to save the forms in an include that then can be used by several programs. This has the same effect as each of the programs defining the forms. The invocation has the same form as described previously. If the forms use global variables, these must be present in each of the including programs.

The second possibility is to use an external call of a form. The following options to the previously described PERFORM are provided:

PERFORM *form(progname) parameterlist.*

or

PERFORM *form* **IN PROGRAM** *progname parameterlist.*

This invokes a form in the *progname* program. The program name must be known at compile-time in first variant. The program name is determined at runtime in the second variant.

In both cases, the program whose form is called is loaded into main memory together with the invoking program. This produces a so-called program group. Because the stack of the *invoking* program is used to pass the parameters and for the management of the local data, there is no difference between an internal and an external call.

This is not the case for global data. Because the invoked form uses the global data of its own program, you cannot expect that an externally invoked form can read or write the global data in the invoking program. If this is required, you must explicitly specify a common memory area as interface between the invoking and the invoked program:

DATA: BEGIN OF COMMON PART *name.*

* common data

END OF COMMON PART *name.*

In Figure 8.3, the PROG1 program invokes the form F2 in the PROG2 program. The form uses a global field COMMDAT of its program. COMMDAT is defined in the COMMON area C of both programs. The trace of COMMDAT in the PROG1 program shows the value "PROG2" that was set by the form. If the COMMDAT field is defined in both programs without COMMON block, COMMDAT in program PROG1 is then empty after calling F2.

Note that external FORM calls are not subject to the syntax test. If, for example, there is an incorrect number of parameters in the PERFORM, the invoking program terminates at runtime with the PERFORM_PARAMETER_MISSING error. The use of function modules can counteract this disadvantage.

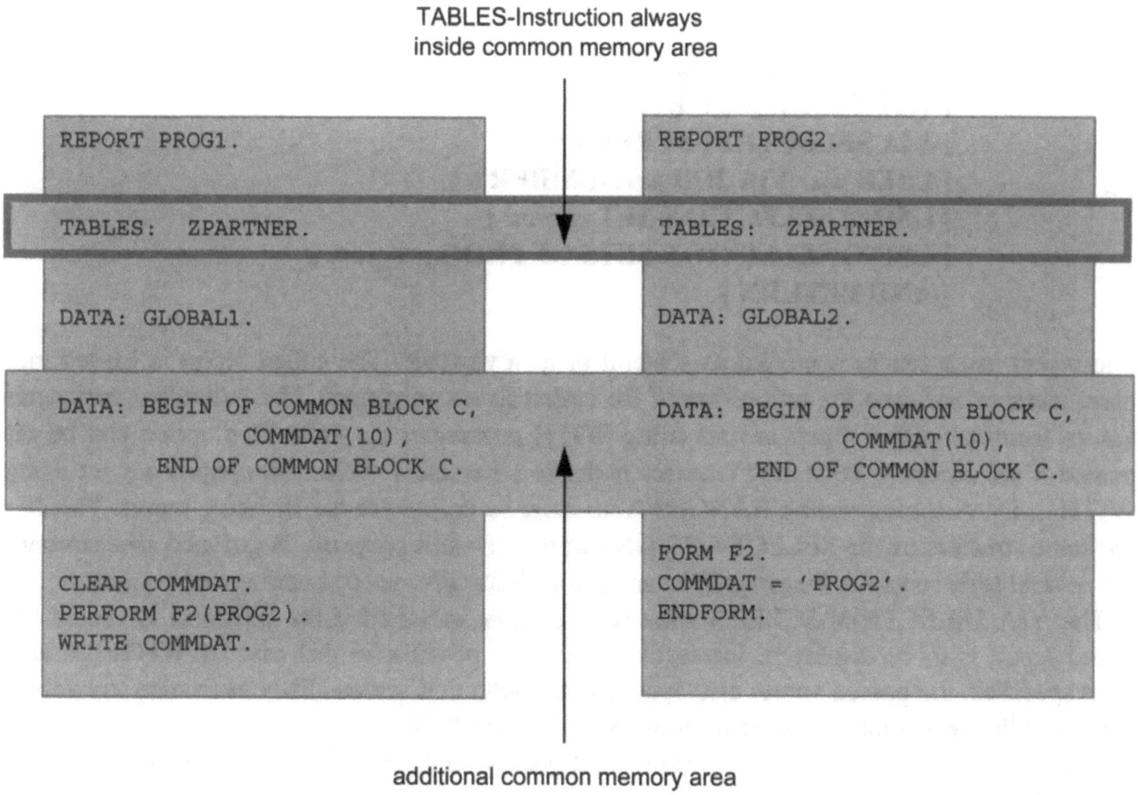

Figure 8.3: Common global data for two programs

8.3 Data Exchange Between Reports

Section 8.2.6 showed how a program can invoke a form of another program. The data transfer is performed using the parameter list of the form or with a common memory area.

It was characteristic that only the code of the called subprograms, but never the program code of the invoking report, was always processed. This provides a communication between program and subprogram. The following three sections demonstrate the communication between various programs.

8.3.1 Start Report with SUBMIT

SUBMIT is a powerful, highly efficient ABAP/4 command. It is used to start a report from another report. The command provides variants and options, not all of which are discussed here. A possible form of the command with frequently used options:

SUBMIT (*report_name*)
[**WITH** *parameter* **Op** *field*]
[**WITH** *selectoption* **IN** *sel*]
[**VIA SELECTION-SCREEN**]
[**USER** *user* **VIA JOB** *job* **NUMBER** n]
[**USING SELECTION-SET** *variant*]
[**USING SELECTION-SETS OF PROG** *program*]
[**AND RETURN**] .

The report name can be specified as a literal or as a variable. The called report is loaded into main memory and then the processing of the called report continued. The individual parameter values from the called report are set using WITH *parameter op field.* This option can be repeated if the report to be started requires multiple parameters. Selection options are set using WITH ... IN. A corresponding RANGES table must be defined in the invoking report. This has the same structure as the SELECT-OPTIONS in the invoked program. A grouped area containing several table rows can be assigned to an option. Naturally, several options are permitted.

The VIA SELECTION-SCREEN must be explicitly specified if the selection screen of the called report is to be displayed. Interactive inputs are possible in this case. If WITH has also been specified, the passed values also appear in the selection screen. They overwrite any values that the called report may have been set in INITIALIZATION.

VIA JOB can be used to set the report as a background job. This is described in detail in Chapter 10.

The USING SELECTION-SET option can be used to start the program with its (own) variant. USING SELECTION-SETS (plural) permits the use of variants of another specified program. This permits variants to be used between programs. Obviously, this is appropriate only for those programs that have the same parameters.

The AND RETURN option causes the processing to be continued after the SUBMIT in the invoking report when the called report ends.

```
REPORT ZR_08_06 LINE-SIZE 70.

DATA    ACCNO LIKE ZACCOUNT-ACCNO.
RANGES  RANGE_AMO FOR ACCNO.

RANGE_AMO-SIGN   = 'I'.
RANGE_AMO-OPTION = 'BT'.
RANGE_AMO-LOW    = '4001'.
```

```
RANGE_AMO-HIGH    = '4003'.  APPEND RANGE_AMO.
WRITE: / 'ZR_07_02 will be started ...'.
SUBMIT ('ZR_07_02') WITH SO_AMO IN RANGE_AMO AND RETURN.
WRITE: / '                          ... is ready.'.
```

```
11.09.1998    Chapter  8: Call of a report with SUBMIT              1
-------------------------------------------------------------------
ZR 07 02 will be started ...
                         ... is ready.
```

The ZR_07_08 report uses SUBMIT ... AND RETURN to invoke the interactive report ZR_07_02. The select option SO_AMO of the invoked report is filled using the RANGE_AMO RANGES table. The basic list and the details list ZR_07_02 appear on the screen of the calling report. Only a *return* to the basic list from ZR_07_02 results in the output of the basic list for ZR_07_08. Thus, the WRITE that is located in front of the SUBMIT appears only after the RETURN.

8.3.2 Data Transfer using EXPORT/IMPORT

A new *internal* mode opens if a report uses SUBMIT to start another report. An external mode, namely a non-modal input window for a session, can have a maximum of nine such internal modes. Although all internal modes have their own memory area (roll area), they can also access a common memory area, the ABAP/4 memory. The following commands are used for this purpose:

EXPORT *field1 field2* ... **TO MEMORY ID** *id.*

and

IMPORT *field1 field2* ... **FROM MEMORY ID** *id.*

Fields, field strings or complete tables can be exported and imported. It is common for the invoking report to export the data before the SUBMIT that the invoked report then imports. The SET PARAMETER and GET PARAMETER commands are used to transfer data.

Please note: An invoked report that is started in another external mode, even while the exporting report is still active, cannot import any data.

In addition to the export into the ABAP/4 memory, it is also possible to export to a database table or to a file. The corresponding import commands are available.

8.3.3 Data Transfer Using SET / GET PARAMETER

Programs can communicate using the so-called SAP memory that operates in various external modes:

SET PARAMETER ***field*** **ID** ***id*****.**
GET PARAMETER ***field*** **ID** ***id*****.**

This memory area is active during the complete session. Parameters remain set even when then the program that set them has terminated. A SET PARAMETER with the same ID value can be used to replace an existing value.

The ZR_08_07 sample program uses EXPORT to place the *value1* field in the ABAP/4 memory. The ZR_08_08 program attempts to read these data using IMPORT or GET PARAMETER. The result depends on whether ZR_08_08 has been started. It is irrelevant whether ZR_08_08 is started in the same or different mode.

The value1 = "11111" can only be read using IMPORT when ZR_08_08 is running or ran in the same mode (and in the same window) as ZR_08_07.

```
REPORT ZR_08_07 LINE-SIZE 70.
DATA VALUE1(10) VALUE '1111111'.
DATA VALUE2(10) VALUE '2222222'.

EXPORT VALUE1 TO MEMORY ID 'ID1'.
SET PARAMETER ID 'ID2' FIELD VALUE2.

WRITE: / 'click to start ZR_08_08.'.

AT LINE-SELECTION.
SUBMIT ('ZR_08_08') AND RETURN.
```

```
REPORT ZR_08_08 LINE-SIZE 70.
DATA VALUE1(10).
DATA VALUE2(10).

IMPORT VALUE1 FROM MEMORY ID 'ID1'.
GET PARAMETER ID 'ID2' FIELD VALUE2.
WRITE: / 'Here is', SY-REPID.
WRITE: / 'VALUE1=', VALUE1, 'VALUE2 =', VALUE2.
```

```
11.09.1998  Chapter  8: IMPORT FROM MEMORY and GET PARAMETER        1
----------------------------------------------------------------------
Here is ZR_08_08
VALUE1= 1111111    VALUE2 = 2222222
```

8.4 Logical Databases

Large application systems, such as an R/3 module, normally have many reports that can access the associated tables. It has been found that those program sections of these reports that are responsible for the data retrieval from the database (SELECT) continually repeat themselves in the same or a similar way. The developer must repeatedly define tables and program complex SELECTs with extensive WHERE-conditions in every report. It would be desirable to separate this redundant code from the reports and to place it in a read program that all reports can access.

A logical database achieves precisely this. It separates the data retrieval from the data processing. The developer who uses a logical database in his report, describes just the processing of the data supplied by the logical database. He can use the GET <table> key word to obtain information from the logical database whether a new record is available in the table work area. Reports that use the logical databases normally do not have any SELECTs of their own.

The developers of processing reports can just concentrate on how the data are to be processed. The logical database relieves them of the complete data retrieval task. A logical database is stored in the Repository as three components:

- Structure description
- Selection options
- Read program.

A supervisory control program coordinates the processing of a database report. This initiates alternately the retrieval routines in the read program and the processing routines in the processing program.

A logical database does not itself contain any executable program. It can only be used in conjunction with the appropriate reports.

8.4.1 Structure Description of a Logical Database

A logical database connects several logically related tables that are defined in the Data Dictionary. They are described by a table hierarchy (= table tree). The relationships between the tables in the logical database correspond to the external key relationships of the associated tables.

Figure 8.4 shows the structure of the ZDF logical database. The ZACCOUNT table forms the root node. The ZACCOUNT and ZDOCHD tables are connected to this table by 1:N relationships. The document header table ZDOCHD is itself a primary table for the document items ZDOCITEM. It can be seen that the relationship between ZACCOUNT and ZDOCHD is not appropriate in a table *tree*. All tables with a common primary table are located at the same level. Relationships between such tables cannot represent a logical database.

The structure of the logical database is stored in the TLBD table. Because each LDB provides only two records, the number of tables in a LDB is limited.

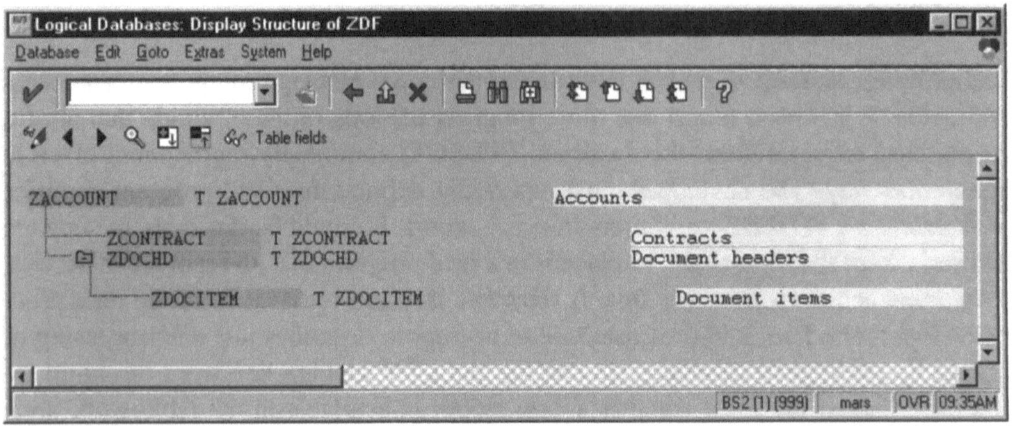

Figure 8.4: Structure of the YDF logical database

8.4.2 Selection Options and Read Program

The selection options and the associated read program can be generated once the structure of an LDB has been determined. The system assigns the program name in the form SAPDB<LDB>. This name cannot be changed. The include for the selection options is named according to the SAP standards in the form DB<LDB>SEL.

The selection options permit the database limits to be set interactively and passed to the read program after the start of a processing program. The parameters specified in the selection options and the SELECT-OPTIONS appear automatically in the selection screen of the processing program and supplement the parameters defined there. The read program can use the entered information.

The system on request generates the following suggestion for the selection options of the ZDF logical database from the database structure.

```
*---------------------------------------------------------------------*
* INCLUDE DBZDFSEL
* It will be automatically included into the database program.
*---------------------------------------------------------------------*
*
* If the source code is automatically generated,
* please perform the following steps:
* 1. Replace ? by suitable names (at most 8 characters).
* 2. Activate SELECT-OPTIONS and PARAMTERS (delete stars).
* 3. Save source code.
* 4. Edit database program
*
* Hint: Syntax-Check is not possible within this Include!
* It will be checked during syntax-check of database program.
*
*---------------------------------------------------------------------*

* SELECT-OPTIONS :  ?  FOR ZACCOUNT-ACCNO.


* Parameter for search pattern selection (Type SY-LDB_SP):
* PARAMETERS p_sp AS SEARCH PATTERN FOR TABLE ZACCOUNT.

* SELECT-OPTIONS :  ?  FOR ZCONTRACT-CONTNO.

* SELECT-OPTIONS :  ?  FOR ZDOCHD-DOCNO.

* SELECT-OPTIONS :
*                   ?  FOR ZDOCITEM-DOCNO,
*                   ?  FOR ZDOCITEM-ITEMNO.


* Enable DYNAMIC SELECTIONS for selected nodes :

* Enable FIELD SELECTION for selected nodes :
```

Depending on the requirements, individual rows can be deleted from or added to DBZDFSEL. The parameters and options can be used for database limits in the read program. The optionally generated read program has the following form:

```
*---------------------------------------------------------------------*
*      DATABASE PROGRAM OF LOGICAL DATABASE ZDF
*---------------------------------------------------------------------*
*
* The automatically generated subroutines (FORMs) are called by
* system routines. Therefore their names must not be changed!!!
*
* If the source code is automatically generated,
* please perform the following steps:
```

```
*
* 1. Replace ? by suitable ABAP statements.
* 2. Activate ABAP statements (delete stars).
* 3. Check syntax of database program.
* 4. Save source code.
*    SELECT-OPTIONS and PARAMETERS will be checked automatically.
*--------------------------------------------------------------------*

*--------------------------------------------------------------------*
* Performance notes
*--------------------------------------------------------------------*
* General information about the use of logical databases is
* contained in the extended help information of transaction SE36.
* Please consider in particular the following aspects:
*
* 1. Use of internal tables:
*    SELECT * FROM table INTO TABLE i_table WHERE ... .
*    LOOP AT i_table.
*      MOVE-CORRESPONDING i_table TO table.
*      PUT table.
*    ENDLOOP.
* 2. Use of OPEN/FETCH CURSOR for nested structures.
* 3. Use of dynamic selections to enable further selection criteria
*    (cf. documentation of SELECTION-SCREEN DYNAMIC SELECTIONS).
* 4. Use of field selection to enable get fields statement in
*    reports
*    (cf. documentation of SELECTION-SCREEN FIELD SELECTION).
* 5. Authority checks already at PAI of selection screen.
*--------------------------------------------------------------------*

PROGRAM SAPDBZDF DEFINING DATABASE ZDF.

TABLES : ZACCOUNT,
         ZCONTRACT,
         ZDOCHD,
         ZDOCITEM.

**********************************************************************
* !!! PLEASE DO NOT CHANGE MANUALLY (BEGIN OF BLOCK) !!!!!!!!!!!!! *
*--------------------------------------------------------------------*
* Data structures for search pattern selection                     *
* !!! PLEASE DO NOT CHANGE MANUALLY (END OF BLOCK) !!!!!!!!!!!!!!! *
**********************************************************************

*--------------------------------------------------------------------*
* BEFORE_EVENT will be called before event EVENT.
* Possible value for EVENT: 'START-OF-SELECTION'.
*--------------------------------------------------------------------*
* FORM BEFORE_EVENT USING EVENT.
*   CASE EVENT.
*     WHEN 'START-OF-SELECTION'.
*
```

```
*   ENDCASE.
* ENDFORM.                                    "BEFORE_EVENT

*-------------------------------------------------------------------*
* AFTER EVENT will be called after event EVENT.
* Possible value for EVENT: 'END-OF-SELECTION'.
*-------------------------------------------------------------------*
* FORM AFTER EVENT USING EVENT.
*   CASE EVENT.
*     WHEN 'END-OF-SELECTION'.
*
*   ENDCASE.
* ENDFORM.                                    "AFTER_EVENT

*-------------------------------------------------------------------*
* Initialize selection screen (processed before first PBO)
*-------------------------------------------------------------------*
FORM INIT.

ENDFORM.                                      "INIT.

*-------------------------------------------------------------------*
* PBO of selection screen (processed before display of screen)
*-------------------------------------------------------------------*
FORM PBO.

ENDFORM.                                      "PBO.

*-------------------------------------------------------------------*
* PAI of selection screen (processed after ENTER)
*-------------------------------------------------------------------*
FORM PAI USING FNAME MARK.

* CASE FNAME.
*   WHEN '*'.
* ENDCASE.

ENDFORM.                                      "PAI

*-------------------------------------------------------------------*
* Call event GET ZACCOUNT
*-------------------------------------------------------------------*
FORM PUT_ZACCOUNT.

* SELECT * FROM ZACCOUNT
*   INTO ZACCOUNT
*   INTO TABLE ? (choose one!)
*   WHERE ACCNO = ?.

    PUT ZACCOUNT.

* ENDSELECT.
ENDFORM.                                      "PUT_ZACCOUNT
```

```
*---------------------------------------------------------------*
* Call event GET ZCONTRACT
*---------------------------------------------------------------*
FORM PUT_ZCONTRACT.

* SELECT * FROM ZCONTRACT
*    INTO ZCONTRACT
*    INTO TABLE ? (choose one!)
*    WHERE CONTNO = ?.

     PUT ZCONTRACT.

* ENDSELECT.
ENDFORM.                                "PUT_ZCONTRACT

*---------------------------------------------------------------*
* Call event GET ZDOCHD
*---------------------------------------------------------------*
FORM PUT_ZDOCHD.

* SELECT * FROM ZDOCHD
*    INTO ZDOCHD
*    INTO TABLE ? (choose one!)
*    WHERE DOCNO = ?.

     PUT ZDOCHD.

* ENDSELECT.
ENDFORM.                                "PUT_ZDOCHD

*---------------------------------------------------------------*
* Call event GET ZDOCITEM
*---------------------------------------------------------------*
FORM PUT_ZDOCITEM.

* SELECT * FROM ZDOCITEM
*    INTO ZDOCITEM
*    INTO TABLE ? (choose one!)
*    WHERE DOCNO = ZDOCHD-DOCNO
*      AND ITEMNO = ?.

     PUT ZDOCITEM.

* ENDSELECT.
ENDFORM.                                "PUT_ZDOCITEM

*---------------------------------------------------------------*
* Authority Check for node ZACCOUNT
*---------------------------------------------------------------*
* FORM AUTHORITYCHECK_ZACCOUNT.
*    AUTHORITY-CHECK ...
* ENDFORM.                              "AUTHORITYCHECK_ZACCOUNT

*---------------------------------------------------------------*
```

```
* Authority Check for node ZCONTRACT
*---------------------------------------------------------------*
* FORM AUTHORITYCHECK_ZCONTRACT.
*   AUTHORITY-CHECK ...
* ENDFORM.                              "AUTHORITYCHECK_ZCONTRACT

*---------------------------------------------------------------*
* Authority Check for node ZDOCHD
*---------------------------------------------------------------*
* FORM AUTHORITYCHECK_ZDOCHD.
*   AUTHORITY-CHECK ...
* ENDFORM.                              "AUTHORITYCHECK_ZDOCHD

*---------------------------------------------------------------*
* Authority Check for node ZDOCITEM
*---------------------------------------------------------------*
* FORM AUTHORITYCHECK_ZDOCITEM.
*   AUTHORITY-CHECK ...
* ENDFORM.                              "AUTHORITYCHECK_ZDOCITEM

*---------------------------------------------------------------*
* PUT_ZDF_SP.
* Processed when search pattern selection is used,
* i.e. user input into PARAMETERS p_sp AS SEARCH PATTERN STRUCTURE.
*---------------------------------------------------------------*
* FORM PUT_ZDF_SP..
* ENDFORM.                              "PUT_ZDF_SP
```

The database program consists exclusively of forms that are invoked from the supervisory program. The forms can be grouped. Forms exist that are invoked before or after each specified event of the processing program:

- AFTER_EVENT
- BEFORE_EVENT
- INIT
- PAI
- PBO

In many cases these forms do not need to be completed. An authorization validation can be performed in the AUTHORITYCHECK_<table> forms. The actual routines for the data selection always have the form

PUT_<table>

These forms are generated for every table in the LDB. They contain principally a selection loop with the appropriate limits and a PUT to the associated table. The control program executes the PUT_<table> command. It contains the execution of the associated GET_<table> in the processing program and the invocation of the PUT forms of all subordinate tables. An executable variant of the DBZDFSEL and SAPDBZDF follows:

```
SELECT-OPTIONS :  SACCNO FOR ZACCOUNT-ACCNO.
```

```
PROGRAM SAPDBZDF DEFINING DATABASE ZDF.

TABLES : ZACCOUNT,
         ZCONTRACT,
         ZDOCHD,
         ZDOCITEM.
*********************************************************************
* !!! PLEASE DO NOT CHANGE MANUALLY (BEGIN OF BLOCK) !!!!!!!!!!!!!! *
*-------------------------------------------------------------------*
* Data structures for search pattern selection                      *
* !!! PLEASE DO NOT CHANGE MANUALLY (END OF BLOCK) !!!!!!!!!!!!!!!! *
*********************************************************************
FORM INIT.
ENDFORM.                                   "INIT.
*-------------------------------------------------------------------*
FORM PBO.
ENDFORM.                                   "PBO.
*-------------------------------------------------------------------*
FORM PAI USING FNAME MARK.
ENDFORM.                                   "PAI
*-------------------------------------------------------------------*
FORM PUT_ZACCOUNT.
 SELECT * FROM ZACCOUNT
   WHERE ACCNO IN SACCNO.
     PUT ZACCOUNT.
 ENDSELECT.
ENDFORM.                                   "PUT_ZACCOUNT
*-------------------------------------------------------------------*
FORM PUT_ZCONTRACT.
 SELECT * FROM ZCONTRACT
   WHERE CONTNO = ZACCOUNT-ACCNO.
     PUT ZCONTRACT.
 ENDSELECT.
ENDFORM.                                   "PUT ZCONTRACT
*-------------------------------------------------------------------*
FORM PUT ZDOCHD.
 SELECT * FROM ZDOCHD
   WHERE ACCNO = ZACCOUNT-ACCNO.
     PUT ZDOCHD.
 ENDSELECT.
ENDFORM.                                   "PUT ZDOCHD
*-------------------------------------------------------------------*
FORM PUT_ZDOCITEM.
 SELECT * FROM ZDOCITEM
   WHERE DOCNO = ZDOCHD-DOCNO.
```

```
        PUT ZDOCITEM.
     ENDSELECT.
   ENDFORM.                                        "PUT_ZDOCITEM
```

8.4.3 Processing Program

If a report wants to use a logical database, its name must be specified in the report attributes (Figure 8.5). The report ZR_08_09 serves as example; here the ZDF logical database reads all documents with their items for the account specified in the selection options. The report declares in the TABLES statement the tables whose data it wishes to process: ZACCOUNT, ZDOCHD and ZDOCITEM. These need not be all the tables of the logical database – the ZCONTRACT is not of interest in this report. The report can initialize parameters or selection options at INITIALIZATION time. SACCNO is initialized here. The report defines those GET events for the specified tables of the LDB that are triggered by the assigned PUT forms in the SAPDBYDS program.

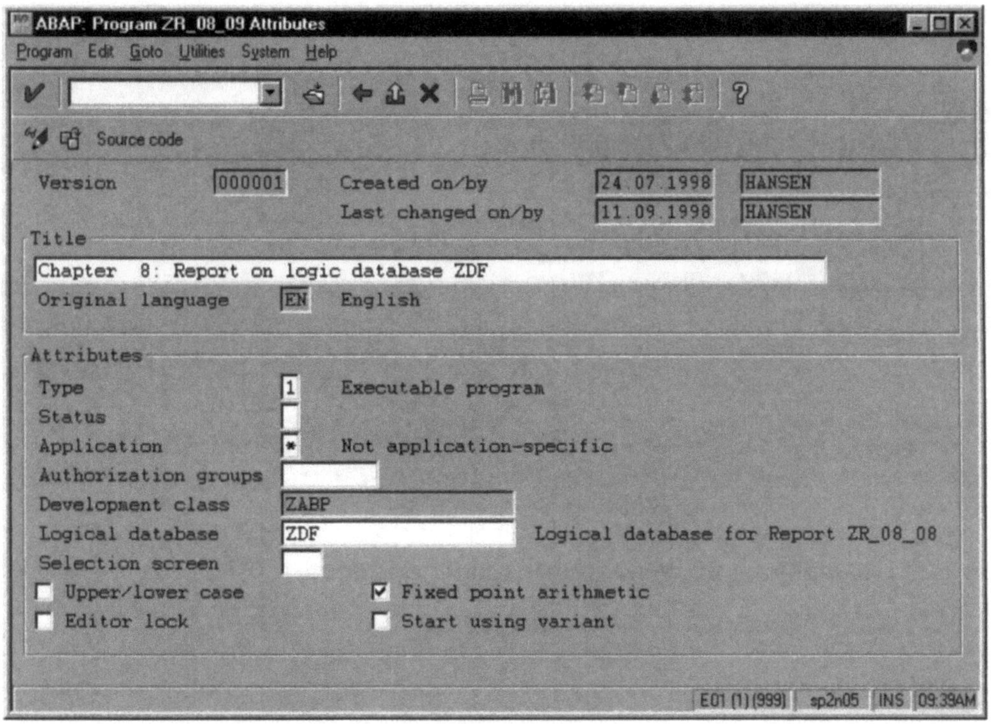

Figure 8.5: Details of the logical database in the report attributes

The events with the LATE option occur when all records of all associated tables have been read for a record in a primary table. GET ZDOCHD LATE will be executed in the report when all document items have been read for a document header. An empty line is output. GET ZACCOUNT LATE is processed when all documents with all items for an account have been read. A line of dashes is output.

```
REPORT ZR_08_09 LINE-SIZE 70.
TABLES: ZACCOUNT, ZDOCHD, ZDOCITEM.

INITIALIZATION.
  SACCNO-OPTION = 'BT'.    SACCNO-SIGN = 'I'.
  SACCNO-LOW    = '4001'.  SACCNO-HIGH = '4003'.
  APPEND SACCNO.

TOP-OF-PAGE.
  WRITE: / 'Acc.No', 10 'Doc.No', 20 'Item.No', 35 'Amount',
           50 'Curr.'.

START-OF-SELECTION.

GET ZACCOUNT.
  WRITE: ZACCOUNT-ACCNO UNDER 'Account'.

GET ZACCOUNT LATE.
  ULINE.

GET ZDOCHD.
  WRITE: / ZDOCHD-DOCNO UNDER 'Doc.No'.

GET ZDOCITEM.
  WRITE: / ZDOCITEM-ITEMNO UNDER 'Item.No',
           (10) ZDOCITEM-AMOUNT UNDER 'Amount',
           ZDOCHD-CURRKY UNDER 'Curr.'.

GET ZDOCHD LATE.
  SKIP.

END-OF-SELECTION.
  WRITE: / 'End'.
```

```
15.09.1998    Chapter  8: Report on logic database ZDF             1
--------------------------------------------------------------------
Acc.No    Doc.No    Item.No         Amount         Curr.
00004001
          00005000
                    001           1.450,00         USD
                    002              50,00         USD

          00005001
                    001           1.450,00         USD
                    002             100,00         USD
```

```
                  003                    45,00        USD
         00005002
                  001                 1.700,00        USD
                  002                   150,00        USD

         00005015
                  001                 2.700,00        USD
-----------------------------------------------------------------
00004002
         00005003
                  001                 1.950,00        USD

         00005004
                  001                 1.950,00        USD
                  002                   100,00        USD
                  003                   200,00        USD
-----------------------------------------------------------------
00004003
         00005005
                  001                 2.200,00        USD
                  002                   180,00        USD

         00005009
                  001                 2.700,00        USD
                  002                   100,00        USD
-----------------------------------------------------------------
End
```

8.4.4 Control Program

The developer has no access to the control program. It controls the interactive execution of the read and processing program using the structure of the LDB. The control program initially reads the information using the logical database from the TLDB table and determines which of these tables have GET events in the report. The control program then invokes the PUT_<table> form in the root table – PUT_ZACCOUNT in this case. The ZACCOUNT select loop is executed. A PUT ZACCOUNT is initiated for each record that is found. The ABAP/4 process then performs the GET ZACCOUNT event in the processing program. ZACCOUNT subsequently invokes the PUT routines of all associated tables in the sequence of their occurrence in the logical database. These in turn contain a corresponding PUT command. This produces a recursive processing of the structure of the LDB using the Depth-First method.

8.5 Function Groups and Function Modules

8.5.1 Concept

In addition to the forms discussed in Section 8.2, function modules provide another structuring capability for ABAP/4 programs. In contrast to forms, function modules are specifically envisaged for the external invocation from programs.

All function modules belong to the system-wide library. In contrast to other programming environments, the R/3 library is an administrative unit rather than a programming unit. The developer cannot create his own libraries; there is always just a single library that contains *all* function modules. Consequently, the names of the function modules must be unique throughout the system.

Function modules only need to be written when a generally-usable functionality is to be provided. However, there are application situations that always require special function modules:

- Locking (ENQUE, DEQUEUE)
- Conversion exits (CONVERSION_EXIT_xxxx_INPUT, CONVERSION_EXIT_xxxx_OUTPUT)
- User exits
- RFC calls
- Authorization validations (AUTHORITY_CHECK)
- Large parts of the R/3 functionality are provided as function modules.

A so-called function group forms the programming unit for the development of function modules. Functionally related function modules are normally combined as a group. In addition to reports and module pools, these function groups also represent a third program type. To some extent, function groups can be compared to DLLs from Windows. In the same manner, the function groups provide a programming unit, have their own global data, and not executable by themselves; A function group can only be loaded and consists of externally callable functions.

8.5.2 Creation of Function Groups

Function groups are created in the same manner as programs. They use the standard include method. The ZDOC function group illustrates this. The system that assigns all source code names derived from the name of the function group is contained in the SAP name space.

```
SAPLZDOC                                  Skeleton program
        INCLUDE LZDOCTOP                  Global data, tables
        INCLUDE LZDOCUnn                  One Include per function module
                INCLUDE LZDOC01           1st module = Z_POST_DOCUMENT
                INCLUDE LZDOC02           2nd module = ...
        ...
        INCLUDE LZDOCFnn                  Forms for all function modules
```

The "Jump" command is used to switch between the source code sections. The somewhat tedious method using Jump/Other Objects is required to reach the global data and the function includes. The Z_POST_DOCUMENT module is considered in the following section.

8.5.3 Creation of Function Modules

Definition of the Interface

In the same manner as for forms, a list of the symbolic parameters is created for the function modules. However, this is not performed in the source code but using the appropriate masks. The source code generated from the mask input must not be changed.

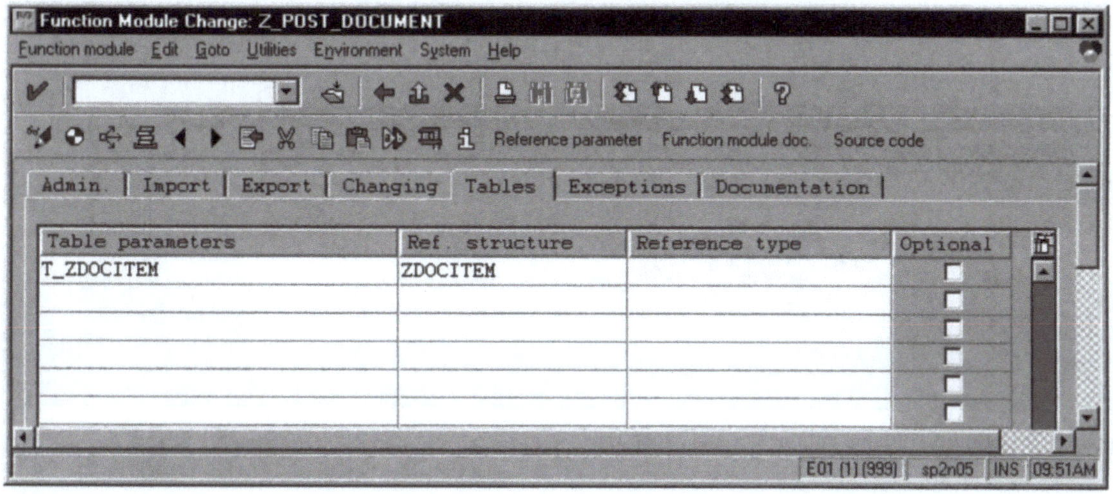

Figure 8.6: Import, Export and Changing parameters of the module Z_POST_DOCUMENT

Figure 8.6 shows the dialog to determine the Import, Export and Changing parameters of the Z_POST_DOCUMENT module.

Whereas import parameters transfer information only into the function module and export parameters transfer information only from the function module, changing-parameter transfers bidirectional. The parameters appear as *named* parameters in the call list. This is the main difference to the positional parameters of the forms. All parameters can be assigned a reference field or a reference type. As with forms, the use of such typed parameters is highly recommended. All parameters can be passed either by reference or by value. The named parameters permit optional parameters to be omitted. In this case, the specified default value is used. Many developers prefix the parameters with "I_" = import, "E_" = export, "C_" = changing, "T_" = table. This improves control of the permitted operations in the source code. E_DOCNO in the example is a pure export parameter that returns to the invoking program the document number that was generated in the module using a number range object. C_DOCHD is a structure that passes bidirectional information.

The specified values here are used to generate a comment in the source code of the function module; the reference fields create a LIKE definition and the reference types create a TYPES definition.

This dialog also defines complex data types as parameters, in particular structures with embedded tables. An additional dialog is provided for the pure table parameters and for the definition of exceptions (See Figure 8.7). The table of the document items has the ZDOCITEM structure. An exception with the name ERROR_NUMBER_RANGE is provided.

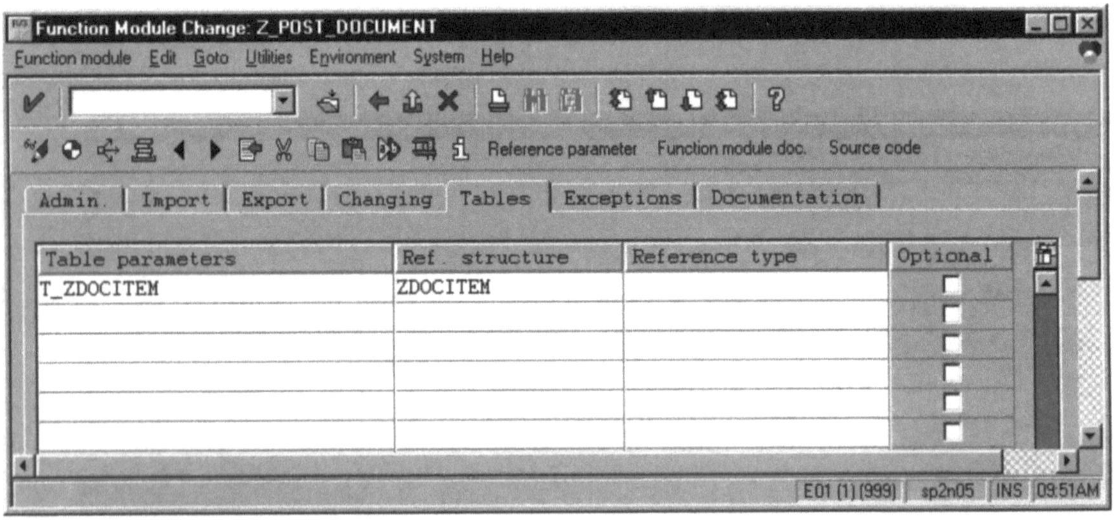

Figure 8.7: Definition of table parameters and exceptions

Global Data and Definitions

Function groups can have their own global data function groupsthat are visible to all function modules and forms of the group without parameters. Table definitions are always made here centrally. The global data of the function groups correspond to the global data from reports or module pools.

It is typical that function modules of a group successively access common global data. The plausibility test of mass data is an example. An initialization module is used that transfers the contents of the validation tables into main memory. The repeated invocation of the actual plausibility module uses these tables.

An Include for each Function Module

Every function module uses an include includesin which the system automatically maintains the interface as comment (LZDOCU01 in this case). This comment is automatically updated after every change to the interface. This means that the developer always sees the current interface in the source code. There is no reason to change this automatically generated comment.

The internal number assignment for document numbers should be used for the updating. Consequently, a call is first made to the NUMBER_GET_NEXT module to obtain a new document number for the number range interval ZDOCNO and the interval 02. This is entered in the header and in the items. INSERT is then used to write the header into the ZDOCHD table. A LOOP is used to write the items in the ZDOCITEM tables. A COMMIT WORK is not performed in the function module.

```
FUNCTION Z_POST_DOCUMENT.
*"----------------------------------------------------------------------
*"*"Local interface:
*"       EXPORTING
*"             VALUE(E_DOCNO) LIKE  ZDOCHD-DOCNO
*"       TABLES
*"              T_ZDOCITEM STRUCTURE  ZDOCITEM
*"       CHANGING
*"             REFERENCE(C_ZDOCHD) LIKE  ZDOCHD STRUCTURE  ZDOCHD
*"       EXCEPTIONS
*"              ERROR_NUMBER_RANGE
*"----------------------------------------------------------------------
DATA DOCNO LIKE ZDOCHD-DOCNO.
DATA QUANTITY LIKE INRI-QUANTITY.
DATA RETCODE LIKE INRI-RETURNCODE.

CALL FUNCTION 'NUMBER_GET_NEXT'
       EXPORTING
            NR_RANGE_NR                 = '02'
            OBJECT                      = 'ZDOCNO'
       IMPORTING
            NUMBER                      = DOCNO
            QUANTITY                    = QUANTITY
            RETURNCODE                  = RETCODE
       EXCEPTIONS
            INTERVAL_NOT_FOUND          = 1
            NUMBER_RANGE_NOT_INTERN     = 2
            OBJECT_NOT_FOUND            = 3
            QUANTITY_IS_0               = 4
            QUANTITY_IS_NOT_1           = 5
            INTERVAL_OVERFLOW           = 6
            OTHERS                      = 7.

IF SY-SUBRC <> 0.
  MESSAGE E023 WITH 'ZDOCNO' '02' RAISING ERROR_NUMBER_RANGE.
ENDIF.

C_ZDOCHD-DOCNO = DOCNO.
INSERT ZDOCHD FROM C_ZDOCHD.
LOOP AT T_ZDOCITEM.
  T_ZDOCITEM-DOCNO = DOCNO.
  T_ZDOCITEM-ITEMNO = SY-TABIX.
  INSERT INTO ZDOCITEM VALUES T_ZDOCITEM.
ENDLOOP.
```

```
ADD 1 TO N.
MESSAGE S025 WITH N.
E_DOCNO = DOCNO.
ENDFUNCTION.
```

The same rules apply inside a function module as those inside a form. The global data can be accessed. Local data can be created. The symbolic parameters are treated like local data. The Z_POST_DOCUMENT module itself first calls the GET_NEXT_NUMBER module.

Every newly developed function module must be activated, otherwise a runtime error occurs on invocation.

Forms in a Special Include

Function groups often use special forms for additional structuring. If a form only belongs to a function module, it can be noted directly after ENDFUNCTION of the function module. Such forms that are to be used from several function modules should be managed in a special include (e.g., LZDOCF001).

Issuing Messages and Exceptions

The MESSAGE command can be used in function modules to issue messages in the same manner as in reports or module pools. A module group can be set as default with MESSAGE-ID in the global data. The messages are set in the message line for online execution and in the joblog for batch execution. "E" type messages adopt a special role. They identify fault or exception situations that occur in the function module.

A simple E-message causes the termination of the function module and the invoking program. However, because this variant does not provide any possibility for the invoking program to influence the fault response, it cannot be recommended. So-called exceptions provide a better handling of exception situations. All exceptions expected in the module are specified *by name* in the dialog that follows Figure 8.7.

RAISE *exception*.

can be used to indicate to the invoking program that a special exception situation has occurred. The function module is terminated without invocation parameters being set. The invoking program receives the control and can itself determine the error response by evaluating the exception (SY-SUBRC). RAISE can be combined with MESSAGE:

MESSAGE *message* **RAISING** *exception*.

The message is not executed in this case, rather only the message variables are set. If necessary, the callers must themselves output the message. Thus, function modules that only use MESSAGE ... RAISING are "speechless".

It would be desirable to have a method that combines the output of E-messages and the initiation of exceptions. This is possible by evaluating the ERROR_MESSAGE system exception. The system creates this when an E-message is created.

8.5.4 Invocation of Function Modules

Function modules are invoked with CALL FUNCTION. In contrast to forms, the parameter lists are specified as

symbolicname = actualname | actualvalue

CALL	**FUNCTION**	*Name*
	IMPORTING	*Exportlist*
	EXPORTING	*Importlist*
	TABLES	*Tablelist*
	EXCEPTIONS	*Exceptionlist.*

Consequently, parameters with default assignment can be omitted. This name-related form of the invocation is more readable and also more flexible than the position-related form of the PERFORM call. The increased writing effort can be reduced by using the *Insert/Sample* command. This command inserts an FBS call with all symbolic parameters and exceptions. The developer only needs to add the actual values.

Particular emphasis is made here that the significance of IMPORTING and EXPORTING is reversed between the function *call* and the function *definition.* It relates to the invoking program for the call. This program imports the parameters that the module has exported and vice versa.

Because the Workbench provides an intuitive test environment (Section 14.2), you do not need to write any program to test the invocation of function modules.

8.5.5 Evaluation of Exceptions, Query of E-Messages

The exceptions defined in a module and the ERROR_MESSAGE system exception can be caught in the invoking program and handled appropriately. Numeric values in this case are assigned to the module's exceptions at its invocation. SY-SUBRC is set to the specified value if an exception occurs in the function module. For example, the numeric values from 1 to 7 are assigned to the seven possible exceptions in the invocation of NUMBER_GET_NEXT in Z_POST_DOCUMENT. However, the assignment could have a different form.

The ERROR_MESSAGE exception must be used if you output an E-message (without RAISING) in a function module as described in Section 8.5.3 but you wish to regain control afterwards.

```
CALL FUNCTION  Fname
     EXPORTING ..
     IMPORTING...
     TABLES ...
     EXCEPTIONS
          ERROR_MESSAGE = 1
          OTHERS               = 7.
IF SY-SUBRC = 1.
     * module canceled by E-massage, this message is put into the
     Joblog
ENDIF.
```

The function module in this case handles the output of the message. However, SY-SUBRC = 1 is used to indicate all error situations to the calling program. SY-MSGNR, for example, can be used to distinguish between errors.

8.5.6 Parallel Invocation of a Function Group by Several Programs

Several programs can use a Windows DLL concurrently. The various programs here have indirect access to the same global data of the DLL. Although this access should be avoided, it permits a general data transfer between different programs.

If several ABAP programs concurrently access function modules of the same function group, a separate version of the function group is loaded into memory for each program. Thus, access to common data by different programs is generally inhibited.

8.5.7 Important Groups of Function Modules

The installation of the specified system contains 5014 function groups with a total of 29 234 function modules. It can be a time-consuming task to find which particular function module can solve the required task from this magnitude of modules. However, in many cases it can be advantageous to continue somewhat longer. A suitable solution already exists for most practical development problems.

The Repository Information System provides one search capability. Figure 8.8 shows the complete selection screen to limit the function modules. The testing with the appropriate use of the '*' placeholder is often helpful. Table 8.2 lists important function groups and frequently-used modules.

Table 8.2: Important function groups

Group	Module	Functions
GRAP	WS_DOWNLOAD	Save file of internal table on the PC
	WS_UPLOAD	Load file from PC into internal table
	WS_FILE_DELETE	Delete file in RAM on the PC
	WS_FILE_COPY	Copy file on the PC
	WS_EXECUTE	Execute a program on the PC
BTCH	JOB_OPEN	Start job planning by program
	JOB_SUBMIT	Add program step to an open job
	JOB_CLOSE	Stop job planning by program
SBDC	BDC_OPEN_GROUP	Open new batch input map
	BDC_INSERT	Fit transaction data into map
	BDC_CLOSE_GROUP	Close batch input map
STXC	START_FORM	Start new form
	END_FORM	End form
	OPEN_FORM	Open form print
	CLOSE_FORM	Close form print
	WRITE_FORM	Output the form

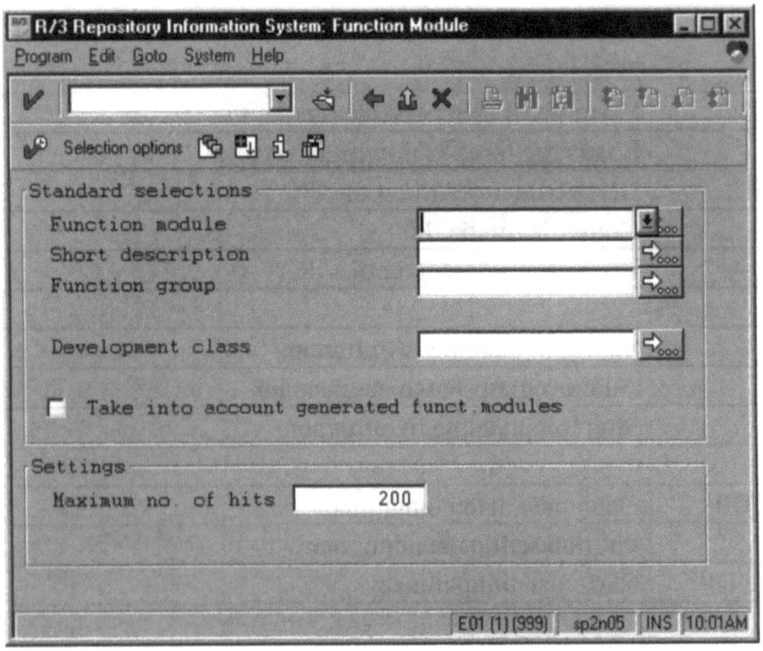

Figure 8.8: Repository information systems for function modules

8.5.8 Conversion Exits

Conversion exits are function modules that perform conversions between the internal and the external format of fields. They always appear as a pair and adhere to the following naming conventions

CONVERSION_EXIT_xxxxx_INPUT
CONVERSION_EXIT_xxxxx_OUTPUT

xxxxx here represents the 5-character designation of a conversion object. This designation can be used as attribute for a domain. If a field is created based on this domain, the OUTPUT exit and the INPUT exit are automatically invoked for outputs (WRITE or screen display) and inputs (PARAMETERS or screen input), respectively. Both modules use the non-typed INPUT and OUTPUT parameters.

The IPADR conversion object that converts between internal and external representations of IP-addresses serves as example. IP-addresses are represented externally in the form such as 193.26.250.3 and internally normally as an unsigned 4-byte number (LONG). Because ABAP/4 supports only signed INT4 numbers, a packed decimal number is used as internal format. P(5) is required to cover value range for LONG of approximately 10 decimal digits; a byte is appended for the sign. Thus, P(6) is used as internal representation.

The INPUT module splits the external representation at the commas into four fields and assigns these to four packed fields P1 ... P4. These are combined to the internal representation P in accordance with the position.

```
FUNCTION CONVERSION_EXIT_IPADR_INPUT.
*"----------------------------------------------------------------------
*"*"Local interface:
*"       IMPORTING
*"             VALUE(INPUT)
*"       EXPORTING
*"             VALUE(OUTPUT)
*"----------------------------------------------------------------------
DATA: C1(3), C2(3), C3(3), C4(3).
DATA: P1(2) TYPE P, P2(2) TYPE P, P3(2) TYPE P, P4(2) TYPE P.
DATA: P(6) TYPE P.
SPLIT INPUT AT '.' INTO C1 C2 C3 C4.
P1 = C1. P2 = C2. P3 = C3. P4 = C4.
P = P4 + 256 * ( P3 + 256 * ( P2 + 256 * P1 ) ) .
OUTPUT = P.
ENDFUNCTION.
```

The OUTPUT module functions in the other direction. It splits the internal representation into the four single bytes, converts them into CHAR fields and uses "," delimiters to concatenate the results into the required external representation.

```
FUNCTION CONVERSION_EXIT_IPADR_OUTPUT.
*"----------------------------------------------------------------------
*"*"Local interface:
*"       IMPORTING
*"             VALUE(INPUT)
*"       EXPORTING
*"             VALUE(OUTPUT)
*"----------------------------------------------------------------------
DATA: B(3).
DATA I TYPE I.
DATA: P(6) TYPE P.
DATA POT(6) TYPE P.
P = INPUT.
POT = 256 * 256 * 256.
I = P DIV POT. B = I. CONCATENATE B '.' INTO OUTPUT.
P = P MOD POT.
POT = 256 * 256.
I = P DIV POT. B = I. CONCATENATE OUTPUT B '.' INTO OUTPUT.
P = P MOD POT.
POT = 256.
I = P DIV POT. B = I. CONCATENATE OUTPUT B '.' INTO OUTPUT.
I = P MOD POT. B = I. CONCATENATE OUTPUT B INTO OUTPUT.
ENDFUNCTION.
```

The following program ZR_08_10 defines a parameter IPADR. This uses LIKE to reference a structure field of the DD, which itself uses a domain with the conversion exit IPADR. The program provides the following selection screen.

```
REPORT  ZR 08 10  LINE-SIZE 70.
PARAMETERS IPADR LIKE CONTAB-IPADR DEFAULT '3239770697'.

WRITE: / IPADR.
```

The following listing results if you execute the program with the specified default parameter assignment:


```
REPORT  ZR 08 10  LINE-SIZE 70.
PARAMETERS IPADR LIKE CONTAB-IPADR DEFAULT '3239770697'.

WRITE: / IPADR.
```


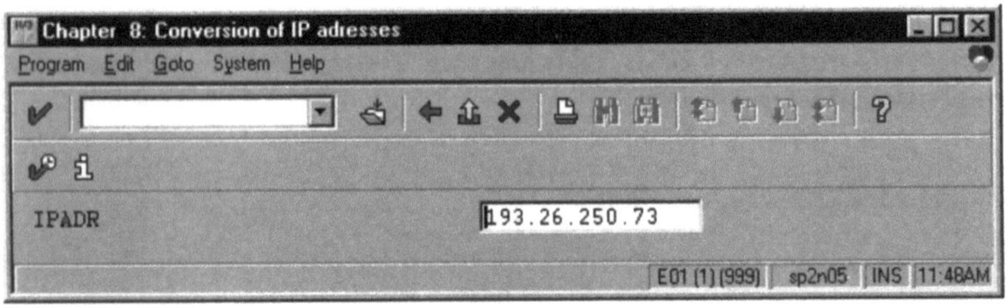

Figure 8.9: Selection screen with parameters in external format

If you execute the program with the entered default assignment of the parameters, the following listing results:

```
11.09.1998                 Conversion of IP addresses                  1
----------------------------------------------------------------------
 193.26.250.73
```

The OUTPUT module automatically converts the ABAP/4 variable P into the external representation specified in the parameter field. Once the program has started, the INPUT module reconverts the variable back into the internal format so that it can be used with WRITE to be transferred again in the external format. The listed internal and external representations are equivalent, i.e., $3239770697 = 193*256^3 + 26*256^2 + 250*256^1 + 73$.

Please note that there is no *explicit* invocation of the conversion modules in the program ZR_08_10, but these are only invoked implicitly during the field transfer from and to the screen and for WRITE. However, it is possible to explicitly invoke the modules at any time, for example in an interface program with external data representation.

8.5.9 Lock Modules

The lock modules described in Chapter 4 can be used to realize the SAP-specific locking logic. The system generates two functions for every created and activated lock object that can be used to lock or release one or more units of the lock object. The EZACCOUNT lock object considered as example manages lock entries in the ZACCOUNT table. The generated lock module ENQUEUE_EZACCOUNT has the following interface:

```
FUNCTION ENQUEUE_EZACCOUNT.
*"----------------------------------------------------------------------
*"*"Local interface:
*"       IMPORTING
*"             VALUE(MODE_ZACCOUNT) LIKE  DD26E-ENQMODE DEFAULT 'E'
*"             VALUE(CLIENT) LIKE  ZACCOUNT-CLIENT DEFAULT SY-MANDT
*"             VALUE(ACCNO) LIKE  ZACCOUNT-ACCNO OPTIONAL
*"             VALUE(X_ACCNO) DEFAULT SPACE
*"             VALUE(_SCOPE) DEFAULT '2'
*"             VALUE(_WAIT) DEFAULT SPACE
*"             VALUE(_COLLECT) LIKE  DDENQ_LIKE-COLLECT DEFAULT ' '
*"       EXCEPTIONS
*"              FOREIGN_LOCK
*"              SYSTEM_FAILURE
*"----------------------------------------------------------------------
* Generierter FuBa zum Sperrobjekt EZACCOUNT
* Bitte diesen Funktionsbaustein nicht modifizieren oder kopieren!
* Informationen zum SAP-Sperrkonzept finden Sie in der ABAP/4-Hilfe
* zum Schlüsselwort 'ENQUEUE'


data:    seqta_tab like seqta occurs 1  with header line,
        __scope like ddenq_like-scope,
        __wait like ddenq_like-waitflag.
__wait =  _wait.
__scope =  _scope.


data: begin of %a_ZACCOUNT,
*         Sperrargument zur Tabelle ZACCOUNT
              CLIENT like ZACCOUNT-CLIENT,
              ACCNO like ZACCOUNT-ACCNO,
       end of %a_ZACCOUNT.
* Initialisierung des Sperrarguments:
call 'C_ENQ_WILDCARD' id 'HEX0' field %a_ZACCOUNT.
```

```
* Zuweisung der Sperrparameter an die Sperrfelder:

if not CLIENT is initial.
   move CLIENT to:
        %a_ZACCOUNT-CLIENT.
endif.

if not ACCNO is initial or
   not x_ACCNO is initial.
   move ACCNO to:
        %a_ZACCOUNT-ACCNO.
endif.

* Füllen der Sperrtabelle:

  __seqta_tab-gname = 'ZACCOUNT'.
  __seqta_tab-gmode = mode_ZACCOUNT.
  __seqta_tab-garg = %a_ZACCOUNT.
append __seqta_tab.


* Absetzen der Sperre:
perform send enqueue(saplsena)
        tables  seqta tab
        using '1' __scope __wait ' ' 'EZACCOUNT' _collect.
ENDFUNCTION.
```

- MODE_ZACCOUNT
  specifies whether the lock is to be maintained as exclusive ("E") or shared ("S").
- CLIENT
  is the client for whom the lock is to be set.
- ACCNO
  Unique (e.g., "5009") or generic (e.g., "5*") account number that is to be locked. The initial value is set if ACCNO is omitted. All records of the object that have not been excluded by other lock attributes will be locked. In this case, the omission of the account number would lock the complete account table.
- X_ACCNO
  This entry is seldom used. It deactivates the generic effect of the initial value in the ACCNO parameter and indicates that the initial value of ACCNO, namely "00000000", is to be locked.
- SCOPE
  specifies the validity range of the lock with regard to a booking task.
- WAIT
  is set to "X" when the lock module should wait for the release of any external locks.
- COLLECT
  indicates that several locks are to be initially collected and the entered as a group.
- If several key attributes describe a lock object, a parameter pair (such as ACCNO, X_ACCNO) is created in the lock module for every sub-attribute.

- If the lock cannot be set, this is indicated by one of the following exceptions:
- FOREIGN_LOCK
  A lock exists already; the name of the lock owner is contained in SY-MSGV1.
- SYSTEM_FAILURE
  The lock could not be set for system-internal reasons.

The generated module DEQUEUE_EZACCOUNT can be used to release a lock.

```
FUNCTION DEQUEUE_EZACCOUNT.
*"----------------------------------------------------------------------
*"*"Local interface:
*"       IMPORTING
*"             VALUE(MODE_ZACCOUNT) LIKE  DD26E-ENQMODE DEFAULT 'E'
*"             VALUE(CLIENT) LIKE  ZACCOUNT-CLIENT DEFAULT SY-MANDT
*"             VALUE(ACCNO) LIKE  ZACCOUNT-ACCNO OPTIONAL
*"             VALUE(X_ACCNO) DEFAULT SPACE
*"             VALUE(_SCOPE) DEFAULT '3'
*"             VALUE(_SYNCHRON) DEFAULT SPACE
*"             VALUE(_COLLECT) LIKE  DDENQ_LIKE-COLLECT DEFAULT ' '
*"----------------------------------------------------------------------
* Generierter FuBa zum Sperrobjekt EZACCOUNT
* Bitte diesen Funktionsbaustein nicht modifizieren oder kopieren!
* Informationen zum SAP-Sperrkonzept finden Sie in der ABAP/4-Hilfe
* zum Schlüsselwort 'ENQUEUE'


data:   seqta_tab like seqta occurs 1  with header line,
        scope like ddenq_like-scope,
        synchron like ddenq_like-synchron.
  __synchron = _synchron.
  __scope = _scope.


data: begin of %a_ZACCOUNT,
*       Sperrargument zur Tabelle ZACCOUNT
            CLIENT like ZACCOUNT-CLIENT,
            ACCNO like ZACCOUNT-ACCNO,
      end of %a_ZACCOUNT.
* Initialisierung des Sperrarguments:
call 'C_ENQ_WILDCARD' id 'HEX0' field %a_ZACCOUNT.

* Zuweisung der Sperrparameter an die Sperrfelder:

if not CLIENT is initial.
   move CLIENT to:
        %a_ZACCOUNT-CLIENT.
endif.
```

```
if not ACCNO is initial or
   not x ACCNO is initial.
   move ACCNO to:
        %a ZACCOUNT-ACCNO.
endif.

* Füllen der Sperrtabelle:

  seqta tab-gname = 'ZACCOUNT'.
  seqta tab-gmode = mode ZACCOUNT.
  seqta tab-garg = %a ZACCOUNT.
append  seqta tab.

* Absetzen der Sperre:
perform send enqueue(saplsena)
        tables  seqta tab
        using '2'  scope ' '  synchron 'EZACCOUNT'  collect.
ENDFUNCTION.
```

The parameters have the same general meaning as for locking.

8.5.10 Number Ranges

Number ranges were described in Chapter 5. The following modules can be used in the program development to access these number ranges:

NUMBER_GET_NEXT	Fetch a new internal number
NUMBER_CHECK	Check an external number
NUMBER_GET_INFO	Fetch information for an interval

The NUMBER_GET_NEXT module invoked in the ZM-09-03 program shows an example of the use.

8.5.11 Form Messages

The RKC_MSG_STRING function module can be used to reconstruct a complete message. The message-ID, the message number and the values of the runtime-dependent message sections must be specified.

```
FUNCTION RKC MSG STRING.
*"local interface:
*"       IMPORTING
*"             ID LIKE SY-MSGID DEFAULT 'KX'
```

```
*"              MTYPE LIKE SY-MSGTY
*"              NUMBER LIKE SY-MSGNO
*"              PAR1 LIKE SY-MSGV1 DEFAULT SPACE
*"              PAR2 LIKE SY-MSGV2 DEFAULT SPACE
*"              PAR3 LIKE SY-MSGV3 DEFAULT SPACE
*"              PAR4 LIKE SY-MSGV4 DEFAULT SPACE
*"        EXPORTING
*"              MSG LIN LIKE CFGNL-MSGLIN
```

For example, the message system variables SY-MSGGR, SY-MSGTY, etc., can be set as parameters in the invocation.

8.6 Authorization Checks

Tools/Administration/User Maintenance/Authorizations (SU03) can be used to create a wide range of authorizations for R/3 and assign these to users. A differentiation is made between object classes, objects and specific authorizations for objects. Figure 8.10 shows the authorization objects for number range maintenance. The following two fields specify the authorization objects for number ranges:

- Activity
- Number range object

The specific object Z_AUTH_DOC authorizes documents in a number range for the *change* (02) and *display* (03) activities.

Authorization checks can be performed on authorization objects. Authorization checks are part of the ABAP/4 language. The

AUTHORITY-CHECK *Object*
 ID *Field1* **FIELD** *Value1*
 ID *Field2* **FIELD** *Value2*
 ...
 ID *Field10* **FIELD** *Value10.*

command can be used to query authorizations for specific objects. A change transaction for number ranges could contain the following call:

```
AUTHORITY-CHECK 'Z AUTH DOC'
    ID 'AKTVT' FIELD '02'
    ID 'BUKRS' FIELD '0010'.
```

SY-SUBRC is processed as return value.

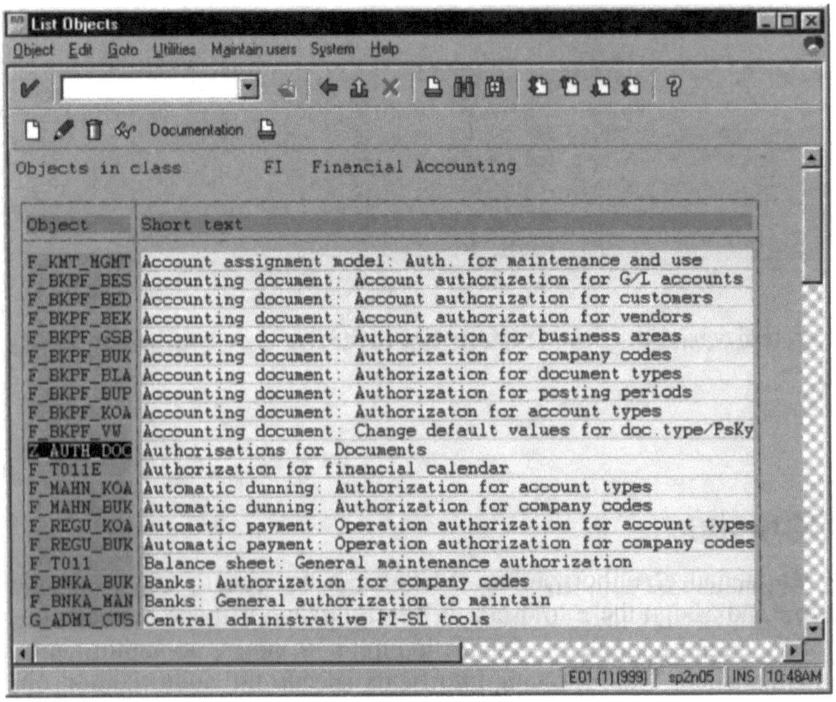

Figure 8.10: Authorization objects for the number range maintenance

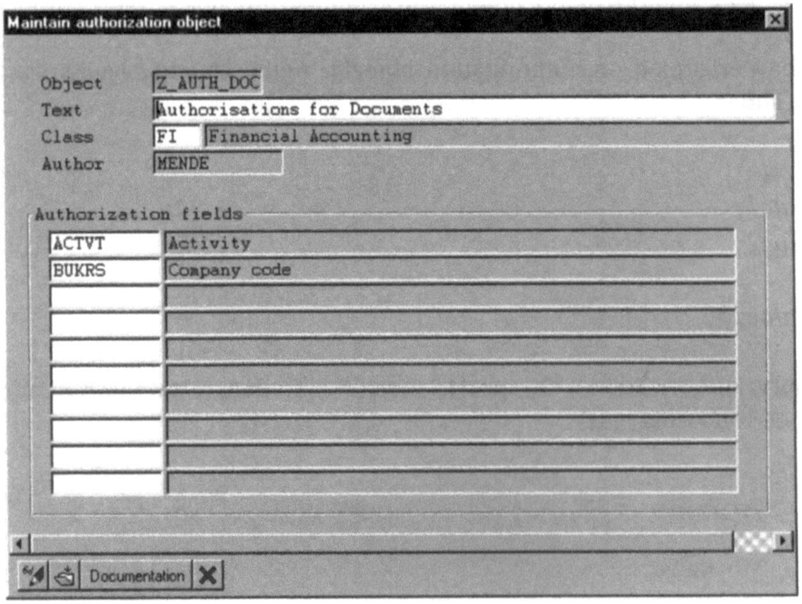

Figure 8.11: Updating an authorization

9 Development of Dialog Transactions

9.1 Concept

Together with the reports discussed in Chapter 7, dialog transactions or dialog programs form the second (directly executable) program type in the ABAP/4 Workbench. Dialog programs perform a dialog with the user in the course of which data can be displayed from or entered into the system. Updating programs are a typical dialog application. Dialog programs are frequently table or record oriented, i.e., they process one or more records from a table or table-pair. Figure 9.1 shows frequently used dialog variants.

Dialog programs are designed for online operation, of which the manual data entry forms the most important function. Although batch execution of dialog programs is not possible, Chapter 12 shows how rerouting of input permits dialog programs to be also used for so-called batch input.

A dialog program initially consists of components that describe the program user interface. These programs are called dynpros in ABAP/4. A dynpro (= **dyn**amic **pro**gram) is a screen (= dialog mask = dialog) with an associated flow control. The dialog masks and flow controls for dynpros are processed in the Screen Painter. With regard to the screen layout, this procedure can be compared with the dialog editors of other development environments, such as Visual Basic or Visual C++.

The flow control is a feature of ABAP/4. It contains control instructions for the dynpro processor, in particular instructions for

- Single field verification
- Group field verification
- ABAP/4 calls
- Exception handling.

A dialog transaction normally requires several dynpros that are processed in a fixed sequence or also user-controlled.

The program logic forms the second important component for a dialog program. This logic provides the dynpros with data or processes the dynpro's data. The program logic for dialog programs consists of so-called modules. A module is a section of ABAP/4 code that can be invoked from the dynpro flow control. A module is not a subprogram, it has no parameter list, and it does not have any local variables. Because a dialog program consists of many modules, it can also be designated as module pool. However, the module pool can define its own subprograms, and the modules themselves can contain subprogram calls.

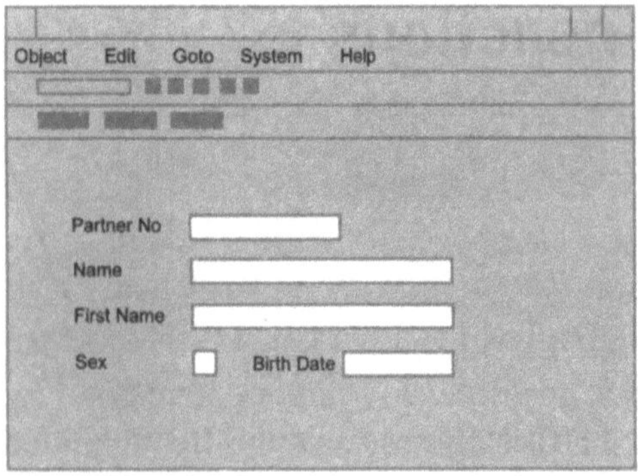

single record:
fields of a table structure
e.g.:
masterdata accounts
masterdata partner

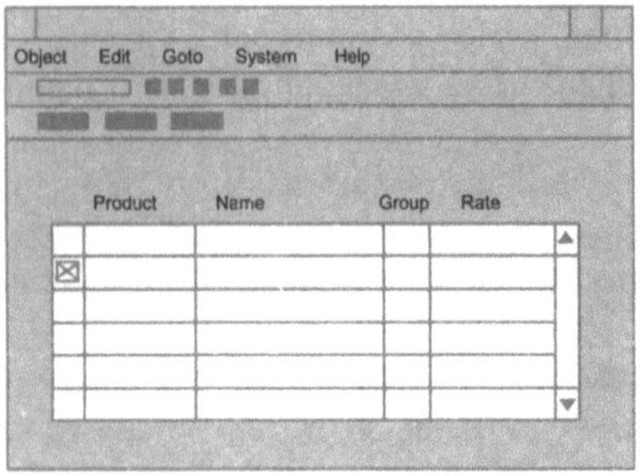

Multiple records:
many records of **one** table
e.g.:
Customizing of tax tables

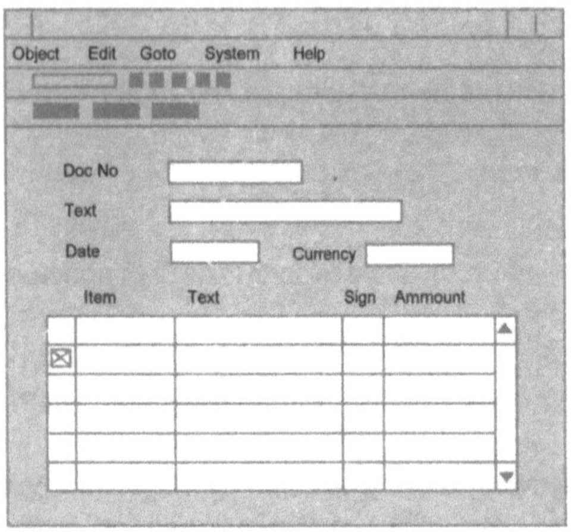

single-multiple records:
one record of primary table
many records of secondary table
e.g.:
document head ZDOCHD with
document items ZDOCITEM

Figure 9.1: Dialog variants

Although a dialog program obviously runs event-controlled, the events used in the interactive reporting have no affect on the dialog programs. The procedure for selection screen layout discussed in Chapter 7 (SELECTION-SCREEN, SELECT-OPTIONS, PARAMETERS, etc.) and the events from the interactive reporting (START-OF-SELECTION, END-OF-SELECTION,

AT LINE-SELECTION) cannot be used in module pools. Because no output list exists, the WRITE command cannot be used in module pools. ABAP/4 defines the following special events for dialog programs:

Table 9.1: Events in dialog programs

Event	Invoked by	Function
PBO = PROCESS BEFORE OUTPUT	Screen processor	Prepare screen data and lay-out
PAI = PROCESS AFTER INPUT	User: ENTER, function keys, buttons, menus	Accept screen data Response to errors Response to input
POH = PROCESS ON HELP-REQUEST	User: F1	User-specific response when F1-key is used
POV = PROCESS ON VALUE-REQUEST	User: F4	User-specific response when F4-key is used

The associated ABAP/4 modules are invoked when these events occur. The exact processing is described in more detail below.

Programmers who are used to dialog programming under Windows (e.g., Visual C++ with MFC) with approximately 100 WM_ messages may be surprised by the small number of events in the ABAP/4 dialog programs. This results from the different architectures of the two systems. A Windows dialog program runs on the same PC in which the user interface is displayed. For example, in situations of rapid mouse movement, it is quite possible that a program must react in real-time to thousands of WM_MOUSEMOVE messages.

R/3 is quite different. The ABAP/4 program must react to all user inputs that may well at distance of 500 km the PC on which the SAPGUI displays the user interface. It would not be sensible to load this WAN connection with constant event transfer. Rather, a few time events are defined in which the required information can be transferred between the user interface and the ABAP/4 program.

9.2 Dialog Program Components and Their Processing

9.2.1 Creation of a Dialog Program

As with a report, a dialog program is created using the Object Browser. The program attributes mask is obtained by entering the program type "M" as module pool (see Figure 9.2).

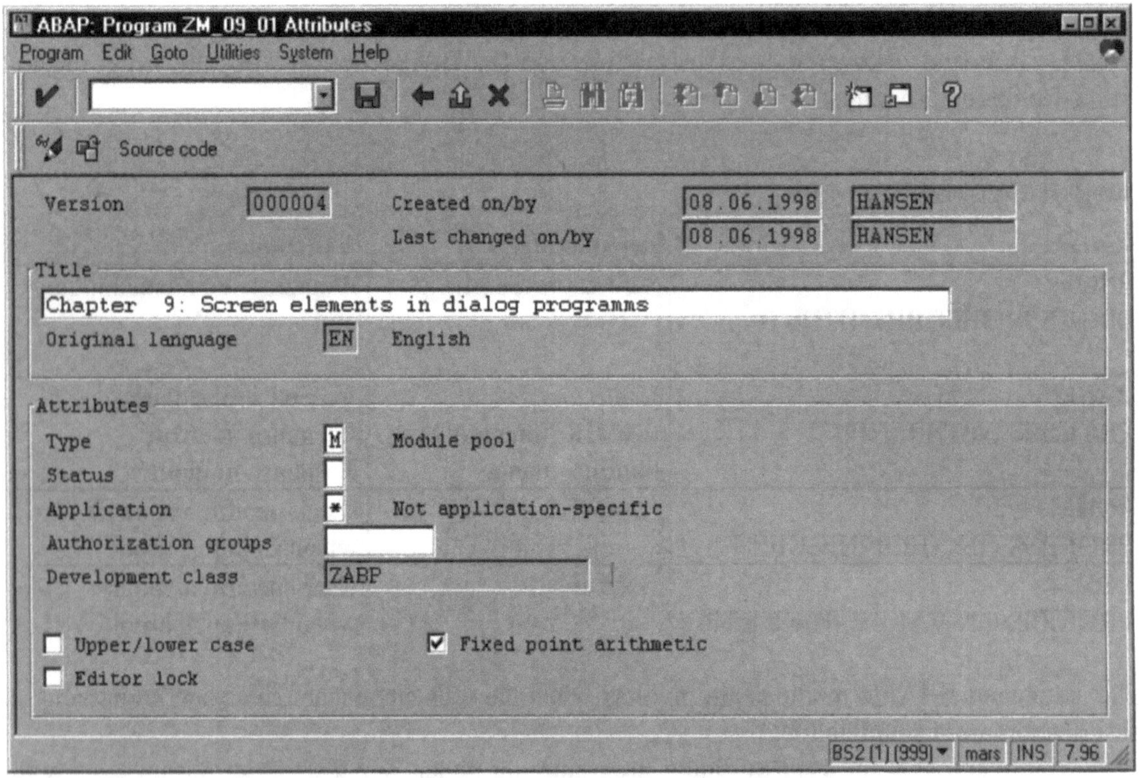

Figure 9.2: Program attributes of a dialog program

A program created in this manner already has its own object list. A double-click on *Program Object Types* in this list displays the possible program components (see Figure 9.3).

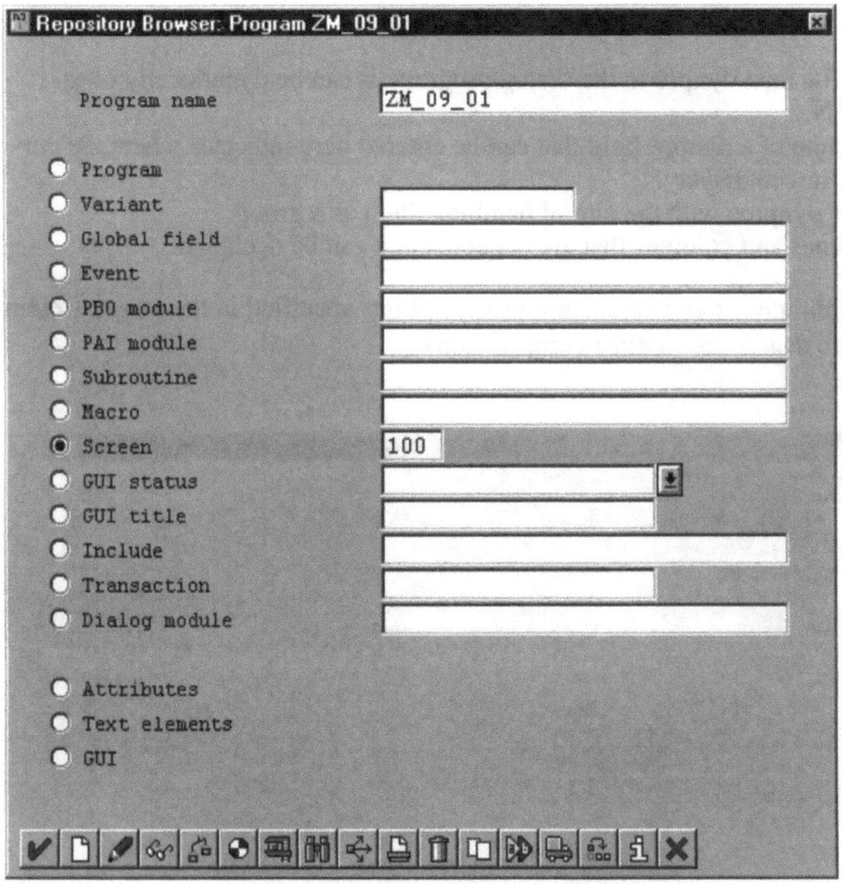

Figure 9.3: Possible components of a dialog program in the Object Browser

9.2.2 Creation and Processing of a Dynpro

As second step, the object list is used as basis for the creation of a dynpro. This provides the dynpro attributes (see Figure 9.4). Details of the dynpro type and the dynpro attributes can be given in addition to the short description.

Dynpro type:

- normal
- modular dialog window
- subscreen

Dynpro attributes:

- *Continuation dynpro:* The next dynpro in the dialog program; it can be dynamically overwritten by SET SCREEN.
- *Cursor position:* The name of a dynpro field that can be entered here indicates where the cursor is to be set after the screen display.
- *Screen group:* Combine dynpros with the aim of handling them as a group.
- *Lines/columns:* Those lines and columns that are occupied and can be occupied.

Refer to the SAP documentation for an explanation of the options specified in the screen (retain data, non-proportional font, deactivate runtime compression).

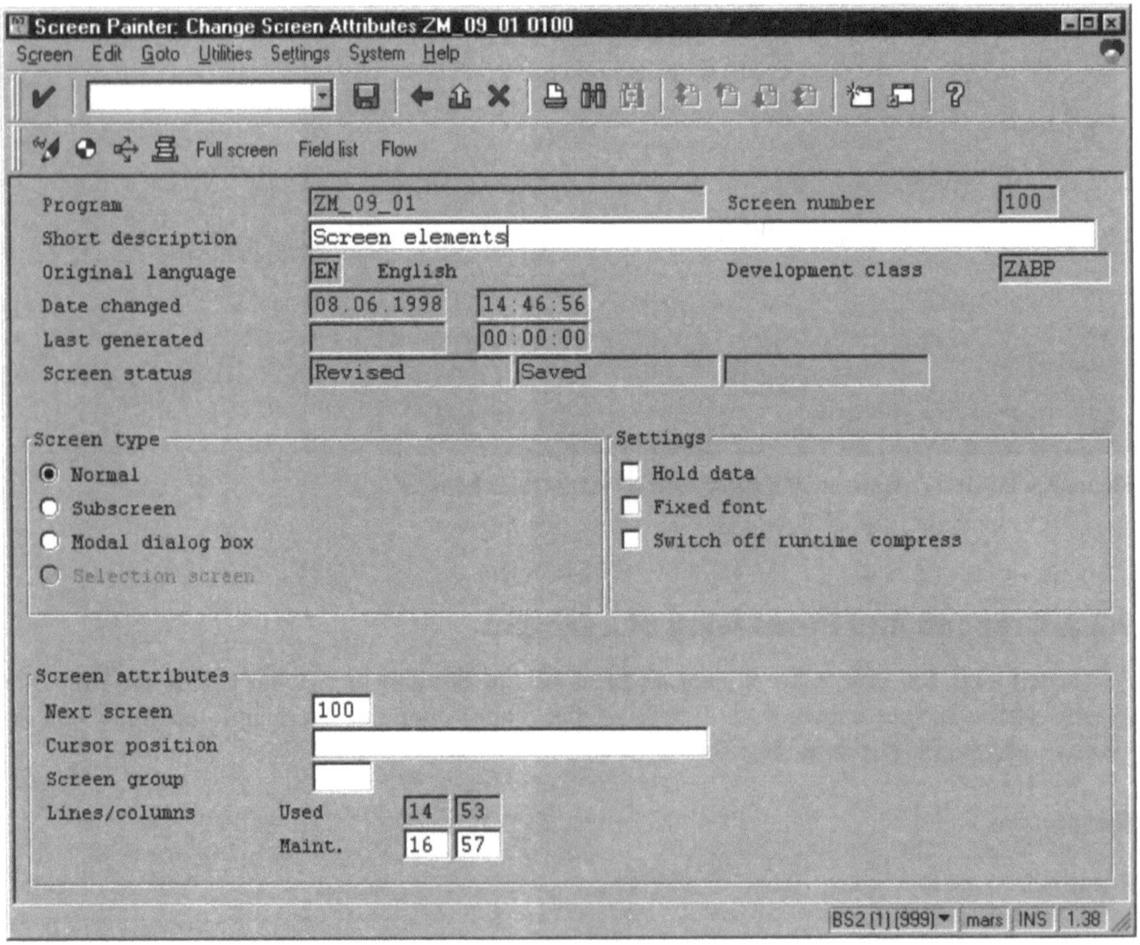

Figure 9.4: Dynpro attributes

The layout of the dynpro can be processed in the Screen Painter once the attributes have been entered and saved. The operation of the fullscreen editor is non-intuitive. The drag-and-drop common in other dialog editors is unfortunately available only under Windows NT.

Static texts are written directly at the required locations. All other elements are entered at the target positions using the appropriate edit formats. "Graphical Element" can be used to convert entered edit formats ("_") into tick fields, selection fields and pushbuttons. Multiple elements can be grouped in block mode and then processed as a group.

Table 9.2 specifies the available graphical base elements that can be used to build the layout of a dynpro. The purely static elements "Text" and "Frame" do not allow any user action at run-time and so do not have any interaction with the associated module pool. The other base elements can be divided into

- storing elements
  - tick fields
  - selection fields
  - input/output fields
  - table fields
- initiating elements
  - pushbuttons

Storing elements save a state or a value. The corresponding ABAP/4 variables with the same name are assigned to them in the module pool. Information is transferred in both directions between ABAP/4 variables and the like-named storing dynpro fields.

Initiating elements are those that initiate the PAI event when the user activates them. Because several such elements can exist on a screen, the corresponding ABAP/4 module must be informed of the initiating element. A corresponding so-called OK code is defined in each dynpro. Initiating elements have a function code that is copied into the OK code before an ABAP/4 module is initiated.

Table 9.2: Element types of the Screen Painter

Type	Type in Screen Painter	Coupling with ABAP/4 variable ?	Triggering of PAI ? FCODE transfer ?
Static text	Text	No	No
Frame	Frame	No	No
Input/output field	I/O	Yes	No
Check box	Check	Yes	No
Selection box	Radio	Yes	No
Pushbutton	Push	No	Yes
Table control	TC	Yes, internal table	No

You may have noticed that storing elements do not cause the triggering of PAI but also initiating elements do not have any information storage. For the operation, this means that you can continue making inputs on a screen until an initiating element is pressed. Pushbuttons, menus, function keys and the ENTER key all have an initiating effect. Figure 9.5 shows dynpro 100 from the ZM-09-01 program that illustrates the use of base elements.

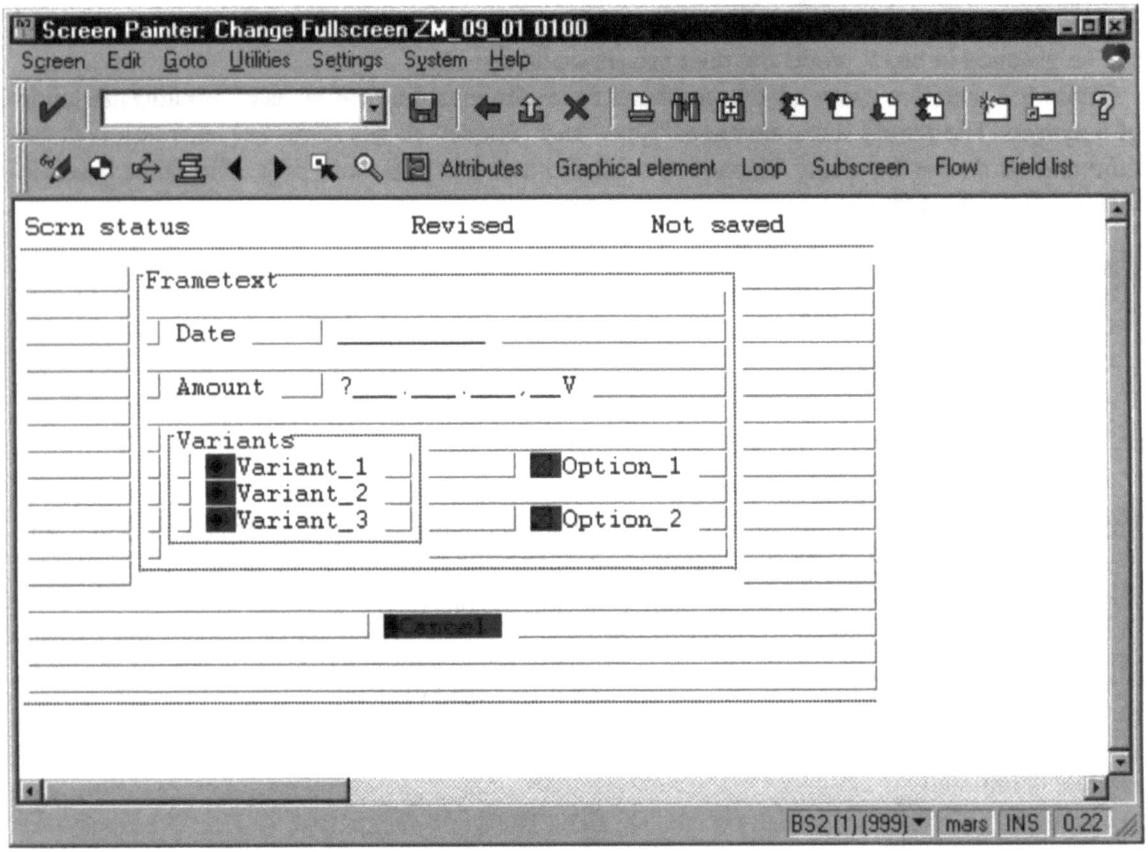

Figure 9.5: Screen with base elements

Attributes can be used to set the properties of a marked dynpro. Figure 9.6 shows the attributes of the BETRAG field as a typical storing element. Important attributes for a storing element are:

- *Field name*: The name specified here is identical to the ABAP/4 field names.
- *Field text*: An edit mask for the formatting of the inputs can be specified here. "?" indicates mandatory input, "V" represents the sign.
- *Length details*: A differentiation is made here between default lengths and displayed lengths The field is made scrollable if the displayed length for I/O fields is longer than the default length.
- *Grouping*: Up to four freely selectable grouping keys can be used to group fields for subsequent common processing. The display and suppression of groups are typical group processing.

- *Format*: The format specified here indicates how the contents of a storing element are to be converted. This type must correspond to the type of the associated ABAP/4 field.
- *Input/output parameters*: Both purely output fields and combined fields are possible.

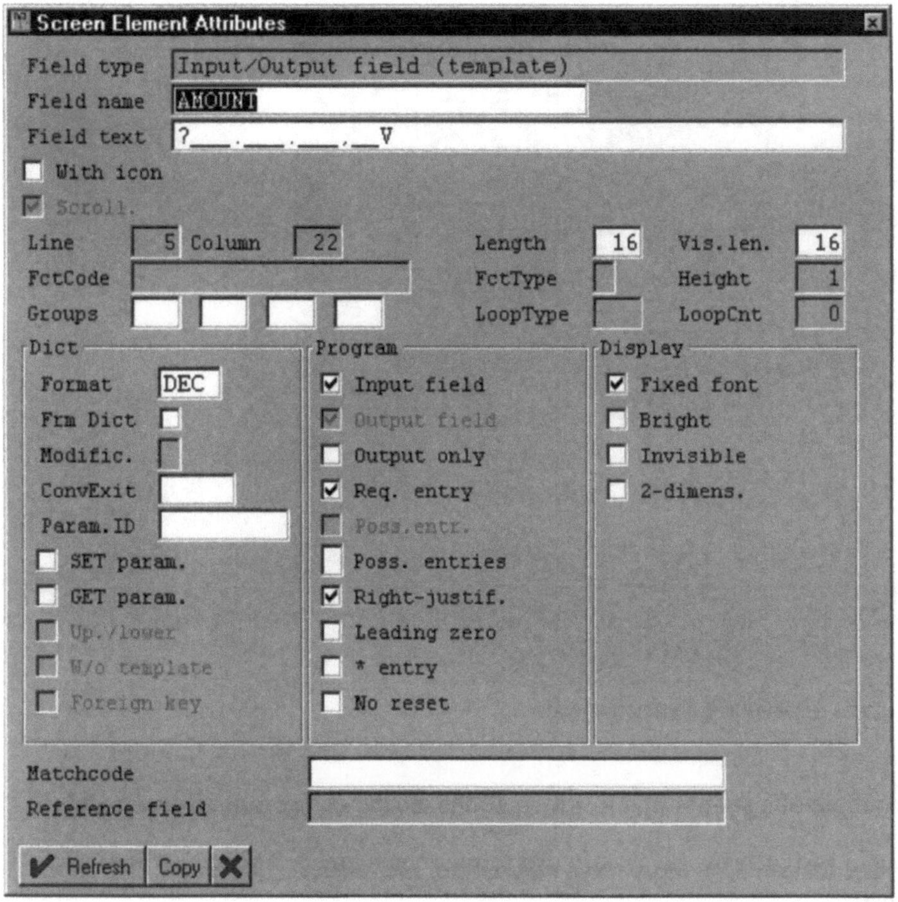

Figure 9.6: Field attributes of a P-field

The OK code of a screen is a special storage element. This does not appear in the user interface, but is only a storage area for the function code of the initiating element. An OK code always has the CHAR type of length 4.

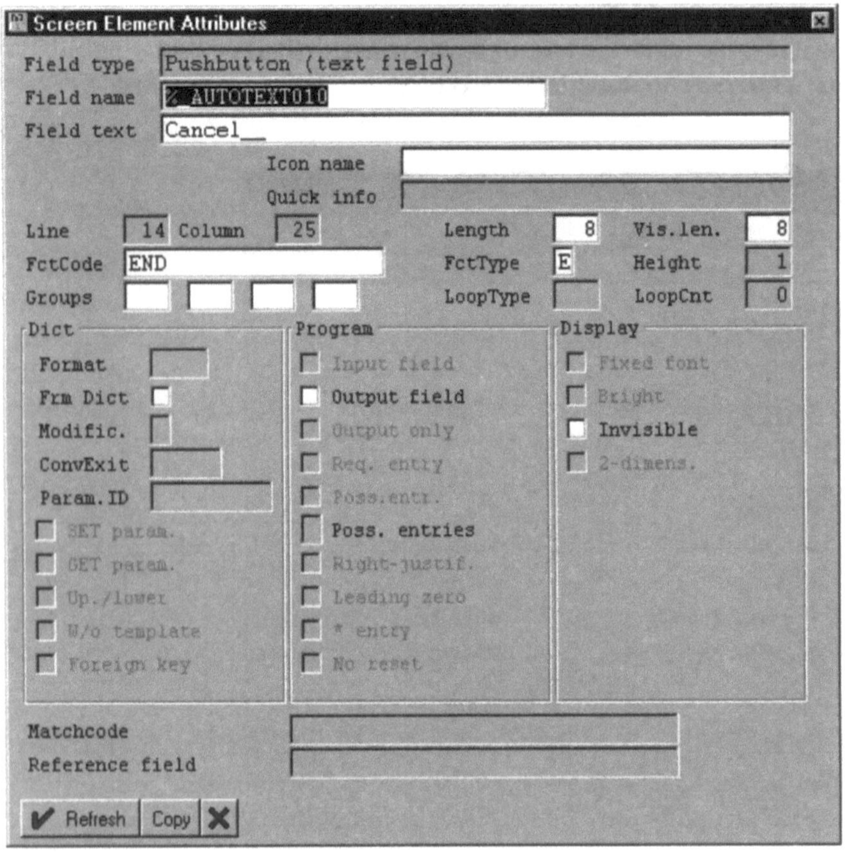

Figure 9.7: Field attributes of a pushbutton with function code

Figure 9.7 uses the example of a pushbutton to illustrate the attributes for initiating elements:

- *Field name*: The name assigned by the system can remain unchanged. This name does not have any significance.
- *Field text*: The field text is used as inscription for pushbuttons.
- *Length*: A differentiation is made here between default lengths and displayed lengths. The default length for pushbuttons is based on the field text. A longer visible length can be specified if the key is to be wider; the text is then centered.
- *Groups*: Up to four freely selectable grouping keys can be used to group fields for subsequent common processing. The display and suppression of groups are typical group processing.
- *Format*: The format specified here indicates how the contents of a storing element are to be converted. This type must correspond to the type of the associated ABAP/4 field.
- *Input/output parameters*: Both purely output fields and combined fields are possible.
- *FctCode*: The identification code of the initiating element is specified here. It is copied into the OK code for the screen before PAI is invoked and so permits the processing program to invoke the function assigned to the initiating element.
- *FctType*: specifies the function code type.

Several views for field lists exist for all elements or fields of a screen. Figure 9.8 shows one such view.

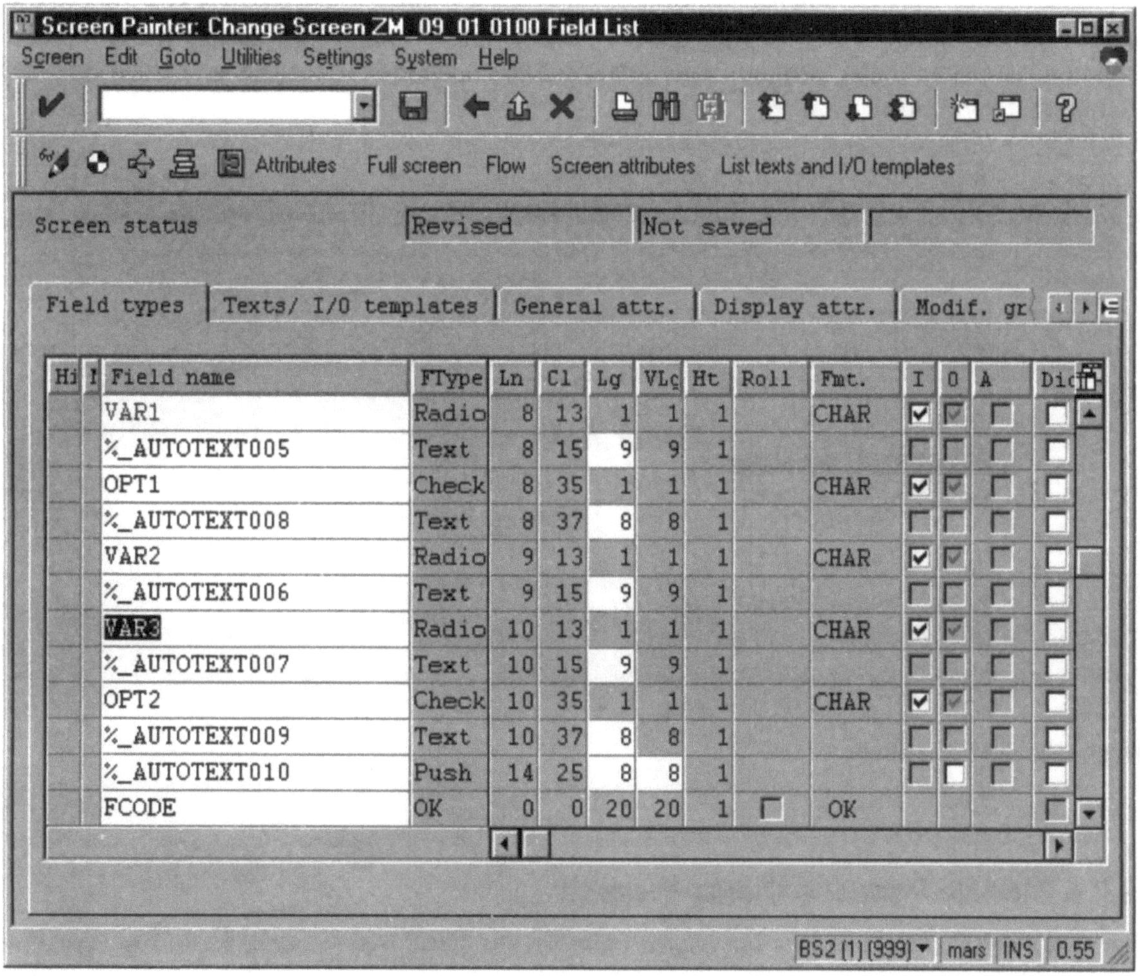

Figure 9.8: Field list

9.2.3 Dynpro Flow Control

You can go directly from the fullscreen editor into the dynpro flow control. This is entered in text form using the ABAP/4 Editor. The flow control contains instructions for the dynpro processor telling it when it is to invoke specific ABAP/4 modules. Note that the flow control itself does not represent any ABAP/4 code. In contrast to ABAP/4, the flow control recognizes very few key words. It permits neither data definitions nor subprogram calls.

A simple flow control is specified when a new dynpro is created. This flow control contains just the PROCESS_BEFORE_OUTPUT and PROCESS_AFTER_INPUT events. The STATUS_0100 and USER_COMMAND_0100 modules are provided in the form of comments as suggested ABAP/4 module names. Simply remove the comment characters if you want to use these module names. A double-click on the module name branches directly to the associated source code of the dialog program after confirmation. Section 9.3 provides a detailed description of the flow control.

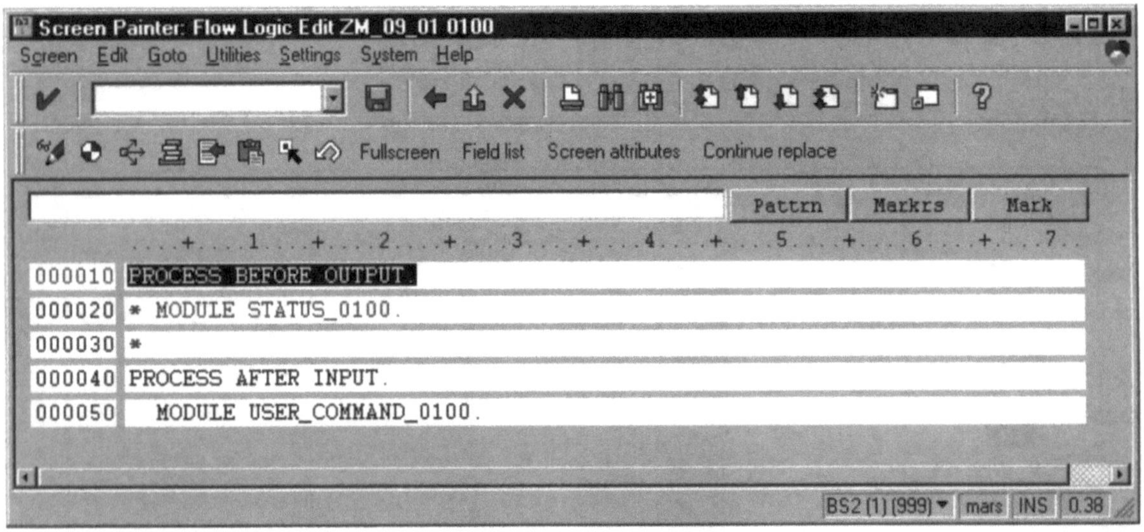

Figure 9.9: Edit flow control

9.2.4 Module Pool of a Dialog Program

The following example shows the source code for the ZM-09-01 module pool. The ABAP/4 fields for the storing dynpro elements are defined as global data. In particular, the OK code has been specified as the FCODE variable. The same name appears in the lower line of the dynpro's field list.

The variables can be set in the STATUS_0100 module. The ABAP/4 OUTPUT key word must be assigned to the module. The set values appear in the dynpro after the module has been processed. Tick fields and selection fields recognize only the "X" status for set and SPACE for not-set.

The INPUT key word must be assigned to the USER_COMMAND module. The values entered in the dynpro can be processed here. A CASE block typically programmed here evaluates the OK code (namely FCODE). Only the *End* key is tested here; it ends the program.

```
PROGRAM  ZM_09_01 LINE-SIZE 72 MESSAGE-ID YO.

DATA:
        DATE TYPE D VALUE '19961224',
        AMOUNT(15) TYPE P DECIMALS 2 VALUE '150500.00',
        VAR1 VALUE ' ',
        VAR2 VALUE 'X',
        VAR3 VALUE ' ',
        OPT1 VALUE 'X',
        OPT2 VALUE 'X',
        FCODE(4).
*---------------------------------------------------------------------*
MODULE USER_COMMAND_0100 INPUT.
IF FCODE = 'END'.
  SET SCREEN 0. LEAVE SCREEN.
ENDIF.
ENDMODULE.                        " USER_COMMAND_0100  INPUT
```

9.2.5 Define Transaction Code

In contrast with a report, a dialog program cannot be started unless it has a so-called four-character transaction code. This can be created using Figure 9.3 as basis. The name of the program to be started and the number of the first dynpro must be specified. This specified code can be entered in the command field of a module with /nYYYY or /oYYYY. The transaction code can also be used to link to the area menu.

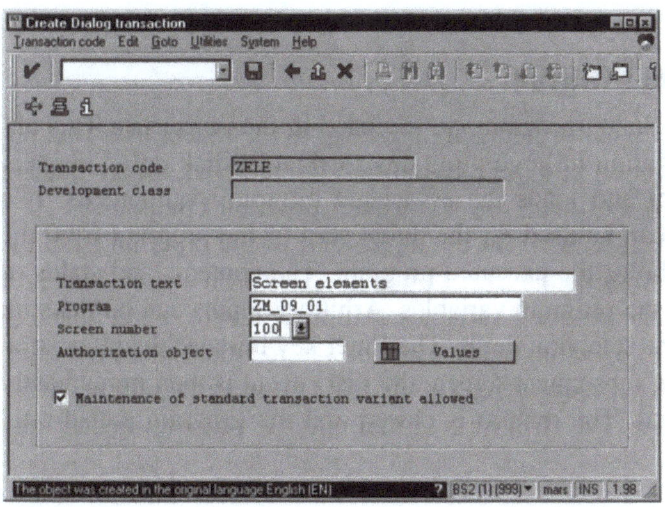

Figure 9.10: Specify the transaction code to start the dialog program

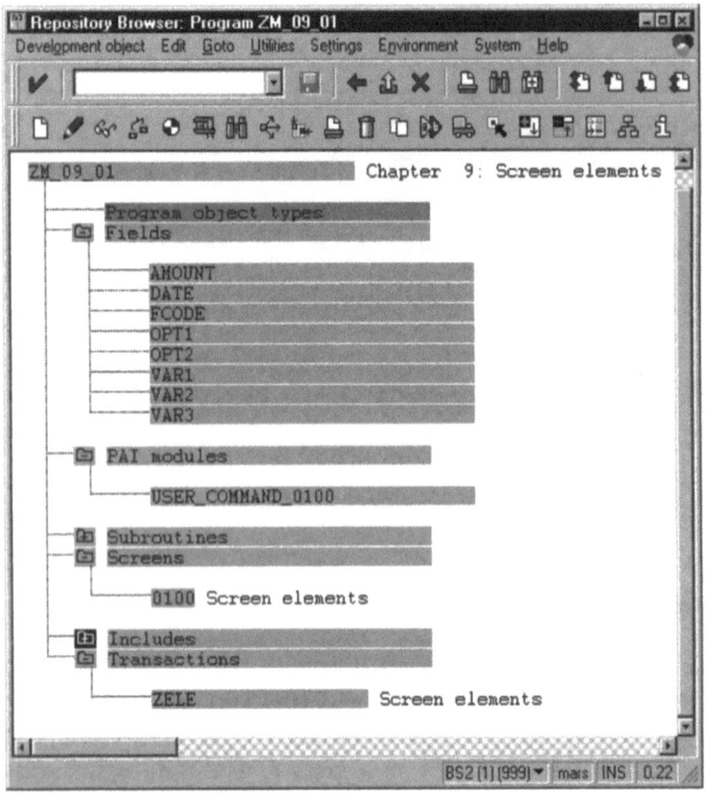

Figure 9.11: Program object in the Object Browser

9.2.6 The Object List of a Dialog Program

All consecutively created elements in a dialog program are recorded in the object list. This object list is particularly suitable for navigation in large programs. A double-click on an element starts the corresponding processing tool and loads the associated program components. If a transaction code has been defined, this can be used for the direct start of the program from the object list using *Execute*. Figure 9.12 shows the executed program. The contents and status of the dynpro fields indicate the values of the program variables. Arbitrary inputs can be made in the document field, the check fields or the selection fields. The Enter key initiates the invocation of PAI. Because dynpro 100 has itself as subsequent screen, the PBO event is then immediately initiated and dynpro 100 again displayed. The dynpro is closed and the program ended only when the End key is pressed.

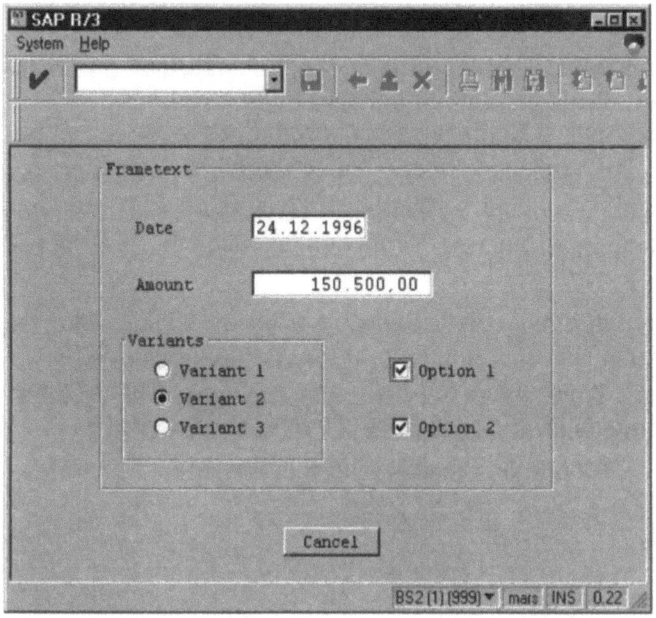

Figure 9.12: Executed program ZM-09-01

9.3 Screen Processing

The dialog processor and the ABAP/4 processor alternately assume control during the processing. This interaction is identical for all screens.

Once a transaction starts, the dialog processor commences with the processing of the screen specified in the transaction attributes (start screen). Section 9.5 describes how the sequence of the screens can be controlled.

9.3.1 Standard Flow

Figure 9.13 shows the standard flow for the screen processing.
The dialog processor initially assumes control (1). This begins with the processing of the flow control in the PROCESS BEFORE OUTPUT section. The control is passed to the ABAP/4 processor to process the specified ABAP/4 module (here STATUS_0100). The module name is naturally arbitrary. The development environment suggests a name and indicates that the status (menu) of the dynpro is normally set in this module.

Various properties of the dynpro fields can also be manipulated. The OUTPUT module also typically has the task of performing read accesses to the database using Open SQL. This module fills all global fields that have name reference to the dynpro. The ABAP/4 processor then returns control to the dialog processor, which subsequently performs the automatic field transport between like-named ABAP/4 fields and dynpro fields (2). The data are converted from internal format into external format during this transport. The output conversion is executed automatically if a conversion exit has been specified for the domain of a dynpro field.

The dynpro is displayed in step (3). The dynpro fields have been initialized with the appropriate values in the module pool. The user can now enter inputs. The SAPGUI has exclusive responsibility for the acceptance of text inputs, and the activation of tick fields and selection fields. Only the activation of a menu command, pushbutton or function key and the ENTER key results in the entry of the data.

Following the data entry and a test, the automatic field transport from the dynpro into the ABAP/4 module is initiated (4). In particular, the function code of the initiating element is set into the associated ABAP/4 function code. Any conversion exits are executed. The AFTER-INPUT module is then invoked from the flow control (here USER_COMMAND_0100).

This module (5) normally performs a CASE loop on the specified function code. The following actions are typical:

- Validate and store the data
- Invoke computation routines or function modules
- Branch to some other dynpro
- Branch to another transaction
- Return to the last dynpro
- Re-invoke the same screen (usually with ENTER).

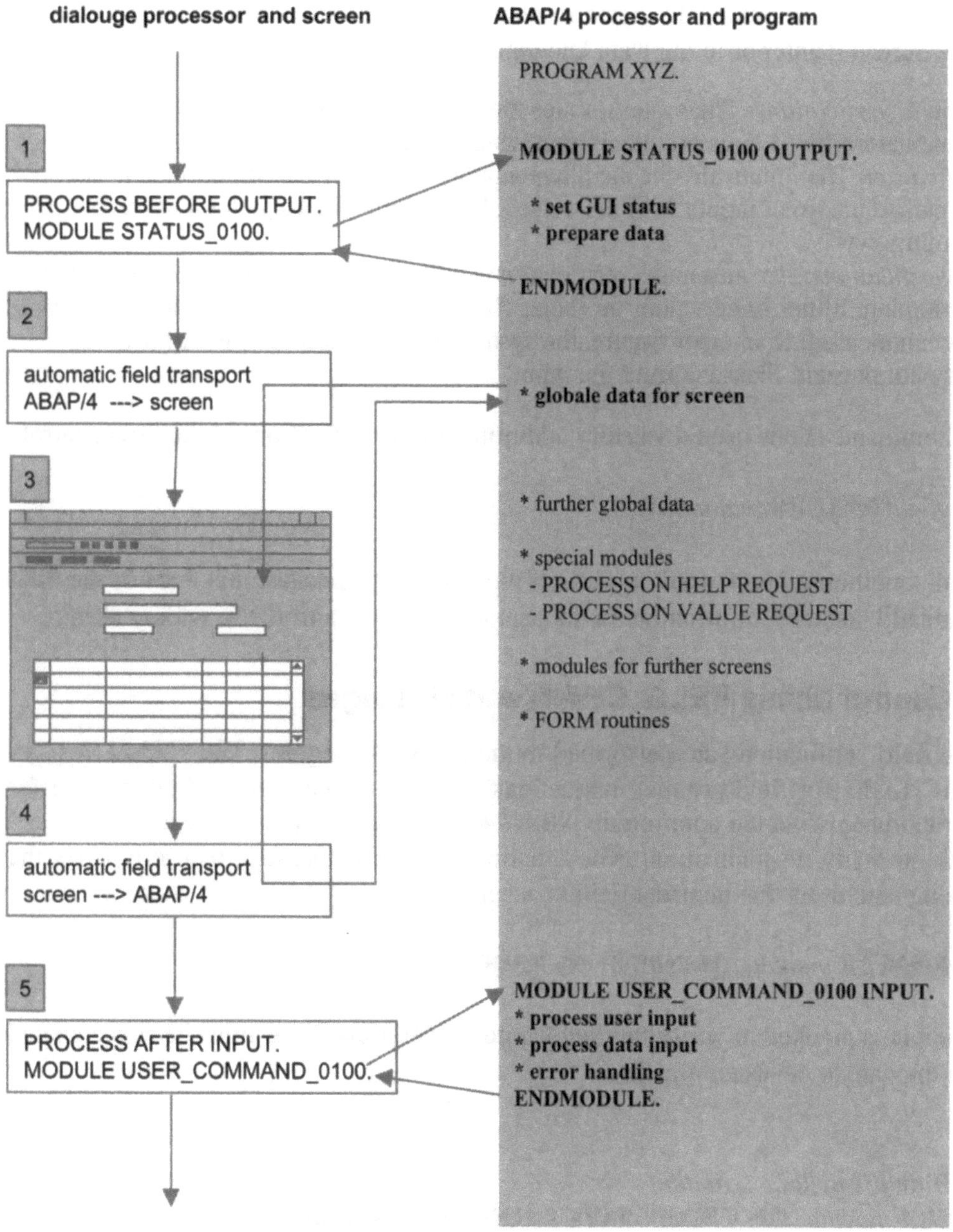

Figure 9.13: Standard flow for screen processing

9.3.2 Automatic Field Verifications

Dialog systems must assume that the user might enter incorrect or incomplete data. Consequently, the data are subjected to various verifications before being entered into the program or database. The system can automatically perform purely formal verifications using the field information in the Screen Painter or in the Data Dictionary. These include:

- *Mandatory field verifications*: The system issues the "Please complete all mandatory fields" message if mandatory fields have not been input when the data are entered.
- *Format verification*: The inputs are checked here against a prespecified input screen. The system responds to incorrect inputs with messages of the form: "Please enter a valid date in the form dd.mm.yyyy".
- *Field value verifications*: An automatic verification is performed using the values specified for the field domain. Either fixed values or values from one of the specified value or verification tables can be used. If an error occurs, the system issues a message of the form: "E: <value> entry not present. Please correct the input".

The following command can be used to specify additional field verifications in the flow control:

FIELD *dynprofield* **VALUES** (*valuelist*).

Multiple logical conditions can be used in place of the value-list. Because this form of the field verification statically includes information on the data in the flow control, it is seldom used.

9.3.3 Flow Control Using FIELD, CHAIN and Messages

Comprehensive field verifications are performed in the ABAP/4 program. The FIELD (for single fields) and CHAIN (for field groups) instructions can be used here in the flow control for PAI. Both instructions invoke the appropriate ABAP/4 modules for the user-specific field verifications. These normally respond in an error situation with an E-message that terminates the normal processing and resets the incorrect field to accept input.

FIELD *field* **MODULE** *module* **[IN INPUT | ON REQUEST].**

The *module* module is invoked to verify the field contents. Multiple fields must be concatenated with CHAIN if they are to be tested together.

CHAIN.
    FIELD: *field1, field2, ... fieldn.*
    MODULE *module* **[ON CHAIN-INPUT | ON CHAIN-REQUEST].**
ENDCHAIN.

If an error occurs in one of the modules, the normal processing is interrupted and all chained fields are reset to be ready for input.

The options specified in parentheses can be used to avoid unnecessary field verifications or to perform field verifications only under certain conditions.

- FIELD ... MODULE ... ON INPUT
  The module for a single field verification is invoked only when the field no longer contains its initial value. It makes no difference whether the field has not be touched at all or whether it has been changed in the meantime but then reset to its initial value.
- CHAIN ... FIELD MODULES ... ON CHAIN-INPUT
  The module is invoked if at least one of the CHAIN fields satisfies the ON INPUT condition.
- ON REQUEST
  The module is invoked if any input has been made to the specified field.
- ON CHAIN-REQUEST
  The module is invoked if at least one CHAIN field satisfies the ON REQUEST condition.

Special conditions apply for the use of ABAP/4 field verifications with regard to the field transport to PAI. The automatic transport is initially performed for all fields that do not appear in FIELD or CHAIN instructions. This permits the programmed field verifications to use previously input values. The FIELD and CHAIN instructions of the control flow are then processed in the sequence of their occurrence. The affected field(s) are first transported and then the associated modules invoked.

9.4 Screen Flow Control

A transaction normally consists of several dynpros. A standard processing sequence is often specified.

9.4.1 Static Screen Flow

Every dynpro has a subsequent dynpro assigned to it in the dynpro attributes. In this case, the PBO of the subsequent dynpro is processed and displayed after the dynpro for the PAI (see Fig. 9.14).

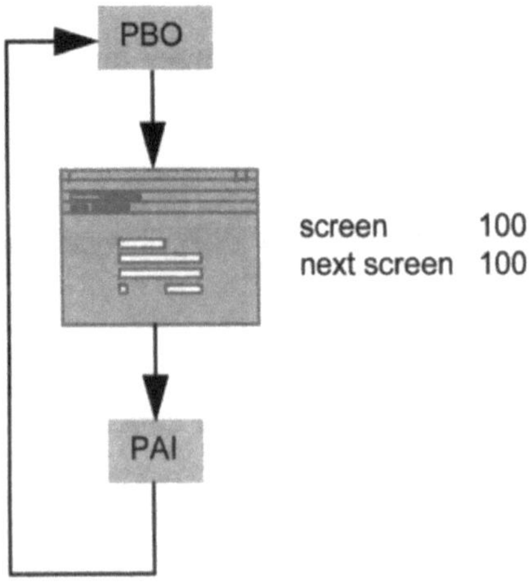

Figure 9.14: A dynpro that references itself as subsequent dynpro

The dynpro itself is always entered as suggested value for the subsequent dynpro. If this value is not changed, the PBO is processed and the dynpro displayed again after every PAI of the dynpro. Figure 9.15 shows a (static) dynpro sequence.

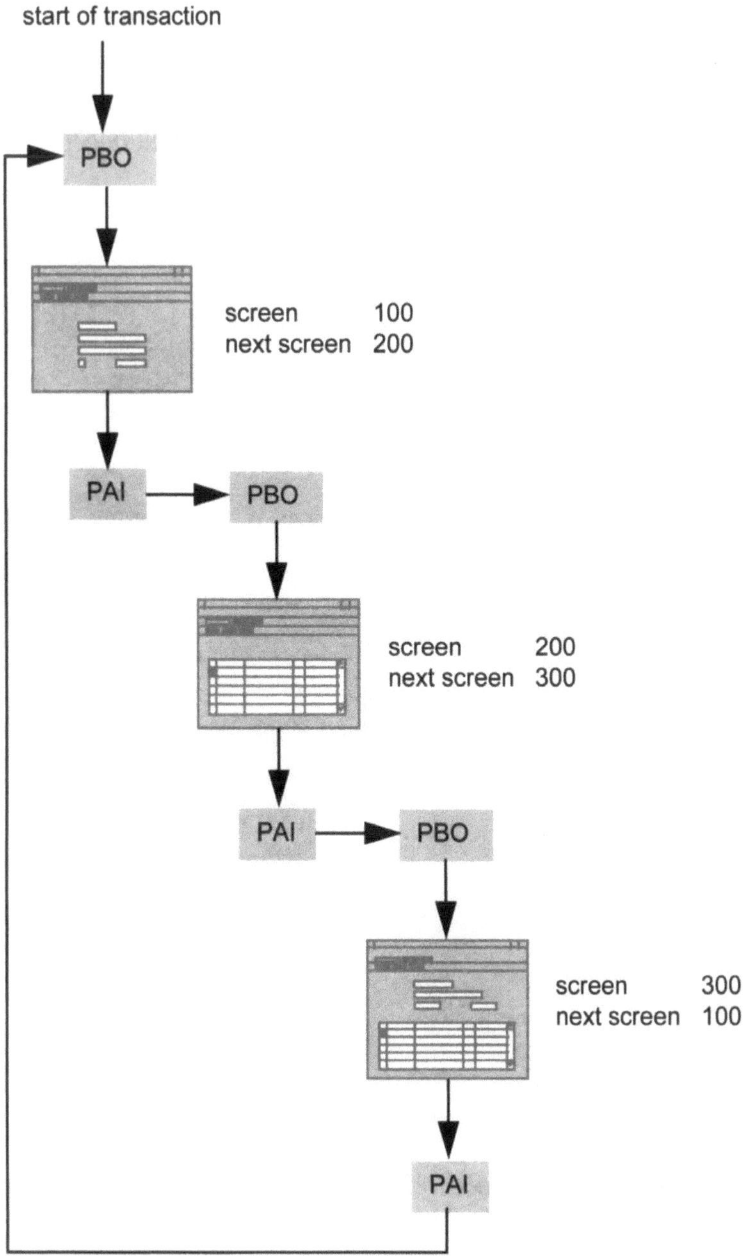

Figure 9.15: Static dynpro sequence

9.4.2 Dynamic Screen Flow

The static screen sequence does not suffice for most dialog transactions. Almost all screens provide the user with menu items or pushbuttons with which he can influence the program flow. Many of these capabilities have associated dynpros that are dynamically invoked depending on the user input.

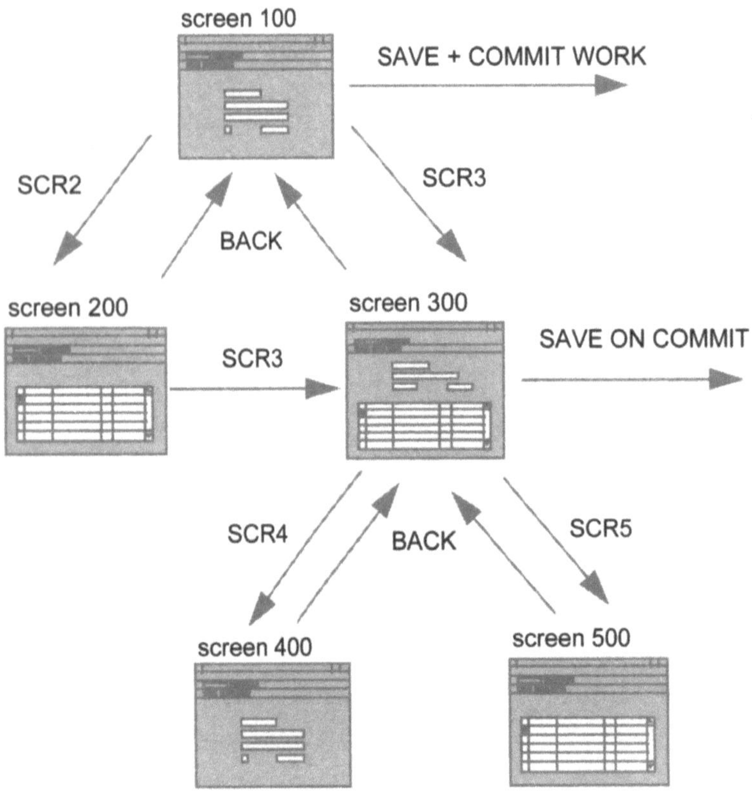

Figure 9.16: Call hierarchy for the dynpros of a transaction

The command to specify a new subsequent dynpro (not for this call) has the form:

SET SCREEN *dynnumber*.

This command overwrites the static subsequent screen in the dynpro attributes. The processing of the current dynpro continues until the next data entry. The

LEAVE SCREEN.

command used immediately after SET SCREEN exits the current dynpro and starts the new dynpro. The

CALL SCREEN *dynnumber.*

command is used to invoke another screen or screen sequence from a screen and then return to the point of invocation. The return to the invoking screen is performed in the invoked screen with SET SCREEN 0. The end of the transaction is prepared if a zero is specified for *dynnumber* in a dynpro that was not invoked with CALL. These screen sequence control commands are used to realize the control flow for large transactions. The used dynpros with their transition capabilities are shown as invocation hierarchies or invocation nets in the design phase (see Figure 9.16). The function codes are noted at the transitions.

9.5 Example 1: Hand Calculator

The following introductory example ZM_09_02 shows a dialog program that realizes a simple hand calculator for the basic arithmetic operations. The operation is as usual with, however, the mouse being used the click the calculator keys. All inputs are added digit by digit to the lower display (X). The first operand is passed to the upper display (Y) when an operation key is pressed. The second operand then can be entered. Confirmation with the "=" key calculates the result, which is placed in the lower display; the upper display is cleared. An attempt to divide by zero displays an error.

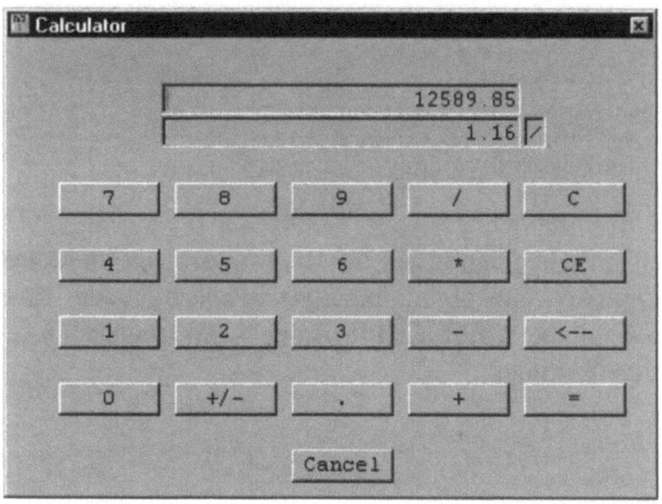

Figure 9.17: Hand calculator as modal dialog window

The hand calculator uses dynpro 100. Output fields form the displays and pushbuttons on the user interface represent the calculator's keys.

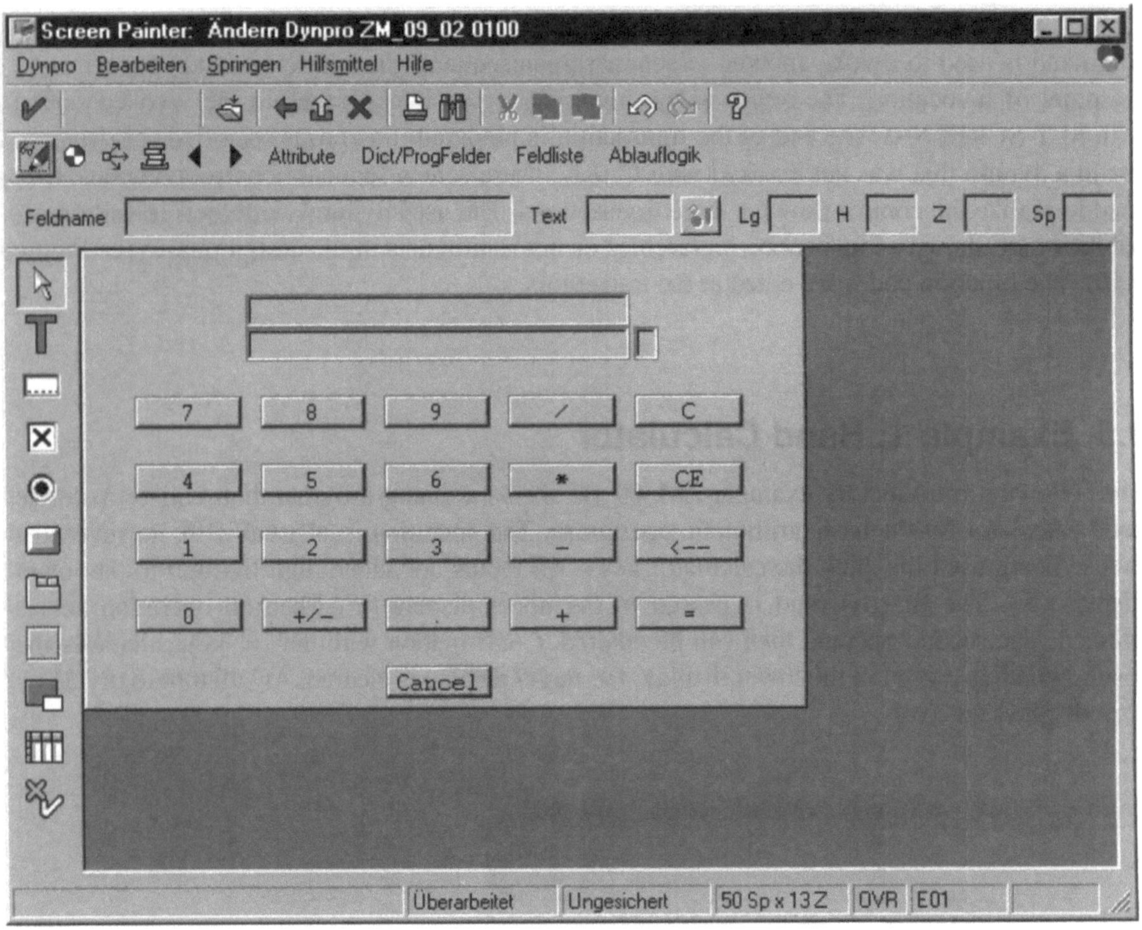

Figure 9.18: Graphical fullscreen editor for dynpro 100 of the hand calculator (German installation)

Figures 9.18 and 9.19 show the graphical fullscreen editor and the lower part of the field-list that lists the elements of the screen. The digit keys directly use the digits as function code. This simplifies working with the function code in the USER_COMMAND_0100 module. Once again, the FCODE field (of type "OK") is the last field.

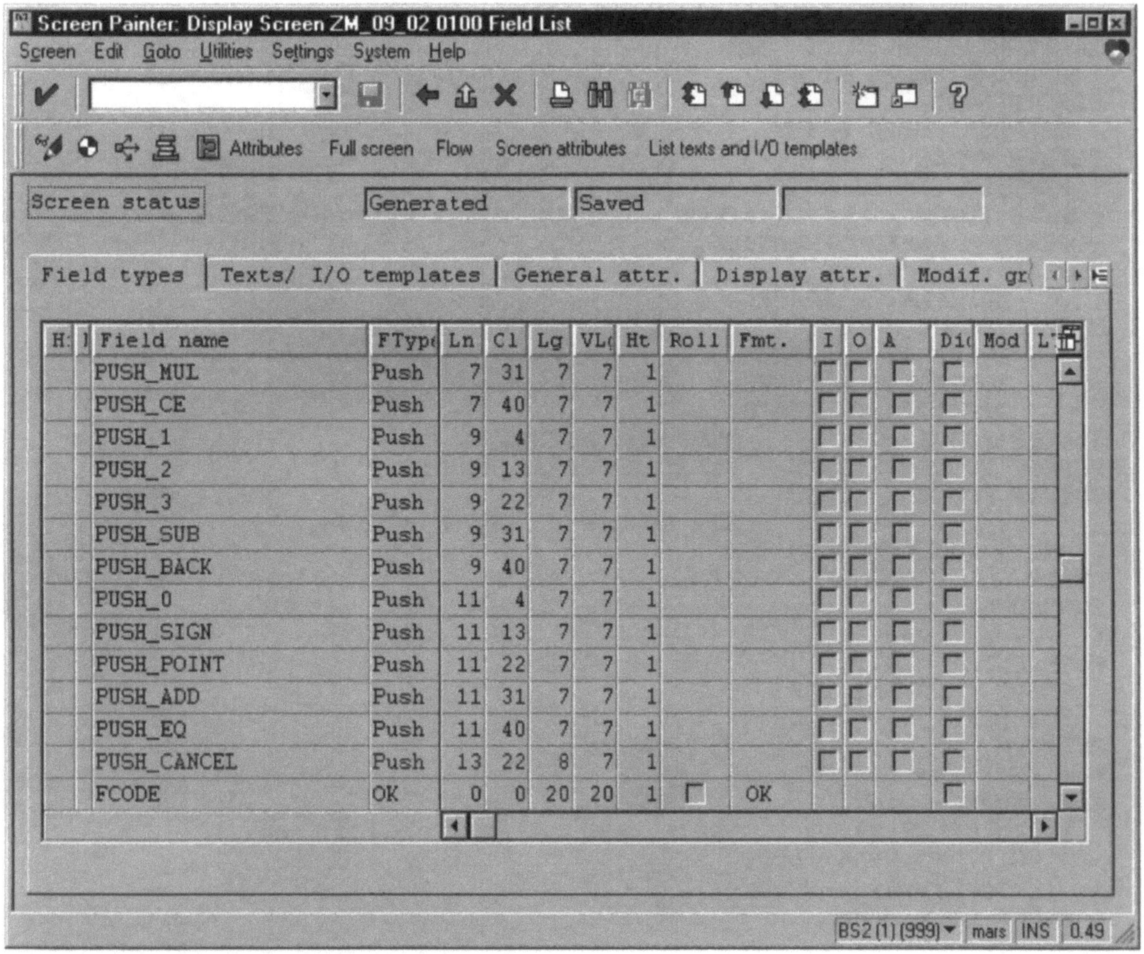

Field name	FType	Ln	Cl	Lg	VL	Ht	Roll	Fmt.
PUSH_MUL	Push	7	31	7	7	1		
PUSH_CE	Push	7	40	7	7	1		
PUSH_1	Push	9	4	7	7	1		
PUSH_2	Push	9	13	7	7	1		
PUSH_3	Push	9	22	7	7	1		
PUSH_SUB	Push	9	31	7	7	1		
PUSH_BACK	Push	9	40	7	7	1		
PUSH_0	Push	11	4	7	7	1		
PUSH_SIGN	Push	11	13	7	7	1		
PUSH_POINT	Push	11	22	7	7	1		
PUSH_ADD	Push	11	31	7	7	1		
PUSH_EQ	Push	11	40	7	7	1		
PUSH_CANCEL	Push	13	22	8	7	1		
FCODE	OK	0	0	20	20	1		OK

Figure 9.19: Field-list of the dynpro elements for the hand calculator

The flow control is only defined for the PROCESS AFTER INPUT event and calls the USER_COMMAND_0100 INPUT module. The following listing shows the complete ABAP/4 source code for the hand calculator.

```
PROGRAM  ZM_09_02 LINE-SIZE 72 MESSAGE-ID Y0.

DATA: XDISPLAY(27),
      YDISPLAY(27),
      OPERATION(1),
      X(12) TYPE P DECIMALS 10,
      Y(12) TYPE P DECIMALS 10,
      FCODE(4).
*---------------------------------------------------------------
MODULE USER_COMMAND_0100 INPUT.
```

```
IF FCODE BETWEEN '0' AND '9'.
  PERFORM ENTER_DIGIT.
ELSEIF FCODE = '.'.
  PERFORM ENTER_POINT.
ELSEIF FCODE = '+/-'.
  PERFORM CHANGE_SIGN.
ELSEIF FCODE = '+' OR FCODE = '-' OR FCODE = '*' OR FCODE = '/'.
  PERFORM ENTER_OPERATION.
ELSEIF FCODE = 'CE'.
      XDISPLAY = SPACE.
ELSEIF FCODE = 'C'.
      XDISPLAY   = SPACE.
      YDISPLAY   = SPACE.
      OPERATION = SPACE.
ELSEIF FCODE = '='.     PERFORM CALCULATE.
ELSEIF FCODE = 'BACK'. SHIFT XDISPLAY RIGHT.
ELSEIF FCODE = 'CANC'.
                       SET SCREEN 0. LEAVE SCREEN.
ELSE.
ENDIF.
ENDMODULE.                  " USER_COMMAND_0100  INPUT
*---------------------------------------------------------------------
FORM ENTER_DIGIT.
  SHIFT XDISPLAY LEFT.
  XDISPLAY+26 = FCODE(1).
ENDFORM.
*---------------------------------------------------------------------
FORM ENTER_POINT.
  IF XDISPLAY NA '.'.  "Point should appear only once
    SHIFT XDISPLAY LEFT.
    XDISPLAY+26 = FCODE(1).
  ENDIF.
ENDFORM.
*---------------------------------------------------------------------
FORM CHANGE_SIGN.
DATA O LIKE SY-FDPOS..
  IF XDISPLAY CA '-'. " Number is negative
    O = SY-FDPOS.
    XDISPLAY+O(1) = ' '.
  ELSE.
    IF XDISPLAY CN ' '.
      O = SY-FDPOS - 1.
      XDISPLAY+O(1)  = '-'.
    ENDIF.
  ENDIF.
ENDFORM.
*---------------------------------------------------------------------
FORM ENTER_OPERATION.
  IF OPERATION = SPACE.
    Y = XDISPLAY.
    YDISPLAY = XDISPLAY.
    XDISPLAY = SPACE.
    OPERATION = FCODE.
```

```
  ENDIF.
ENDFORM.
*---------------------------------------------------------------------
FORM CALCULATE.
CHECK OPERATION NE SPACE.
X = XDISPLAY.
CASE OPERATION.
  WHEN '+'. X = Y + X.
  WHEN '-'. X = Y - X.
  WHEN '*'. X = Y * X.
  WHEN '/'. IF X <> '0.0'. X = Y / X. ENDIF.
ENDCASE.
IF OPERATION = '/' AND X = '0.0'.
  MESSAGE I020.
ELSE.
  YDISPLAY = SPACE.
  PERFORM PACKED2CHAR USING X XDISPLAY.
  OPERATION = SPACE.
ENDIF.
ENDFORM.
*---------------------------------------------------------------------
FORM PACKED2CHAR USING VALUE(X) TYPE P STR.
DATA S(27).
S = X.
SHIFT S RIGHT.
IF X < '0.0'.
  SHIFT S LEFT DELETING LEADING ' '.
  SHIFT S RIGHT.
  S(1) = '-'.
ENDIF.
SHIFT S RIGHT DELETING TRAILING ' 0.'.
STR = S.
ENDFORM.
*--------------------------------------------------------------------*
MODULE USER_COMMAND_0050 INPUT.
  SET TITLEBAR '100'.
  CALL SCREEN 100 STARTING AT 10 5.
  SET SCREEN 0. LEAVE SCREEN.
ENDMODULE.                  " USER_COMMAND_0050  INPUT
```

The three display fields XDISPLAY, YDISPLAY and OPERATION are defined as CHAR fields in the global data. This has the advantage that the numeric inputs can be easily added to the existing display. The displays are converted to the corresponding P-variables X and Y that are used for the computation. The USER_COMMAND_0100 module consists of several IF-ELSEIF branches in which the function code inputs are processed. Because this branch type permits combining of groups of inputs, it is more appropriate here rather than a CASE. Thus, all numeric keys are handled in the same manner. Subprograms have been written for the actions initiated from each of the keys. Because only a few global data items are required, it is possible to avoid the use of parameters.

The ENTER_DIGIT routine for numeric input is particularly simple. It shifts the contents of XDISPLAY one position to the left and writes a new digit in the vacated position. The input of the decimal point in the ENTER_POINT is handled identically, although a test here ensures that a decimal point has not already been input. The backspace is handled directly in the module as SHIFT XDISPLAY RIGHT without special form.

The input of an operation places the calculator in another state. This is indicated by OPERATION <> SPACE. XDISPLAY is copied to YDISPLAY and cleared for the input of the second operand. The P-variable Y is set using the Y = YDISPLAY assignment. This uses the automatic type conversion CHAR→P.

Pressing the "=" key initiates the calculation using the CALCULATE form. The X variable from the display is first determined. The calculation is then performed in accordance with the specified operation. The result contained in X must be placed in the display.

A problem arises here. The conversion P→CHAR for packed numbers is performed using the number of decimal places specified as DECIMALS. However, the decimal representation should be realized with a variable number of decimal places. Furthermore, the sign should not come after the number as is usual for P-numbers but rather at the front. This is achieved in the PACKED2CHAR form.

The P-number X is initially converted into the local CHAR variable S. SHIFT RIGHT removes the trailing sign. If X is negative, S is shifted left and any leading blanks removed. A '-' is then prefixed. S is then repeatedly shifted right to remove any trailing blanks, zeros or the decimal point.

9.6 Screen Layout Features

9.6.1 Dynamic Screen Modification

The static screen layout is defined in the Screen Painter. If required, the field properties specified there can be changed dynamically in the program at PBO time. The switching between display and change mode is a typical example used throughout R/3. A user action at runtime switches certain fields to be input or non-input. The properties of the dynpro fields for the current dynpro have been entered into the SCREEN internal table that the system provides for this purpose.

Table 9.4: SCREEN system table fields

Field	Length	Type	Meaning
SCREEN-NAME	30	C	field name
SCREEN-GROUP1	3	C	field group 1
SCREEN-GROUP2	3	C	field group 2
SCREEN-GROUP3	3	C	field group 3
SCREEN-GROUP4	3	C	field group 4
SCREEN-REQUIRED	1	C	required entry field
SCREEN-INPUT	1	C	field ready for input
SCREEN-OUTPUT	1	C	output field
SCREEN-INTENSIFIED	1	C	intensified field
SCREEN-INVISIBLE	1	C	hidden field
SCREEN-LENGTH	1	X	length of field
SCREEN-ACTIVE	1	C	active field

In the same manner as normal tables, values for the individual fields or complete field groups within PBO can be changed in a LOOP. The following program code that changes all fields of the "EING" group to be input-ready using a form is typical. All fields of the group are set inactive when the ON constant is passed.

```
LOOP AT SCREEN.
  CHECK SCREEN-GROUP1 = 'EING'.
  SCREEN-INPUT = STATUS.
  MODIFY SCREEN.
ENDLOOP.
ENDFORM.
```

The MODIFY command that writes the changes for the header line back into the table body is important. The usual form LOOP AT SCREEN WHERE ... for internal tables is not permitted here.

9.6.2 Table Controls

Table controls are complex dynpro elements for the display and input of data having a tabular structure. They have almost completely replaced the Step loops used in earlier R/3 versions.

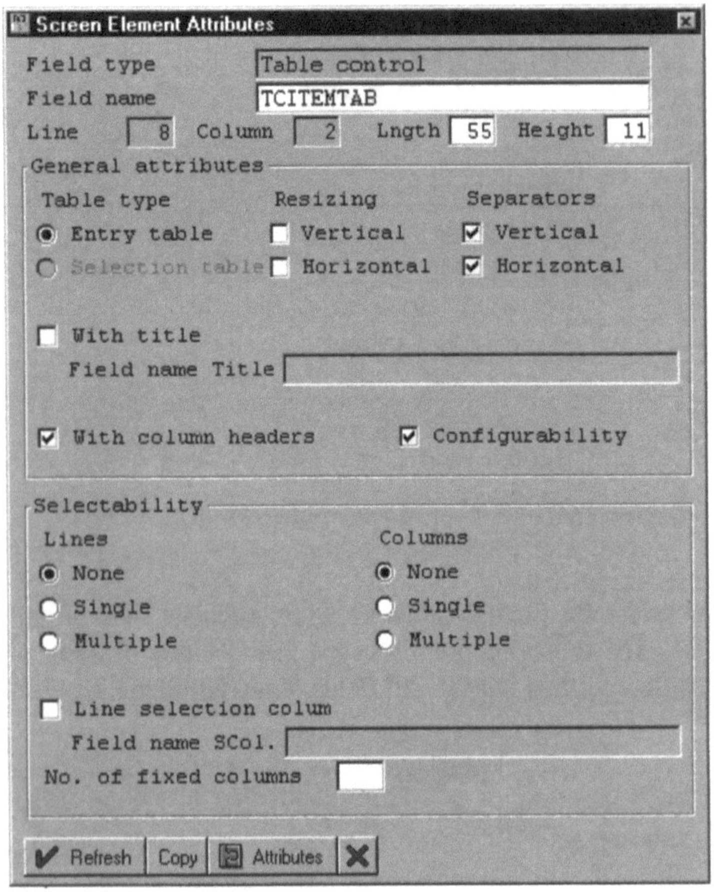

Figure 9.20: Attributes of a table control in the Screen Painter

Table controls are created on the dynpro; the following important properties are initialized:

- Number and width of the columns
- Column field designations
- Column headings
- Number of rows
- Selection capabilities of rows
- Separator lines

Most of the table control properties can also be changed at runtime using a data structure that has been created in the module pool. The input screen for the table control fields shown in Figure 9.21 itself uses a table control.

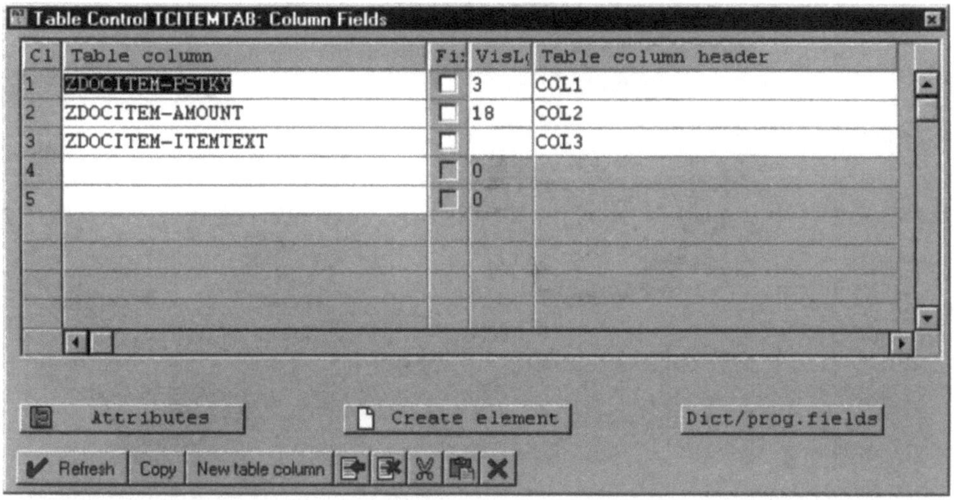

Figure 9.21: Column input for a table control

Every table control created on a dynpro in the Screen Painter is connected with a data structure of TABLEVIEW type in the module pool using CONTROLS.

CONTROLS: *controlname* **TYPE TABLEVIEW USING SCREEN** *scrno***.**

The TABLEVIEW type contains all status information of the table control for the screen. The type of the control is defined using a TYPE-POOL as CXTAB_CONTROL structure with embedded COLS table of CXTAB_COLUMN type:

```
TYPE-POOL CXTAB .

TYPES:
       BEGIN OF CXTAB_COLUMN,
         SCREEN    LIKE SCREEN,       "Attributes structure SCREEN
         INDEX     TYPE I,            "Position of a column on the
                                      screen
         SELECTED,                    "Indicator 'column selected'
         VISLENGTH LIKE ICON-OLENG,"Visualised length of a column
         INVISIBLE,                   "Indicator 'column invisible'
       END   OF CXTAB_COLUMN,

       BEGIN OF CXTAB_CONTROL,
         FIXED_COLS      TYPE I, "Number of fixed columns
         LINES           TYPE I, "Number of lines to display
         TOP_LINE        TYPE I, "Top line during next PBO
         CURRENT_LINE    TYPE I, "Current line during LOOP/ENDLOOP
```

```
          LEFT_COL       TYPE I, "Fist scrollable column after fixed
                                  area
          LINE_SEL_MODE TYPE I, "Line-selection   : none(0),
                                  single(1),
          COL_SEL_MODE  TYPE I, "Column-selection:         multiple(2)
          LINE_SELECTOR,         "Indicator: 'With line-selection
                                  column'
          V_SCROLL,              "not used
          H_GRID,                "Indicator: 'Horizontal  grid-lines'
          V_GRID,                "Indicator: 'Vertikal    grid-lines'
          COLS          TYPE CXTAB_COLUMN OCCURS 10,
          INVISIBLE,
END    OF CXTAB_CONTROL,

        BEGIN OF CXTAB_TABSTRIP,
          ACTIVETAB LIKE SCREEN-NAME,
          %_SCROLLPOSITION LIKE SCREEN-NAME,
          INVISIBLE,
        END OF CXTAB_TABSTRIP.
```

TOP_LINE and CURRENT_LINE are the most important properties. These are used to control the data exchange with the dynpro. Note that this structure does not contain any user data but only status information for the control. The user data are normally stored in an additional internal table.

Unfortunately, the field transport for a table control cannot be achieved using a simple name comparison between control fields and fields of an internal table. Additional loops constructions have been added to the flow control for the line-oriented field transport:

LOOP AT *Itab* [**WITH CONTROL** *control*]
[**INTO** *WA*]
[**CURSOR** *firstrow*]
[**FROM** *ITabrowfrom*]
[**TO** *ITabrowuntils*].
MODUL *module.*
ENDLOOP.

Although the LOOP instruction *must* be listed for both PBO and PAI, it may be empty in some circumstances. Figure 9.22 shows the interaction between flow control with LOOP instructions and the corresponding ABAP/4 modules.

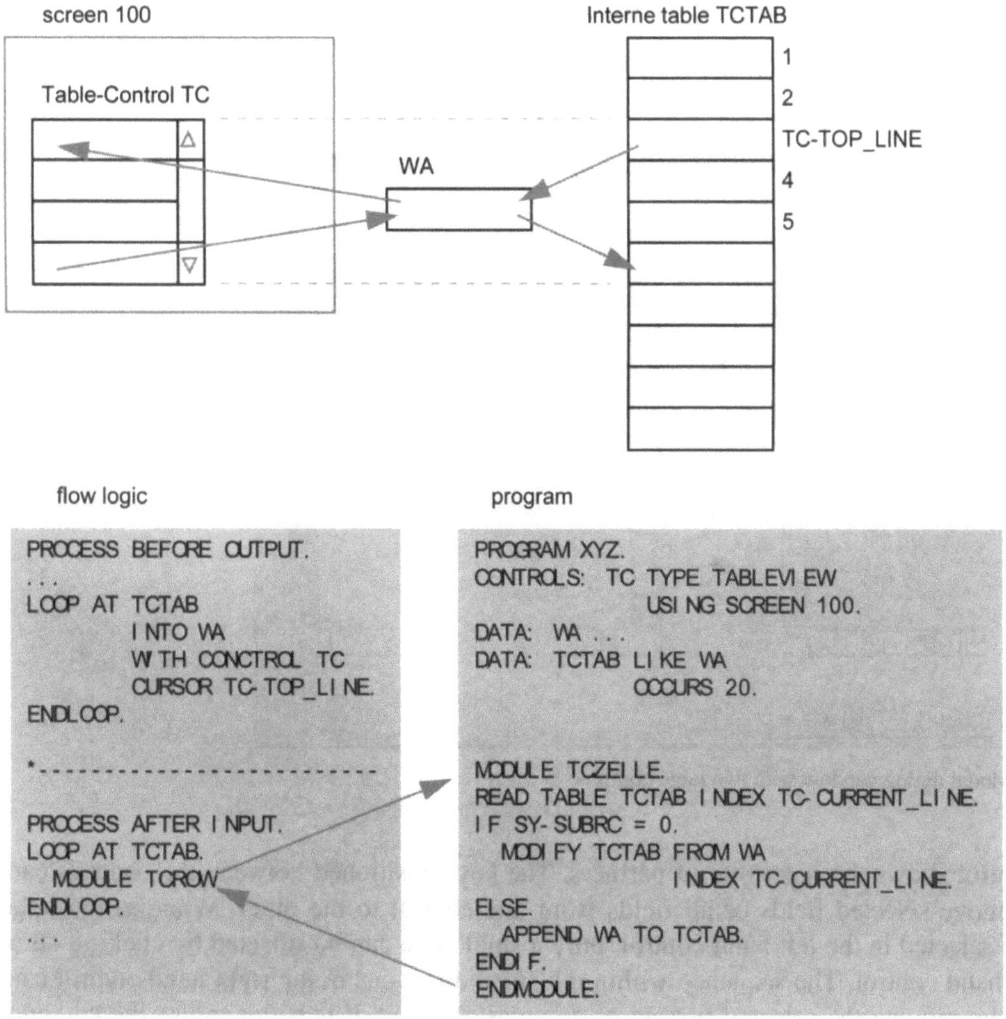

Figure 9.22: Field transport between the internal table TCTAB, the work area WA and the table control TC

9.7 Example 2: Two Table Controls on a Dynpro

It is possible to place several table controls on a dynpro. A typical application is the selection of elements from a repertoire but with the restriction that a sequence must be specified for the selected elements.

9.7.1 Dynpro as Modal Dialog Window

Figure 9.23 shows a modal dialog window for partner selection.

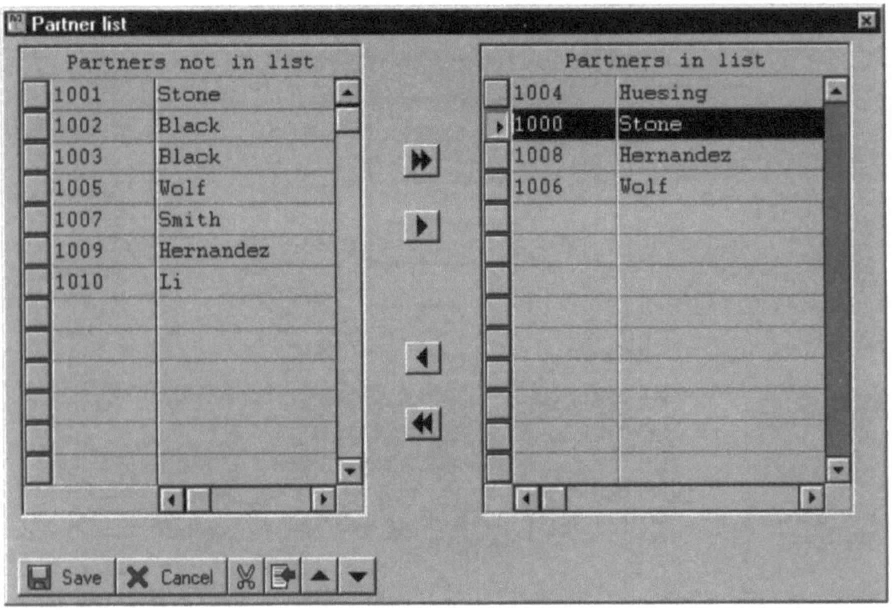

Figure 9.23: Modal dialog window with two table controls

The left control shows the repertoire of partners. The keys positioned between the controls can be used to move selected fields or all fields from one control to the other. Whereas multiple lines can be selected in the left hand control, only a single line can be selected by clicking on it in the right hand control. The sequence within the entered persons in the right hand control can be changed by moving the selected line up or down as required. It is better to use the *Cut* and *Insert* keys if the number of entered persons is larger than the line count of the control.

9.7.2 Report as Main Program

The main program ZR_09_04 is designed as program. The table controls are created as CTRL1 and CTRL2 variables; their data are contained in the IPART1 and IPART2 internal tables. In addition to the fields from YPARTNER, these have a selection field that shows in the program whether a line has been selected. All partners are read into the IPART1 work repertoire after the program start. SET SCREEN 50 invokes an empty dynpro that serves as frame for the modal dialog window 100. A direct call of dynpro 100 can be used to display this as a non-modal window. Dynpro 50 has dynpro 100 as next dynpro. The main program logic is contained in the forms. The MOVE_SELECTED_RIGHT form is considered as an example of a form that accesses both controls. A loop over the internal table of the left hand control (IPART1) retrieves either all lines (ALLKZ = "X") or only the selected lines (SELFIELD NOT INITIAL). Such a retrieved line is copied to IPART2 and added to IPART2 using APPEND. It is then removed from IPART1.

The SELECTED_UP and SELECTED_DOWN forms operate only on the IPART2 table. Both initially determine in a loop whether a partner has been selected in the IPART2, and, if yes, which partner. The INDEX variable contains the line number of the partner to be moved (SELPARTNER). This line is deleted and the deleted partner added above or below. The CUT_SELECTED and PASTE forms operate similarly. However, the cut partner is buffered in a global variable (CUTPARTNER). The storage of these entered and sorted persons is omitted in the program. The sorted selection of fields for the list display is a frequent application.

```
REPORT ZR_09_04 MESSAGE-ID Y1.

TABLES: YPARTNER.

DATA: BEGIN OF IPART1 OCCURS 100,
        SELFIELD.
        INCLUDE STRUCTURE YPARTNER.
DATA: END OF IPART1.

DATA: BEGIN OF IPART2 OCCURS 100,
        SELFIELD.
        INCLUDE STRUCTURE YPARTNER.
DATA: END OF IPART2.

CONTROLS: CTRL1 TYPE TABLEVIEW USING SCREEN 100,
          CTRL2 TYPE TABLEVIEW USING SCREEN 100.

DATA CUTPARTNER LIKE YPARTNER.

SELECT * FROM YPARTNER.
  MOVE-CORRESPONDING YPARTNER TO IPART1.
  APPEND IPART1.
ENDSELECT.
SET SCREEN 50.
*-------------------------------------------------------------------
MODULE STATUS_0100 OUTPUT.
  SET PF-STATUS 'STAT0100'.
  SET TITLEBAR  'TIT' WITH 'Partner Selection'.
ENDMODULE.                               " STATUS_0100  OUTPUT
*-------------------------------------------------------------------
MODULE USER_COMMAND_0100 INPUT.
  CASE SY-UCOMM.
    WHEN 'BACK'. SET SCREEN 0.
    WHEN 'EXIT'. SET SCREEN 0.
    WHEN 'ABEN'. SET SCREEN 0.
    WHEN 'MOVR'. PERFORM MOVE_SELECTED_RIGHT USING SPACE.
    WHEN 'MOVL'. PERFORM MOVE_SELECTED_LEFT USING SPACE.
    WHEN 'ALLR'. PERFORM MOVE_SELECTED_RIGHT USING 'X'.
```

```
    WHEN 'ALLL'. PERFORM MOVE_SELECTED_LEFT USING 'X'.
    WHEN 'CUT'.  PERFORM CUT_SELECTED.
    WHEN 'PAST'. PERFORM PASTE.
    WHEN 'DOWN'. PERFORM DOWN_SELECTED.
    WHEN 'UP  '. PERFORM UP_SELECTED.
  ENDCASE.
  LEAVE SCREEN.
ENDMODULE.
*---------------------------------------------------------------------
MODULE INIT_0100 OUTPUT.
  CLEAR SY-UCOMM.
ENDMODULE.
*---------------------------------------------------------------------
FORM MOVE_SELECTED_RIGHT USING ALLKZ.
  LOOP AT IPART1.
    IF ALLKZ <> 'X'.
      CHECK NOT ( IPART1-SELFIELD IS INITIAL ).
    ENDIF.
    CLEAR IPART1-SELFIELD.
    MOVE-CORRESPONDING IPART1 TO IPART2.
    APPEND IPART2.
    DELETE IPART1.
  ENDLOOP.
ENDFORM.
*---------------------------------------------------------------------
FORM MOVE_SELECTED_LEFT USING ALLKZ.
  LOOP AT IPART2.
    IF ALLKZ <> 'X'.
      CHECK NOT ( IPART2-SELFIELD IS INITIAL ).
    ENDIF.
    CLEAR IPART2-SELFIELD.
    MOVE-CORRESPONDING IPART2 TO IPART1.
    APPEND IPART1.
    DELETE IPART2.
  ENDLOOP.
  SORT IPART1 BY PARTNR.
ENDFORM.
*---------------------------------------------------------------------
MODULE PAI_CTRL1 INPUT.
* CHECK NOT ( IPART1-SELFIELD IS INITIAL ).
  MODIFY IPART1 INDEX CTRL1-CURRENT_LINE.
ENDMODULE.
*---------------------------------------------------------------------
MODULE PAI_CTRL2 INPUT.
* CHECK NOT ( IPART2-SELFIELD IS INITIAL ).
  MODIFY IPART2 INDEX CTRL2-CURRENT_LINE.
ENDMODULE.
*---------------------------------------------------------------------
MODULE PBO_CTRL1 OUTPUT.
*
ENDMODULE.
```

```
*---------------------------------------------------------------------
MODULE PBO_CTRL2 OUTPUT.
*
ENDMODULE.
*---------------------------------------------------------------------
MODULE ABEND_0100 INPUT.
  SET SCREEN 0. LEAVE SCREEN.
ENDMODULE.
*---------------------------------------------------------------------
FORM CUT_SELECTED.
  DATA INDEX LIKE SY-TABIX VALUE 0.
  IF NOT ( CUTPARTNER IS INITIAL ).
    IPART1 = CUTPARTNER.
    IPART1-SELFIELD = SPACE.
    APPEND IPART1.
    SORT IPART1 BY PARTNR.
  ENDIF.
  LOOP AT IPART2 WHERE NOT ( SELFIELD IS INITIAL ) .
    CUTPARTNER = IPART2.
    INDEX = SY-TABIX.
    EXIT.
  ENDLOOP.
  IF NOT ( CUTPARTNER IS INITIAL ).
    DELETE IPART2 INDEX INDEX.
  ENDIF.
ENDFORM.
*---------------------------------------------------------------------
FORM PASTE.
  DATA INDEX LIKE SY-TABIX VALUE 0.
  IF NOT CUTPARTNER IS INITIAL.
    MESSAGE S001 WITH 'Nothing to be entered.'.
    EXIT.
  ENDIF.
  LOOP AT IPART2 WHERE NOT ( SELFIELD IS INITIAL ) .
    INDEX = SY-TABIX.
    IPART2-SELFIELD = SPACE.
    MODIFY IPART2.
    EXIT.
  ENDLOOP.
  CHECK INDEX > 1.
  INDEX = INDEX - 1.
  INSERT CUTPARTNER INTO IPART2 INDEX INDEX.
ENDFORM.
*---------------------------------------------------------------------
FORM DOWN_SELECTED.
  DATA SELPARTNER LIKE YPARTNER.
  DATA INDEX LIKE SY-TABIX.
  CLEAR: SELPARTNER, SY-TFILL.
  LOOP AT IPART2 WHERE NOT ( SELFIELD IS INITIAL ) .
    SELPARTNER = IPART2.
    INDEX = SY-TABIX.
  ENDLOOP.
  DESCRIBE TABLE IPART2 LINES SY-TFILL.
```

```
  IF NOT ( SELPARTNER IS INITIAL ).
    CHECK INDEX < SY-TFILL.
    DELETE IPART2 INDEX INDEX.
    INDEX = INDEX + 1.
    INSERT SELPARTNER INTO IPART2 INDEX INDEX.
  ENDIF.
ENDFORM.
*---------------------------------------------------------------------
FORM UP_SELECTED.
  DATA SELPARTNER LIKE YPARTNER.
  DATA INDEX LIKE SY-TABIX.
  CLEAR SELPARTNER.
  LOOP AT IPART2 WHERE NOT ( SELFIELD IS INITIAL ) .
    SELPARTNER = IPART2.
    INDEX = SY-TABIX.
  ENDLOOP.
  IF NOT ( SELPARTNER IS INITIAL ).
    CHECK INDEX > 1.
    DELETE IPART2 INDEX INDEX.
    INDEX = INDEX - 1.
    INSERT SELPARTNER INTO IPART2 INDEX INDEX.
  ENDIF.
ENDFORM.
*--------------------------------------------------------------------*
MODULE USER_COMMAND_0050 INPUT.
  CALL SCREEN 100 STARTING AT 10 5.
  SET SCREEN 0. LEAVE SCREEN.
ENDMODULE.
*---------------------------------------------------------------------
MODULE STATUS_0050 OUTPUT.
  SY-UCOMM = 'ONLI'.
ENDMODULE.                              " STATUS_0050  OUTPUT
*---------------------------------------------------------------------
```

9.7.3 Flow Control

The flow control is simple. It contains at PBO time for every control a loop over the associated internal table; the CTRLX-TOP_LINE value is used as offset. Loops in the same sequence are also noted for PAI. The invoked PAI_CTRL1 and PAI_CTRL2 modules accept the changed table contents in the program.

```
PROCESS BEFORE OUTPUT.
  MODULE STATUS_0100.
  LOOP AT IPART1 WITH CONTROL CTRL1 CURSOR CTRL1-TOP_LINE.
    MODULE PBO_CTRL1.
  ENDLOOP.
  LOOP AT IPART2 WITH CONTROL CTRL2 CURSOR CTRL2-TOP_LINE.
    MODULE PBO_CTRL2.
  ENDLOOP.
```

```
  MODULE INIT 0100.
PROCESS AFTER INPUT.
  MODULE ABEND 0100 AT EXIT-COMMAND.
  LOOP AT IPART1. " WITH CONTROL CTRL1.
    MODULE PAI_CTRL1.
  ENDLOOP.
  LOOP AT IPART2. " WITH CONTROL CTRL1.
    MODULE PAI CTRL2.
  ENDLOOP.
  MODULE USER_COMMAND_0100.
```

9.8 Database Operations

The hand calculator program discussed in Section 9.5 only serves to determine and display the calculated results. It does not contain any database access. However, most dialog programs use Open SQL to make read and write access to the database.

The changes (updates) to the database represent the most difficult problem. The starting point for the considerations is the fact that a transaction during the processing of several dynpros may change the work process many times. An automatic database COMMIT is performed for every change. This means that all changes to the database (INSERT, DELETE, MODIFY, UPDATE) made in the PAI of the dynpro without options take effect immediately in the database.

An example is a transaction to store partner data that use several screens (100 = general data, 200 = addresses, 300 = bank accounts). It only makes sense to store the data when all screens have been displayed and all fields have been completed. There is also no point in storing the general data, the address or the bank data, by themselves. The following section discusses solutions for this conflict.

9.8.1 Inline Updating

The simplest method is to collect all the data to be updated over screen limits in structures or internal tables and to save as a unit at a single place at the end of the transaction. It cannot hurt to set an explicit COMMIT WORK here. If an error occurs, a ROLLBACK WORK can be used to recreate a consistent state. The following command should be mentioned in this context:

INSERT *table* **FROM TABLE** *itab* **ACCEPTING DUPLICATE KEYS.**

It is more efficient than a single INSERT within a loop over the internal table. The ACCEPTING DUPLICATE KEYS option avoids possible runtime errors if duplicate keys occur.

9.8.2 Grouped Updating with PERFORM ON COMMIT

In this method, any individual updates in the screens are combined in a form that is invoked with the ON COMMIT option. Such calls initially cause an indicator to be set in the forms for the updating at the next COMMIT WORK. As with the inline updating, this should be placed at the end of the task after the *store* or *save* command. Forms with ON COMMIT may not themselves contain any COMMIT WORK or ROLLBACK WORK. The sequence of the processing of the noted forms corresponds to the sequence of their invocation. The LEVEL option can be used to explicitly change the sequence. Updates with ON COMMIT always run synchronously, i.e., the command following COMMIT WORK is processed only after the update has completed successfully.

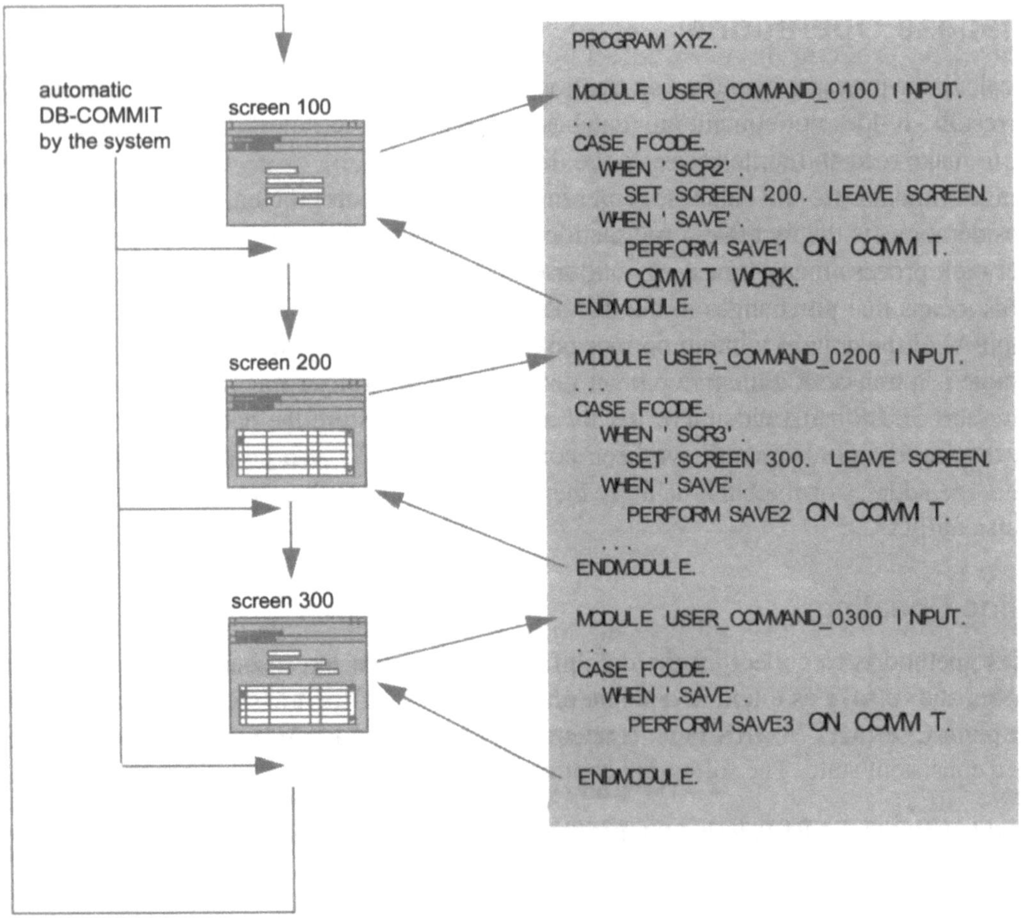

Figure 9.24: Updating with ON COMMIT

Figure 9.24 shows a specific screen sequence (100 → 200 → 300 → 100) in which the COMMIT WORK takes place in the first screen after the 200 and 300 screens have also been processed.

No parameters can be passed to subprograms that are invoked with ON COMMIT. Such subprograms must use global data or EXPORT TO MEMORY. In particular, when global data are used, it should be appreciated that their values can change between the time of invocation (set indicator) and the time of execution (COMMIT WORK), which can cause undesirable results.

9.8.3 Grouped Updating with PERFORM IN UPDATE TASK

Mass updates in the database (bookings) can be initiated using special function modules in the form

CALL FUNCTION *function* **IN UPDATE TASK EXPORTING** *export_ list.*

The booking modules must be marked appropriately in the library. The module names are stored together with the invocation parameters in the appropriate report tables. These are normally processed asynchronously from special updates. A COMMIT WORK initiates the start of the asynchronous processing. The program is then continued without waiting for the update result. In special cases, the AND WAIT option can be used to force a synchronization.

The asynchronous processing means that an update module cannot export any parameters to the caller, because it is quite possible that the update is no longer running at this time. The same applies for exceptions, which the caller also cannot process. Note that the above mentioned EXPORTING designation applies to the caller and indicates the *imported* parameters from the module.

9.8.4 Grouped Updating with PERFORM IN BACKGROUND TASK

A call of the form

PERFORM *function* **IN BACKGROUND TASK DEST** *remote_host.*

initiates asynchronous updates on remote computer systems. As with a normal update, the function calls are grouped with the parameter values in report tables and then passed to the remote system at the COMMIT WORK using RFC (refer to Chapter 13).

9.9 Example 3: Updating Action

A simple updating action with the following characteristics is discussed:

- Single record / multiple record document acquisition in a *single* screen
- Item data in a Table Control

- Database update with internal number assignment
- Locking logic for updated account

9.9.1 Dialog

Figure 9.25 shows the screen for the updating dialog. The elements for a document header ZDOCHD are input in the header fields. The document number is not entered but generated by the system during the store operation.

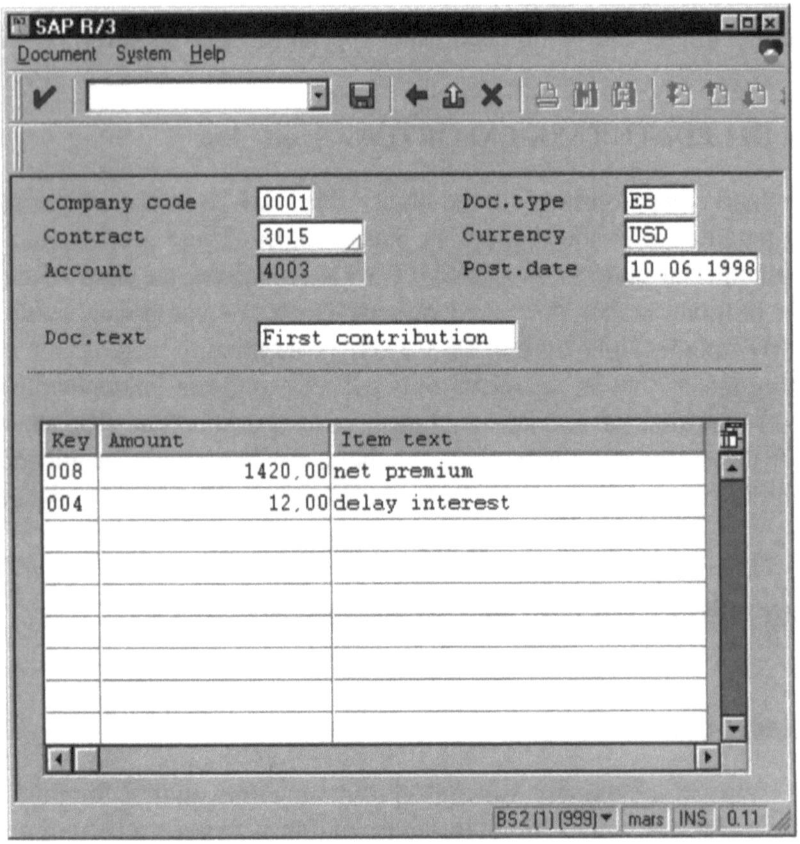

Figure 9.25: Update transaction with table view

The table control contains the item data corresponding to ZDOCITEM. Any number of items can be entered.

Company code, booking date and currency are preassigned but can be overwritten. Input help using F4 is provided for the document type. The contract numbers can be determined using the matchcode object described in Chapter 4. Because just a single account is assigned to each contract, the account number is not entered but read when the Enter key is pressed after the contract number has been entered. Any number of items can be entered into the table. The *Docu-*

ment/Book command performs a grouped inline update of the complete document with subsequent COMMIT WORK.

9.9.2 Module Pool

The module pool as global data initially defines the required database tables. The table work area ZDOCHD is linked here using the corresponding field names with the header fields of the dynpro. The ABAP/4 program records the document items in an internal table POSTAB. This has the ZDOCITEM structure. The TCPOSTAB variable of type CONTROLS is created in the program as counterpart to the table view on the screen.

```
PROGRAM  ZM_09_03 MESSAGE-ID Y0.
TABLES: ZDOCHD, ZDOCITEM, ZCONTRACT, ZACCOUNT.

CONTROLS: TCITEMTAB TYPE TABLEVIEW USING SCREEN 100.
DATA:     ITEMTAB LIKE ZDOCITEM OCCURS 5 WITH HEADER LINE.
DATA:     FCODE(4).
DATA:     DOCNO LIKE ZDOCHD-DOCNO.
*---------------------------------------------------------------------*
MODULE PBO 0100 OUTPUT.
  SET PF-STATUS 'ST0100'.
  IF ZDOCHD-COMCODE  IS INITIAL. ZDOCHD-COMCODE = '0001'.   ENDIF.
  IF ZDOCHD-PSTDAT   IS INITIAL. ZDOCHD-PSTDAT  = SY-DATUM. ENDIF.
  IF ZDOCHD-CURRKY   IS INITIAL. ZDOCHD-CURRKY  = 'USD'.    ENDIF.
  IF ZDOCHD-CONTNO NE SPACE AND ZDOCHD-ACCNO EQ SPACE.
    SELECT SINGLE * FROM ZCONTRACT WHERE CONTNO = ZDOCHD-CONTNO.
    IF SY-SUBRC = 0.
      ZDOCHD-ACCNO = ZCONTRACT-ACCNO.
      CALL FUNCTION 'ENQUEUE_EZACCOUNT'
           EXPORTING
                KONTNR          = ZDOCHD-ACCNO
           EXCEPTIONS
                FOREIGN_LOCK   = 1
                SYSTEM_FAILURE = 2
                OTHERS          = 3.
      IF SY-SUBRC = 1.
        MESSAGE S024 WITH ZDOCHD-ACCNO ZCONTRACT-CONTNO SY-MSGV2.
        ZDOCHD-ACCNO = 0.
        SET SCREEN 100. LEAVE SCREEN.
      ENDIF.
    ENDIF.
  ENDIF.
ENDMODULE.                          " PBO_0100  OUTPUT
*---------------------------------------------------------------------
MODULE PAI 0100 INPUT.
  READ TABLE ITEMTAB INDEX TCITEMTAB-CURRENT_LINE.
  IF SY-SUBRC = 0.
    MODIFY ITEMTAB FROM ZDOCITEM INDEX TCITEMTAB-CURRENT_LINE.
  ELSE.
    APPEND ZDOCITEM TO ITEMTAB.
```

```
  ENDIF.
ENDMODULE.                                    " PAI_0100  INPUT
*-------------------------------------------------------------------*
MODULE USER_COMMAND_0100 INPUT.
  CASE FCODE.
    WHEN 'EXIT'.
      SET SCREEN 0.
      LEAVE SCREEN.
    WHEN 'BUCH'.
      CALL FUNCTION 'Z_POST_DOCUMENT'
           IMPORTING
                E_DOCNO              = DOCNO
           TABLES
                T_ZDOCITEM           = ITEMTAB
           CHANGING
                C_ZDOCHD             = ZDOCHD
           EXCEPTIONS
                ERROR_NUMBER_RANGE   = 1
                OTHERS               = 2.
      IF SY-SUBRC = 0.
        COMMIT WORK.
        MESSAGE S022 WITH DOCNO.
        CALL FUNCTION 'DEQUEUE_EZACCOUNT'
             EXPORTING
                  KONTNR = ZDOCHD-ACCNO
             EXCEPTIONS
                  OTHERS = 1.
      ELSE.
        MESSAGE ID SY-MSGID TYPE SY-MSGTY  NUMBER SY-MSGNO
                WITH SY-MSGV1 SY-MSGV2 SY-MSGV3 SY-MSGV4.
      ENDIF.
    WHEN OTHERS.
  ENDCASE.
ENDMODULE.                                    " USER_COMMAND_0100  INPUT
*-------------------------------------------------------------------*
```

9.9.3 Flow Control

The flow control uses the PBO_0100, PAI_0100 and USER_COMMAND_0100 modules. The LOOP-ENDLOOP block used for the data exchange with the TCPOSTAB table view represents a special feature. This is created as independent, modularized element in the Screen Painter. The ZDOCITEM-BUGRD, ZDOCITEM-BETRW, etc. DDIC designations are used as column names. This is necessary to permit the use of the corresponding input help. The loop in PROCESS BEFORE OUTPUT operates over the internal POSTAB table specified in the module pool. It loads each record of it into the ZDOCITEM table work area that is used for the automatic field transport to a row of the table view.

```
PROCESS BEFORE OUTPUT.
MODULE PBO 0100.
LOOP AT POSTAB INTO YBELPOS
   CURSOR TCPOSTAB-TOP_LINE WITH CONTROL TCPOSTAB.
ENDLOOP.

PROCESS AFTER INPUT.
LOOP AT POSTAB.
  MODULE PAI_0100.
ENDLOOP.
MODULE USER_COMMAND_0100.
```

9.10 Transaction Manager for Complex Business Transactions

9.10.1 Concept

Processing of complex business transactions using R/3 standard transactions
Complex and very case-specific business transactions (BT) arise in many business areas (financial services, industry, public service, medical facilities). The SAP R/3 system can currently only partially satisfy the user demands for the effective processing of such BTs. The universal concept of a standard software system is badly suited to meet such extremely case-specific requirements. Normally, multiple SAP transactions, each with several dialog masks, must be processed in order to be able to process a complex BT in the R/3 system. A SAP transaction can be either completely processed or not at all. No means of buffering data are provided. The subsequent assignment of the transaction results to specific business transactions is either not possible or very difficult. The SAP standard transactions provide inadequate support for additional definitions of business rules or validations.

The following conclusions can be made for the processing of complex, case-specific business transactions in the SAP R/3 system:

- High input effort for the processing of the business transactions
- No case-specific checks in the system and consequently frequent occurrence of errors
- Inadequate support provided for the management of complex business transactions
- Difficult to incorporate external systems.

This unsatisfactory situation was the reason for the development of a software system aimed at compensating for these deficiencies of the SAP R/3 system and at ensuring effective business transaction processing.

Aims for the development of the transaction manager

The development of the transaction manager should achieve the following goals:

- Significantly reduced effort for the input of complex business transactions
- Significant simplification of the input process for the user
- Reduction of input errors
- Transparent management of the business transactions
- Support for the external interfaces to old systems or non-SAP systems.

Initial results

The following example comes from a large Swiss insurance company. The transaction manager described here runs in this company under R/3, Release 3.xx. It is used in this insurance company as follows:

- Productive operation since 1.1.97
- 37 different BT types have been modeled
- Implementation effort per BT type: approximately 5 days
- 12 000 business transactions per month
- External interfaces (RFC) to various old systems.

The following results have been achieved already:

The time savings compared with the use of SAP standard transactions average 70% (over 80% in some cases)

- High acceptance of the product in both the user departments and the data processing departments
- Significantly reduced demands made on the clerks for the business transactions
- Significantly lower error rate compared with the processing using standard transactions
- Complete adherence to accounting regulations (e.g. four-eyes security principle).

A specific business transaction is used to illustrate these results.

The "termination of service" from the company would require that the clerk to perform the following SAP transactions in the traditional processing the business transaction:

1. FK01: Create a creditor
2. FB02: Process a booking document to input the required bookings for the business transaction
3. ZUMI: Input the supplementary information for payments (customer-specific transaction)

Just for the input of the necessary updates for the document would require the clerk to work through a total of 85 (!) SAP standard dynpros for this business transaction.

The business transaction is currently being input in parallel in an old system and passed to the SAP R/3 system using RFC. The missing items from the business transaction are added on its acceptance; the business transaction is then checked against the SAP R/3 system and various special business rules. Currently approximately 300 external BTs are accepted per day. The effective effort for the processing of a transaction for this business transaction could be reduced to 25% of the original effort. This result was achieved through the consistent implementation of the following requirements for the realization of the transaction manager:

- Intuitive, business process-oriented data input with minimized effort
- Support of the data input through the use of default assignments and case-specific processing rules
- Provision for the storing of incomplete job states
- Compact, transaction-controlled processing of a fully input BT
- Monitoring of the progress of various processing states of the BT
- Simple definition and inclusion of new BT types
- Support for external interfaces

The consistent use of the transaction manager offers a major rationalization potential. The saving in processing time compensates already after a few weeks for the increased one-off implementation effort for the new business transactions.

Solution concept – meta-transactions and transaction manager

The aim of the development of the transaction manager was to represent complex business transactions company-specific in the SAP R/3 system and so permit an effective processing of these business transactions with as few errors as possible. The transaction manager combines several SAP R/3 standard transactions to form a business transaction-oriented processing unit (meta-transaction) and relieves the user for the longwinded processing of many single dynpros.

All data relevant for the business transaction are entered in a single BT form. A BT form here is a dialog transaction specifically adapted to the associated business transaction. The layout of the form is independent to the executing SAP R/3 standard transactions. The implementation of several form masks with interaction mask logic adapted to the associated business transaction is possible for complex business transactions.

To minimize the implementation effort for the form creation, the complete form logic (reading the BT, storing, scrolling, etc.) has been implemented independent of the business transaction. This technique limits the effort for the implementation of new form masks for the design of a new user interface and the modification of those data structures used (substructures).

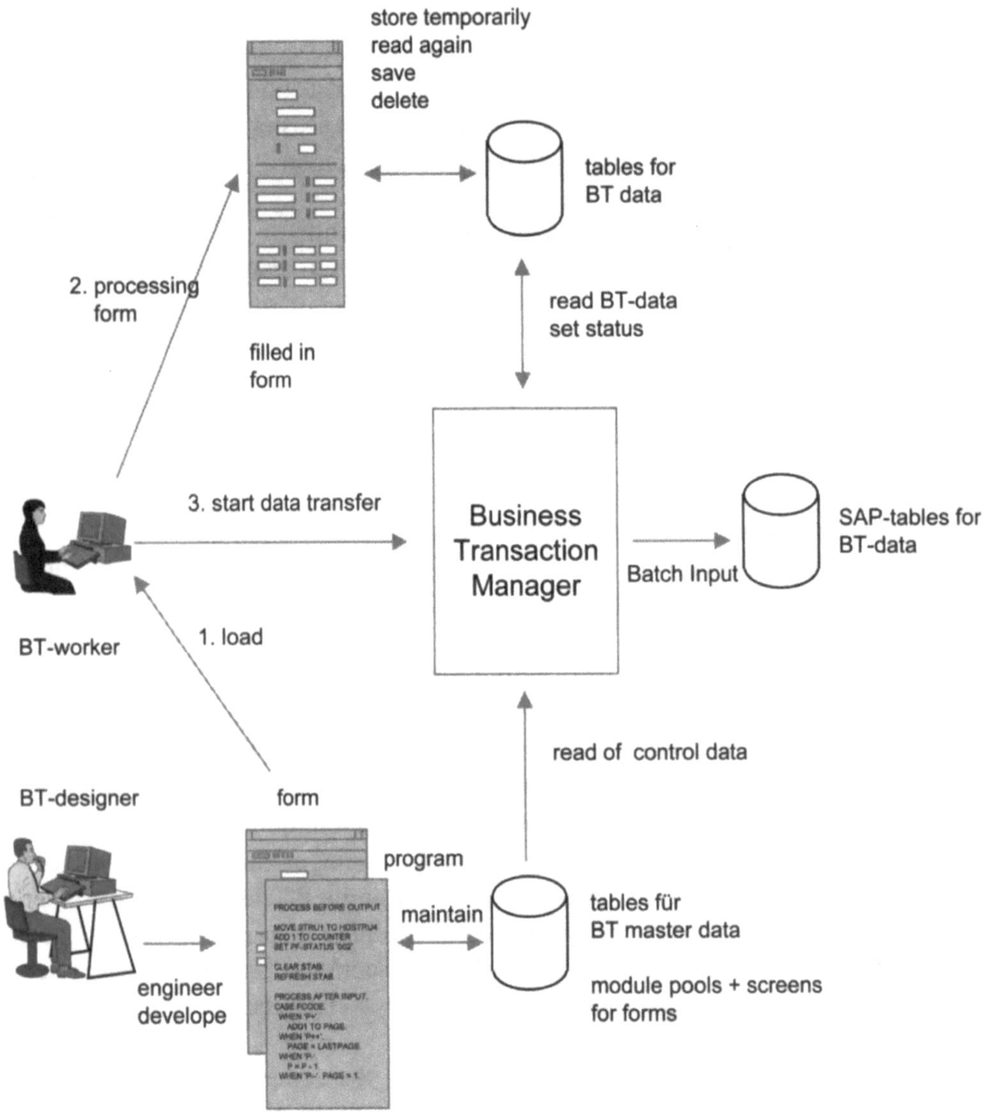

Figure 9.26: Function principle of the transaction manager

One of the main demands made on the transaction manager was that all validations of the standard transactions of the SAP R/3 systems be performed in the BT form. This requirement is satisfied by including the data elements of the SAP standard transactions in the form data structures. The use of the rule logic from the transaction manager permits in the BT form and during the subsequent acceptance of the business transaction in the SAP Standard the input data to be converted, plausibility checks performed on the data, data selected from the SAP system or the flow logic of the SAP system influenced.

In addition, user-specific business rules can be defined for processing BT forms. This technique and the ability to use a default assignment to initialize all BT forms for specific business transactions and language, provides the user with effective processing of the business transactions.

The data input in the forms can be optionally stored in business transaction-independent document tables and through the subsequent invocation of SAP R/3 standard transactions to be processed in the R/3 system.

The transaction manager uses the standardized BDC interfaces of the SAP R/3 system to pass the data to the SAP R/3 system. The following interfaces are currently supported:

- Accept data from the document database using batch input sessions
- Direct invocation of SAP standard transactions (call transactions)

The transaction manager's control tables are used to determine the SAP R/3 transactions to be processed for the associated business transaction. The form data are read from the form tables and processed per page and subitem. The transaction manager has been divided into three basic component groups:

- BT-specific components
- Components that operate between BTs
- SAP-specific components

The BT-specific components include the form masks and the special BT rule logic used for processing the business transaction.

The components that operate between BTs are routines having with functionality that is independent of both individual business transactions and standard SAP R/3 (e.g., database routines, multiple document processing, etc.).

The SAP-specific components constitute those parts of the transaction manager that are required for the access to the standard transactions of the SAP R/3 system.

This intentional division of the functionality of the transaction manager simplifies the modification and maintenance of the transaction manager. If a business transaction changes, this requires only modifications to the form masks and the associated BT rules. The same applies for further developments in the standard SAP R/3 system. Any changes in SAP R/3 require only modifications to the SAP-specific components of the transaction manager.

9.10.2 Transaction Manager Data Model

The transaction manager operates table controlled. All tables are stored as transparent tables in R/3. Figure 9.27 shows the SAP SERM model of the transaction manager.

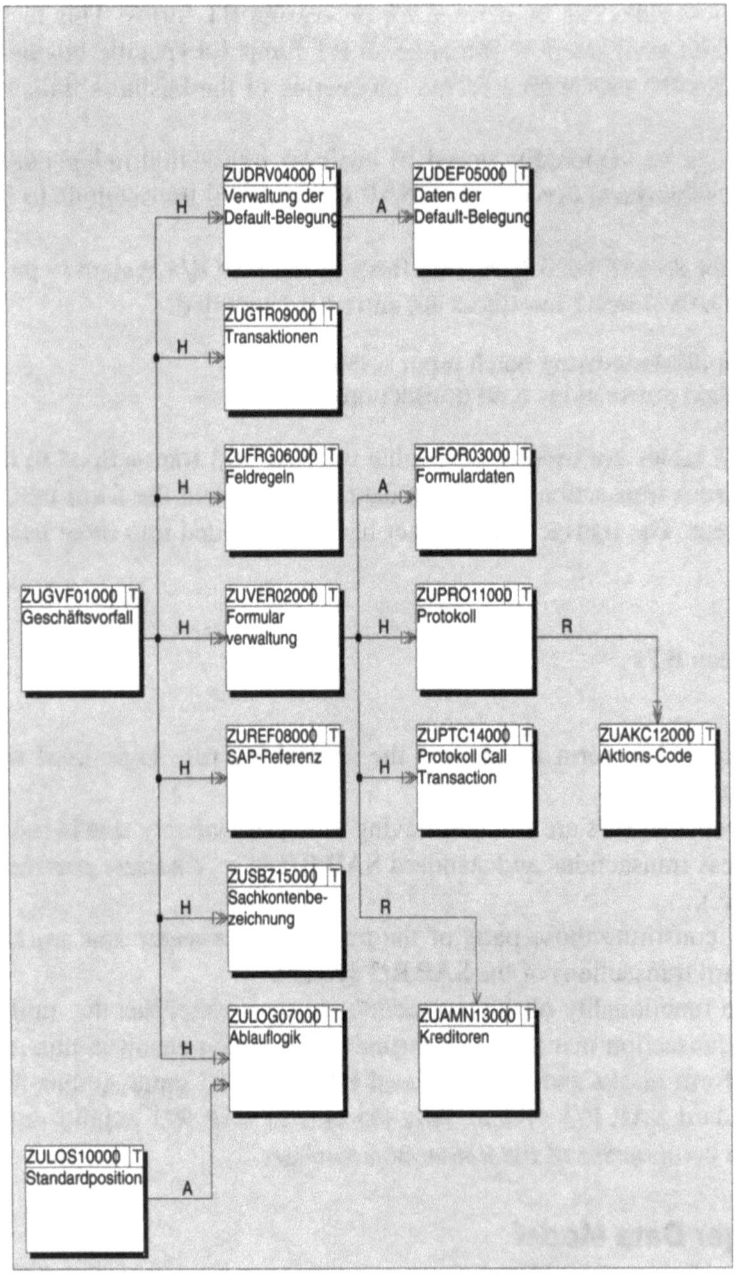

Figure 9.27: SAP SERM model of the transaction manager

Master data

The "Geschäftsvorfall" (Business Transaction) table contains the following information for all types of business transactions:

- BT number = transaction code of the meta-transaction = form type
- Description of the BT
- Fixed values for header fields (company code, document type)
- Dynpro number and module pool of the form user interface
- Change date

The following SAP transactions invoked for the processing of a BT are entered in the "Transaktionen" (Transactions) table in the appropriate sequence:

- BT number
- Running transaction number
- Transaction code
- Transaction designation

The processing steps (dynpros) to be performed for every SAP transaction are noted in the "SAP-Referenz" (SAP Reference) table. A processing step corresponds to a dynpro, the number of which is also specified. All fields to be filled on the dynpro are assigned a reference to the corresponding form field. The processing mode specifies whether the field may contain a fixed value. The SAP Reference table contains the following items:

- BT number
- Running transaction number
- Item number of the transaction
- Form field
- SAP field
- Processing type
- Field value

Transaction data = form data

The forms are started and filled using normal SAP transaction codes. The administration data for a form are entered in the "Formularverwaltung" (Form Administration) table:

- BT number
- Running form number
- Processing clerk
- Document date
- Booking date

The associated item data for the forms are contained in the "Formulardaten" (Form Data) table:

- BT number
- Running form number
- Subitem in the form
- Structure name of the subitem in the form
- Structure length
- Structure data

The same number of rows for a completed form are created as there are different structures in this form. All data for a structure are stored in a non-interpreted form as CHAR string and split into individual fields only at processing-time.

9.10.3 Components and Functions of the Transaction Manager

Manual creation of a form

Every type of BT has its own entry interface: a form. Forms are saved in the Workbench as dialog programs. In most cases, a form has a single page, i.e., the dialog program has only one dynpro. However, multiple dynpros are generally permitted.

The BT form masks are based on documents. The form created for each business transaction can consist of several pages (dynpros). The pages themselves are divided into several subareas (Figure 9.28). Subarea 0 has a special significance; the form header data are defined in it. A unique data structure is defined in the Data Dictionary for every subarea. This structure is used for the data transfer between the form-dynpro and the function module for access to the BT tables.

The use of the data elements of the SAP standard transactions permits the integration of parts of the validation logic of the original transactions in the BT form mask. It is possible to define plausibility and conversion rules for all dynpro fields of the form.

The data entry logic for a BT is combined in a module pool. The inter-BT parts are implemented just once:

- Initialization functions
- Input functions
- Plausibility checks
- Processing functions
- Service functions
- Error handling

The initialization of the form mask includes the authorization check, the creation of the form mask, the default settings for fixed values and the acceptance of any defined default or previous values. The initialization functions are processed within the PBO section of the program.

The data input is performed document-oriented for all form masks. It is assumed that a document consists of a document header and several document items. The document header data and data common for several document items are entered in the document header.

The plausibility check of the form data covers the validation of the data entered at the field level. In addition to the validations that are also subsequently performed in the SAP R/3 standard transaction, the plausibility check can also have user-specific validations.

The processing functions can be activated using the menu, the menubar, the function keys or the pushbuttons. These functions permit the creation of a new business transaction, the saving of the business transaction in the document database (document preliminary input), the processing of the business transaction (transfer to SAP), the termination of the business transaction, the deletion of the form mask, changing a stored business transaction or deleting a stored business transaction.

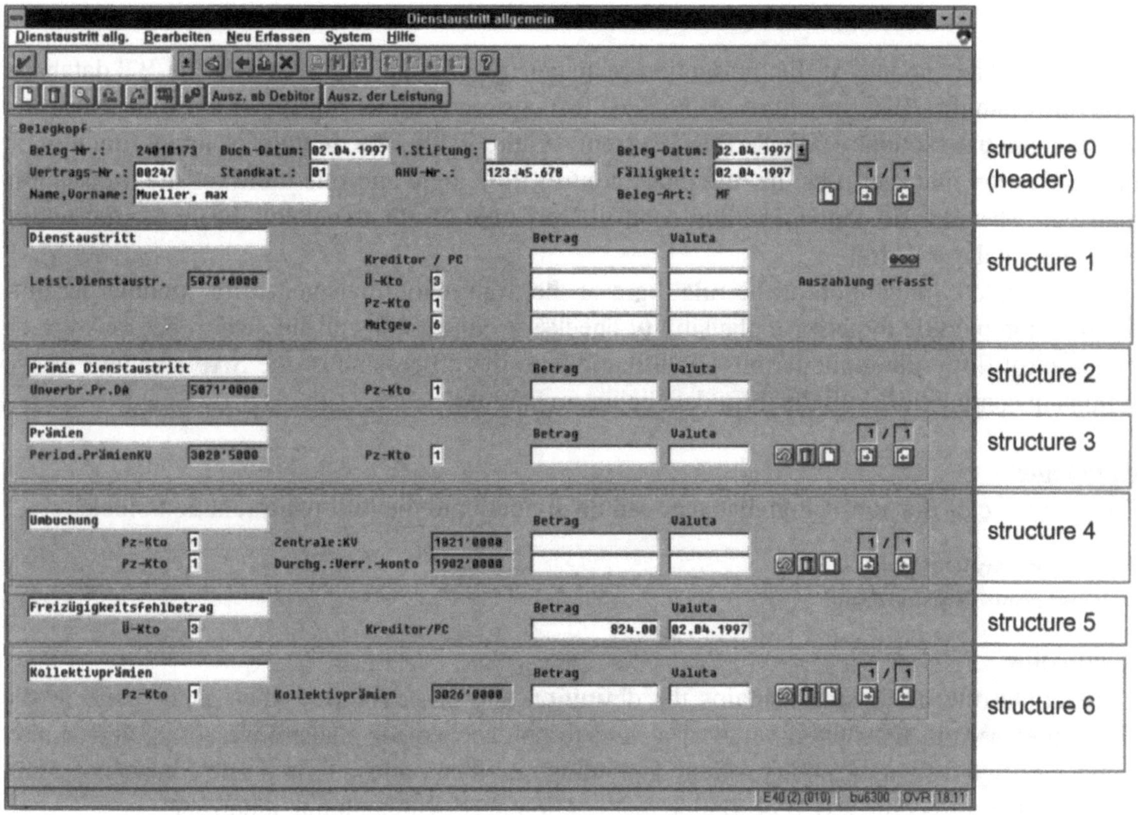

Figure 9.28: Single page form with 6 subareas (structures)

The service functions can be activated using the menu, the menubar or with pushbuttons. These functions support the user through the provision of universal search and display functions for the document database and with the definition of default values (user-specific and business transaction-oriented).

The error handling is dependent on the method used to transfer data to the SAP R/3 system. When data are passed to the SAP R/3 system using a call of the standard transactions (CALL

TRANSACTION), a message table containing all error messages that occurred in the transactions will be created if an error occurs.

Computer-generated forms – form interfaces

It is possible to enter BTs in external systems (host systems, laptop) and to transfer these to the transaction manager. The following methods are supported:

- Remote Function Call (RFC)
- Batch Input
- Sequential files

The transferred data can be given the default assignments of the transaction manager.

BT Transfer

The BT transfer module of the transaction manager realizes the conversion of the BT database structures into the BDC structures of the SAP R/3 system and the transfer of these structures to the standard transactions of the SAP R/3 system (Figure 9.29). The module as kernel function of the transaction manager uses the reference, control flow logic and rule tables of the transaction manager. The specific conversion and control flow logic of the associated business transaction is defined in these tables.

The complete integration of the rule logic of the transaction manager in the module permits the function module to perform plausibility checks or conversions of the data to be transferred. The control flow rule logic permits modifications to the processing of the SAP standard transactions in conjunction with the form data being transferred.

Rule logic

The rule logic of the transaction manager can be divided into the following function blocks:

- Field rule processing
- Flow control processing

Field rules

The field rule processing contains the definition and processing of rules at the field level. Field rules permit the entered value of a field to be checked for plausibility, to convert it into some specified format or modify a field depending on other values. A field rule consists of a encapsulated user-specific ABAP/4 routine that is referenced with a unique identifier.

The field rules are assigned to the individual fields using the control type in the reference tables ("Feldregeln" (Field Rules) and "SAP-Referenz" (SAP Reference)) of the transaction manager. A rule can be assigned to several fields.

The transaction manager currently supports the following field types within the field rule processing:

- Form fields of the BT-form
- Dynpro fields of the SAP transactions to be processed

The dynpro fields of the SAP standard transactions in the "SAP-Referenz" (SAP Reference) table are assigned using the associated processing rules while the form fields are being referenced using the "Feldregeln" (Field Rules) table.

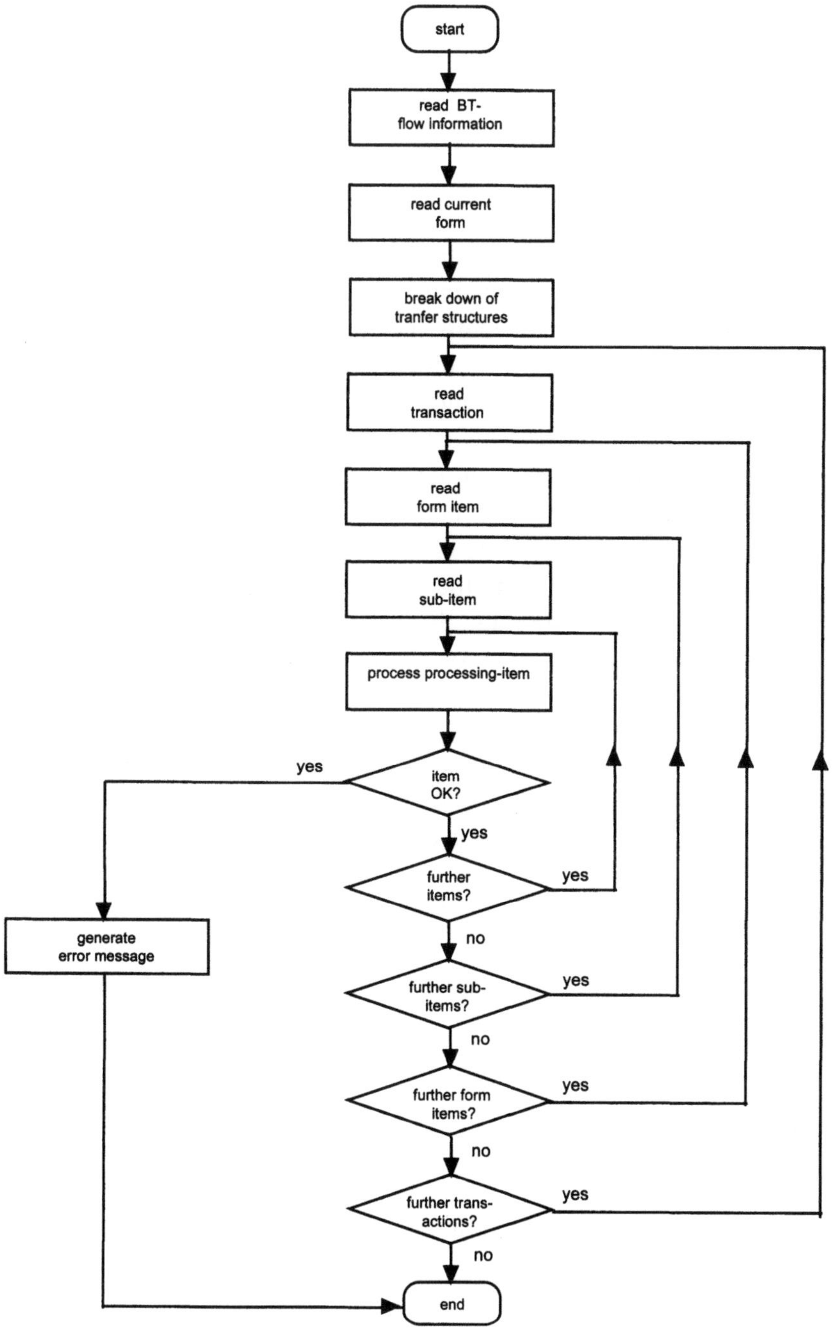

Figure 9.29: Acceptance of BT-data from form tables

The transaction manager provides a function module for the field rule processing. This function module currently contains the definitions for all field rules. To simplify defining rules, this function module implements several global routines for access to the current data of the form to be processed. The following field rule classes are differentiated for the field rule processing in the transaction manager:

- Conversion rules
- Plausibility rules
- Inter-document rules
- Special rules (e.g., for payments)

Procedure rules

The procedure rule processing covers all components required for the control of the flow of the SAP standard transactions. As in the field rule processing, a procedure rule consists of an ABAP/4 routine and a unique identifier. The procedure table of the transaction manager ("Ablauflogik" (Procedure Logic)) is used to assign the individual rules to the SAP standard transactions. The processing logic of the transaction manager uses this table to process the SAP transactions in the appropriate sequence for the associated business transactions. If this sequence is to be modified according to the data entered in the BT-form, procedure rules are assigned to the SAP standard transactions in the procedure table. Definitions can be made in this table whether the associated rule is to be processed before or after the specified transaction. The result of the flow rule processing is a processing item in the procedure table where the processing is to be continued. This rule definition can determine this item absolutely or virtually. The transaction manager provides a function module for the procedure rule processing.

Logging

A special function module in the "Protokoll" (Log) table is used to log all transaction manager actions. Various transaction manager components make use of this module. To avoid uncontrolled actions within the BT processing, the log module is one of the transaction manager kernel functions.

In addition to the BT type and the current BT form number, the module logs the associated actions, its return code, the current user, and the time and date when the action was performed. At the same time, the function module updates the status of the associated BT-form in the "Formularverwaltung" (Form Administration) table.

A special report is provided to perform simple analyses of the log table.

Administration of the transaction manager

Maintenance the control tables

Special dialog transactions have been developed for the maintenance of the BT control logic and flow logic of transaction manager (Figure 9.30).

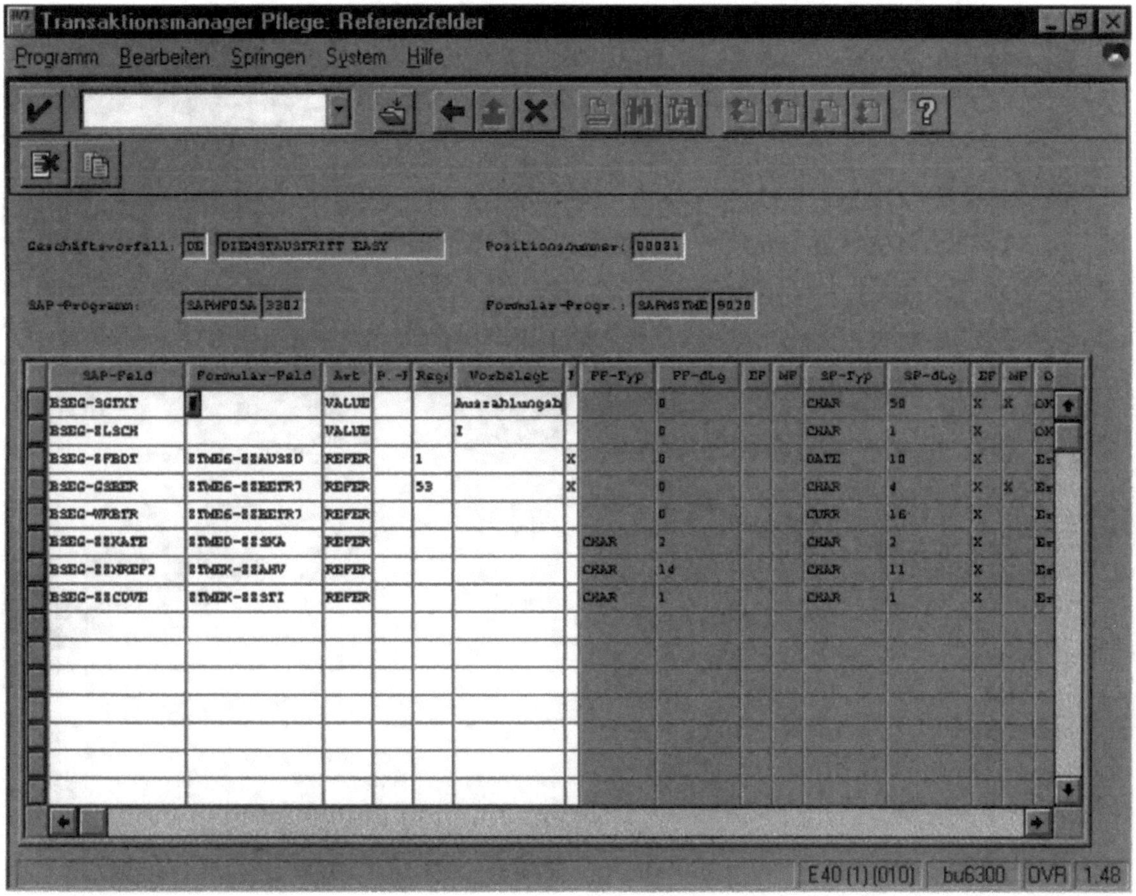

Figure 9.30: Maintenance of the BT types

Monitor

The transaction manager monitor was developed to support to processing of a large number of BTs. The monitor can be used to display the various processing states, the current user and date information of the BT. Various processing functions of the transaction manager can be initiated from the monitor (Figure 9.31).

Transaction manager and workflow

Although the transaction manager is not a replacement for SAP R/3 Workflow, its evaluation of processing rules and the result-controlled processing of transactions performs some of the tasks of a workflow. However, in contrast to Workflow, no complex business processes with multiple business transactions are represented in the transaction manager, but various SAP standard transactions combined as a business transaction-related processing unit. These BT transactions are presented to the user as normal SAP transactions (forms) in the form of a business transaction-related optimized user interface with the appropriate processing rules. It is both possible and desirable to incorporate R/3 in the business workflow.

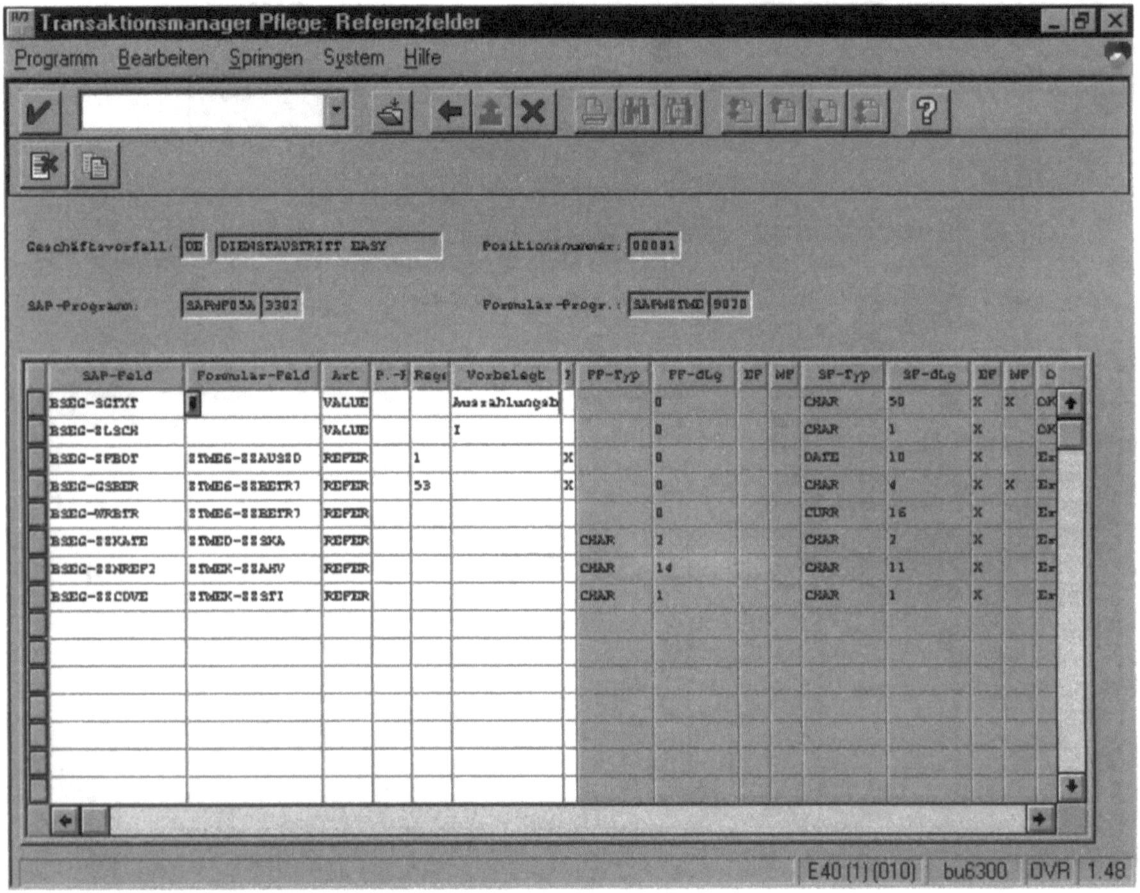

Figure 9.31: Transaction manager monitor

Transaction manager and SAPForms

SAP from Release 3.1 provides with SAPForms a tool to link the business workflow with external systems. In perspective, SAPForms can be used to couple the transaction manager to external systems. SAPForms cannot handle the previously described tasks of the transaction manager.

10 Background Processing

10.1 Concept

R/3 permits the processing of Reports both direct (online) and in background. The batch control processes the so-called batch jobs defined for the background processing, also known as batch processing. In the simplest case, a single report can be executed in background from the menu (Figure 10.1).

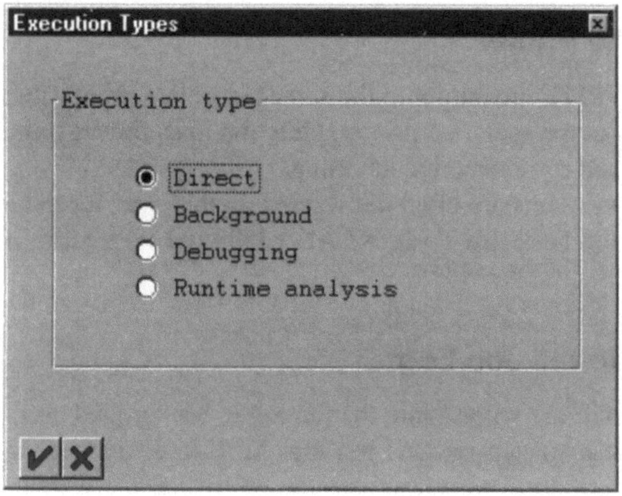

Figure 10.1: Types of execution for a report

In the general case, a job can contain several reports (steps) that are processed sequentially. Background processing is used for

- the processing of large data volumes
- the processing of complex algorithms
- the automated execution of periodically recurring tasks.

The words background processing indicate that no interaction takes place with the user. All inputs and outputs for a batch job are performed using mass storage (database, files) or rerouted to this. In contrast to pure batch systems that were widely used at the operating system level of mainframe computers, R/3 permits the parallel operation of dialog and batch processing. Every user can execute several batch jobs in background in parallel to his dialog program.

10.1.1 Control of the Background Processing

A job is created either interactively or from a program and then passed to the job control for processing. The job control monitors the conditions that have been defined for the start of the processing of the jobs (times, events, other jobs), and independently starts with the processing of the individual job steps.

10.1.2 Rerouting of Parameter Inputs to Variants

Parameters or selection options in the selection screen are normally passed to an interactive report. When a report with parameters is started as a step of a batch job, the parameters are read from the database using a variant. This variant must be specified during the interactive definition of the program step. If the job is formed from a program and the steps set using SUBMIT, the variants are created automatically from the parameters passed using WITH.

10.1.3 Reroute WRITE Output to the Printer

The list lines from a report produced with WRITE are output to the screen in online processing. In background processing, they are rerouted to the specified printer. Only the lines for the basic list can be printed. Drill-down lists are reserved for interactive reporting.

In particular during the test phase, paper print-outs are often not wanted. In this case, it can be useful not to specify a printer but to read the basic list using READ LINE and then place it completely in the job log.

10.1.4 Reroute MESSAGE Output to the Job Log

The report messages produced with MESSAGE are written into the job log in background processing. Messages from the job control are also written into the job log. An E-level message at program or form level terminates the step.

10.2 Interactive Processing with the Job Control

10.2.1 Create and Change of a Job

Jobs are created from the *System/Services/Jobs/Define Jobs* menu item or with the SM36 transaction (Figure 10.2).

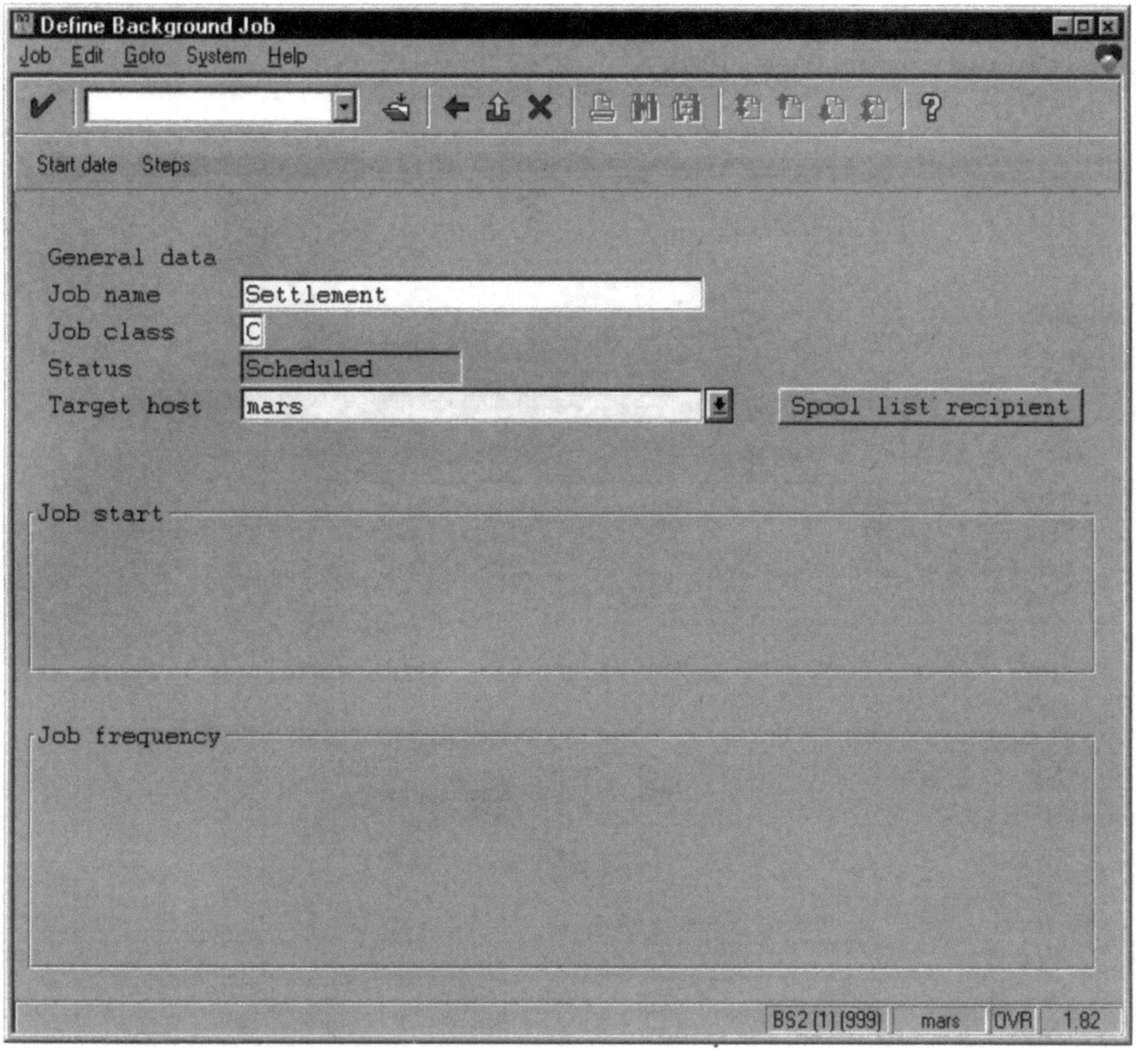

Figure 10.2: Definition of background jobs

The jobname is not a key identifier for a job. Several different jobs can run with the same name. The jobclass represents a priority, "A" indicates the highest priority, "C" indicates the lowest priority. User jobs are normally assigned jobclass "C".

The target computer of the job is an application server available in the associated R/3 system. If the job uses just the database of the system, there is no reason to specify a specific target computer. It is better to allow the system to find a suitable server and so achieve workload balancing. The target computer should be specified only when the report requires server-specific resources (e.g., the file system). Similarly, you can at runtime determine in the report from SY-HOST the server on which the program is running.

The *Steps* key can be used to create the program steps of the job. These can be ABAP/4 reports or external programs (Figure 10.3).

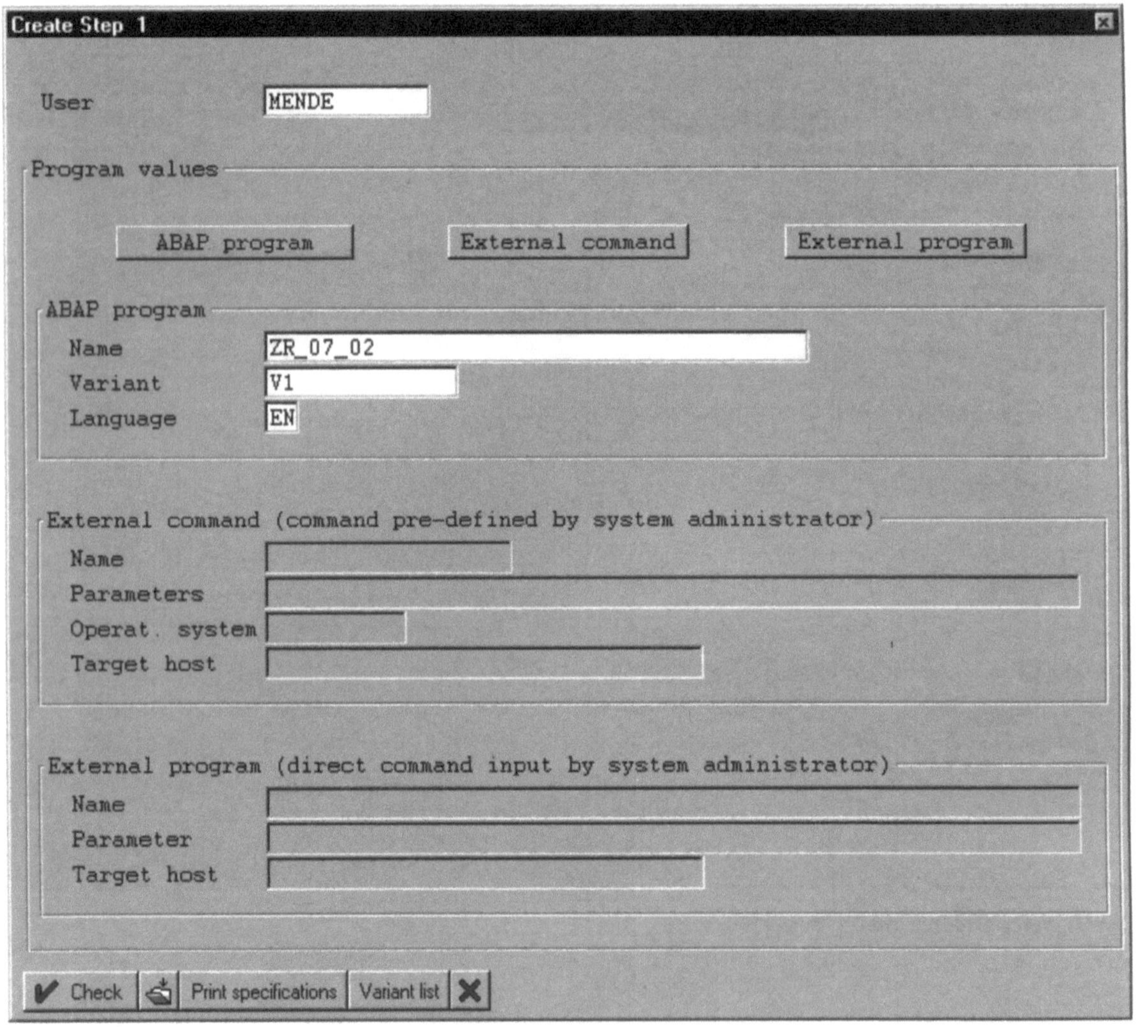

Figure 10.3: Create a step (program) for a batch job

The *Start Date* pushbutton is used to formulate the condition for the start of the job. The following variants are possible:

- *Start time controlled:*
  - immediately
  - start date (date and time, optionally repetition period)
  - start date in the company calendar (calendar, day in month, period)

- *Start job controlled:* A preceding job is specified. The job should start when this predecessor job ends. The start of the new job can also be made dependent on the status of the preceding job.
- *Start event controlled:* A job can start when a specific event occurs.
- *Start operation mode controlled:* The job should run only for specific operating modes.

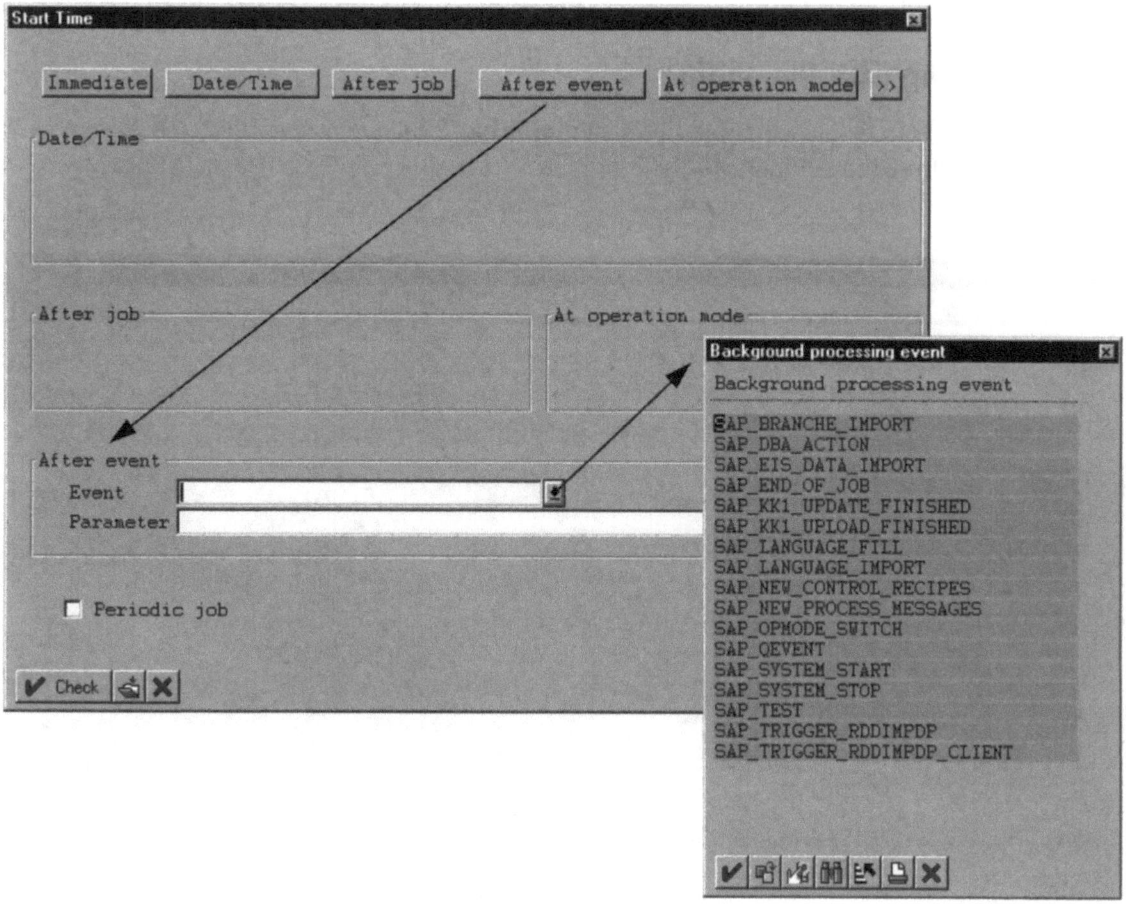

Figure 10.4: Specification of the "after event" start conditions

The appropriate variant must be specified for ABAP/4 reports with parameters. If a job consists of several steps, these are processed in sequence. *Start Date* can be used to specify various conditions for the start of a report. The following variants are possible:

- *Date and time:* A future date and time can be specified. The job will be released for processing at this time.
- *Preceding job:* The specification of a preceding job permits sequences of jobs to be processed. A distinction is made whether the preceding job was canceled or completed without error.

- *Event:* An initiating event can be specified here (Figure 10.4). SAP_* events are predefined and are initiated appropriately from the system. New events from Release 3.0 are defined within Workflow. They can be initiated from within R/3 using the BP_EVENT_RAISE function module.
- *Operation mode:* A job is started automatically when the operating mode changes.
- *Company calendar:* A company calendar can be specified in addition to the period. This variant is useful for the period execution of batch processes.

10.2.2 Working with the Joblist

The joblist is used to display the jobs. It is started using *System/Services/Jobs/Job overview* or with the SM37 transaction (Figure 10.5).

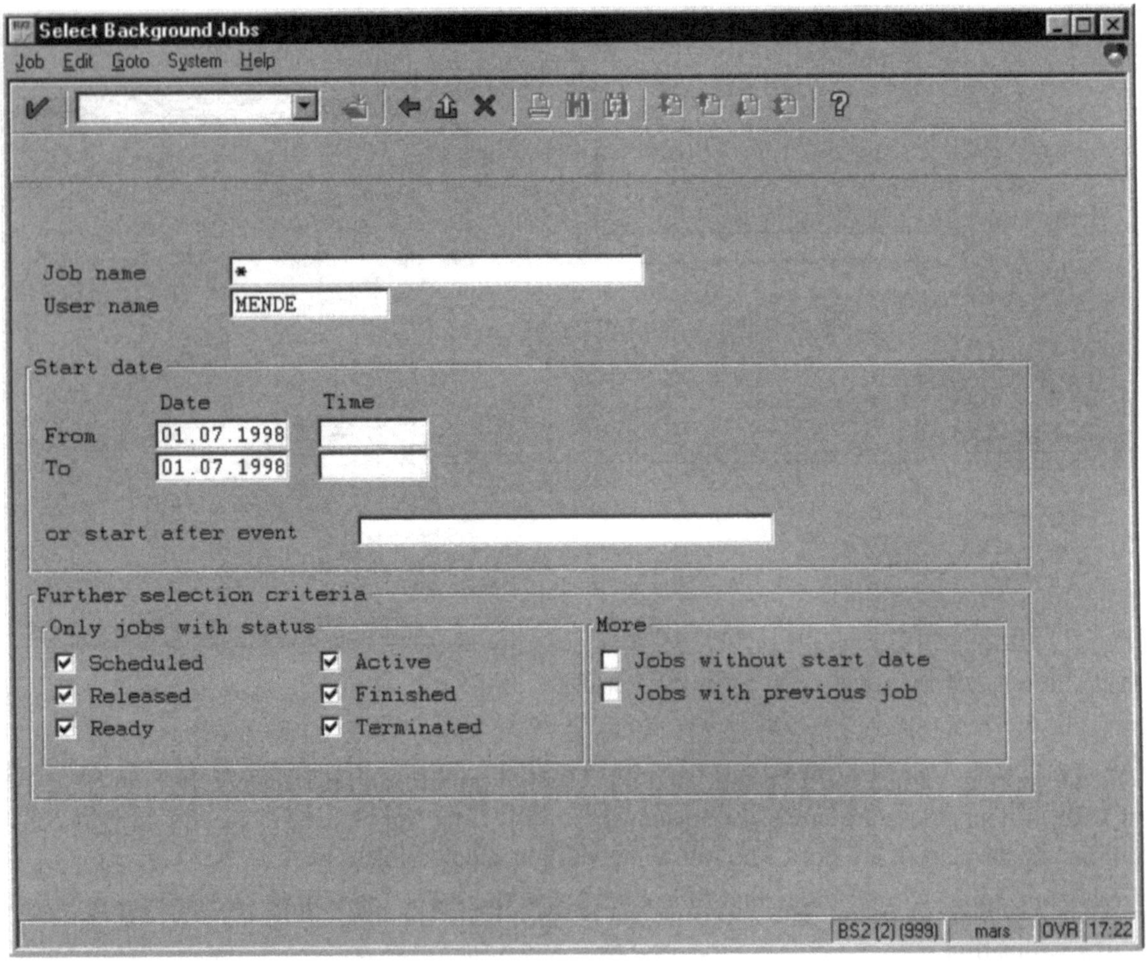

Figure 10.5: Initial form of the joblist

The figure contains various selection criteria for jobs. In particular, it shows six different states that a job can adopt :

- *Scheduled:* The job has been defined (start time, steps, etc.) and saved but reset. In this job status, because the job has not been released, the job is *not* started when the start time is reached.
- *Released:* The job has been released for processing. The job receives the *ready* status when the start time is reached. *Job/Planning/Reset* may have been used previously to set the status to planned.
- *Ready:* The job awaits execution. The user can no longer change its status.
- *Active:* The job is running.
- *Finished:* The job completed successfully.
- *Terminated:* A program step of the jobs was terminated with MESSAGE Ennn or with a system error.

Figure 10.6 contains the transition diagram for the job states. The job is set into the *released* state when it is saved.

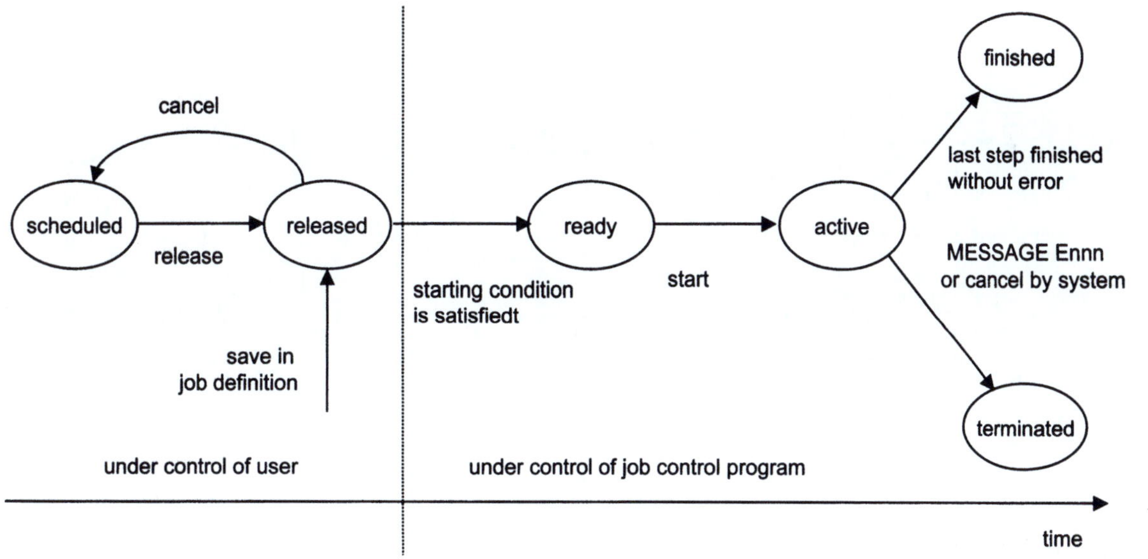

Figure 10.6: Transition diagram for the states of a background job

The job is under user control during the first two states. As soon as the job has attained the *ready* state, it can no longer by reset by the user but can only be canceled.

The actual job overview appears once the job has been localized (Figure 10.7). *Update* can be used to refresh the display. The *Job* menu permits various actions depending on the job status, for example:

- reset
- release
- repeat
- copy
- change
- cancel.

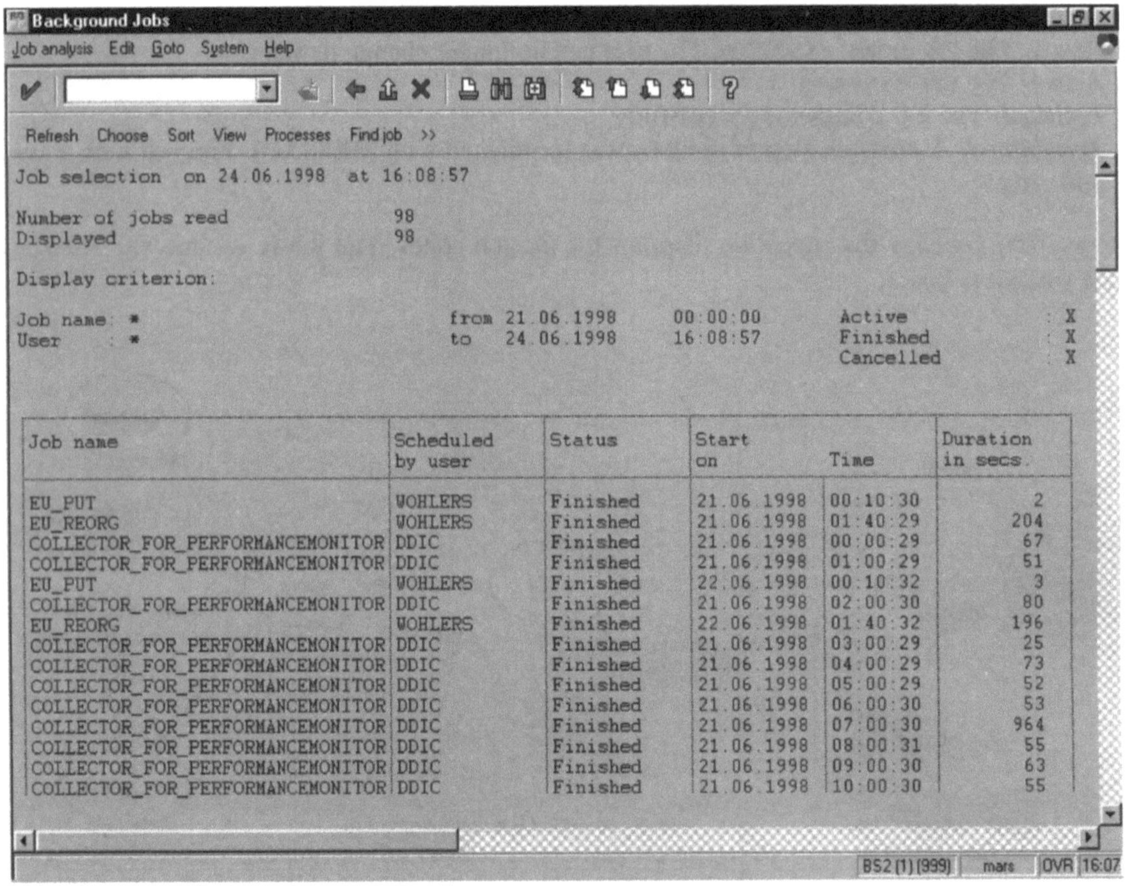

Figure 10.7: Job overview with status display

A double-click on a completed or canceled job displays the associated log (Figure 10.8). Section 10.4.4 describes how to set the output list for a report in the job log. Section 10.4.5 shows how to read the job log into an internal table.

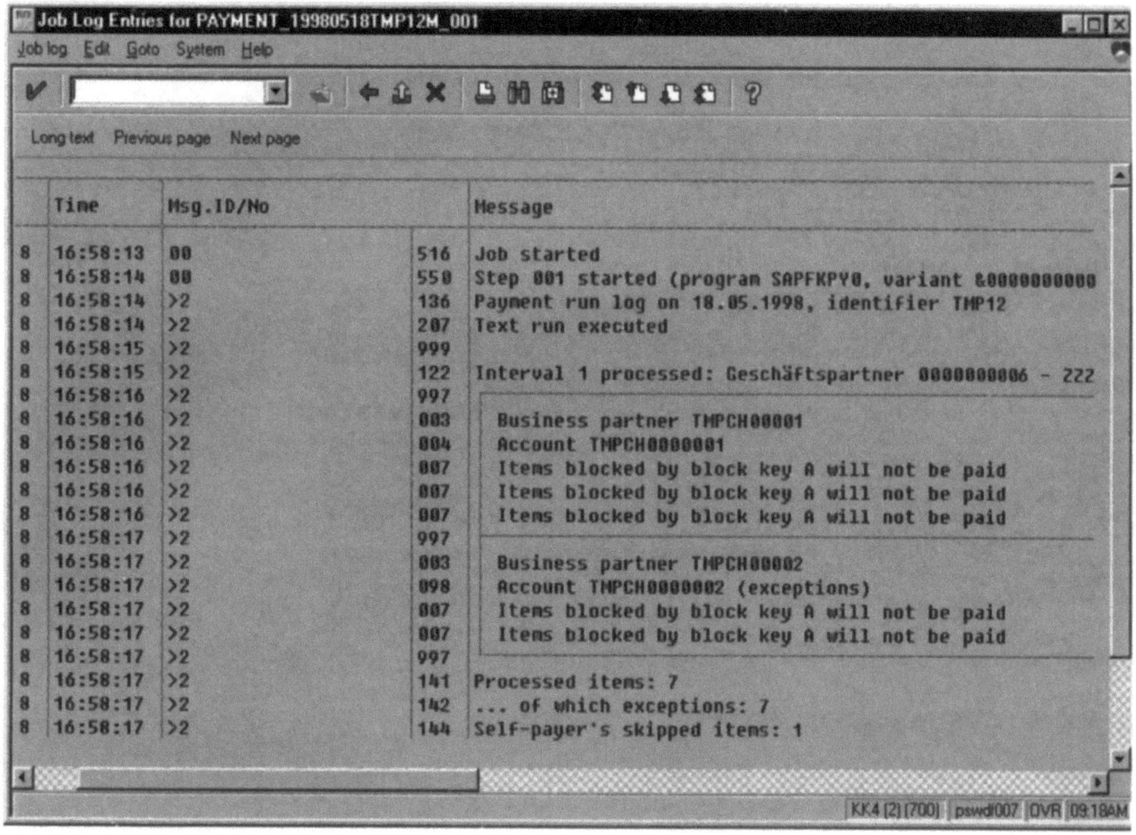

Figure 10.8: Display of a job log

10.3 Programming the Job Control – an Example

The ZR_10_01 program shows how JOB_OPEN is used to create a job. JOBCOUNT is the result. SUBMIT ... VIA JOB is then used to define the ZR_07_02 report as the only program step of the job. The passed parameters or selection options are stored automatically in a variant. This starts with "&". The actual start conditions are passed at JOB_CLOSE. The program permits an immediate start or start at a specified time.

```
REPORT ZR_10_01 MESSAGE-ID Y0 LINE-SIZE 70.

TABLES: SSCRFIELDS, YKONTO.
DATA    ACTION LIKE SSCRFIELDS-UCOMM.
DATA    ACCNO LIKE ZACCOUNT-ACCNO.
CONSTANTS NO_TIME LIKE SY-UZEIT VALUE '
```

```
*---------------------------------------------------------------------
SELECT-OPTIONS:
    SO_ANO FOR ACCNO DEFAULT '4000' TO '4010'.
PARAMETERS:
    P_SYSTEM(20) DEFAULT 'ds0015' LOWER CASE,
    P_STARTD LIKE SY-DATUM,
    P_STARTT LIKE SY-UZEIT,
    P_IMMED DEFAULT 'X'.
*---------------------------------------------------------------------
INITIALIZATION.
    P_STARTD = SY-DATUM.
    P_STARTT = SY-UZEIT + 20.       " Es geht in 20 Sekunden los
    P_SYSTEM = SY-HOST.             " Batch unbedingt auf diesem
Rechner
                                    " Rechner starten
*---------------------------------------------------------------------
START-OF-SELECTION.
IF P_IMMED = 'X'.
  " Creating and immediately starting batch job for report ZR_07_02
  PERFORM  SUBMIT_REPORT_VIA_JOB USING 'X'.
ELSE.
  " Create and schedule batch job for report ZR_07_02
  PERFORM  SUBMIT_REPORT_VIA_JOB USING SPACE.
ENDIF.

SET SCREEN 0. LEAVE SCREEN.

*---------------------------------------------------------------------
FORM SUBMIT_REPORT_VIA_JOB USING IMMED_KZ.
DATA STARTDATE LIKE SY-DATUM.
DATA STARTTIME LIKE SY-UZEIT.
DATA JOBNAME(32).
DATA JOBCOUNT LIKE TBTCJOB-JOBCOUNT.

* create jon name
CONCATENATE 'ZR_07_02/' SY-DATUM '/' SY-UZEIT INTO JOBNAME.

* create new job
CALL FUNCTION 'JOB_OPEN' EXPORTING  JOBGROUP  = ' '
                                    JOBNAME   = JOBNAME
                         IMPORTING  JOBCOUNT  = JOBCOUNT
                         EXCEPTIONS ALREADY_LOCKED     = 1
                                    JOBCOUNT_CANTGEN   = 2
                                    JOBGROUP_MISSING   = 3
                                    JOBNAME_MISSING    = 4
                                    LOCK_FAILED        = 5
                                    OLD_DATABASE       = 6
                                    PLAN_NOAUTH        = 7
                                    START_PAST         = 8
                                    OTHERS             = 99.
 IF SY-SUBRC > 0.
   MESSAGE S011 WITH SY-SUBRC JOBNAME.
   EXIT.
 ENDIF.
```

```
SUBMIT ('ZR_07_02') TO SAP-SPOOL WITHOUT SPOOL DYNPRO
                DESTINATION 'MUP1'
                IMMEDIATELY 'X'
                KEEP IN SPOOL ' '
                SAP COVER PAGE ' '
                USER SY-UNAME
                VIA JOB JOBNAME NUMBER JOBCOUNT
                WITH SO_ANO IN SO_ANO
                AND RETURN.
IF SY-SUBRC > 0.
  MESSAGE E012 WITH SY-SUBRC 'ZR-07-02'.
  EXIT.
ENDIF.

* Job is scheduled and released
STARTDATE  = P_STARTD.
STARTTIME  = P_STARTT.
IF IMMED_KZ = 'X'.
CALL FUNCTION 'JOB_CLOSE' EXPORTING JOBCOUNT     = JOBCOUNT
                                    JOBNAME      = JOBNAME
                                    STRTIMMED    = 'X'
                                    TARGETSYSTEM = P_SYSTEM
                          EXCEPTIONS ALREADY_LOCKED     = 1
                                     JOBCOUNT_CANTGEN   = 2
                                     JOBGROUP_MISSING   = 3
                                     JOBNAME_MISSING    = 4
                                     LOCK_FAILED        = 5
                                     OLD_DATABASE       = 6
                                     PLAN_NOAUTH        = 7
                                     START_PAST         = 8
                                     CANT_START_IMMEDIATE = 9
                                     JOB_CLOSE_FAILED   = 10
                                     OTHERS             = 99.
  IF SY-SUBRC GT 0.
    MESSAGE E013 WITH SY-SUBRC JOBNAME.
  ELSE.
    MESSAGE S014 WITH 'ZR_07_02' JOBNAME.
  ENDIF.
ELSE.
CALL FUNCTION 'JOB_CLOSE' EXPORTING JOBCOUNT     = JOBCOUNT
                                    JOBNAME      = JOBNAME
                                    SDLSTRTDT    = STARTDATE
                                    SDLSTRTTM    = STARTTIME
                                    TARGETSYSTEM = P_SYSTEM
                          EXCEPTIONS ALREADY_LOCKED     = 1
                                     JOBCOUNT_CANTGEN   = 2
                                     JOBGROUP_MISSING   = 3
                                     JOBNAME_MISSING    = 4
                                     LOCK_FAILED        = 5
                                     OLD_DATABASE       = 6
                                     PLAN_NOAUTH        = 7
                                     START_PAST         = 8
                                     CANT_START_IMMEDIATE = 9
```

```
                                        JOB CLOSE FAILED      = 10
                                        OTHERS                = 99.
  IF SY-SUBRC GT 0.
    MESSAGE E015 WITH SY-SUBRC JOBNAME.
  ELSE.
    MESSAGE S016 WITH 'ZR_07_02' JOBNAME.
  ENDIF.
ENDIF.
ENDFORM.
*---------------------------------------------------------------
```

10.4 Special Questions Concerning the Background Processing

10.4.1 Workload Balancing

If possible, no target computer should be specified. In this case the system can itself determine the target computer and so achieve a load balancing between the various application servers. The target computer should be specified only when special resources (e.g., the file system) of a specific server are required.

10.4.2 Parallel Background Processing

If large data volumes are to be processed in batch, it can be appropriate to run the batch in parallel on several application servers. An example is the accounting run for a large insurance company. Such an accounting run updates the due items for all associated insurance accounts. Prerequisite for a parallel operation is that the available work (the number of accounts) can be usefully divided into intervals, which then can be processed on multiple servers. Figure 10.9 illustrates the principle.

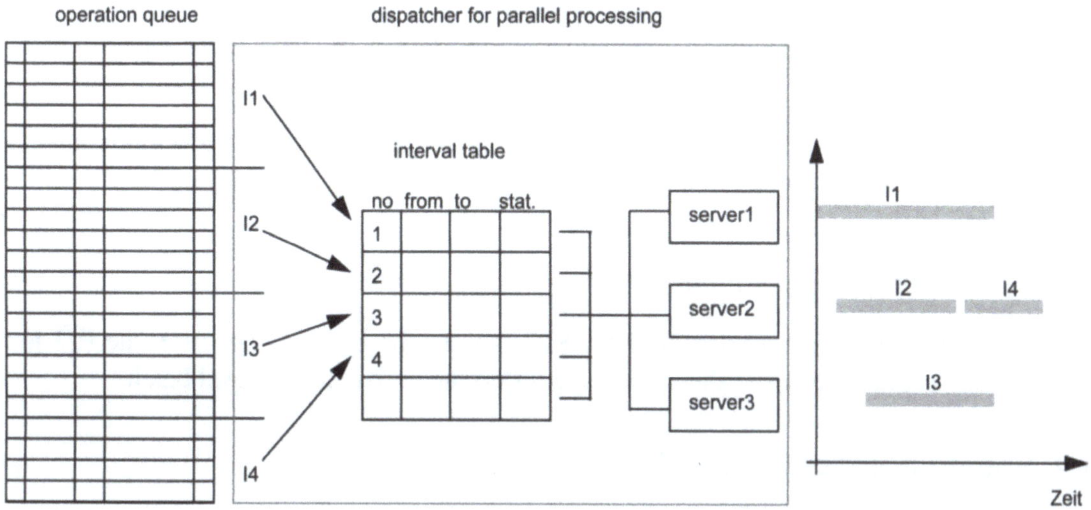

Figure 10.9: Parallelization of a batch job by interval assignment of the available work

A dispatcher program assigns the available work into intervals of the same general size so that all records are processed just once. The interval assignment is written into a table before the start of the parallel run. This table also maintains the processing status for each interval. The dispatcher starts the same batch on each available server. The dispatcher contains a report with the following general processing structure:

```
DO.
  PERFORM READ INTERVALL USING NO FROM UNTIL RETCODE.
  IF RETCODE > 0 EXIT. ENDIF.
  PERFORM PROCESS INTERVALL USING FROM UNTIL.
  PERFORM CLOSE_INTERVALL USING NO.
ENDDO.
PERFORM LIGHT_OFF.
```

The parallel-running jobs request the individual intervals still awaiting processing and locks them for others. The data of the interval are then processed. Finally, the interval is marked as *ready* and is unlocked. To obtain information on the end of the parallel run, each job can use the status field in the interval table to determine whether it processed the last interval or whether all other intervals have already been processed.

10.4.3 Integration in the External Workflow

In the heterogeneous computer worlds typical nowadays, workflow or batch processes that access external systems represent a challenge. Two questions arise in conjunction with R/3 batch processes that run within a higher-level batch control:

- How can an R/3 batch job be started externally?
- How can an R/3 batch job supply a completion or cancellation message to the external environment?

The sapevt program that runs on an application server can initiate an event that starts an R/3 batch job. The program has the following call syntax:

sapevt *event*
[–p *parameter*] [–t] [–pf = *profile*] [name = *SAPID* nr = *instance*]

A detailed description is contained in [Will]. CPIC can also be used to start from the R/3 job control external programs that pass the appropriate information to a higher-level batch.

10.4.4 Setting a Report List in the Job Log

As described in Chapter 7, a report can at any time read the list it created . The following form performs this and uses a message of the type "S" to set the read list lines in the job log:

```
FORM LIST_TO_JOBLOG USING VALUE(class) VALUE(NUMBER).
DATA: S1(72), S2(72), Z.
DATA: L TYPE I, O TYPE I.
CHECK SY-BATCH = 'X'.
  DO.
    READ LINE SY-INDEX.
    IF SY-SUBRC = 0.
      L = STRLEN( SY-LISEL ).
      IF L < 40.
        MESSAGE ID CLASS TYPE 'S' NUMBER NUMBER WITH SY-LISEL.
      ELSE. " division of parameter
        O = 40.
        DO.
          Z = SY-LISEL+O(1).
          O = O + 1.
          IF Z <> ' '. EXIT. ENDIF.
        ENDDO.
        S1 = SY-LISEL(O).
        L = L - O.
        S2 = SY-LISEL+O(L).
        MESSAGE ID KLASSE TYPE 'S' NUMBER NUMBER WITH S1 S2.
      ENDIF.
    ELSE.
      EXIT.
    ENDIF.
  ENDDO.
ENDFORM.
```

The associated message must have been created before the form is called. Because the placeholder variables SY-MSGVn are only 50 character long, the SY-LISEL line may need to be divided into two parts. Consequently, two placeholders must be provided in the message. If required, an indentation can be performed (> _ _ &_&). A blank must separate the two placeholders, otherwise they would together be interpreted as an '&'. With a certain amount of effort, it would also be possible to suppress the blank characters that occur at the peer.

10.4.5 Reading the Job Log

The BP_JOBLOG_READ function module can be used to read the job log into an internal table where it can be further processed (download). This requires that both the job name and the job count are known. If the job count is not known, an appropriate SELECT can be used to determined it from the TBTCO table. The example shows the log for report ZR_06_01 that was started in background, however, its outputs are rerouted to the log as described above. The additional blank character can be seen at position 40.

```
REPORT  ZR_10_02 LINE-SIZE 70.
TABLES: TBTCO.
DATA:   LOGTAB LIKE TBTC5 OCCURS 20 WITH HEADER LINE.
SELECT * FROM TBTCO WHERE JOBNAME = 'ZR_06_21'.
* EXIT.
ENDSELECT.
IF SY-DBCNT > 0.
  CALL FUNCTION 'BP_JOBLOG_READ'
     EXPORTING
          CLIENT                    = SY-MANDT
          JOBCOUNT                  = TBTCO-JOBCOUNT
*         JOBLOG                    = ' '
          JOBNAME                   = 'ZR_06_21'
     TABLES
          JOBLOGTBL                 = LOGTAB
     EXCEPTIONS
          CANT_READ_JOBLOG          = 1
          JOBCOUNT_MISSING          = 2
          JOBLOG_DOES_NOT_EXIST     = 3
          JOBLOG_IS_EMPTY           = 4
          JOBLOG_NAME_MISSING       = 5
          JOBNAME_MISSING           = 6
          JOB_DOES_NOT_EXIST        = 7
          OTHERS                    = 8.

ENDIF.
LOOP AT LOGTAB.
  WRITE / LOGTAB-TEXT.
ENDLOOP.
```

```
Job started
Step 001 started (program ZR_06_21, variant , user name HANSEN)
>  15.06.98 Chapter  6: Selection of all par tners with ZIP-Code =
>  ----------------------------------- ----------------------
>     1 Mr          Frank      Black       9240 7 San Bernadino    0000
>     2 Mrs Dr.     Jane       Black       9240 7 San Bernadino    0000
>     3 Mrs         Wanda      Huesing     9301 3 Carpenteria      0000
>     4 Mr          John       Smith       9002 8 Santa Barbara    0000
>     5 Mr Dr.      Paul       Stone       9002 8 Hollywood        0000
>     6 Mrs         Sharon     Stone       9002 8 Hollywood        0000
>
>     Count of selected partners: 6
Job finished
```

11 File Interfaces

Large R/3 systems are frequently introduced to replace or supplement existing host systems. Here it is typical that large data quantities need to be sent to the new R/3 system either once (migration) or periodically. ABAP/4 is frequently used to develop such file interfaces.

11.1 Read and Write Files on the Application Server

ABAP/4 refers to sequential files on the application server as datasets. The most important ABAP/4 commands for datasets are:

OPEN DATASET *dataset.*
READ DATASET *dataset* **INTO** *field.*
TRANSFER *field* **TO** *dataset.*
CLOSE DATASET *dataset.*
DELETE DATASET *dataset*

Dataset is a file name that is valid in the operating system of the application server. It is assumed that this is UNIX. Note that the DATASET key word is missing from the TRANSFER command. Because this command is not used in other contexts, the key word is not required. All commands set SY-SUBRC.

0: OK = File has been opened, line has been read
4: End of file
8: File not opened

Datasets are often processed in batch. Note that a file system can be attached to a special application server. In such a case, this application server must be specified as the destination computer when the batch job is submitted.

11.1.1 Opening of Datasets

The command with its most commonly used options has the form:

OPEN DATASET *dataset*
    [FOR OUTPUT | FOR INPUT | FOR APPENDING]
    [IN BINARY MODE | IN TEXT MODE].

The default setting is always the first value in brackets. FOR OUTPUT opens a new file or overwrites an existing file. FOR APPENDING adds the output at the end of an existing file. FOR INPUT requires that the file exists. Binary mode transfers the bytes with the subsequent READ without interpretation, whereas text mode recognizes the line structure and removes line delimiters.

11.1.2 Read from Datasets

The command to read from a file that has been opened with OPEN DATASET has the form:

READ DATASET *dataset* **INTO** *field* [**LENGTH** *long*].

Bytes are read into the *field* field or field string. In binary mode, the number of bytes read is the same as the field length. In text mode, a line is read. The *long* field in both cases contains the number of bytes read.

11.1.3 Write in Datasets

The command to write to a file that has been opened with OPEN DATASET has the form:

TRANSFER *field* **TO** *dataset* [**LENGTH** *long*].

In binary mode, all the bytes contained in *field* are written into the file. In text mode, any trailing blank characters are suppressed and an end-of-line is added. The *long* field contains the number of characters to be output.

11.1.4 Close Datasets

The

CLOSE DATASET *dataset.*

command closes a file that was opened with OPEN DATASET.

11.1.5 Delete Datasets

The command to delete datasets on the application server has the form:

DELETE DATASET *dataset.*

11.2 Read and Write PC Files

The R/3 system reads and writes PC files for various purposes, for example,

- Upload or download ABAP/4 source code
- Save a report list.

ABAP/4 does not provide any specific commands for the development of tailored interfaces for the file system of the attached PCs. The appropriate function modules must be used here:

WS_UPLOAD	Read a PC file
WS_DOWNLOAD	Write a PC file

WS here indicates the workstation. In contrast to the DATASET commands, the WS-function-modules use internal tables as parameter. A command always processes a complete file. As with datasets, a differentiation is made between binary mode and text mode. Because it is possible that no workstation is active during the batch run, PC files can only be processed online.

11.2.1 Read a PC File

An example is used to show how a text file of the presentation server can be read into the ABAP/4 table ITAB and from there output linewise to the /tmp UNIX directory of the attached application server.

Text file:

```
Line 1<CR><LF>
<CR><LF>
<CR><LF>
Line 4, because lines 2 and 3 are empty <EOF>
```

```
REPORT  ZR_11_01 LINE-SIZE 70.
DATA: BEGIN OF ITAB OCCURS 10,
        LINE(72),
      END OF ITAB.
DATA DOSFILE  LIKE RLGRAP-FILENAME VALUE 'C:\TEMP\TEST.TXT'.
DATA UNIXFILE LIKE RLGRAP-FILENAME VALUE '/tmp/test.txt'.
DATA DOSBYTES  TYPE I VALUE 0.
DATA UNIXBYTES TYPE I VALUE 0.
DATA LINENBYTES TYPE I.
CALL FUNCTION 'WS_UPLOAD'
     EXPORTING
          FILENAME                = DOSFILE
     IMPORTING
          FILELENGTH              = DOSBYTES
     TABLES
```

```
        DATA_TAB                = ITAB
    EXCEPTIONS
        CONVERSION_ERROR        = 1
        FILE_OPEN_ERROR         = 2
        FILE_READ_ERROR         = 3
        INVALID_TABLE_WIDTH = 4
        INVALID_TYPE            = 5
        NO_BATCH                = 6
        UNKNOWN_ERROR           = 7
        OTHERS                  = 8.
OPEN DATASET UNIXFILE FOR OUTPUT IN TEXT MODE.
LOOP AT ITAB.
  TRANSFER ITAB-LINE TO UNIXFILE.
  UNIXBYTES = UNIXBYTES + STRLEN( ITAB-LINE ).
ENDLOOP.
CLOSE DATASET UNIXFILE.
WRITE: / 'DOS :', (3)DOSBYTES, 'Bytes read from', (20)DOSFILE.
WRITE: / 'UNIX:', (3)UNIXBYTES, 'Bytes transferred to',
                         (5)SY-HOST,'::', (20)UNIXFILE.
```

```
23.09.98 Chapter 11: Read a file from the workstation, output      1
----------------------------------------------------------------------
DOS : 51  Bytes read from C:\TEMP\TEST.TXT
UNIX: 45  Bytes transferred to sp2n0 :: /tmp/test.txt
```

WS_UPLOAD uses typed parameters for the file name. If a variable is used as parameter, this must be of the required type. The function module reports that 51 characters have been read; these are all characters including the line delimiter <CR> and <LF>, but excluding the end-of-file <EOF>. Only the sum of the line bytes is sent to UNIX, namely 3*2 = 6 bytes fewer. The SY-HOST system variable specifies the application server on which the report runs.

This program is useful in that it permits test data produced on the PC to be passed to the application server without requiring a specific transfer program.

11.2.2 Write a PC File

The following report reads a specified program into an internal table, adds a five-digit sequencing with 10 increments, and outputs the source code to a text file with the corresponding name.

```
REPORT  ZR_11_02 LINE-SIZE 70.
DATA: BEGIN OF ITAB OCCURS 10,
        LINE(72),
      END OF ITAB.
DATA REPORTNAME(10) VALUE 'ZR_11_04'.
DATA DOSFILE  LIKE RLGRAP-FILENAME.
DATA DOSFILETYPE  LIKE RLGRAP-FILETYPE VALUE 'ASC'.
DATA LINENO(5) TYPE N VALUE 0.
```

```
DATA DOSBYTES TYPE I.
CONCATENATE 'C:\BE\ABAP\' REPORTNAME(8) '.LST' INTO DOSFILE.
READ REPORT REPORTNAME INTO ITAB.
LOOP AT ITAB.
  ADD 10 TO LINENO.
  ITAB-LINE+6     = ITAB-LINE.
  ITAB-LINE(5)    = LINENO.
  ITAB-LINE+5(1)  = ' '.
  MODIFY ITAB.
ENDLOOP.
CALL FUNCTION 'WS_DOWNLOAD'
     EXPORTING
          FILENAME              = DOSFILE
          FILETYPE              = DOSFILETYPE
     IMPORTING
          FILELENGTH            = DOSBYTES
     TABLES
          DATA_TAB              = ITAB
     EXCEPTIONS
          FILE_OPEN_ERROR       = 1
          FILE_WRITE_ERROR      = 2
          INVALID_FILESIZE      = 3
          INVALID_TABLE_WIDTH   = 4
          INVALID_TYPE          = 5
          NO_BATCH              = 6
          UNKNOWN_ERROR         = 7
          OTHERS                = 8.
WRITE: / 'Report', REPORTNAME, 'written to file', (25)DOSFILE.
```

```
23.09.98 Chapter 11: Download of a report with line numbers          1
-------------------------------------------------------------------------
Report ZR_11_04    written to file C:\BE\ABAP\ZR_11_04.LST
```

This program can be used, for example, to make source code available for documentation.

11.3 Processing of the Data from an ASCII File

In practice, ASCII files are normally used as interface files. Because these transfer all data in external format, they provide good portability over system boundaries. Different line types and lengths are used to transfer different record structures. The readability of the data simplifies their manual checking.

Special problems normally arise with the data import of text files into the R/3 system. It must be assumed that even when the interface has been precisely defined, the data cannot be accepted from the read data lines into the ABAP fields without performing the required tests. These tests must initially exclude general errors that could cause a program failure. The attempt to read non-numeric values into numeric fields is such an example. Subsequent tests concern the contents of the imported data.

11.3.1 Split Lines into Individual Fields

Every line of an ASCII import file transfers a record having a specified structure. All structure elements are available in their own external (readable) form. Although a global assignment of the form "fieldarray = line" into an interface program does not cause a program failure, it produces incorrect results for packed decimal fields and binary fields.

Consequently, a read data line must be split into the fields corresponding to the assigned structure. The following program demonstrates the procedure for the PERSON structure that is defined internally in the program. The ASSIGN COMPONENT is used in a DO loop to assign the n-th component to the <field> field symbol. Its offset in the PERSON structure is computed using DESCRIBE DISTANCE BETWEEN. The target type results from DESCRIBE FIELD... TYPE and the external length from DESCRIBE FIELD ... OUTPUT-LENGTH.

```
REPORT  ZR_11_03 LINE-SIZE 70.
DATA: BEGIN OF PERSON,
         NAME(10),
         AGE(3) TYPE N,
         SALARY(7) TYPE P DECIMALS 2,
      END OF PERSON.
DATA: LINE(30) VALUE 'Smith      45  4.200,00'.
DATA: NO TYPE I, OFF TYPE I, LONG TYPE I, TYP(1).
DATA: TOKEN(30).
FIELD-SYMBOLS: <FIELD>.

PERSON = LINE. WRITE: / PERSON.
SKIP.
WRITE: / 'No', 8 'Type', 16 'Length', 34 'Token'.
DO 3 TIMES.
  ASSIGN COMPONENT SY-INDEX OF STRUCTURE PERSON TO <FIELD>.
  DESCRIBE DISTANCE BETWEEN <FIELD> AND PERSON-NAME INTO OFF.
  DESCRIBE FIELD <FIELD> OUTPUT-LENGTH LONG.
  DESCRIBE FIELD <FIELD> TYPE TYP.
  TOKEN = LINE+OFF(LONG).
  WRITE:  /(2) SY-INDEX UNDER 'No', TYP UNDER 'Type',
           (2) LONG UNDER 'Length', TOKEN UNDER 'Token'.
ENDDO.
```

```
18.06.98 Chapter 11: Split lines into single fields              1
--------------------------------------------------------------------
Smith      45  4.200,

No     Type    Length          Token
1      C       10              Smith
2      N       3               45
3      P       15                4.200,00
```

The n-th subfield of the line is extracted using an assignment with offset and length details. A test is then performed to determine whether the subfield can be assigned to the target type.

11.3.2 Convert Fields into the Internal Format

The requirement to convert input data is already known from dialog programs. At the PAI time, all dynpro fields are transformed from the external format into the internal ABAP/4 format using automatic field conversions. Checks are performed before the actual transformation during this INPUT conversion. For dialog programs, the user is requested to make a new entry if the input was incorrect (e.g., a non-numeric value in an amount field).

The same errors in the data can occur for file input as for the dialog case. Possible causes here are:

- The supplying system sends unexpected data or does not send the data in the correct sequence.
- Various factors have invalidated the data.
- The R/3 system has changed its interface without informing the supplying system.

It is generally possible to use the same routines from the dialog programming to check the data and to convert into the internal format.

Unfortunately, the conversion and check routines for the basic data types used in the field validations of the PAI cannot be invoked explicitly in ABAP/4. Consequently, user-routines must be used to convert the individual data types.

- *Datatype C*: Validation and conversion routines are not required here.
- *Datatype N*: A validation is required using the following code

```
L = STRLEN( Token ).
IF Token CO '0123456789'. ENDIF.
IF SY-FDPOS >= L.
* OK
ELSE.
* Error
ENDIF.
```

The usual conversion exit CONVERSION_EXIT_NUMCV_INPUT can also be invoked.

- *Datatype D*: German installations normally use DD.MM.YYYY as external format. This must be transformed to the internal form YYYYMMDD. CONVERSION_EXIT_SDATE_INPUT should be used for this conversion. This conversion exit tests the input and performs the conversion if the test was successful.
- *Datatype P*: The following form shows a possible C-P conversion for strings that contain the '+-0123456789,' characters. The sign can be prefixed or suffixed but cannot occur more than once. A comma represents the decimal delimiter; it also cannot occur more than once. Alphabetic letters and other characters set the return code.

```
FORM C2P USING STR TYPE C X TYPE P RC LIKE SY-SUBRC.
DATA S(50) .
DATA L LIKE SY-INDEX.
DATA VZ.

X = '0.0'.
S = STR.

SHIFT S LEFT DELETING LEADING SPACE.
L = STRLEN( S ).
IF NOT ( S CO '0123456789+-,' ).
  IF SY-FDPOS < L. RC = 1. EXIT. ENDIF.
ENDIF.
* There are only integers of 00123456789+-

* Decimal sign is allowed only once
REPLACE ',' WITH '.' INTO S.
IF SY-SUBRC = 0.  " 1st occurrence --> OK
  SEARCH S FOR ','.
  IF SY-SUBRC = 0.    " 2nd occurrence --> Error
    RC = 1. EXIT.
  ENDIF.
ENDIF.

* '-'-symbol is only allowed at the beginning
L = STRLEN( S ) - 1.
SEARCH S FOR '-'.
IF SY-SUBRC = 0.  " minus sign exists
  IF NOT ( SY-FDPOS = 0 OR SY-FDPOS = L ).
    RC = 1. EXIT.
  ENDIF.
  REPLACE '-' WITH SPACE INTO S.  " cancel minus sign
  VZ = '-'.
  SEARCH S FOR '-'.
  IF SY-SUBRC = 0. RC = 1. EXIT. ENDIF.
  SEARCH S FOR '+'.
  IF SY-SUBRC = 0. RC = 1. EXIT. ENDIF.
ELSE.             " no minus sign
* '+'-sign is only allowed to appear at the end or at the start
  SEARCH S FOR '+'.
```

```
    IF SY-SUBRC = 0.   " plus sign existed
      IF NOT ( SY-FDPOS = 0 OR SY-FDPOS = L ).
        RC = 1. EXIT.
      ENDIF.
      REPLACE '+' WITH SPACE INTO S.
      VZ = '+'.
      SEARCH S FOR '+'.
      IF SY-SUBRC = 0. RC = 1. EXIT. ENDIF.
    ENDIF.
  ENDIF.
  RC = 0.
  X = S.
  ENDFORM.
```

11.3.3 Plausibility Test of the Data

Plausibility tests on the data assume successfully converted and filled ABAP/4 fields. They test

- whether accumulator values belong to the value range
- the value ranges for numeric fields and data fields

In addition to tests of individual fields, field combinations can be tested. The requirement to test a field using an associated control table occurs frequently. Two extreme cases are conceivable to solve this problem:

- Preload all entries from the control table into an internal table that READ TABLE *table* WITH KEY reads for every validation. This method avoids having to read records from the database, but may read records from the database that are not required. This method is appropriate for control tables that have few records.
- Validate every incoming field value using SELECT SINGLE to read from the database table. This method may read the same record many times. It is appropriate for small data volumes.

A combined method is best for large data volumes and control tables that contain many entries. The records read from the database table are buffered in an internal table. The validation initially searches for the record in the internal table. The validation is positive if it is found. If the record is not found, a search for the corresponding record is made in the database table. The validation is positive if it is found there. The record in this case is added to the internal table using APPEND. A subsequent occurrence of the value finds the entry in the internal table.

The following program demonstrates this buffering using the example of the ZPSTKY customizing table. All booking reasons to be tested using this table are created in the interval 1 .. 9 with the random number function RANDOM_I2. Five attempts are made with the value counts 5, 10, 100, 1 000 and 10 000. The log shows that a saving results compared to read the complete table when the number of values to be tested is of the same order of magnitude as the number of entries in the validation table. If it is to be expected that all values of the control table are required, it is better to read these using SELECT ... INTO TABLE.

```
REPORT  ZR_11_05 LINE-SIZE 70.
TABLES: ZPOSTKEY.

DATA:   BEGIN OF SIMULA OCCURS 5,
          COUNT TYPE I,
          DBCOUNT TYPE I,
          ITABCOUNT TYPE I,
        END OF SIMULA.

DATA:   POSTKEYTAB LIKE ZPOSTKEY OCCURS 20 WITH HEADER LINE.
DATA:   PSTKY LIKE ZPOSTKEY-PSTKY.
DATA:   RNDVALUE LIKE DATATYPE-INTEGER2.

CLEAR SIMULA.
SIMULA-COUNT =     5. APPEND SIMULA.
SIMULA-COUNT =    10. APPEND SIMULA.
SIMULA-COUNT =   100. APPEND SIMULA.
SIMULA-COUNT =  1000. APPEND SIMULA.
SIMULA-COUNT = 10000. APPEND SIMULA.

WRITE: / 'Count',  15'Database hits', 30'Internal hits'.
LOOP AT SIMULA.
  CLEAR POSTKEYTAB. REFRESH POSTKEYTAB.
  DO SIMULA-COUNT TIMES.
    CALL FUNCTION 'RANDOM_I2'
         EXPORTING
              RND_MIN    = 1
              RND_MAX    = 9
         IMPORTING
              RND_VALUE = RNDVALUE
         EXCEPTIONS
              OTHERS     = 1.
    PSTKY = RNDVALUE.
    READ TABLE POSTKEYTAB WITH KEY PSTKY = PSTKY.
    IF SY-SUBRC > 0.
      SELECT SINGLE * FROM ZPOSTKEY WHERE PSTKY = PSTKY.
      IF SY-SUBRC = 0.
        ADD 1 TO SIMULA-DBCOUNT.
        APPEND ZPOSTKEY TO POSTKEYTAB.
      ENDIF.
    ELSE.
      ADD 1 TO SIMULA-ITABCOUNT.
    ENDIF.
  ENDDO.
  WRITE: /(7) SIMULA-COUNT, 15(5) SIMULA-DBCOUNT,
          30(7) SIMULA-ITABCOUNT.
ENDLOOP.
```

```
Count          Database hits  Internal hits
     5              5             0
    10              7             3
   100              9            91
 1.000              9           991
10.000              9         9.991
```

11.4 Logical File Interfaces (LFI)

In exactly the same way as for logical databases, a division can be made between obtaining the data (database program) and the data processing (processing program) in the development of file interface for the data import. This section shows the integration in the database program for the file interface of the functions described in Section 11.3.

- Open file
- Read file
- Split file lines
- Perform conversion tests
- Close file.

The report that automatically creates the database program as a logical database-defined file interface is of particular interest.

The sample data from Chapter 3 taken from an ASCII file should be used as example. The file should have the following general structure:

```
ZINS       Start of File
ZMASTER    Start of Master Data
ZACCOUNT   1  400020  P
ZACCOUNT   1  400030  P
ZACCOUNT   1  400040  PX
ZACCOUNT   1  400050  K
ZPRODUCT   1  705      SV   KV car fully-comprehensive insured, V4
ZPRODUCT   1  706      SV   KV car fully-comprehensive insured, V6
ZPRODUCT   1  723      SV   KV car fully-comprehensive insured, V12
ZCONTRACT  1  60600    400010  706      1000200119960723  20060712
ZCONTRACT  1  60700    400070  802      1000200519960723  20060712
ZCONTRACT  1  60800    400080  804      1000200619960723  20060712
ZCONTRACT  1  60900    400090  803      1000200719960723  20060712
ZCONTRACT  1  70100    400100  701      1000200819960723  20060712
ZPOST      Start of Posting Datas
ZDOCHD     1  642010001   EP   DEM  19960824  Booking text
ZDOCITEM   1  642010001  400010  60100   UMB  10          Postext
ZDOCITEM   1  642010002  400010  60100   UMB  20          Postext
ZDOCITEM   1  642010003  400010  60100   UMB  30          Postext
```

```
ZDOCHD     1  642010011   EP    DEM  19960824  Booking text
ZDOCITEM   1  642010011  400020  60200    UMB  100              Postext
ZDOCITEM   1  642010012  400020  60200    UMB  200              Postext
```

A line identification of fixed length (here 10) specifies the structure of the associated line. The sequence in which the various line types can occur in the file is defined. The master data, identified with the ZMASTER control line, are transferred first. The transaction data (ZPOST) then follow. The transaction data (documents) should be entered as a heading line (ZDOCHD) followed by an arbitrary number of item lines (ZDOCITEM).

In an ideal situation, the associated processing program should also be built as a logical database, i.e., it should always contain the GET events for the line structures present in the line structures.

```
REPORT XYZ.
TABLES: ZINS, ZMASTER, ZPARTNER, ZACCOUNT, ZPRODUCT, ZCONTRACT,
        ZPOST, ZDOCHD, ZDOCITEM
GET ZPARTNER.        " partner-master-data read - MODIFY DB
GET ZACCOUNT.        " account-master-data read - MODIFY DB
GET ZMASTER LATE.    " end of master-data
GET ZDOCHD.          " header book position - note
GET ZDOCITEM.        " open items book position document
GET ZDOCHD LATE.     " document read totally, plausibility check
GET ZPOST LATE.      " end of temporary data
GET ZINS LATE.       " end of data transfer
```

11.4.1 Data and File Structure of a LFI in the Data Dictionary

It must first be determined which types of data records (line formats) are to be transferred to the file, and in which sequence. Of the nine different line structures used in the above example, only six transfer user data. These are the line types: ZPARTNER, ZACCOUNT, ZPRODUCT, ZCONTRACT, ZDOCHD and ZDOCITEM. These line types correspond to the tables created in the Data Dictionary. The other line types (ZINS, ZMASTER and ZPOST) are used only for the file structuring and to control the read process. They are stored as structures in the Data Dictionary.

The logical database ZDS created in the DDIC contains the defined line structures in a tree structure. This tree structure must represent the sequence of the lines in the interface file (Figure 11.1).

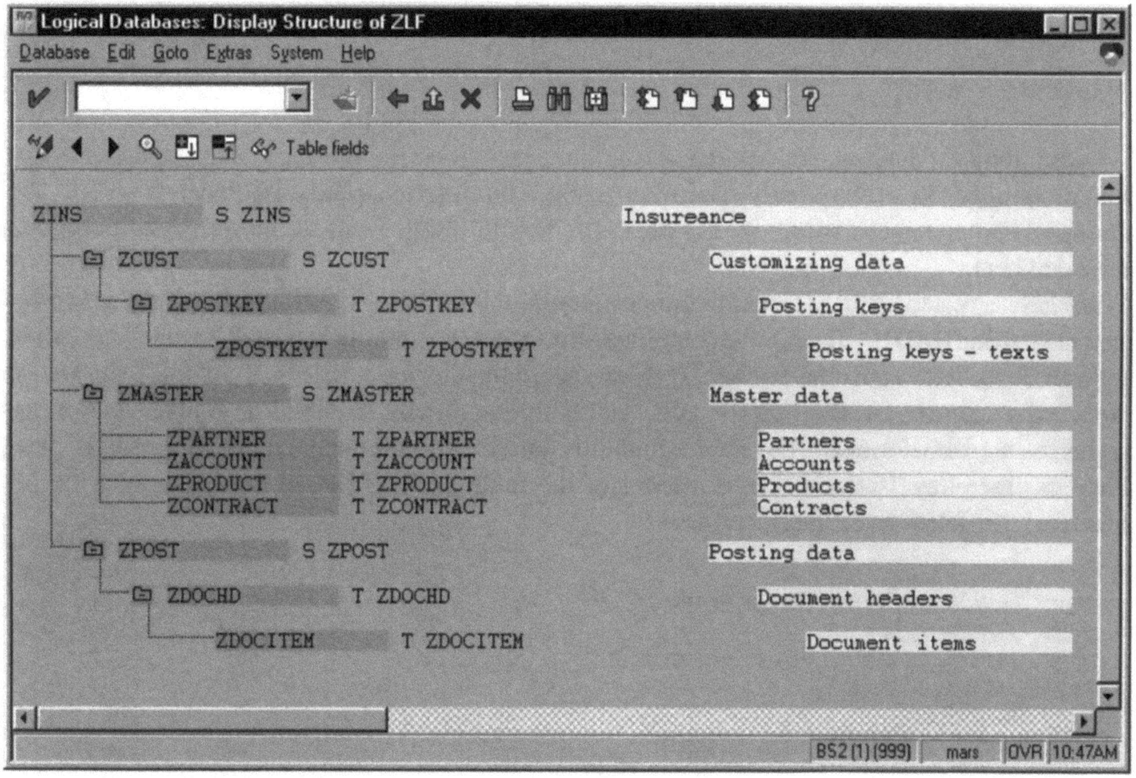

Figure 11.1: ZDS logical file interface

11.4.2 Database Program for the File Interface

The database program for the ZDS logical file interface is described using the SAPDBZDS program as example. The TABLES declaration must contain all structures and tables of the assigned logical ZDS database. The DDIC tables DD01L, DD03L and DD04L are included to receive information on the table and structure fields at runtime:

```
TABLES:     DD01L, DD03L, DD04L,
            ZINS,
            ZCUST,
            ZPSTKY,
            ZPSTKYT,
            ZMASTER,
            ZPARTNER,
            ZACCOUNT,
            ZPRODUCT,
            ZCONTRACT,
            ZPOST,
```

```
          ZDOCHD,
          ZDOCITEM.
```

As with a logical database, the database program of a logical file interface consists just of forms that are invoked from the primary control program. The first function is BEFORE_EVENT. The actions to be performed before the START–OF–SELECTION event of the processing program are coded here.

Initially, a nested SELECT reads into an internal table FIELDTAB all tables and structures for ZDS from DD03L. Because the interface file transfers data in external format, the output lengths of the fields must be known. They are determined using a SELECT SINGLE for the assigned data element in the DD04L table and a further SELECT SINGLE for the domain assigned to the data element. The internal table is sorted into table name and field position order after this three-level select. The sequence of the fields in FIELDTAB corresponds to the sequence of the fields in the interface lines.

```
FORM BEFORE_EVENT USING EVENT.
DATA BYTES TYPE I.
DATA FNAME LIKE RLGRAP-FILENAME.
FNAME = FILENAME.
  CASE EVENT.
    WHEN 'START-OF-SELECTION'.
       SELECT * FROM DD03L WHERE
         AS4LOCAL = 'A' AND
         FIELDNAME NE '.INCLUDE' AND (
         TABNAME = 'ZINS' OR
         TABNAME = 'ZCUST' OR
         TABNAME = 'ZPSTKY' OR
         TABNAME = 'ZPSTKYT' OR
         TABNAME = 'ZMASTER' OR
         TABNAME = 'ZPARTNER' OR
         TABNAME = 'ZACCOUNT' OR
         TABNAME = 'ZPRODUCT' OR
         TABNAME = 'ZCONTRACT' OR
         TABNAME = 'ZPOST' OR
         TABNAME = 'ZDOCHD' OR
         TABNAME = 'ZDOCITEM' ) .
         MOVE-CORRESPONDING DD03L TO FIELDTAB.
         SELECT * FROM DD04L WHERE ROLLNAME = DD03L-ROLLNAME.
           SELECT * FROM DD01L WHERE DOMNAME = DD04L-DOMNAME.
             FIELDTAB-OUTPUTLEN = DD01L-OUTPUTLEN.
             APPEND FIELDTAB.
             EXIT.
           ENDSELECT.
           EXIT.
         ENDSELECT.
       ENDSELECT.
       SORT FIELDTAB BY TABNAME POSITION.
*
```

```
      CLEAR STRUTAB. REFRESH STRUTAB.
      STRUTAB-STRUNAME = 'ZINS'.
      APPEND STRUTAB.
      STRUTAB-STRUNAME = 'ZCUST'.
      APPEND STRUTAB.
      STRUTAB-STRUNAME = 'ZPSTKY'.
      APPEND STRUTAB.
      STRUTAB-STRUNAME = 'ZPSTKYT'.
      APPEND STRUTAB.
      STRUTAB-STRUNAME = 'ZMASTER'.
      APPEND STRUTAB.
      STRUTAB-STRUNAME = 'ZPARTNER'.
      APPEND STRUTAB.
      STRUTAB-STRUNAME = 'ZACCOUNT'.
      APPEND STRUTAB.
      STRUTAB-STRUNAME = 'ZPRODUCT'.
      APPEND STRUTAB.
      STRUTAB-STRUNAME = 'ZCONTRACT'.
      APPEND STRUTAB.
      STRUTAB-STRUNAME = 'ZPOST'.
      APPEND STRUTAB.
      STRUTAB-STRUNAME = 'ZDOCHD'.
      APPEND STRUTAB.
      STRUTAB-STRUNAME = 'ZDOCITEM'.
      APPEND STRUTAB.
*
      IF FILENAME(1) = '/'.
        OPEN DATASET FILENAME FOR INPUT IN TEXT MODE.
      ELSE.
        CALL FUNCTION 'WS_UPLOAD'
             EXPORTING
              FILENAME               = FNAME
             IMPORTING
                  FILELENGTH             = BYTES
             TABLES
                  DATA_TAB               = FILETAB
             EXCEPTIONS
                  CONVERSION_ERROR     = 1
                  FILE_OPEN_ERROR      = 2
                  FILE_READ_ERROR      = 3
                  INVALID_TABLE_WIDTH = 4
                  INVALID_TYPE         = 5
                  NO_BATCH             = 6
                  UNKNOWN_ERROR        = 7
                  OTHERS               = 8.
      ENDIF.
      IF SY-SUBRC > 0. STOP. ENDIF.
  ENDCASE.
ENDFORM.
```

The internal table STRUTAB contains all names of the line formats associated with ZDS. The file is then opened for reading. The first character of the file name is used to differentiate between PC files and application server files. A "/" indicates a file on the UNIX application server. All other file names are interpreted as being DOS files. An OPEN DATASET is coded for UNIX files, DOS files are read into an internal table FILETAB. The global variable ROW is used for the line-oriented processing in both cases.

Although the code in the AFTER_EVENT form specifies that the file is to be closed at the end of the processing, this needs to be explicitly specified only for UNIX files.

```
FORM AFTER_EVENT USING EVENT.
   CASE EVENT.
     WHEN 'END-OF-SELECTION'.
 IF FILENAME(1) = '/'.
      CLOSE DATASET FILENAME.
 ENDIF.
   ENDCASE.
 ENDFORM.
```

A parameterless form with the name PUT_<structure> is present in the database program for every line structure contained in the LFI structure. Nine forms with the names PUT_ZINS, PUT_ZMASTER, PUT_ZPARTNER, etc. exist for the above example. Except for the structure name, each of these PUT forms is identical. The PUT_ZDOCHD form is shown as example.

```
FORM PUT_ZDOCHD.
DATA STRUNAME(30).
DO.
  IF ROW = SPACE.
    IF FILENAME(1) = '/'.
      READ DATASET FILENAME INTO ROW.
      NUMBROWS = NUMBROWS + 1.
    ELSE.
      NUMBROWS = NUMBROWS + 1.
      READ TABLE FILETAB INDEX NUMBROWS.
      ROW = FILETAB-ROW.
    ENDIF.
    IF SY-SUBRC > 0. EXIT. ENDIF.
  ENDIF.
  STRUNAME = ROW(10).
  READ TABLE STRUTAB WITH KEY STRUNAME = STRUNAME.
  IF SY-SUBRC = 0.          " no comment line
    IF STRUNAME = 'ZDOCHD'.
      PERFORM SPLITLINE USING ROW STRUNAME.
      ROW = SPACE.
      PUT ZDOCHD.
    ELSE.
      EXIT.
    ENDIF.
  ELSE.                     " comment line is not read
    ROW = SPACE.
```

```
ENDIF.
ENDDO.
ENDFORM.
```

The DO loop continues to read lines from the file as long the STRUNAME line identifier remains the same as the associated structure name <structure>. The SPLITLINE form splits the line into its component parts. These are individually tested for convertibility and are assigned to the target fields of the associated structure. Once a line has been fully processed, PUT <structure> is used to initiate the GET event in the processing program and to invoke PUT form of the subordinate or the secondary structure. The line is deleted once the processing has completed successfully. If a line has not been processed, it is not deleted and is available for processing by the next form. All lines whose line identifiers were not found in the STRUTAB table of the line formats are considered to be comments and are ignored.

The PUT forms have an almost identical appearance; the significant difference is in the *source code* that follows the PUT key word. This difference is responsible that the PUT forms are *not* replaced by a single form with the table name as parameter. This parameter must contain a section of source code; this is only possible for macros. Indeed, the forms can be represented using a macro, which, however, does not improve the readability. The forms are in any case generated.

The parsing of a read line and the test for conversion errors are integrated in the database program. The SPLITLINE form performs a loop over all fields of the passed format. The corresponding section of the line using offset and length is assigned to a CHAR variable D.

```
FORM SPLITLINE USING ROW STRUNAME.
FIELD-SYMBOLS <datafieldref>.
FIELD-SYMBOLS <errorfieldref>.
DATA FIELD(45).
DATA D(30).
DATA O TYPE I.
DATA L TYPE I.
DATA RC LIKE SY-SUBRC.

O = 10.
READ TABLE STRUTAB INDEX 1.
CONCATENATE STRUTAB-STRUNAME '-FEHLER' INTO FIELD.
ASSIGN (FIELD) TO <errorfieldref>.
LOOP AT FIELDTAB WHERE TABNAME = STRUNAME.
  L = FIELDTAB-OUTPUTLEN.  " external format will be transferred
  D = ROW+O(L).
  CONCATENATE FIELDTAB-TABNAME '-' FIELDTAB-FIELDNAME INTO FIELD.
  ASSIGN (FIELD) TO <datafieldref>.
  PERFORM CHECKFORMAT USING D FIELDTAB-INTTYPE RC.
  IF RC = 0.
    <datafieldref> = D.
    <errorfieldref> = SPACE.
```

```
   ELSE.
*    MESSAGE ID ...  TYPE 'S' NUMBER ...
*            WITH NUMBROWS STRUNAME FIELD.
     CLEAR <datafieldref>.
     <errorfieldref> = 'X'.
   ENDIF.
   O = O + L.
ENDLOOP.

ENDFORM.
```

The CHECKFORMAT test function checks whether the data element D is an element of type *fieldtype*.

```
FORM CHECKFORMAT USING FIELD FIELDTYPE RC.
DATA L TYPE I.
L = STRLEN( FIELD ).
RC = 1.
CASE FIELDTYPE.
  WHEN 'C'.
    RC = 0.
  WHEN 'N'.
    IF FIELD CO '0123456789'. ENDIF.
    IF SY-FDPOS >= L. RC = 0.
    ELSE.             RC = 1.
    ENDIF.
  WHEN 'D'.
    IF FIELD CO '.0123456789'. ENDIF.
    IF SY-FDPOS >= L. RC = 0.
    ELSE.             RC = 1.
    ENDIF.
  WHEN 'X'.
    IF FIELD CO '0123456789ABCDEF'. ENDIF.
    IF SY-FDPOS >= L. RC = 0.
    ELSE.             RC = 1.
    ENDIF.
  WHEN 'P'.
    IF FIELD CO '+-.0123456789'. ENDIF.
    IF SY-FDPOS >= L. RC = 0.
    ELSE.             RC = 1.
    ENDIF.
ENDCASE.
ENDFORM.
```

If the validation was successful, the data element D is indirectly assigned to the structure field using a field symbol. Otherwise, MESSAGE is used to issue an error message. The WITH-parameters provide the message with information on the data line, structure and field names. Messages and functional groups must have been created before this variant can be used. In batch, all issued messages are collected in the log file. The processing program must be informed of all errors that occurred. The use of a special error field in the top-structure of the LFI is appropriate here; if an error occurs, the database program sets the corresponding PUT <structure> before issuing the error.

The programming of the CHECKFORMAT form shows only the general logic and does not realize any complete error checking. The DATE_CHECK_PLAUSIBILITY and CHECK_AND_CONVERT_NUMERICS function modules can be used for further checking.

11.4.3 Select Options of a Logical Database Interface

The name of the file to be processed should be passed as parameter to the processing program. It must be made known to the database program. As usual, the SELECT options of the logical database are used. In the case of ZDS, the include DBSELZDS is created using the logical database ZDS and modified as follows:

```
PARAMETER FILENAME(150) DEFAULT 'C:\BE\ABAP\ZDS.TXT
                        LOWER CASE FOR TABLE ZINS.
```

The default value of the file name appears in the parameter of the processing program and can be overwritten there. The table reference of the parameter (FOR TABLE) always applies to the top structure of the LFI.

11.4.4 Processing Program for a Logical File Interface

The processing program of an LFI does not differ from the processing program for an LDB. The name of the assigned logical database must be specified in the report attributes. In addition to the GET <structure> events, in particular the GET <structure> LATE events are of interest for effective processing. For example, the occurrence of GET ZDOCHD LATE indicates that a further document has been read completely. Its content then can be subjected to a plausibility check and subsequently stored. Structures that are only used to control the read process (ZINS, ZCUST, ZMASTER, ZPOST) do not need to be added to the TABLES declaration of the processing program.

Figure 11.2 demonstrates the interaction of processing program, database program and control program. The GENLDS report described in the following section can be used to generate the database program and the selection options from the structure of the logical file interface.

11.4.5 Generating the Database Program for an LFI

The ZR_11_04 report can be used to generate the database program for an LFI using just the structure information of the LFI. The following program description shows the line numbers for ZR_11_04 in parentheses. ZR_11_04 expects two parameters (540–550):

- The name of the logical database that describes the structure of the LFI
- The complete default file name of the file to be processed.

Read the structure information for the LFI from the TLDB table

The structure of an LDB or an LFI is stored in the TLDB table. This contains the fields shown in Table 11.1.

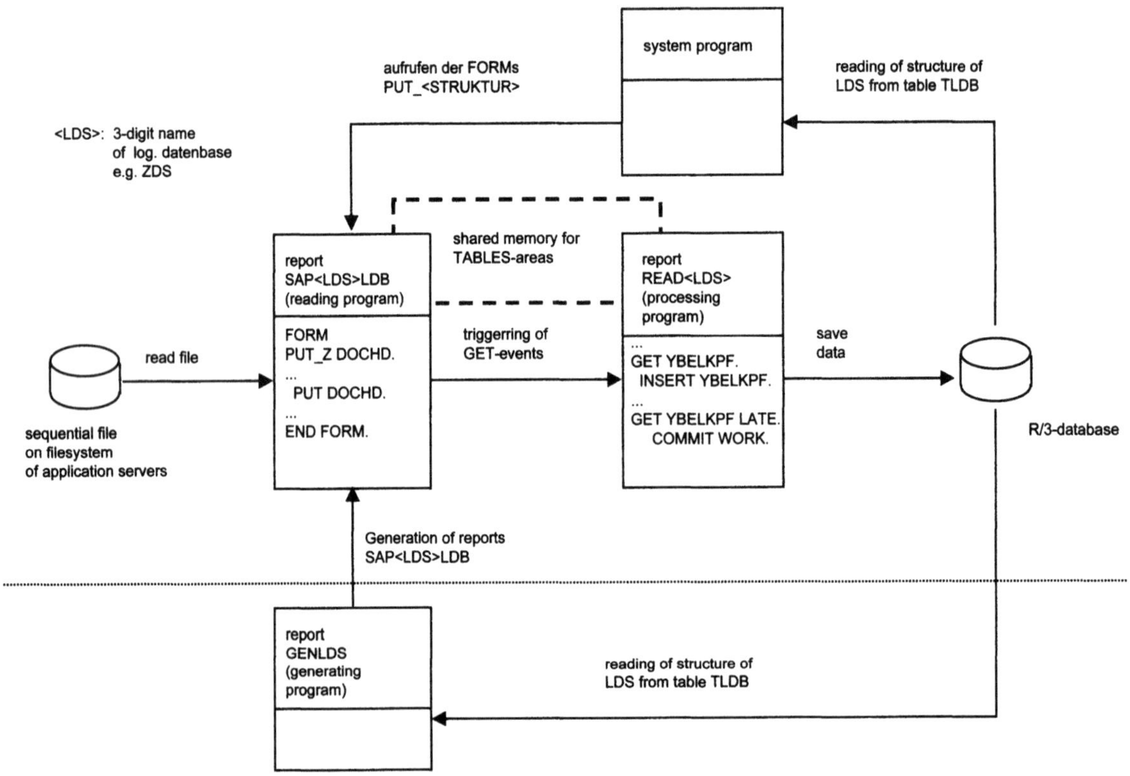

Figure 11.2: Components of a logical file interface

Table 11.1: Structure information of a logical database in the TLDB table

Key	Name	Type	Length	Description
X	DBNAME	CHAR	2	Name of LDB / LFI
X	SYSTEM	CHAR	1	Last character of the name
X	IDENTIFICATION	CHAR	1	Type of information in ENTRY
	ENTRY	CHAR	200	Various information

DBNAME and SYSTEM together form the three-character name of the LFI or LDB. The IDENTIFICATION field specifies the type of information in the ENTRY field. The entries with the identification "P" (primary tables) and "S" (secondary tables) are important for the structure of the LFI:

```
P=          ZINS    ZCUST    ZPSTKY   ZINS     ZMASTER  ZMASTER  ZMASTER ..
S=ZINS     ZCUST    ZPSTKY   ZPSTKYT  ZMASTER  ZPARTNER ZACCOUNT  PRODUCT
```

The longest of the structure or table names contained in these two records determines the raster with which the lines are written. The raster is determined from the number of leading blank characters in the record with the P-identification. The raster is 8 in the example. It is determined from the ZPARTNER string. Those structure names present are read in raster increments from the record with the S-identification and stored in the internal table STRUTAB (600-890).

Create a compilable program

The database program to be generated is built in the internal table PROGTAB (490–510) in ZR_11_04 starting at line 910. Macros A1 to A5 (160–310) are used to reduce the size. These connect the specified number of parameters to the new program line that is added with APPEND. Because macros do no permit any empty parameters, the "#" character is used instead of the required blank character. This is replaced with a blank character before the program is output (2900–2930).

The LOOP STRUTAB at the following location in the generated program handles dependency of the codes on the LFI structure:

- TABLES declaration (950–1010)
- SELECT to DD03L to determine the fields of all structures of a LFI (1290–1350)
- PUT_<structure> for every structure (1490–1520).

Display, download and insert the generated database program and the include

The generated program and the include are shown as list (2890–2960, 3100–3170) and, if required, can be downloaded to a PC file. In addition, the internally generated program sources added to the library as report under the name SAPDB<LFI> (2990) or as include DB<LFI>SEL (3200). SAPDB<LFI> can be generated automatically without requiring any changes. Any old programs present in the library will be overwritten without warning.

The generating program can be extended if necessary. For example, the frame of the processing program can be generated also with the possible tables and their PUT events or PUT LATE events.

Advanced notes

When large data volumes are transferred, it is usual to perform a COMMIT WORK on the database after a certain number of records have been accepted. A suitable restart procedure to accept the data would be required in this case. The easiest method is to create a table that contains all the information required for the transmission (LFI, date, file name, number of determined lines, status). An UPDATE with the current values for the current transmission must be made on this table before every COMMIT. The used database program must also read the appropriate record from this table after opening the file and continue the processing at the specified position. This provides a consistent state for a ROLLBACK.

```
*-------------------------------------------------------------------
* Report for generation of the database program for a logical
* file interface (LFI)
* Principle:
*   LFI defined as a logical database, consisting of DDIC-structures
*   and DDIC-tables
*   Every structure or table stands for a single line type
* Input:
*   Name of the logical file interface (database) <LFI>
*   Default filename for the database program
* To be generated:
*   Database program SAPDB<LFI>
*   Include for SELECT-Options DB<LFI>SEL
*-------------------------------------------------------------------
REPORT ZR_11_04  LINE-SIZE 70.

* Macros A1 to A5 to append lines of code to the internal pgm table
DEFINE A1.
  PROGTAB-ZEILE = &1. APPEND PROGTAB.
END-OF-DEFINITION.
DEFINE A2.
  CONCATENATE &1 &2 INTO PROGTAB-ZEILE. APPEND PROGTAB.
END-OF-DEFINITION.
DEFINE A3.
  CONCATENATE &1 &2 &3 INTO PROGTAB-ZEILE. APPEND PROGTAB.
END-OF-DEFINITION.
DEFINE A4.
  CONCATENATE &1 &2 &3 &4 INTO PROGTAB-ZEILE. APPEND PROGTAB.
END-OF-DEFINITION.
DEFINE A5.
  CONCATENATE &1 &2 &3 &4 &5 INTO PROGTAB-ZEILE. APPEND PROGTAB.
END-OF-DEFINITION.
TABLES: TRDIR,                  " ABAP/4 programs
        DD03L.       " fields from structures and tables
TABLES: TLDB.                   " logical databases Release 3.xx
TABLES: LDBN.                   " logical databases release 4.xx
DATA    PEINTRAG LIKE TLDB-EINTRAG.
DATA    SEINTRAG LIKE TLDB-EINTRAG.
DATA    RASTER TYPE I.
DATA    O TYPE I.
DATA    PROGNAME(12).                " database program SAPDB<LDB>
DATA    SELNAME(12).     " include for select options DB<LDB>SEL

* Table of table and structure names of the LFI
DATA:   BEGIN OF STRUTAB OCCURS 20,
           STRUNAME(30),
           STRUTYPE(1),          " only for release 4.xx
        END OF STRUTAB.
DATA    ANZSTRUTAB TYPE I VALUE 0.

* table of generated source code
DATA:   BEGIN OF PROGTAB OCCURS 400,
           ZEILE(72),
```

```
        END OF PROGTAB.
*-----------------------------------------------------------------------
PARAMETERS: LDB(3) DEFAULT 'ZLF',
            FILENAME(150) DEFAULT 'C:\BE\ABAP\ZLF.TXT' LOWER CASE,
            TEST DEFAULT 'X'.
*-----------------------------------------------------------------------
CLEAR STRUTAB. REFRESH STRUTAB.
CLEAR PROGTAB. REFRESH PROGTAB.

* Reading the database information from the DDIC - release-dependent
IF SY-SAPRL CA '4'.                          " Release is 4.xx
  SELECT STRUCTURE TYPE INTO (STRUTAB-STRUNAME, STRUTAB-STRUTYPE)
         FROM LDBN WHERE LDBNAME = LDB
                   AND PARENTNODE = SPACE.  "top table or struct
    APPEND STRUTAB.
  ENDSELECT.

  SELECT STRUCTURE TYPE INTO (STRUTAB-STRUNAME, STRUTAB-STRUTYPE)
         FROM LDBN WHERE LDBNAME = LDB
                   AND PARENTNODE <> SPACE.
    APPEND STRUTAB.
  ENDSELECT.
ELSE.
  SELECT SINGLE * FROM TLDB
     WHERE  DBNAME = LDB(2) AND SYSTEM = LDB+2(1) AND KENNUNG = 'P'.
  PEINTRAG = TLDB-EINTRAG.

  SELECT SINGLE * FROM TLDB
     WHERE  DBNAME = LDB(2) AND SYSTEM = LDB+2(1) AND KENNUNG = 'S'.
  SEINTRAG = TLDB-EINTRAG.

  RASTER = 0.
  DO.
    IF PEINTRAG(1) = SPACE.
      RASTER = RASTER + 1.
      SHIFT PEINTRAG LEFT.
    ELSE.
      EXIT.
    ENDIF.
  ENDDO.

  O = 0.
  DO.
    STRUTAB-STRUNAME = SEINTRAG+O(RASTER).
    IF STRUTAB-STRUNAME NE SPACE.
      APPEND STRUTAB.
      O = O + RASTER.
    ELSE.
      EXIT.
    ENDIF.
  ENDDO.
ENDIF.
DESCRIBE TABLE STRUTAB LINES ANZSTRUTAB.
```

```
*-----------------------------------------------------------------
*----- report name with reference to logical database
A5 'REPORT SAPDB' LDB '#DEFINING DATABASE#' LDB '.'.

*----- tables and struct. in logical databases - release-dependent
IF SY-SAPRL CA '4'.        " release 4.xx
  A1 'NODES:'.
  LOOP AT STRUTAB WHERE STRUTYPE = 'S'.
      A3 '############' STRUTAB-STRUNAME ','.
  ENDLOOP.
  TRANSLATE PROGTAB-ZEILE USING ',.'.
  DESCRIBE TABLE PROGTAB LINES SY-TFILL.
  MODIFY PROGTAB INDEX SY-TFILL.

  A1 'TABLES:'.
  LOOP AT STRUTAB WHERE STRUTYPE = 'T'.
      A3 '############' STRUTAB-STRUNAME ','.
  ENDLOOP.
  TRANSLATE PROGTAB-ZEILE USING ',.'.
  DESCRIBE TABLE PROGTAB LINES SY-TFILL.
  MODIFY PROGTAB INDEX SY-TFILL.
ELSE.
  A1 'TABLES:     DD01L, DD03L, DD04L,'.
  LOOP AT STRUTAB.
    IF SY-TABIX LT ANZSTRUTAB.
      A3 '############' STRUTAB-STRUNAME ','.
    ELSE.
      A3 '############' STRUTAB-STRUNAME '.'.
    ENDIF.
  ENDLOOP.
ENDIF.
*----- parameters and data
A1 'DATA:        BEGIN OF STRUTAB OCCURS 20,'.
A1 '               STRUNAME(15),'.
A1 '             END OF STRUTAB.'.
A1 'DATA:        BEGIN OF FILETAB OCCURS 1000,'.
A1 '               ZEILE(250),'.
A1 '             END OF FILETAB.'.
A1 'DATA:        BEGIN OF FELDTAB OCCURS 30.'.
A1 '               INCLUDE STRUCTURE DD03L.'.
A1 'DATA:          OUTPUTLEN  LIKE DD01L-OUTPUTLEN,'.
A1 '             END OF FELDTAB.'.
A1 'DATA         ZEILE(250) VALUE SPACE.'.
A1 'DATA         ANZZEILEN TYPE I VALUE ''0''.'.
A1 '*----------------------------------------------------------'.
A1 '*----------------------------------------------------------'.

*----- FORMs
A1 'FORM BEFORE EVENT USING EVENT.'.
A1 'DATA BYTES TYPE I.'.
A1 'DATA FNAME LIKE RLGRAP-FILENAME.'.
A1 'FNAME = FILENAME.'.
A1 '  CASE EVENT.'.
```

```
A1 '    WHEN ''START-OF-SELECTION''.'.
A1 '       SELECT * FROM DD03L WHERE'.
A1 '         AS4LOCAL = ''A'' AND'.
A1 '         FIELDNAME NE ''.INCLUDE'' AND ('.
LOOP AT STRUTAB.
  IF SY-TABIX < ANZSTRUTAB.
    A3 '           TABNAME = ''' STRUTAB-STRUNAME ''' OR'.
  ELSE.
    A3 '           TABNAME = ''' STRUTAB-STRUNAME ''' ) .'.
  ENDIF.
ENDLOOP.
A1 '         MOVE-CORRESPONDING DD03L TO FELDTAB.'.
A1 '         SELECT * FROM DD04L WHERE ROLLNAME = DD03L-ROLLNAME.'.
A1 '           SELECT * FROM DD01L WHERE DOMNAME = DD04L-DOMNAME.'.
A1 '             FELDTAB-OUTPUTLEN = DD01L-OUTPUTLEN.'.
A1 '             APPEND FELDTAB.'.
A1 '             EXIT.'.
A1 '           ENDSELECT.'.
A1 '           EXIT.'.
A1 '         ENDSELECT.'.
A1 '       ENDSELECT.'.
A1 '       SORT FELDTAB BY TABNAME POSITION.'.
A1 '*'.
A1 '       CLEAR STRUTAB. REFRESH STRUTAB.'.
LOOP AT STRUTAB.
  A3 '         STRUTAB-STRUNAME = ''' STRUTAB-STRUNAME '''.'.
  A1 '         APPEND STRUTAB.'.
ENDLOOP.
A1 '*'.
A1 '       IF FILENAME(1) = ''/''.'.
A1 '         OPEN DATASET FILENAME FOR INPUT IN TEXT MODE.'.
A1 '       ELSE.'.
A1 '         CALL FUNCTION ''WS UPLOAD'''.
A1 '              EXPORTING'.
A1 '               FILENAME                = FNAME'.
A1 '              IMPORTING'.
A1 '                   FILELENGTH             = BYTES'.
A1 '              TABLES'.
A1 '                   DATA_TAB               = FILETAB'.
A1 '              EXCEPTIONS'.
A1 '                   CONVERSION ERROR     = 1'.
A1 '                   FILE OPEN ERROR      = 2'.
A1 '                   FILE READ ERROR      = 3'.
A1 '                   INVALID TABLE WIDTH  = 4'.
A1 '                   INVALID TYPE         = 5'.
A1 '                   NO BATCH             = 6'.
A1 '                   UNKNOWN ERROR        = 7'.
A1 '                   OTHERS               = 8.'.
A1 '       ENDIF.'.
A1 '       IF SY-SUBRC > 0. STOP. ENDIF.'.
A1 '   ENDCASE.'.
A1 ' ENDFORM.'.
A1 '*-----------------------------------------------------------'.
```

```
A1 'FORM AFTER EVENT USING EVENT.'.
A1 '   CASE EVENT.'.
A1 '     WHEN ''END-OF-SELECTION''.'.
A1 ' IF FILENAME(1) = ''/''.'.
A1 '      CLOSE DATASET FILENAME.'.
A1 ' ENDIF.'.
A1 '   ENDCASE.'.
A1 ' ENDFORM.'.
A1 '*---------------------------------------------------------------'.
A1 '*---------------------------------------------------------------'.
A1 '* The FORMs PUT <Struname> are to be called by the system.'.
A1 '* These names should not be changed.'.
LOOP AT STRUTAB.
 A1 '*-------------------------------------------------------------'.
  A3 'FORM PUT_' STRUTAB-STRUNAME '.'.
  A1 'DATA STRUNAME(30).'.
  A1 'DO.'.
  A1 '  IF ZEILE = SPACE.'.
  A1 '    IF FILENAME(1) = ''/''.'.
  A1 '      READ DATASET FILENAME INTO ZEILE.'.
  A1 '      ANZZEILEN = ANZZEILEN + 1.'.
  A1 '    ELSE.'.
  A1 '      ANZZEILEN = ANZZEILEN + 1.'.
  A1 '      READ TABLE FILETAB INDEX ANZZEILEN.'.
  A1 '      ZEILE = FILETAB-ZEILE.'.
  A1 '    ENDIF.'.
  A1 '    IF SY-SUBRC > 0. EXIT. ENDIF.'.
  A1 '  ENDIF.'.
  A1 '  STRUNAME = ZEILE(10).'.
  A1 '  READ TABLE STRUTAB WITH KEY STRUNAME = STRUNAME.'.
  A1 '  IF SY-SUBRC = 0.        " no comment line in input file'.
  A3 '    IF STRUNAME = ''' STRUTAB-STRUNAME '''.'.
  A1 '      PERFORM SPLITLINE USING ZEILE STRUNAME.'.
  A1 '      ZEILE = SPACE.'.
  A3 '      PUT#' STRUTAB-STRUNAME '.'.
  A1 '    ELSE.'.
  A1 '      EXIT.'.
  A1 '    ENDIF.'.
  A1 '  ELSE.                 " bypassed comment line in input file'.
  A1 '    ZEILE = SPACE.'.
  A1 'ENDIF.'.
  A1 'ENDDO.'.
  A1 'ENDFORM.'.
ENDLOOP.
A1 '*---------------------------------------------------------------'.
A1 'FORM PBO.  ENDFORM. '.
A1 'FORM PAI USING FNAME MARK. ENDFORM. '.
A1 '*---------------------------------------------------------------'.
A1 'FORM SPLITLINE USING ZEILE STRUNAME.'.
A1 'FIELD-SYMBOLS <DataFieldRef>.'.
A1 'FIELD-SYMBOLS <ErrorFieldRef>.'.
A1 'DATA FELD(45).'.
A1 'DATA D(30).'.
```

```
A1 'DATA O TYPE I.'.
A1 'DATA L TYPE I.'.
A1 'DATA RC LIKE SY-SUBRC.'.
A1 'O = 10.'.
A1 'READ TABLE STRUTAB INDEX 1.'.
A1 'CONCATENATE STRUTAB-STRUNAME ''-ERROR'' INTO FELD.'.
A1 'ASSIGN (FELD) TO <ErrorFieldRef>.'.
A1 'LOOP AT FELDTAB WHERE TABNAME = STRUNAME.'.
A1 '  L = FELDTAB-OUTPUTLEN.  " external format'.
A1 '  D = ZEILE+O(L).'.
A1 'CONCATENATE FELDTAB-TABNAME ''-'' FELDTAB-FIELDNAME INTO FELD.'.
A1 '  ASSIGN (FELD) TO <DataFieldRef>.'.
A1 '  PERFORM CHECKFORMAT USING D FELDTAB-INTTYPE RC.'.
A1 '  IF RC = 0.'.
A1 '    <DataFieldRef> = D.'.
A1 '    <ErrorFieldRef> = SPACE.'.
A1 '  ELSE.'.
A1 '*   MESSAGE ID ...  TYPE ''S'' NUMBER ...'.
A1 '*           WITH ANZZEILEN STRUNAME FELD.'.
A1 '    CLEAR <DataFieldRef>.'.
A1 '    <ErrorFieldRef> = ''X''.'.
A1 '  ENDIF.'.
A1 '  O = O + L.'.
A1 'ENDLOOP.'.
A1 'ENDFORM.'.
A1 '*-------------------------------------------------------------'.
A1 'FORM CHECKFORMAT USING FELD FELDTYP RC.'.
A1 'DATA L TYPE I.'.
A1 'L = STRLEN( FELD ).'.
A1 'RC = 1.'.
A1 'CASE FELDTYP.'.
A1 '  WHEN ''C''.'.
A1 '    RC = 0.'.
A1 '  WHEN ''N''.'.
A1 '    IF FELD CO ''0123456789''. ENDIF.'.
A1 '    IF SY-FDPOS >= L. RC = 0.'.
A1 '    ELSE.             RC = 1.'.
A1 '    ENDIF.'.
A1 '  WHEN ''D''.'.
A1 '    IF FELD CO ''.0123456789''. ENDIF.'.
A1 '    IF SY-FDPOS >= L. RC = 0.'.
A1 '    ELSE.             RC = 1.'.
A1 '    ENDIF.'.
A1 '  WHEN ''X''.'.
A1 '    IF FELD CO ''0123456789ABCDEF''. ENDIF.'.
A1 '    IF SY-FDPOS >= L. RC = 0.'.
A1 '    ELSE.             RC = 1.'.
A1 '    ENDIF.'.
A1 '  WHEN ''P''.'.
A1 '    IF FELD CO ''+-.0123456789''. ENDIF.'.
A1 '    IF SY-FDPOS >= L. RC = 0.'.
A1 '    ELSE.             RC = 1.'.
A1 '    ENDIF.'.
```

```
  A1 'ENDCASE.'.
  A1 'ENDFORM.'.

  ULINE.
  LOOP AT PROGTAB.
    TRANSLATE PROGTAB-ZEILE USING '# '.
    MODIFY PROGTAB.
    WRITE: / PROGTAB-ZEILE.
  ENDLOOP.

  CONCATENATE 'SAPDB' LDB INTO PROGNAME.
  IF TEST = SPACE.
    INSERT REPORT PROGNAME FROM PROGTAB.
    SELECT SINGLE * FROM TRDIR WHERE NAME = PROGNAME.
    TRDIR-LDBNAME = LDB.
    MODIFY TRDIR.
  ENDIF.
  *
  * generating the SELECT options - release-dependent
  CLEAR PROGTAB. REFRESH PROGTAB.
  READ TABLE STRUTAB INDEX 1.
    A3 'PARAMETERS  FILENAME(150) DEFAULT#''' FILENAME ''' LOWER
CASE'.
  IF SY-SAPRL CA '4'.
    IF STRUTAB-STRUTYPE = 'T'.
    A3 '                          FOR TABLE#' STRUTAB-STRUNAME '.'.
    ELSE.
    A3 '                          FOR NODE#' STRUTAB-STRUNAME '.'.
    ENDIF.
  ELSE.
    A3 '                          FOR TABLE#' STRUTAB-STRUNAME '.'.
  ENDIF.
  ULINE.
  WRITE: / 'generated SELECT options:'.
  ULINE.
  LOOP AT PROGTAB.
    TRANSLATE PROGTAB-ZEILE USING '# '.
    MODIFY PROGTAB.
    WRITE: / PROGTAB-ZEILE.
  ENDLOOP.

  CONCATENATE 'DB' LDB 'SEL' INTO SELNAME.
  IF TEST = SPACE.
    INSERT REPORT SELNAME FROM PROGTAB.
    SELECT SINGLE * FROM TRDIR WHERE NAME = SELNAME.
    TRDIR-SUBC = 'I'.       " switch type to 'I' = Include
    MODIFY TRDIR.
  ENDIF.
```

12 Batch Input

12.1 Concept

The term *batch input* sometimes causes confusion with R/3 users and consultants. Does this refer to the processing of input data that were created in batch? Or is it the batch processing of input data? Or do both apply?

Batch input is used for the reliable import of large, usually computer-generated, data volumes into the R/3 system. The input data procedure makes use of the normal dialog transactions of the system. The main difference to normal dialog operation is that the input data for the dialog transactions does not come from user inputs (mouse, keyboard) but is read from specially prepared data files. These data files are called batch input sessions. They are usually populated manually, stored in the appropriate tables and then *processed.* During the processing of a batch input session, their data are passed to the dynpro fields of the transactions in the same manner as for dialog operation. Simulated user inputs (continue, save, back) pass the data to the system after performing the usual field validations. Thus, the batch input process can be understood as being input rerouting for dialog transactions. The classic batch input process consists of two parts:

- Data acceptance and creation of session
- Session processing

The two steps can be performed independent of each other directly in background (batch). One of the variants will be used depending on the data quantity or processing time involved. Typical situations for the use of batch input are:

- Acceptance of large data volumes using a file from non-SAP systems
  Session creation: batch
  Session processing: batch
- Acceptance of mid-sized data volumes using a file or RFC from non-SAP systems
  Session creation: direct
  Session processing: batch
- Acceptance of small data volumes within R/3 (customizing)
  Session creation: direct
  Session processing: direct

The last example shows that batch input is possible without using batch. If this seldom application situation is ignored, batch input can be designated as being "batch execution of dialog programs using computer-generated input data". Batch input can be compared with the background execution of reports with variant. Variants also represent an input rerouting for the report parameters. Rather than specifying just a few parameters in the report variant, batch input populates a complete session with input data.

Because of the comprehensive field validations performed on the dynpros, it can normally be assumed that the session processing runs much longer than the session creation.

In addition to the classic batch input using sessions, there is also a variant with CALL TRANSACTION in which batch input data are passed directly using an internal table.

The following DDIC structures are used for the creation and processing of batch input data:

Table 12.1: Important structures for batch input

Structure	Field	Type, Length	Meaning
BDCDATA			Batch input new table field structure
	PROGRAM	CHAR8	Program name
	DYNPRO	NUM4	Dynpro number
	DYNBEGIN	CHAR1	Flag whether new dynpro
	FNAM	CHAR35	Field name on the dynpro
	FVAL	CHAR132	Field value in external format
BDCTH			Batch input transaction header
	MTYPE	CHAR1	Message type
	STATE	CHAR1	Status
	TCODE	CHAR4	Transaction code

The actual batch input data are stored in an internal table having the structure BDCDATA. The DYNBEGIN switch controls whether the first two fields or last two fields of a table entry apply. DYNBEGIN = "X" always applies in the first line of a table; the program name and dynpro number are specified. The lines that follow with DYNBEGIN = SPACE contain the field name and field values for fields of the associated dynpro. A new line with DYNBEGIN = "X" identifies a new dynpro or/and a new program.

The simulated function code or key code adopts a special role; the BDC_OKCODE value is entered in FNAM. The associated field value contains either the required key code (/11, /5 or /3) or the assigned function code (EDIT, SAVE, BACK, END, etc.). Field names and codes can be determined from the running transaction. The right mouse button displays the function keys permitted for the dynpro; F1 and then the *Technical Help* key provides the field name.

The table fields in table views also have a special feature. In addition to the name, these fields are specified with an index in parentheses suffixed to the field name.

12.2 Classic Batch Input Using Sessions

12.2.1 Creation of Sessions

Several transaction invocations for the session creation are saved in the database with a common name as a so-called session or group. Every transaction call contains a transaction header with the structure BDCTH. The following function modules are used for the program-controlled creation of sessions

BDC_OPEN_GROUP	Open a new session
BDC_INSERT	Insert a transaction call (multiple)
BDC_CLOSE_GROUP	Close a session

These functions are explained using the ZR_12_01 program that takes the batch input data from a file. This program uses the ZBF logical file interface that describes the hierarchical interrelationship between sessions, transactions and dynpros. The top structure ZBDCSESS contains the clients, the sessions and the user names. The two subordinate structures correspond to the above BDC structures. The file structure corresponds to the structure of the logical database. Two sessions are to be created.

```
* Textfile for logical file interface ZBF:
*
* ZBDCSESS
*      |
*      |----BDCTH
*             |
*             |-------BDCDATA
*
* Report ZR 12 01 reads the file and creates the given
* batch input sessions.
*
*
*        10        20        30        40        50        60
*23456789|123456789|123456789|123456789|123456789|123456789|123456|
*
* Batch input data for the view of ZPOSTKEY and ZPOSTKEYT using SM30
ZBDCSESS  999ZPOSTKEY    MENDE
BDCTH     M1SM30
ZBDCDATA  SAPMSVMA0100X
ZBDCDATA                 VIEWNAME                          ZPOSTKEY
ZBDCDATA                 BDC OKCODE                        /5
ZBDCDATA  SAPLZGEN0001X
ZBDCDATA                 BDC OKCODE                        /5
ZBDCDATA  SAPLZGEN0001X
ZBDCDATA                 ZPOSTKEY-PSTKY(1)                 10
ZBDCDATA                 ZPOSTKEYT-PSTKYTXT(1)             net prem.
ZBDCDATA                 ZPOSTKEY-PSTKY(2)                 20
```

```
ZBDCDATA                ZPOSTKEYT-PSTKYTXT(2)              refund
ZBDCDATA                ZPOSTKEY-PSTKY(3)                  30
ZBDCDATA                ZPOSTKEYT-PSTKYTXT(3)              interest
ZBDCDATA                BDC_OKCODE                         /11
ZBDCDATA  SAPLZGEN0001X
ZBDCDATA                BDC_OKCODE                         /3
ZBDCDATA  SAPLZGEN0001X
ZBDCDATA                BDC_OKCODE                         ENDE

* Batch input data for posting transaction ZDOC (ZM_09_03)
ZBDCSESS  999Posting     MENDE
BDCTH     M1ZDOC
ZBDCDATA  ZM_09_030100X
ZBDCDATA                ZDOCHD-COMCODE                     0001
ZBDCDATA                ZDOCHD-CONTNO                      3013
ZBDCDATA                ZDOCHD-CURRKY                      USD
ZBDCDATA                ZDOCHD-PSTDAT                      25.06.1998
ZBDCDATA                ZDOCHD-DOCTEXT                     Batch Inp.
ZBDCDATA                ZDOCHD-DOCTYPE                     FB
ZBDCDATA                ZDOCITEM-PSTKY(1)                  1
ZBDCDATA                ZDOCITEM-AMOUNT(1)                 1024,00
ZBDCDATA                ZDOCITEM-ITEMTEXT(1)               net prem.
ZBDCDATA                ZDOCITEM-PSTKY(2)                  2
ZBDCDATA                ZDOCITEM-AMOUNT(2)                 12,10
ZBDCDATA                ZDOCITEM-ITEMTEXT(2)               refund
ZBDCDATA                BDC_OKCODE                         /13
ZBDCDATA  ZM_09_030100X
ZBDCDATA                BDC_OKCODE                         BUCH
```

The first session with the name ZPOSTKEY should pass the posting reasons with the descriptive texts to the ZPOSTKEY and ZPOSTKEYT tables. The extended table maintenance update SM30 with the update view previously generated for the table should be used here. The SAPMSVMA-0100 dynpro sets the value ZPOSTKEY for the VIEWNAME field. /5 is the function code for the "Update" key. SAPLYCNV-0001 is then invoked and BDC_OKCODE /5 used to release new fields. The values are set in these fields. The numbers specified in parentheses correspond to the line numbers of the table control. BDC_OKCODE /11 saves the new entries and BDC_OKCODE /3 performs the return.

The second session contains posting data for the posting transaction ZDOC of the examples. A document consisting of header and three items is accepted. Note that because ZDOCHD-ACCNO field is not an input field, it cannot be entered using batch input. This field is filled after a contract number is entered (directly or using match-code). BDC_OKCODE /13 in the batch input initiates a data release to fill the field. The "BUCH" function code posts the data.

ZR_11_04 from YBF is used to generate the SAPDBYBF interface program. The ZR_12_01 report processes the file. GET ZBDCSESS opens a new session. A new transaction header BDCTH clears the internal table BDCTAB. Every new BDCDATA inserts a line in BDCTAB; the first line always represents a new dynpro and all continuation lines contain pairs with field and value.

A BDC_INSERT is invoked after the last BDCDATA record of a transaction. The forms used in the program encapsulate the function modules. Because they make no use of global data (also no internal tables), they can be called from any other programs.

```
REPORT  ZR 12 01 MESSAGE-ID Z0 LINE-SIZE 70.
NODES: ZBDCSESS, BDCTH, ZBDCDATA.

DATA BDCTAB LIKE BDCDATA OCCURS 100 WITH HEADER LINE.

GET ZBDCSESS.
  WRITE:/ 'Session opened :', ZBDCSESS-GROUPID.
  PERFORM BDC OPEN GROUP
          USING ZBDCSESS-CLIENT ZBDCSESS-GROUPID ZBDCSESS-USERID.

GET BDCTH.
  CLEAR BDCTAB. REFRESH BDCTAB.

GET ZBDCDATA.
  IF ZBDCDATA-DYNBEGIN = 'X'.
    PERFORM BDC DYNPRO TABLES BDCTAB
                       USING  ZBDCDATA-PROGRAM ZBDCDATA-DYNPRO.
  ELSE.
    PERFORM BDC_FIELD  TABLES BDCTAB
                       USING  ZBDCDATA-FNAM ZBDCDATA-FVAL.
  ENDIF.

GET BDCTH LATE.
  PERFORM BDC INSERT TABLES BDCTAB
                     USING  BDCTH-TCODE.

GET ZBDCSESS LATE.
  PERFORM BDC_CLOSE_GROUP.
  WRITE:/ 'Session created:', ZBDCSESS-GROUPID.

END-OF-SELECTION.
COMMIT WORK.
*-------------------------------------------------------------------
FORM BDC_OPEN_GROUP USING CLIENT GROUP USER.
  CALL FUNCTION 'BDC_OPEN_GROUP'
       EXPORTING  CLIENT            = CLIENT
                  GROUP             = GROUP
                  USER              = USER
                  KEEP              = 'X'.
ENDFORM.
*-------------------------------------------------------------------
FORM BDC_INSERT TABLES BDCTAB USING TCODE.
  CALL FUNCTION 'BDC_INSERT' EXPORTING TCODE           = TCODE
                                TABLES DYNPROTAB = BDCTAB.
ENDFORM.
*-------------------------------------------------------------------
```

```
FORM BDC_CLOSE_GROUP.
  CALL FUNCTION 'BDC_CLOSE_GROUP'.
ENDFORM.
*----------------------------------------------------------------
FORM BDC_DYNPRO TABLES BDCTAB STRUCTURE BDCDATA
                USING PROGRAM DYNPRO.
  CLEAR BDCTAB.
  BDCTAB-PROGRAM  = PROGRAM.
  BDCTAB-DYNPRO   = DYNPRO.
  BDCTAB-DYNBEGIN = 'X'.
  APPEND BDCTAB.
ENDFORM.
*----------------------------------------------------------------
FORM BDC_FIELD TABLES BDCTAB STRUCTURE BDCDATA USING FNAM FVAL.
  CLEAR BDCTAB.
  BDCTAB-FNAM = FNAM.
  BDCTAB-FVAL = FVAL.
  APPEND BDCTAB.
ENDFORM.
```

```
26.06.98 Chapter 12: Create batch input folders from a file      1
--------------------------------------------------------------------
Session opened : ZPOSTKEY
Session created: ZPOSTKEY
Session opened : Posting
Session created: Posting
```

The ZR_12_01 program together with the ZBF logical file interface can be used in many different ways. It can reliably accept any data (transaction data, master data, customizing and DDIC data) using the associated transactions.

12.2.2 Session Management and Session Processing

System/Services/Batch Input or SM35 provide the session management . The status of the created sessions can be shown. The ZR_12_01 program created both the above sessions.

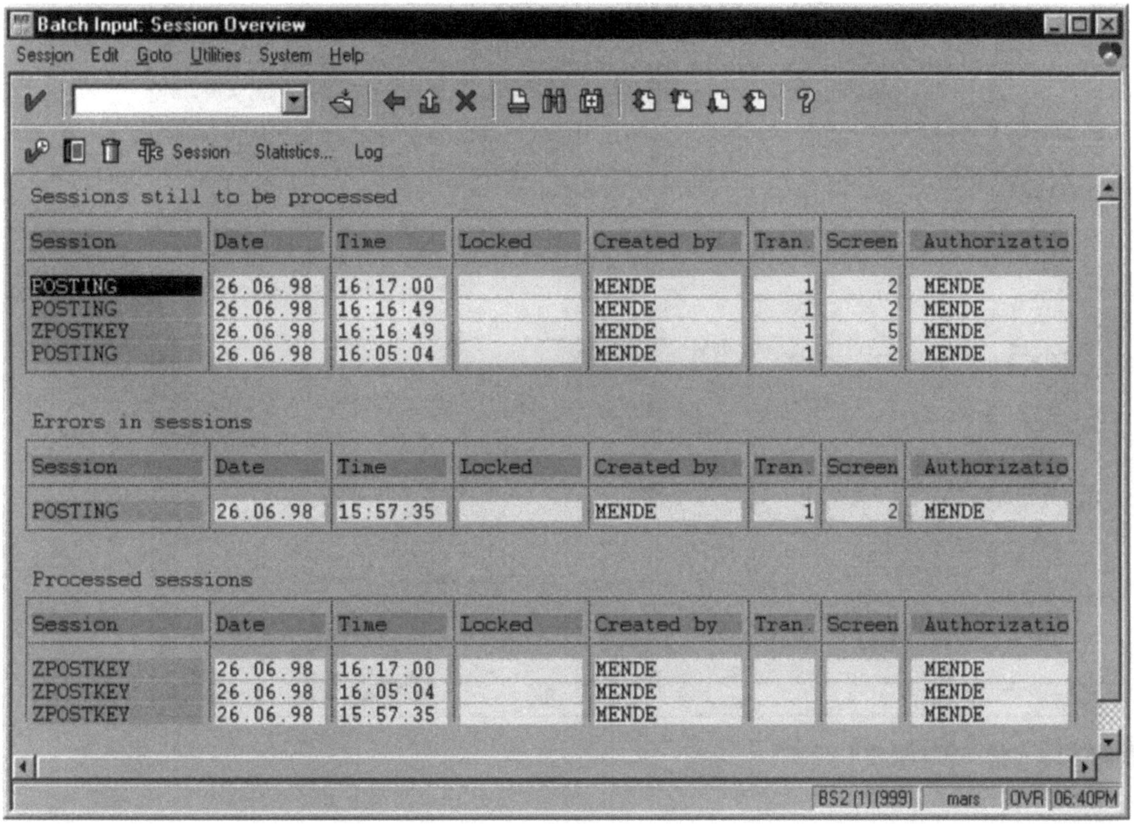

Figure 12.1: Session overview sorted according to session status

The selection of a session initially displays its transaction calls. The selection of a transaction call displays its dynpros with all associated data.

The sessions can be processed in several ways. At the beginning, in particular during the program test, it is desirable to trace the processing of the sessions. In this case, the dynpros are filled with batch input data and displayed. The BDC_OKCODE is placed in the command field and executed only when the ENTER key is pressed. This enables the individual steps to be traced. A log exists for every processed session.

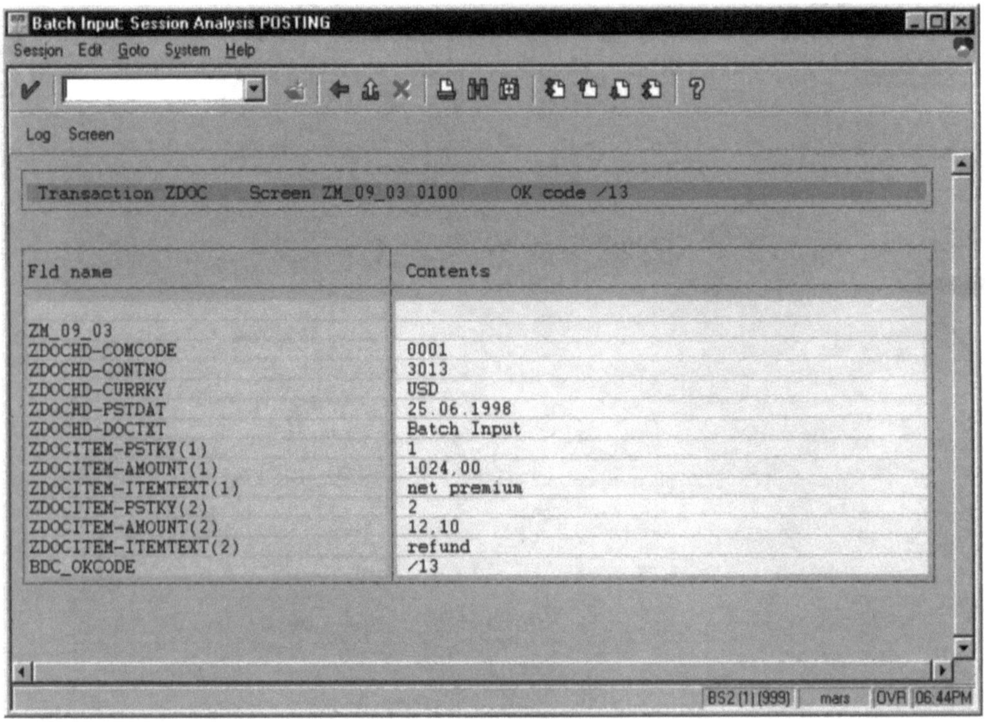

Figure 12.2: Data display of a session

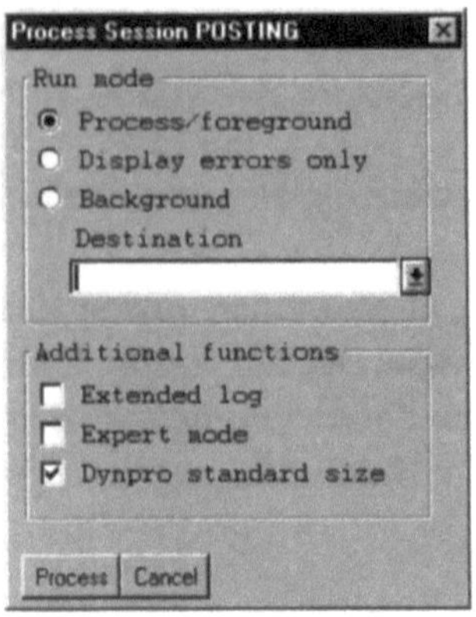

Figure 12.3: Processing capabilities for a session

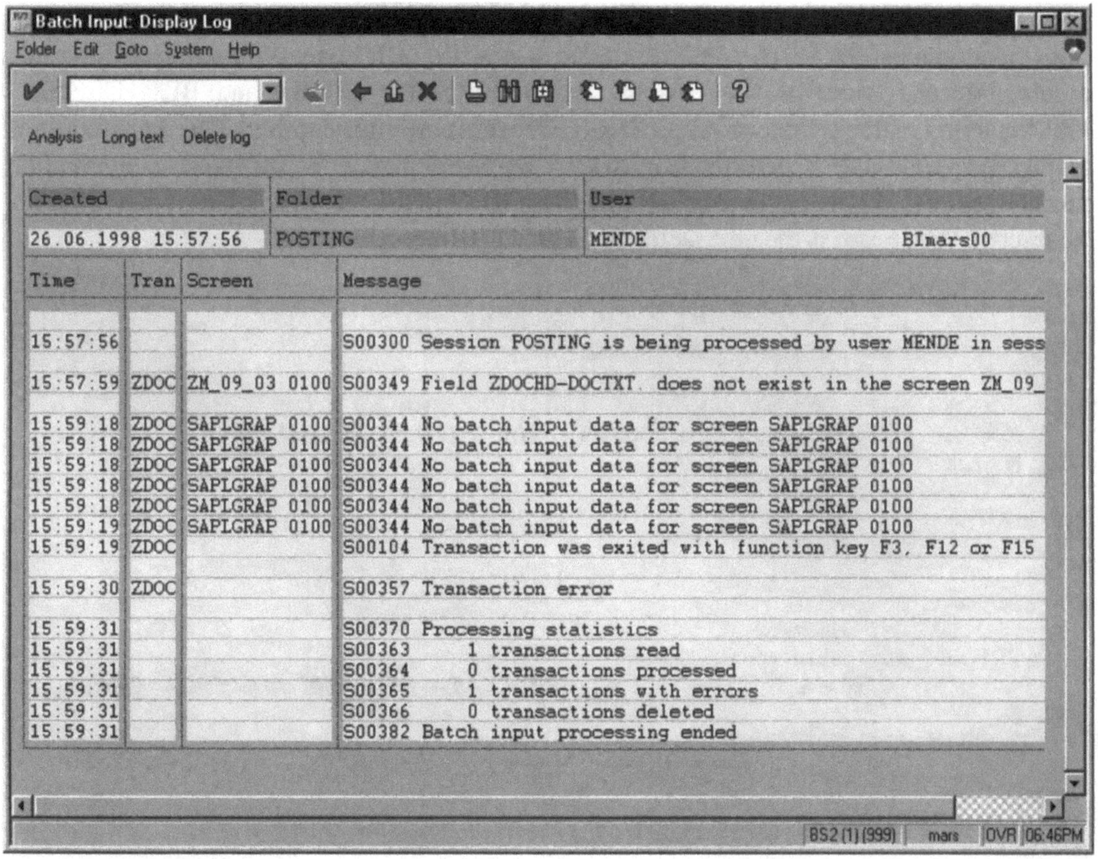

Figure 12.4: Processing log for a session

12.3 Batch Input Using CALL TRANSACTION

The saving of data in sessions can be avoided if the BDCTAB internal table of the invoked transaction BDCTH-TCODE is passed directly in a CALL TRANSACTION. The general form of this command, which corresponds to the SUBMIT for reports, has the form:

CALL TRANCACTION *trans* **USING** *BDCTab*
[MODE *mode* **MESSAGES INTO** *messtab*] **.**

Trans is the transaction code, *BDCTab* is an internal table of BDCDATA type. The mode specifies whether or not the processing of the transaction is to be shown. All messages initiated in the transactions can be stored in an internal table *MessTab* for subsequent processing.

CALL TRANSACTION is faster than the session variant. The ZR_12_02 program processes the same input data as ZR_12_01. As with these, it uses the ZBF logical file interface for batch input data. Because there are no sessions, the BDC_OPEN_GROUP and BDC_CLOSE_-GROUP function calls and the corresponding GET events are not required. The preparation of the dynpro and field data is performed in exactly the same manner as for the session creation. The forms from ZR_12_01 are invoked. Rather than BDC_INSERT, CALL TRANSACTION is called directly. The result is the same as for the ZR_12_01 report.

```
REPORT  ZR 12 02 MESSAGE-ID Z0 LINE-SIZE 70.
NODES: ZBDCSESS, BDCTH, ZBDCDATA.

DATA BDCTAB LIKE BDCDATA OCCURS 100 WITH HEADER LINE.
DATA MSGTAB LIKE BDCMSGCOLL OCCURS 100 WITH HEADER LINE.
DATA MSGTXT(70).

GET BDCTH.
  CLEAR BDCTAB. REFRESH BDCTAB.

GET ZBDCDATA.
  IF ZBDCDATA-DYNBEGIN = 'X'.
    PERFORM BDC DYNPRO(ZR 12 01)
            TABLES BDCTAB USING  ZBDCDATA-PROGRAM ZBDCDATA-DYNPRO.
  ELSE.
    PERFORM BDC FIELD(ZR 12 01)
            TABLES BDCTAB USING  ZBDCDATA-FNAM ZBDCDATA-FVAL.
  ENDIF.

GET BDCTH LATE.
 CLEAR MSGTAB. REFRESH MSGTAB.
  CALL TRANSACTION BDCTH-TCODE USING BDCTAB MODE  'A'.   "'N'.
  WRITE: / 'Transaction called:', BDCTH-TCODE.
END-OF-SELECTION.

21.07.98 Chapter 12: Batch input with CALL TRANSACTION             1
--------------------------------------------------------------------
Transaction called: SM30
Transaction called: ZDOC
```

13 Desktop Integration

13.1 Remote Function Call (RFC)

Remote Function Call (RFC) means the call of functions outside system boundaries. The remote system can be another R/3 system, an application server (UNIX) or a PC. If an ABAP/4 program initiates an RFC in an R/3 system, the processing of the lower-level RFC mechanisms is not visible. If the processing is successful, the user hardly notices any difference compared to a normal call of a function module.

13.1.1 RFC Between R/3 Systems

If ABAP/4 is to execute RFC calls as an RFC client, the SM59 transaction must have been used previously to enter an RFC connection in the system. Figure 13.1 shows how such a connection is created to another R/3 system. The system name (SY-SYSID) of the target system is specified as RFC destination. The target machine in this case is the symbolic IP address "mars". The "Test Connection" button can be used to test the specified connection.

The ZR_13_01 program shows the invocation of the Y_SALDO functions module on the "BS1" system. The module must be created there in the 900 client. *RFC Support* must be ticked in the administration data of the module. The Y_SALDO module does not need to be available on the invoking system. In this case, it cannot also be added to the editor using *Process/Statement Pattern.*

However, any type information from the Data Dictionary used in the interface of the module must also be present in the invoking system.

```
REPORT  ZR_13_01 MESSAGE-ID Z0 LINE-SIZE 70.
DATA SALDO(7) TYPE P DECIMALS 2.

CLEAR SALDO.
CALL FUNCTION 'Y_SALDO'
  DESTINATION 'BS1'
  EXPORTING I_VERTRAG = '12345'
  IMPORTING E_SALDO    =  SALDO.

WRITE: / 'Balance =', SALDO.
```

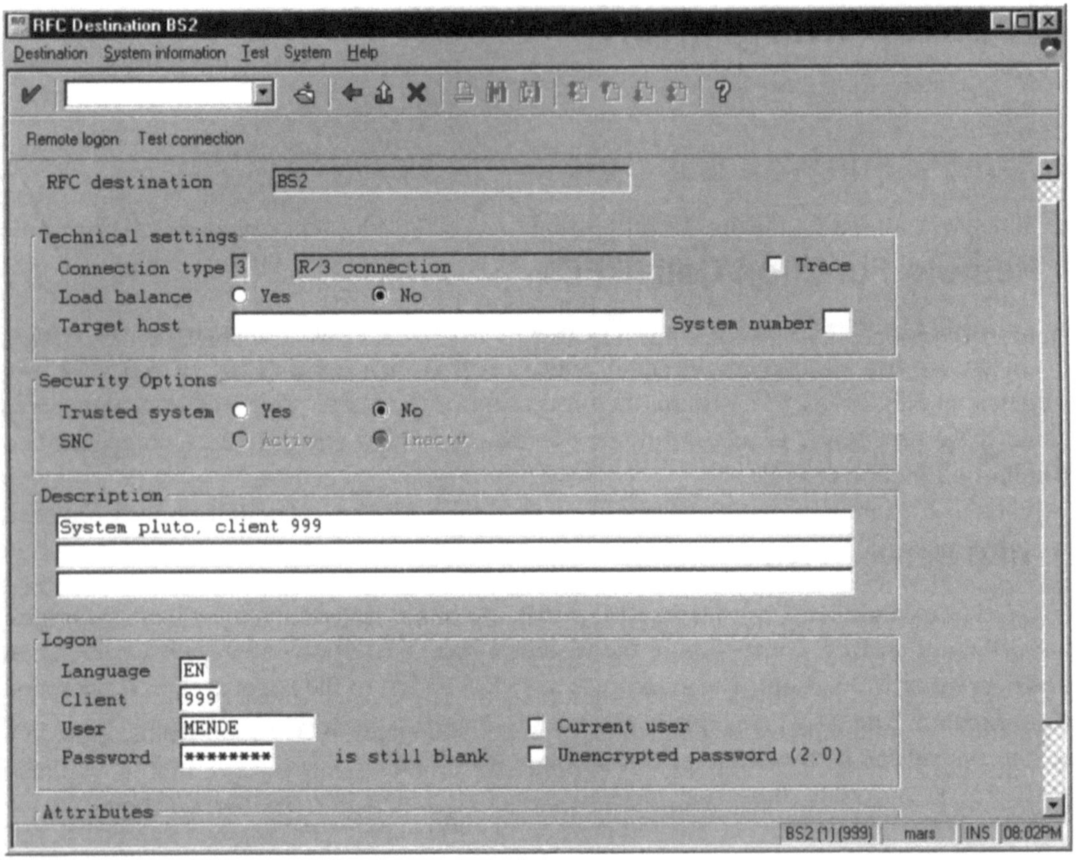

Figure 13.1: Entering an RFC connection between different R/3 systems

13.1.2 RFC with External Systems– the RFC SDK

The RFC between R/3 and external systems is more complicated than the RFC within R/3 systems. This section discusses the RFC connections between PC programs and the R/3 system. These connections can be used in a similar manner for RFC connections between a program on an application server and an R/3 system. Depending on who opens the connection, a differentiation is made between two types of RFC:

- RFC client program on the PC: the PC program opens the connection
- RFC server on the PC: R/3 opens the connection.

To establish an RFC connection with a PC, it is not necessary that the SAPGUI is installed on this PC. SAP provides the RFC SDK to develop and test RFC programs on the PC. This SDK supports various UNIX operating systems and PC operating systems:

- Windows 3.1

- Windows NT
- OS/2.

The RFC programming in C under Windows is also discussed. The RFC SDK includes the following components:

Table 13.1: Required components of the RFC SDK under Windows 3.1

Type	File Name	Content / Use
Header files	SAPRFC.H	Defines, data types and prototypes of the RFC functions
	SAPITAB.H	Data types and prototypes for table parameters
Libraries	LIBRFC16.LIB	Static part for LIBRFC16.DLL
DLLs	LIBRFC16.DLL	Code of the RFC SDK
Help	RFC.HLP	Well-structured, comprehensive Windows help

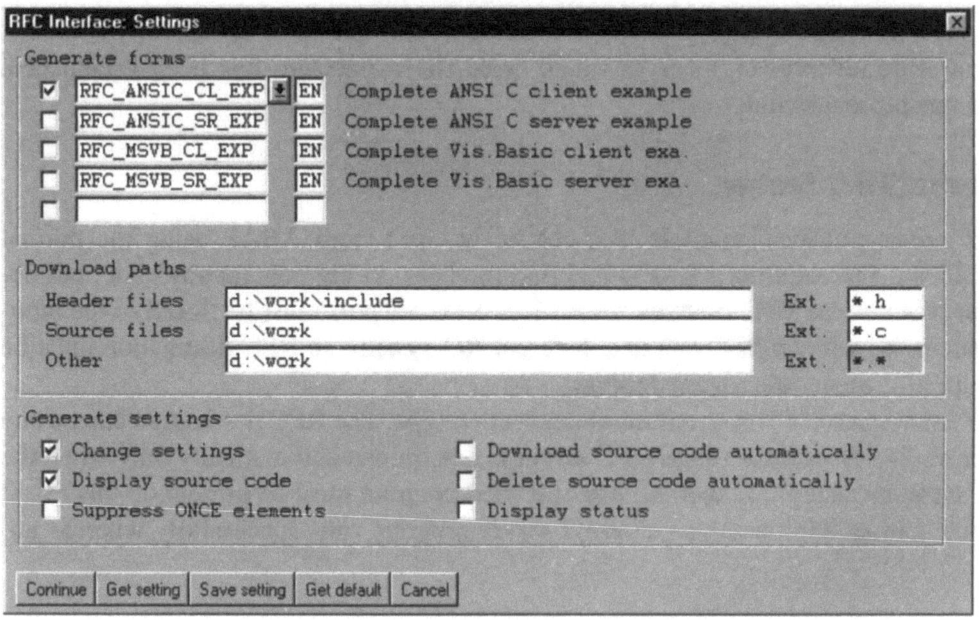

Figure 13.2: Initial screen of the RFC generator of the function library

Helps provide a detailed description of the use of the RFC API. In addition, the RFC Generator integrated in the R/3 system can generate complete code examples for specified ABAP/4 function modules for both RFC clients and RFC server, and store these on the PC. The *Extras* command accesses the RFC Generator in the function library. This introduction to the RFC programming is highly recommended.

13.1.3 External RFC Clients

External RFC clients can invoke those ABAP/4 function modules that are marked as such. Because the external client initializes the connection, it is not necessary to specify a special RFC destination (SM59). The RFC client program has the following general structure (the error handling has been omitted):

```
RfcEnvironment(...);                /* Initialize error handling   */
rfc_handle = RfcOpen(...);          /* Open RFC connection         */
rfc_rc = RfcCallReceive(...);       /* Call a RFC function module  */
RfcClose(...);                   /* Close RFC connection        */
```

RfcOpen( ) opens the connection to an R/3 system specified in the program or in the SAPRFC.INI file. The *RfcCallReceive*( ) function combines the calls of *RfcCall*( ) and *RfcReceive*( ). The name and parameter list of the invoked function module is specified. Obviously, several calls of RfcCallReceive( ) can be made once the connection has been established. RfcClose( ) closes the connection.

13.1.4 External RFC Server

External RFC server provides functions that can be invoked from ABAP using the normal CALL FUNCTION. The required ABAP/4 function modules do not contain any code, but define just the interface of the RFC modules within R/3. *RFC Support* must be ticked in the module administration. As with an RFC call to a different R/3 system, an RFC destination must be specified. Figure 13.2 shows the required inputs.

The TCP/IP connection ("T") is specified as connection type. The RFC destination can be any name in this case. The IP address of the RFC server is determined automatically only when the connection to the associated PC is opened. The specified program must be present on this PC. It is quite possible that an RFC with one external server program runs successfully whereas another fails.

There are two ways of activating RFC servers:

- Startup: The specified program is started on invocation of the RFC module on the PC and then automatically ended on completion. A new invocation restarts the program.
- Registration: The user manually starts the specified program on the PC, which then registers itself in R/3 using the specified program-ID. Any number of subsequent function calls then can be made from R/3. The server program must be ended manually.

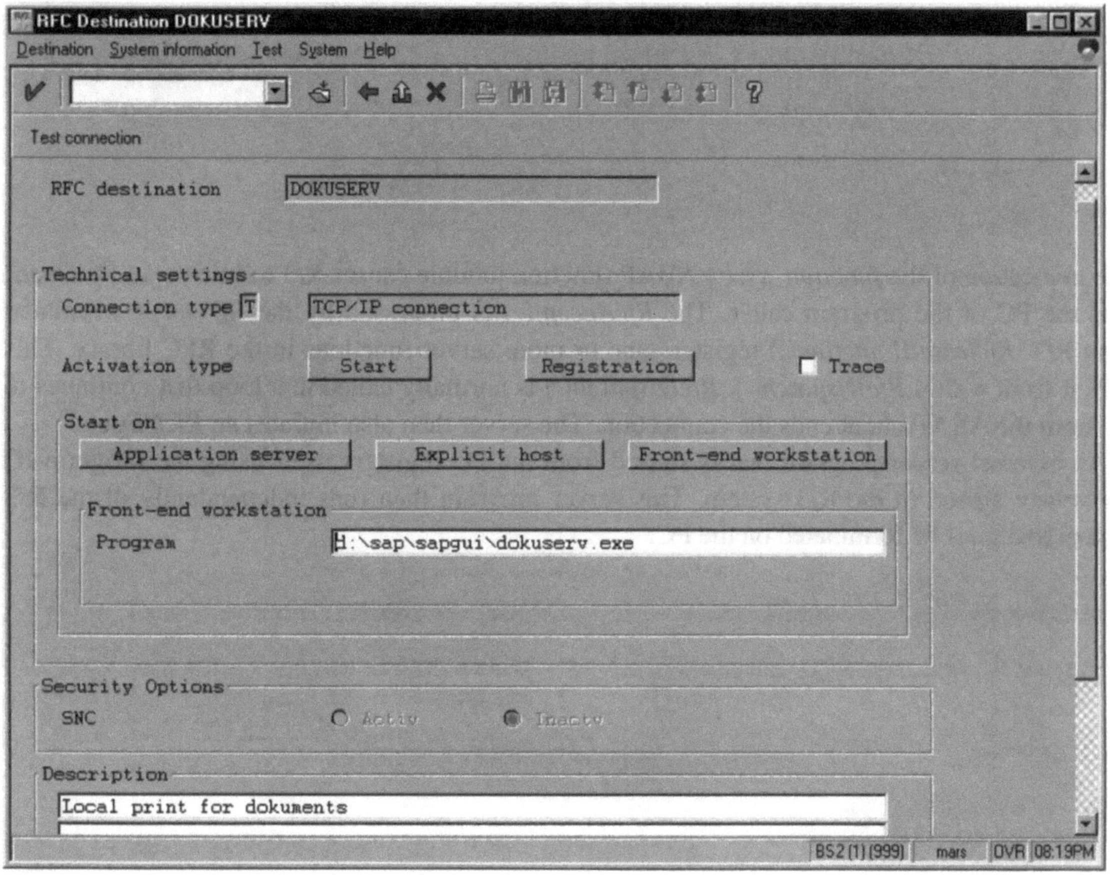

Figure 13.3: RFC destination for a PC server program

A server program that is started from R/3 has the following highly simplified structure:

```
rfc_handle = RfcAccept(...);       /* RFC connection from R/3     */
rfc_rc = RfcInstallFunction(...);/* Install function function_xyz */
do                                 /* Wait for function call */
```

```
  {
    rfc_rc = RfcDispatch(...);              /* Process call */

  } while ( rfc_rc == RFC_OK );

RfcClose(...);                            /* End of program */


static RFC_RC function_xyz(RFC_HANDLE rfc_handle)
{
  rfc_rc = RfcGetData(...);                   /* Get parameter data  */
  ...
  rfc_rc = RfcSendData(...);                  /* Set parameter data */
  ...
  return 0;
}
```

The invocation of the *function_xyz*( ) ABAP function module causes R/3 to initiate an *RfcOpen*( ) on the PC of the program caller. The *RfcAccept*( ) is processed by the *RfcOpen*( ) initiated from R/3. *RfcInstallFunction*( ) registers one or more server functions in the RFC library. This calls it from within *RfcDispatch*( ). *RfcDispatch*( ) is normally called in a loop that continues to run until the ABAP client ends the connection. The server then also initiates an *RfcClose*( ).

An external server program that is started from the PC registers itself using the program-ID previously agreed in the R/3 system. This server program then runs independently of the R/3 system and must be terminated on the PC.

```
rfc_handle = RfcAccept(...);        /* RFC connection from local PC */

rfc_rc = RfcInstallFunction(...);/* Install function function_xyz */
                                  /* within R/3 */

do                                /* Wait for call */
  {

    rfc_rc = RfcListen(...);      /* Poll */
    if   rfc_rc == RFC_RETRY
         {
                                  /* free time for server */
         }
    else rfc_rc = RfcDispatch(...);    /* process call */

  } while ( rfc_rc == RFC_OK );

RfcClose(...);                                 /* End of program */


static RFC_RC function_xyz(RFC_HANDLE rfc_handle)
{
```

```
   rfc_rc = RfcGetData(...);                    /* Get parameter data */
   ...
   rfc_rc = RfcSendData(...);                   /* Set parameter data */
   ...
   return 0;
}
```

13.2 Desktop Integration with OLE

13.2.1 ABAP/4 as OLE Client on Desktop Servers (Excel, WinWord)

ABAP/4 provides from Release 3.0 the following OLE language elements that can be used to access the OLE2 server on the PC:

CREATE OBJECT *object class* **[LANGUAGE** *lang* **].**
SET PROPERTY OF *object P = field | literal.*
GET PROPERTY OF *object P = field.*
CALL METHOD OF *object method*
EXPORTING *#1 = field1 | literal1 ... #n ... fieldn | literaln.*
FREE OBJECT *object.*

The OLE commands are directly oriented to the terms used in object-oriented programming. Objects have properties that can be read or set. They provide parameterized methods that can be executed. To create an object of an OLE2 server class, the affected class must be connected in R/3. As usual, SY-SUBRC indicates the success or failure of the commands.
WORD.BASIC for WinWord and EXCEL.APPLICATION for Excel are two frequently used classes. The following section discusses these two classes in more detail. The properties and methods correspond to those provided by WORD-BASIC and EXCEL-BASIC. You can use the program help for these languages to obtained detailed information about the properties and methods. For example, the
DateiÖffen (FileOpen) "C:\BE\KAP\MAHNDOC.DOC" command
is used in a WORD-BASIC macro to load an existing file, whereas ABAP/4 uses simply

```
CREATE OBJECT WORD " WORD.BASIC"  LANGUAGE 'D'.
CALL METHOD OF WORD 'DATEIÖFFNEN'
                           EXPORTING #1 = 'C:\BE\KAP\MAHNDOC.DOC'.
```

Optional parameters (conversion, password, write-protect, etc.) can also be specified. The form of the commands is somewhat unusual, because fields that receive a value are written to the right of the assignment character. For example, to read an Excel cell into the ABAP/4 field VALUE:

```
GET PROPERTY OF ZELLE 'Value' = VALUE .
```

An English version of Word also functions with German methods and properties. It is always simpler for the developer to set the language for his OLE object to match that available in the PC help text.

The ZR_13_02 program displays a report that takes records from an Excel table in accordance with Figure 13.4. The language has been set by default to English.

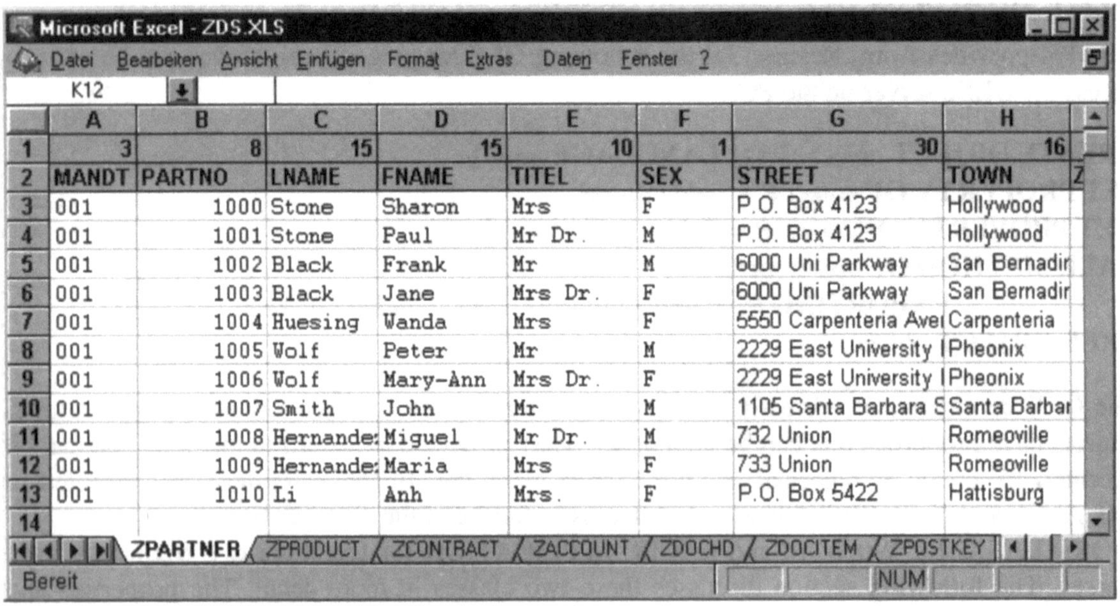

	A	B	C	D	E	F	G	H
1	3	8	15	15	10	1	30	16
2	MANDT	PARTNO	LNAME	FNAME	TITEL	SEX	STREET	TOWN
3	001	1000	Stone	Sharon	Mrs	F	P.O. Box 4123	Hollywood
4	001	1001	Stone	Paul	Mr Dr.	M	P.O. Box 4123	Hollywood
5	001	1002	Black	Frank	Mr	M	6000 Uni Parkway	San Bernadir
6	001	1003	Black	Jane	Mrs Dr.	F	6000 Uni Parkway	San Bernadir
7	001	1004	Huesing	Wanda	Mrs	F	5550 Carpenteria Ave	Carpenteria
8	001	1005	Wolf	Peter	Mr	M	2229 East University	Pheonix
9	001	1006	Wolf	Mary-Ann	Mrs Dr.	F	2229 East University	Pheonix
10	001	1007	Smith	John	Mr	M	1105 Santa Barbara S	Santa Barbar
11	001	1008	Hernande	Miguel	Mr Dr.	M	732 Union	Romeoville
12	001	1009	Hernande	Maria	Mrs	F	733 Union	Romeoville
13	001	1010	Li	Anh	Mrs.	F	P.O. Box 5422	Hattisburg
14								

Figure 13.4: Excel folder that is accessed from ZR_13_02 using OLE

The OLE2INCL and EXCEL__C Includes make various definitions available to the program. The EXCEL, FOLDER, SHEET and CELL OLE objects are then defined. The program's OLE calls refer to these objects.

```
CREATE OBJECT EXCEL 'EXCEL.Application'.
SET PROPERTY OF EXCEL 'Visible' = 1.
```

The above code starts Excel on the PC. Excel operates in the background if the 'Visible' property is not set. It is often better during the development to follow the individual actions on the screen.

The Workbooks method of the EXCEL object creates a folder object whose 'OPEN' method opens the specified folder.

The program initially reads in a DO loop from line 2 all field names into the internal table FIELDTAB. Then a further DO loop is used to read all values of a partner record. Although only WRITE is used to make the output here, it could also contain a MODIFY to the ZPARTNER table.

The WorkSheet method creates a table object and the ZPARTNER table is activated in the LOAD_TABLE form.

The Cells method of the table object is invoked in the READ_CELL form. The method receives the line and column in the table as parameters. The cell is activated and the value is read.

```
CALL METHOD OF TABELLE 'Cells' = CELL
               EXPORTING #1 = ROW  #2 = COL.
CALL METHOD OF CELL 'Activate'.
GET PROPERTY OF CELL 'Value' = VALUE.
```

```
REPORT  ZR_13_02 LINE-SIZE 70.
TABLES: ZPARTNER.

INCLUDE OLE2INCL.
INCLUDE EXCEL_C.

CONSTANTS: EXCELFILE(30) VALUE 'C:\BE\ABAP\ZLS.XLS'.

DATA EXCEL   TYPE OLE2_OBJECT.
DATA FOLDER  TYPE OLE2_OBJECT.
DATA SHEET   TYPE OLE2_OBJECT.
DATA CELL    TYPE OLE2_OBJECT.

CREATE OBJECT EXCEL 'EXCEL.Application'.
SET PROPERTY OF EXCEL 'Visible' = 1.
CALL METHOD OF EXCEL 'WORKBOOKS' = FOLDER.
CALL METHOD OF FOLDER 'OPEN' EXPORTING #1 = EXCELFILE.
PERFORM LOAD_TABLE_VALUES USING 'ZPARTNER'.
CALL METHOD OF EXCEL 'QUIT'.
FREE OBJECT EXCEL.
*--------------------------------------------------------------------
FORM LOAD_TABLE_VALUES USING VALUE(TABNAME) LIKE DD03L-TABNAME.
DATA:  FIELDTAB(30) OCCURS 10 WITH HEADER LINE.
DATA FIELDCOUNT TYPE I.
DATA FIELDNAME(30).
DATA FULLNAME(30).
DATA FIELDVALUE(30).
DATA: COLUMN TYPE I, ROW TYPE I.
FIELD-SYMBOLS: <FS>.
```

```
CALL METHOD OF EXCEL 'WorkSheets' = SHEET
                EXPORTING #1 = TABNAME .
CALL METHOD OF SHEET 'Activate'.

* find field names in row 2
COLUMN = 1.
DO.
  PERFORM READ_CELL USING 2 COLUMN FIELDTAB.
  IF FIELDTAB = SPACE.
    EXIT.
  ENDIF.
  APPEND FIELDTAB.
  COLUMN = COLUMN + 1.
ENDDO.
DESCRIBE TABLE FIELDTAB LINES FIELDCOUNT.
* read the field valus row by row
ROW = 3.
DO.
  PERFORM READ_CELL USING ROW 1 FIELDVALUE.  " 1. COLUMN
  IF FIELDVALUE NE SPACE.
    DO FIELDCOUNT TIMES.
      PERFORM READ_CELL USING ROW SY-INDEX FIELDVALUE.
      IF FIELDVALUE NE SPACE.
        READ TABLE FIELDTAB INDEX SY-INDEX.
        CONCATENATE TABNAME '-' FIELDTAB INTO FULLNAME.
        ASSIGN (FULLNAME) TO <FS>." TYPE FIELDTAB-INTTYPE.
*        FIELDVALUE = FIELDVALUE(FIELDTAB-LENG).
        <FS> = FIELDVALUE.
        WRITE: / FULLNAME, '=', <FS>.
      ENDIF.
    ENDDO.
    ROW = ROW + 1.
    IF ROW > 5. EXIT. ENDIF.
    ULINE.
*   MODIFY ZPARTNER.   " to insert data into database, remove comment
  ELSE.                " no further rows
    EXIT.
  ENDIF.
ENDDO.
ENDFORM.
*---------------------------------------------------------------------
FORM READ_CELL USING VALUE(ROW) VALUE(COLUMN) VAL.
CALL METHOD OF SHEET 'Cells' = CELL
               EXPORTING #1 = ROW  #2 = COLUMN.
CALL METHOD OF CELL 'Activate'.
GET PROPERTY OF CELL 'Value' = VAL .
ENDFORM.
```

```
29.05.1998  Chapter 13: ABAP as an OLE-Client at EXCEL Server      1
--------------------------------------------------------------------
ZPARTNER-CLIENT                  = 999
ZPARTNER-PARTNO                  = 00001000
ZPARTNER-LNAME                   = Stone
ZPARTNER-FNAME                   = Sharon
ZPARTNER-TITEL                   = Mrs
ZPARTNER-SEX                     = F
ZPARTNER-STREET                  = P.O. Box 4123
ZPARTNER-TOWN                    = Hollywood
ZPARTNER-CIPCODE                 = 90028
ZPARTNER-STATE                   = CA
--------------------------------------------------------------------
ZPARTNER-CLIENT                  = 999
ZPARTNER-PARTNO                  = 00001001
ZPARTNER-LNAME                   = Stone
ZPARTNER-FNAME                   = Paul
ZPARTNER-TITEL                   = Mr Dr.
ZPARTNER-SEX                     = M
ZPARTNER-STREET                  = P.O. Box 4123
ZPARTNER-TOWN                    = Hollywood
ZPARTNER-CIPCODE                 = 90028
ZPARTNER-STATE                   = CA
```

The ZR_13_03 program illustrates the interaction of ABAP/4 and WinWord. It creates dunning notices for overdue items using the principle of form letters. German has been selected as language for the methods and properties.

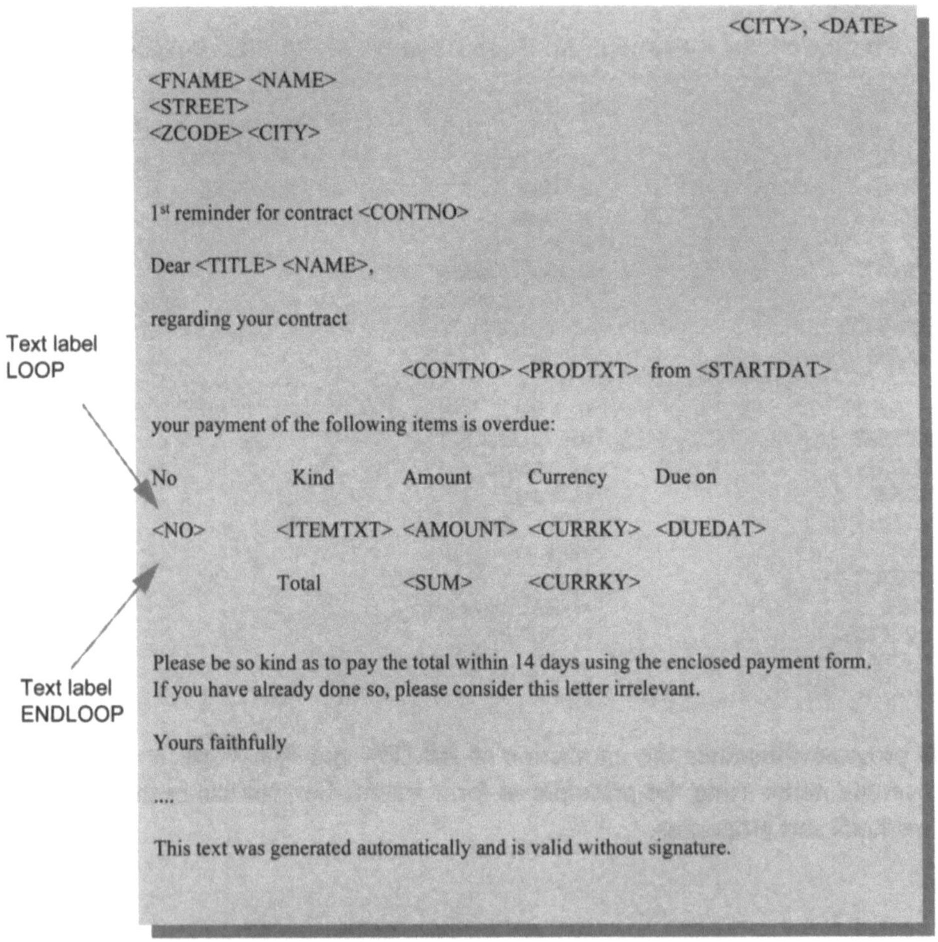

<CITY>, <DATE>

<FNAME> <NAME>
<STREET>
<ZCODE> <CITY>

1st reminder for contract <CONTNO>

Dear <TITLE> <NAME>,

regarding your contract

<CONTNO> <PRODTXT> from <STARTDAT>

your payment of the following items is overdue:

No	Kind	Amount	Currency	Due on
<NO>	<ITEMTXT>	<AMOUNT>	<CURRKY>	<DUEDAT>
	Total	<SUM>	<CURRKY>	

Please be so kind as to pay the total within 14 days using the enclosed payment form.
If you have already done so, please consider this letter irrelevant.

Yours faithfully

....

This text was generated automatically and is valid without signature.

Figure 13.5: Master document for a dunning notice

The SELECT commands show the highly simplified dunning process that determines the overdue items. To simplify the processing, only one document is determined. The overdue items for this document are set into the internal table ITEMTAB and should appear on the dunning notice.

The connection to Word is established as in the pervious example. The dunning notice is stored as master document with placeholders of the form <NAME>, <CITY>, etc. (Figure 13.5).

The dunning notice is opened and all placeholders successively replaced with the values determined in the program. The REPLACE form defined for this purpose contains the *Bearbeiten-Suchen* (ProcessSearch) and *Einfügen* (Insert) calls.

The line for the open items forms a special case. This line is enclosed in the LOOP and ENDLOOP text marks. These are not visible in the text. Arrows in Figure 13.5 indicate the position of the text marks. The program initially searches for the LOOP text mark, and then marks the text up to ENDLOOP. The line marked in such a way will continue to be duplicated with *BearbeitenEinfügen* (EditInsert) until the number of lines is the same as the number of open items in the internal table POSTAB. The write cursor is then set to the LOOP text cursor. All line fields in all lines are now replaced in a loop over ITEMTAB. This permits a table structure to represent a master document.

Because packed-decimal numbers or binary-coded numbers must be converted before they are passed to WinWord, WRITE TO is used to set the currency amount into an appropriate CHAR field.

Once all placeholders have been replaced, the document is printed and then discarded. This retains the master document.

```
REPORT  ZR_13_03 LINE-SIZE 70.
INCLUDE OLE2INCL.
TABLES:      ZPARTNER, ZCONTRACT, ZPRODUCT,
             ZDOCHD, ZDOCITEM, ZPOSTKEY, ZPOSTKEYT.
CONSTANTS:   DOCNAME(50) VALUE 'C:\BE\KAP\DUNNING.DOC'.
DATA:        BEGIN OF ITEMTAB OCCURS 10,
               ITEMTEXT LIKE ZDOCITEM-ITEMTEXT,
               AMOUNT(15),
               CURRKY LIKE ZDOCHD-CURRKY,
               DUEDAT(10),
             END OF ITEMTAB.
DATA         DUNDAT LIKE SY-DATUM VALUE '19980602'.
DATA         CSUM(15).
DATA         WORD TYPE OLE2_OBJECT.
DATA         CURNO(1) TYPE N.
DATA         SUM LIKE ZDOCITEM-AMOUNT.
DATA         DATE(10).

* determine the dunning items
SELECT * FROM ZDOCITEM WHERE DOCNO = '5004'
                           AND DUEDAT < DUNDAT.
  SELECT SINGLE * FROM ZPOSTKEYT
                     WHERE LANGU = 'E' AND PSTKY = ZDOCITEM-PSTKY.
  SELECT SINGLE * FROM ZDOCHD WHERE DOCNO = ZDOCITEM-DOCNO.
  SELECT SINGLE * FROM ZCONTRACT WHERE CONTNO = ZDOCHD-CONTNO.
  SELECT SINGLE * FROM ZPARTNER WHERE PARTNO = ZCONTRACT-PARTNO.
  SELECT SINGLE * FROM ZPRODUCT WHERE PRODNO = ZCONTRACT-PRODNO.
  ITEMTAB-ITEMTEXT = ZPOSTKEYT-PSTKYTXT.
  WRITE  ZDOCITEM-AMOUNT TO ITEMTAB-AMOUNT RIGHT-JUSTIFIED.
  ADD ZDOCITEM-AMOUNT TO SUM.
  ITEMTAB-CURRKY = ZDOCHD-CURRKY.
  WRITE ZDOCITEM-DUEDAT TO ITEMTAB-DUEDAT.
  APPEND ITEMTAB.
ENDSELECT.
```

```
* open WORD server und load file
CREATE OBJECT WORD 'Word.Basic' LANGUAGE 'D'.
CALL METHOD OF WORD 'DateiÖffnen' EXPORTING #1 = DOCNAME.

* find and replace < ... >
PERFORM REPLACE USING '<CITY>'      'Boston'.
WRITE SY-DATUM TO DATE.
PERFORM REPLACE USING '<DATE>'      DATE.
PERFORM REPLACE USING '<FNAME>'     ZPARTNER-FNAME.
PERFORM REPLACE USING '<NAME>'      ZPARTNER-LNAME.
PERFORM REPLACE USING '<STREET>'    ZPARTNER-STREET.
PERFORM REPLACE USING '<ZCODE>'     ZPARTNER-ZIP.
PERFORM REPLACE USING '<CITY>'      ZPARTNER-TOWN.
PERFORM REPLACE USING '<CONTNO>'    ZCONTRACT-CONTNO.
PERFORM REPLACE USING '<TITLE>'     ZPARTNER-TITLE.
PERFORM REPLACE USING '<NAME>'      ZPARTNER-LNAME.
PERFORM REPLACE USING '<CONTNO>'    ZCONTRACT-CONTNO.
PERFORM REPLACE USING '<PRODTXT>'   ZPRODUCT-PRODTXT.
WRITE ZCONTRACT-STARTDAT TO DATE.
PERFORM REPLACE USING '<STARTDAT>'  DATE.

* find the text label LOOP and mark the text from here to
* text label ENDLOOP
CALL METHOD OF WORD 'BearbeitengeheZu' EXPORTING #1 = 'LOOP'.
CALL METHOD OF WORD 'MarkierungErweitern'.
CALL METHOD OF WORD 'BearbeitengeheZu' EXPORTING #1 = 'ENDLOOP'.
CALL METHOD OF WORD 'BearbeitenKopieren'.
*CALL METHOD OF WORD 'BearbeitenEinfügen'.

* LOOP in document gets as many lines as ITEMTAB has
DESCRIBE TABLE ITEMTAB LINES SY-TFILL.
DO SY-TFILL TIMES.
  CALL METHOD OF WORD 'BearbeitenEinfügen'.
ENDDO.

* back to the start of the LOOP and insert the LOOP lines
CALL METHOD OF WORD 'BearbeitengeheZu' EXPORTING #1 = 'LOOP'.
LOOP AT ITEMTAB.
  CURNO = SY-TABIX.
  PERFORM REPLACE USING '<NO>'      CURNO.
  PERFORM REPLACE USING '<ITEMTXT>' ITEMTAB-ITEMTEXT.
  PERFORM REPLACE USING '<AMOUNT>'  ITEMTAB-AMOUNT.
  PERFORM REPLACE USING '<CURRKY>'  ITEMTAB-CURRKY.
  PERFORM REPLACE USING '<DUEDAT>'  ITEMTAB-DUEDAT.
ENDLOOP.

* total of items
WRITE SUM TO CSUM.
PERFORM REPLACE USING '<SUM>'   CSUM.
PERFORM REPLACE USING '<CURRKY>'   ITEMTAB-CURRKY.

* print and save dunning
CALL METHOD OF WORD 'DateiDrucken'.
```

```
CALL METHOD OF WORD 'DateiSpeichernUnter'
                    EXPORTING #1 = 'C:\BE\KAP\M.DOC'.
CALL METHOD OF WORD 'DateiSchließen' EXPORTING #1 = 2.

* release object
FREE OBJECT WORD.
*-------------------------------------------------------------------
FORM REPLACE USING WHAT WITH.
  CALL METHOD OF WORD 'BearbeitenSuchen' EXPORTING #1 = WHAT.
  CALL METHOD OF WORD 'Einfügen' EXPORTING #1 = WITH.
ENDFORM.
.
```

Because the name and sequence of the fields to be replaced in the master document must also be known in the program, this method is inflexible. If fields are changed in the master document, the program must be modified accordingly.

Boston, 21.07.1998

Frank Black
6000 Uni Parkway
92407 San Bernadino

1st reminder for contract 00003001

Dear Mr Black,

regarding your contract

00003001 life insurance from 23.07.1996

your payment of the following items is overdue:

No	Kind	Amount	Currency	Due on
1	net premium	1.950,00	USD	01.03.1997
2	delay interest	100,00	USD	01.03.1997
3	back payment	200,00	USD	01.03.1997
	Total	2.250,00	USD	

Please be so kind as to pay the total within 14 days using the enclosed payment form.
If you have already done so, please consider this letter irrelevant.

Yours faithfully

....

This text was generated automatically and is valid without signature.

Figure 13.6: Dunning notice created with the master document from Figure 13.5

It is possible to make the creation of documents more variable by using only designations of the DDIC as placeholders. This permits the required data designations in the program to be read from the master document, the data to be obtained and inserted.

A true dunning using large amounts of data would maintain dunning schedules (dunning process) with several dunning levels and a dunning history. Before each dunning, the dunning history would be used to determine the next dunning level is to be performed according to the dunning schedule. An appropriate master document is created for each of the possible dunning levels.

The shown program requires approximately 12 seconds on the PC to produce the print file. Although this is too slow for the processing of mass data, this method is well-suited for rapid prototyping. Figure 13.6 shows the complete document produced with the ZR_13_03 program.

13.2.2 Desktop Clients to ABAP/4 Servers

OLE calls can be passed to an R/3 OLE server SAPServ from various programming languages. The methods of the server correspond to the ABAP/4 function modules. The following example shows an Excel subroutine that opens the connection, invokes a function module and then closes the connection.

```
Sub ReadCurrency()
Dim SAPServer Als Object
Dim SAPConn Als Object

Dim Result Als Boolesch
Dim Password Als Boolesch
Dim Currency Als ZeichenF

' Get connection to R/3 and log in
Set SAPServer = CreateObject("RFC.ServerObject.1")
Set SAPConn = SAPServer.Connection

SAPConn.User = "MENDE"
SAPConn.Destination = "BV1"
SAPConn.Client = "001"
SAPConn.System = "21"
SAPConn.HostName = "pluto"
SAPConn.Language = "D"
SAPConn.GatewayHost = "berlin"
SAPConn.GatewayService = "berlin"
'
' Enter password
Password = InputBox("Enter Password")
SAPConn.Password = Password

Wenn SAPConn.Öffnen <> Wahr Dann
   MsgBox ("No connection.")
   SAPServer.Application.Quit
   Verlasse Sub
Ende Wenn
'
' Call of function module as method call of object SAPServer
Result = SAPServer.Y_GET_WAERS_FROM_BUKRS(BUKRS:="0001" ,
                                          WAERS:= Currency)
```

```
Wenn Result <> Wahr Dann
   MsgBox ("Function Call Failed")
   SAPServer.Application.Quit
   Verlasse Sub
Ende Wenn

' Close connection
SAPServer.Quit Falsch
Ende Sub
```

14 Development Aids

Efficient tools for fault localization and program analysis are essential for the development of large application systems. The range of such tools provided by R/3 is summarized here.

14.1 Pretty Printer and Program Checks

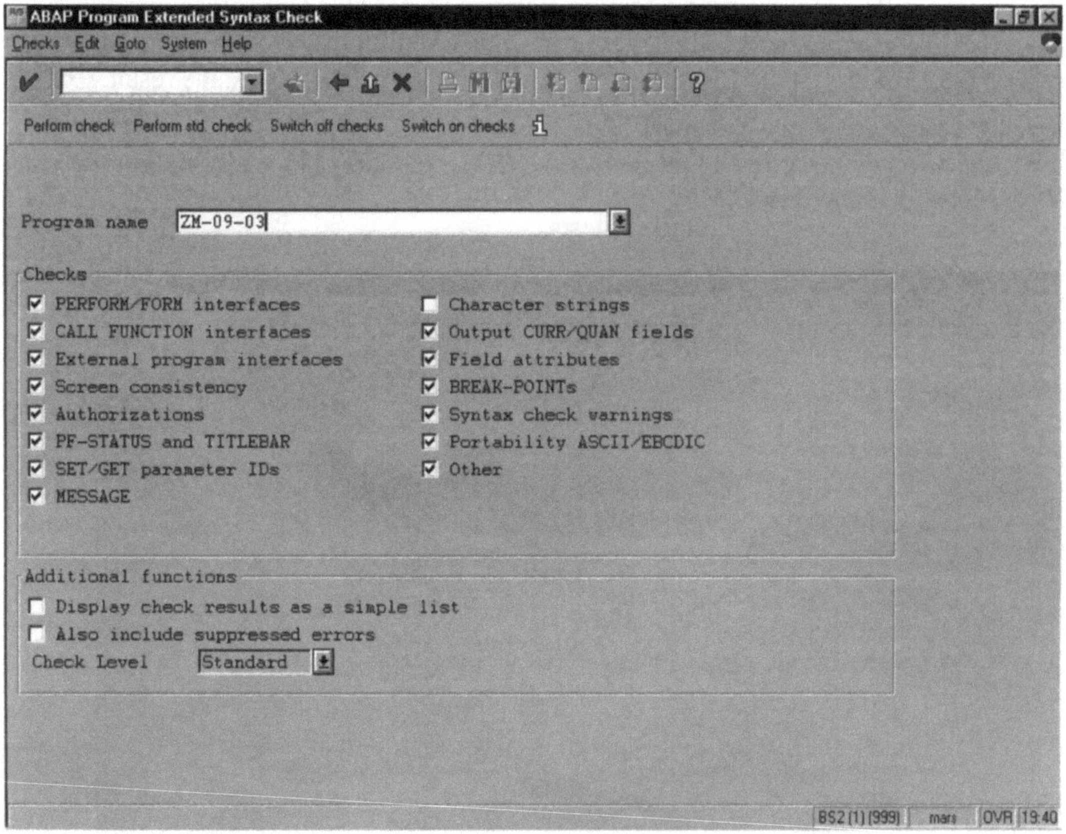

Figure 14.1: Extended syntax check of an ABAP/4 program

The consistent and orderly formatting of large source codes has an effect on their readability and maintainability that should not be underestimated. The ABAP/4 Editor provides with *Program/Pretty Printer* a formatting program that formats source code without requiring any additional effort. Two blank characters are used to form the various nesting levels. Matching command groups, such as LOOP-ENDLOOP, SELECT-ENDSELECT and IF-ELSE-ELSEIF are aligned. The use of the pretty printer can be particularly recommended for large development teams where the source code may need to be read by several developers.

The greater the number of errors that can be already recognized by the syntax checker, the fewer runtime errors and short dumps you get. If you consistently use the capabilities of ABAP/4, such as initialization of variables and type-checking of parameters, you can avoid many runtime errors by providing the syntax checker with additional information. Unfortunately, the standard syntax check invoked from the symbolbar or with the *Program/Check/Current Program* command does not perform all possible validations. For example, you receive the "*No syntax errors found*" message even when the checked program passes an incorrect parameter list to a called function module. A runtime error would be the result. Consequently, in longer intervals, but always before the completion of a program, it is desirable to perform an extended check. It is started using *Program/Check/Extended Program Check* and provides the capability to select specific checks, see Figure 14.1. The validation can take quite some time for a large program if you mark all tests.

Figure 14.2 shows the overview of an extended check. A double-click on an error or warning provides the corresponding details.

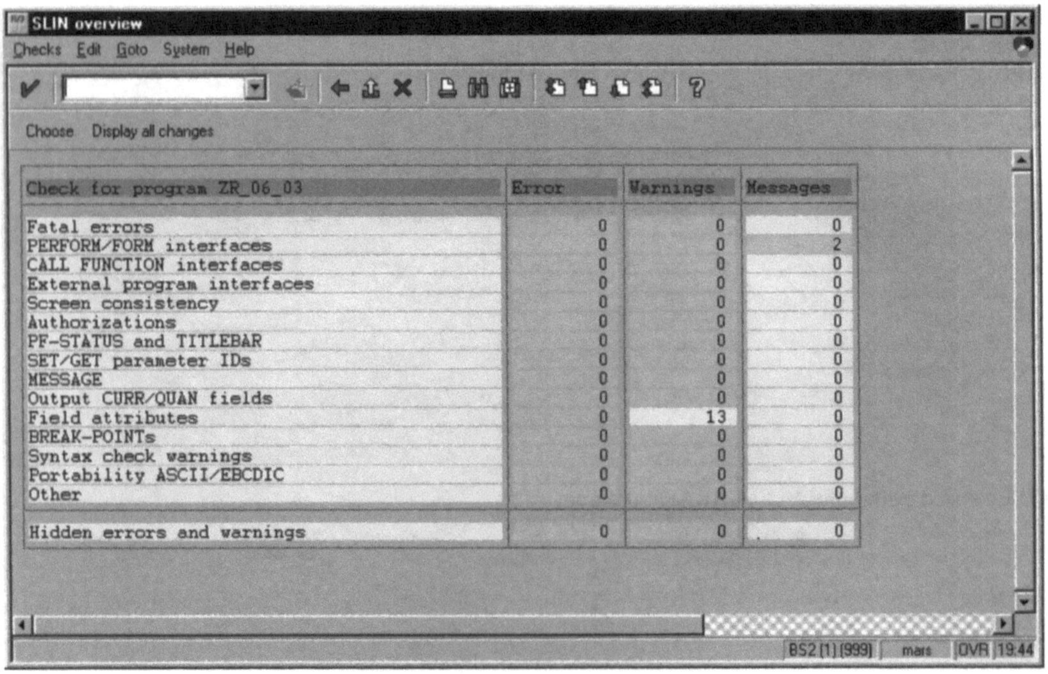

Figure 14.2: Result overview after an extended check

14.2 Testing of Function Modules

Function modules are designed to perform limited tasks and use only the interface to exchange information with the calling program. Function modules cannot access global data of the calling program. Consequently, it is possible and also useful to test function modules during their development without requiring the calling program. R/3 provides a very powerful test environment for this situation; the Z_CONTRACTS_TO_ACCOUNT module illustrates the use of this test environment. The module has one import parameter: the account number. An internal table of all contracts for this account is returned as the result.

```
FUNCTION Z_CONTRACTS_TO_ACCOUNT.
*"----------------------------------------------------------------
*"*"Local interface:
*"       IMPORTING
*"             VALUE(I_ACCNO) LIKE  ZACCOUNT-ACCNO
*"       TABLES
*"              T_CONTRACT STRUCTURE  ZCONTRACT
*"       EXCEPTIONS
*"              ACCOUNT_FALSE
*"----------------------------------------------------------------
SELECT SINGLE * FROM ZACCOUNT WHERE ACCNO = I_ACCNO.
IF SY-SUBRC > 0.
  RAISE ACCOUNT_FALSE.
ENDIF.

SELECT * FROM ZCONTRACT INTO TABLE T_CONTRACT
                 WHERE ACCNO = I_ACCNO.
ENDFUNCTION.
```

Once the function module has been coded and activated, *Process* from the function group list can be used to start the test environment. The test environment presents a dynpro on which all import parameters of the module can be entered (Figure 14.3). The input fields for all export parameters are displayed after *Process*. Import structures can also be entered interactively.

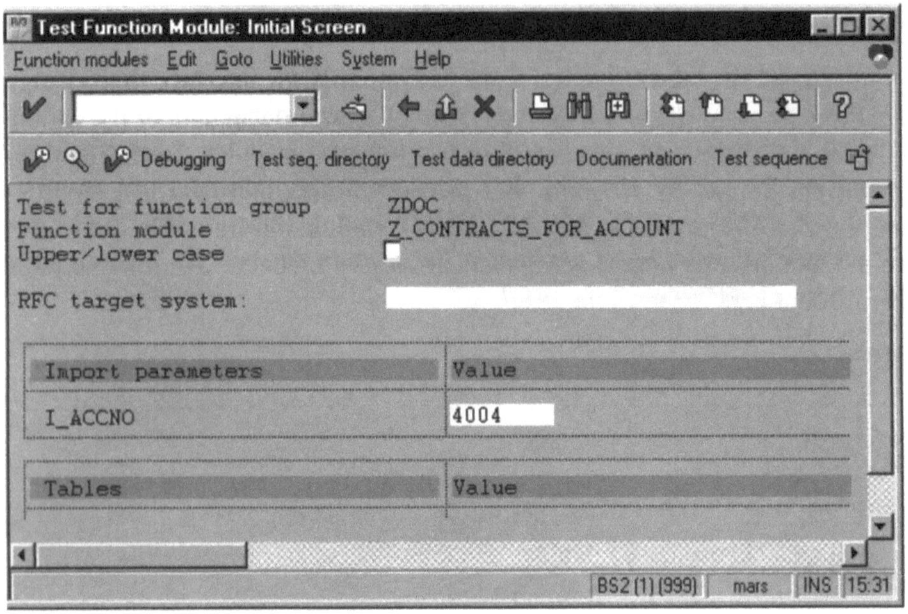

Figure 14.3: Testing of function modules

The values of all export parameters are displayed once the test has been started (Figure 14.4).

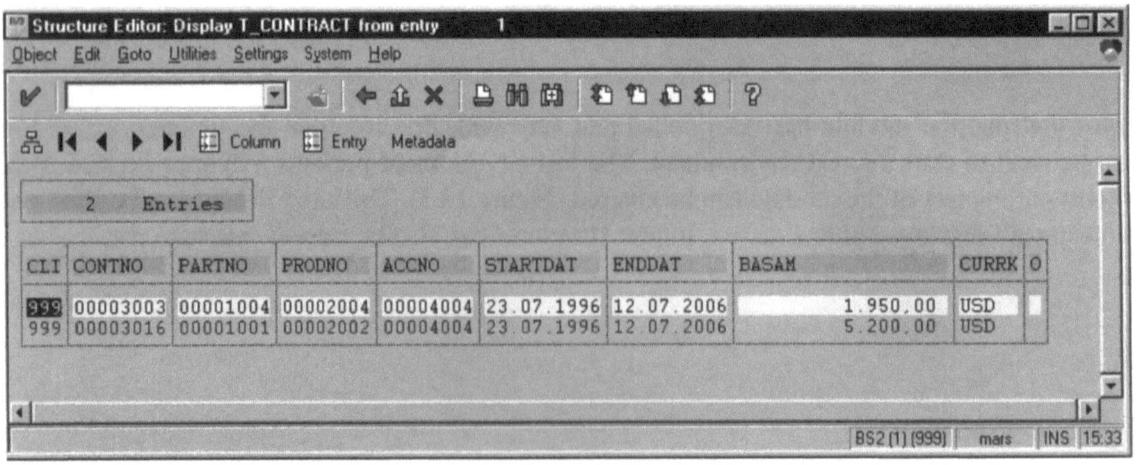

Figure 14.4: Result screen for the test of Z_CONTRACTS_FOR_ACCOUNT

The line count before and after the execution is initially specified for table parameters. A double-click on a table name displays the table contents.

To permit the reuse of test cases that have extensive import parameters, it is possible to store such test cases with appropriate comments for the test data (Figure 14.5).

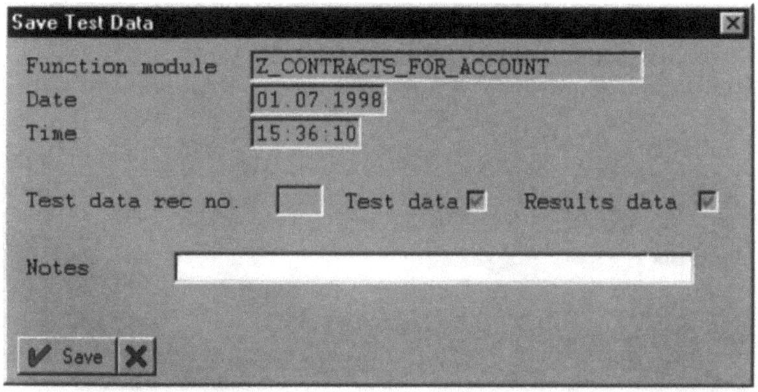

Figure 14.5: Save test data

Saved test cases can be later retrieved from the test directory and re-executed. It is also possible to define and process complete test sequences.

This test environment provides the user with an excellent test tool. Unlike the Debugger, this test tool can be used by personnel who have only limited experience with the Workbench (user department).

14.3 Dump Analysis

Even extended program checks cannot eliminate all runtime errors. In certain critical error situations, the ABAP processor terminates the program and produces a short dump (Figure 14.6). The short dump is displayed immediately in online operation. In batch operation, it can be displayed using the *Tools/Administration/Monitor/Dump/Analysis* command. The error name (DBIF_NTAB_FIELD_NOT_FOUND) and the following explanatory line normally suffice to clarify the error. The short dump provides further information on

- the system environment,
- the user and the transaction
- the fault location in the program (source code)
- the values of the system fields
- the values of selected program variables.

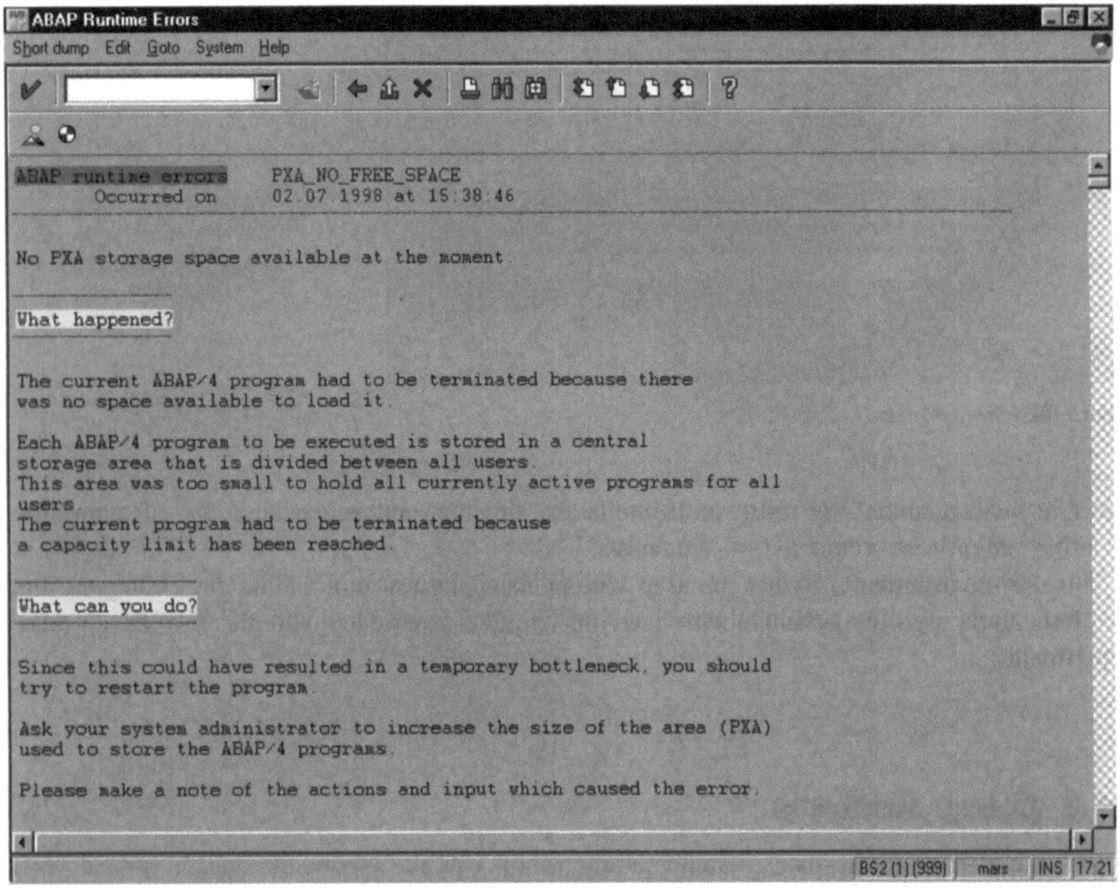

Figure 14.6: Short dump for an incorrect dynamic SELECT

14.4 Debugger

All modern programming environments provide symbolic debuggers for error localization in programs at the source code level. The principle is the same in all cases. So-called breakpoints are used to insert interrupts in the lines where the program is to pause. If the program reaches a breakpoint, it stops and the debugger is activated. The user can now inspect his program at source code level, for example, he can access program variables using their symbolic names or he can view invocation hierarchies. Compiler languages buy this capability through increased processing during compiling and linking and also in the resulting larger EXE files. An executable program does not normally contain any symbolic information but only the addresses of variables and functions. Because the symbolic information is always present at runtime for interpreter languages such as BASIC and ABAP/4, these languages do not require any special preparations for debugging.

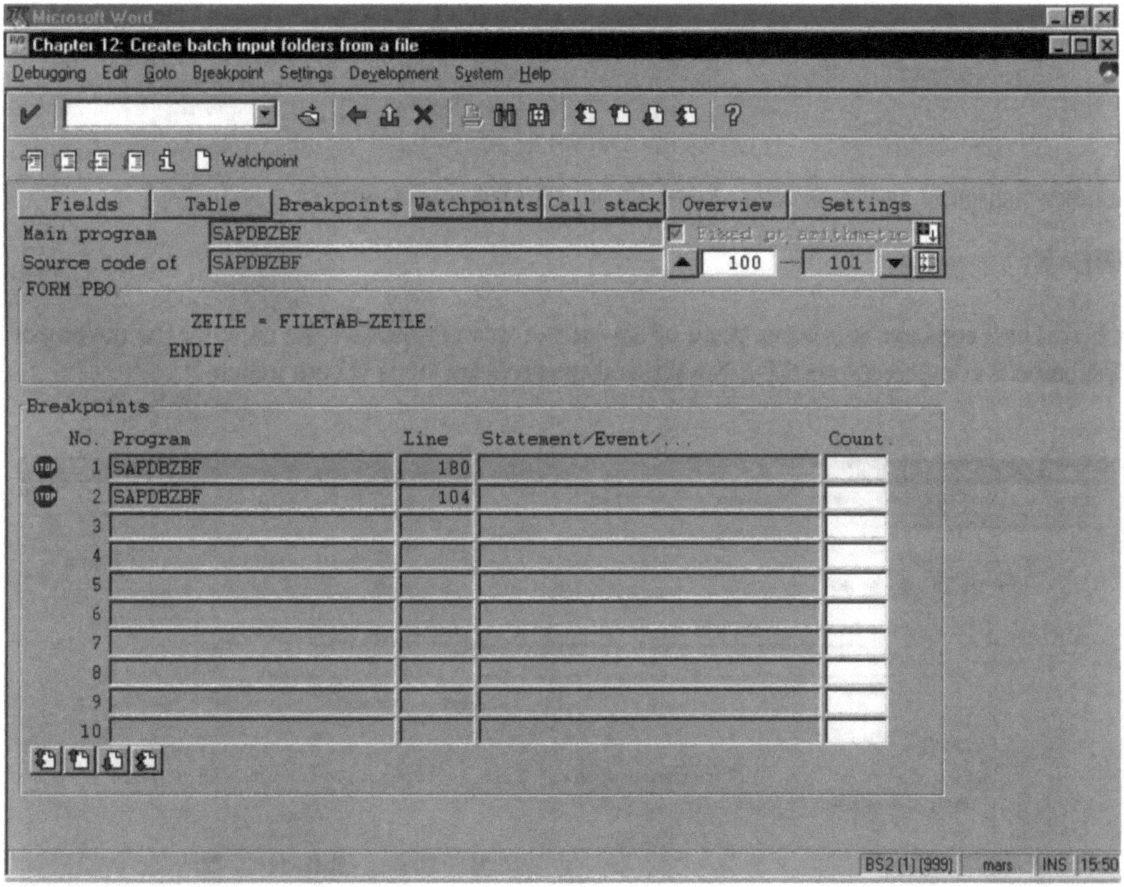

Figure 14.7: Debugger in 'V' mode

Breakpoints in ABAP/4 programs are normally set directly in the Editor. The *Breakpoints* command can be used to provide a list of the breakpoints. Individual breakpoints can be deactivated temporarily or deleted. Special ABAP/4 commands are also available to add breakpoints to the source code:

BREAK-POINT.

In this variant, the program always pauses at the line that contains the command. This has the advantage that the breakpoint remains at this source code location, even when extensive program modifications have been made. However, unpleasant surprises are possible if you forget to remove breakpoints from the program before it is put into productive use. In many cases it is desirable to invoke the command only under specific circumstances, e.g., only when the program runs on a specific system:

```
IF SY-SYSID = 'PLUTO'.
  BREAK-POINT.
ENDIF.
```

Another restrictive variant is offered directly as ABAP/4 command:

BREAK *username.*

A literal or a constant is used in place of *username*; this is typically the name of the developer. This name is compared with SY-UNAME and the program stops if both match.

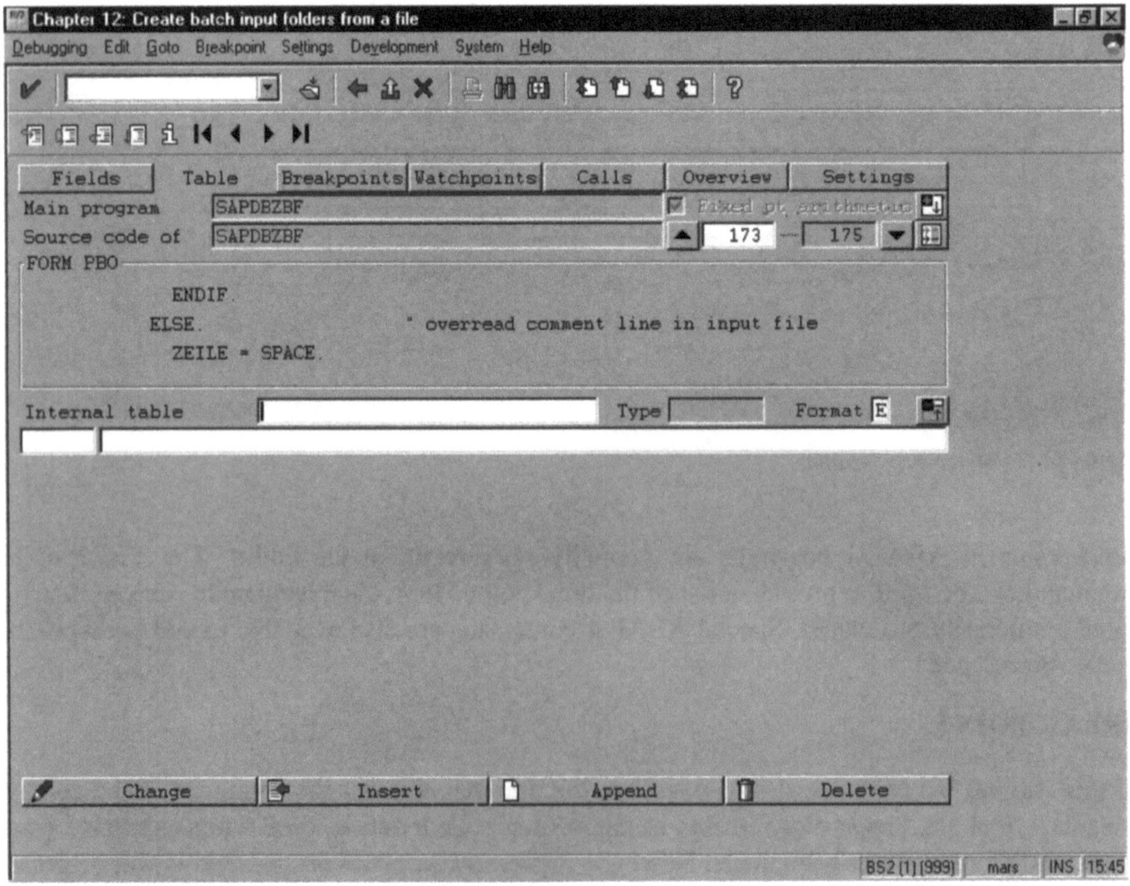

Figure 14.8: Debugger table mode

When breakpoints have been set, the Debugger is started automatically during the program execution if a breakpoint is reached. If you do not want to set any breakpoints, you can also directly start the report in debugging mode. The execution then stops at the first line of the report. Figure 14.7 shows the Debugger in "V" mode (variables). The user can now

- continue processing the program (like-wise)
- process forms and functions or jump into these
- display and change variables
- perform COMMIT WORK or ROLLBACK WORK.

The "T" mode is provided for the display of internal tables (Figure 14.8). Breakpoints have no effect in batch operation. If possible, do not set any breakpoints within select loops when debugging programs with database access.

14.5 SQL Trace

SQL Trace can be used to view the SQL accesses that Open SQL makes to the associated database. The *SystemlUtilities/SQL Trace* command must be used to activate the trace. The required program is then started. The trace can be obtained as list. The trace option then should be switched off.

Detail and *Explain SQL* can be used to obtain details and explanations for the associated SQL command. SQL Trace can also be used to obtain the sequence with which tables were accessed in the program.

14.6 Runtime Analyses

Error-free programs provide no guarantee that all requirements are satisfied with regard to performance. The runtime demands made on batch and online programs differ only quantitatively. Whereas the time savings for batch programs often represent hours or even days, 20 seconds can decide on the acceptance or non-acceptance of online programs.

The runtime analysis is an important tool to check the performance and to make specific tuning of programs. It is started using *System/Utilities/Runtime Analysis* (Figure 14.10).

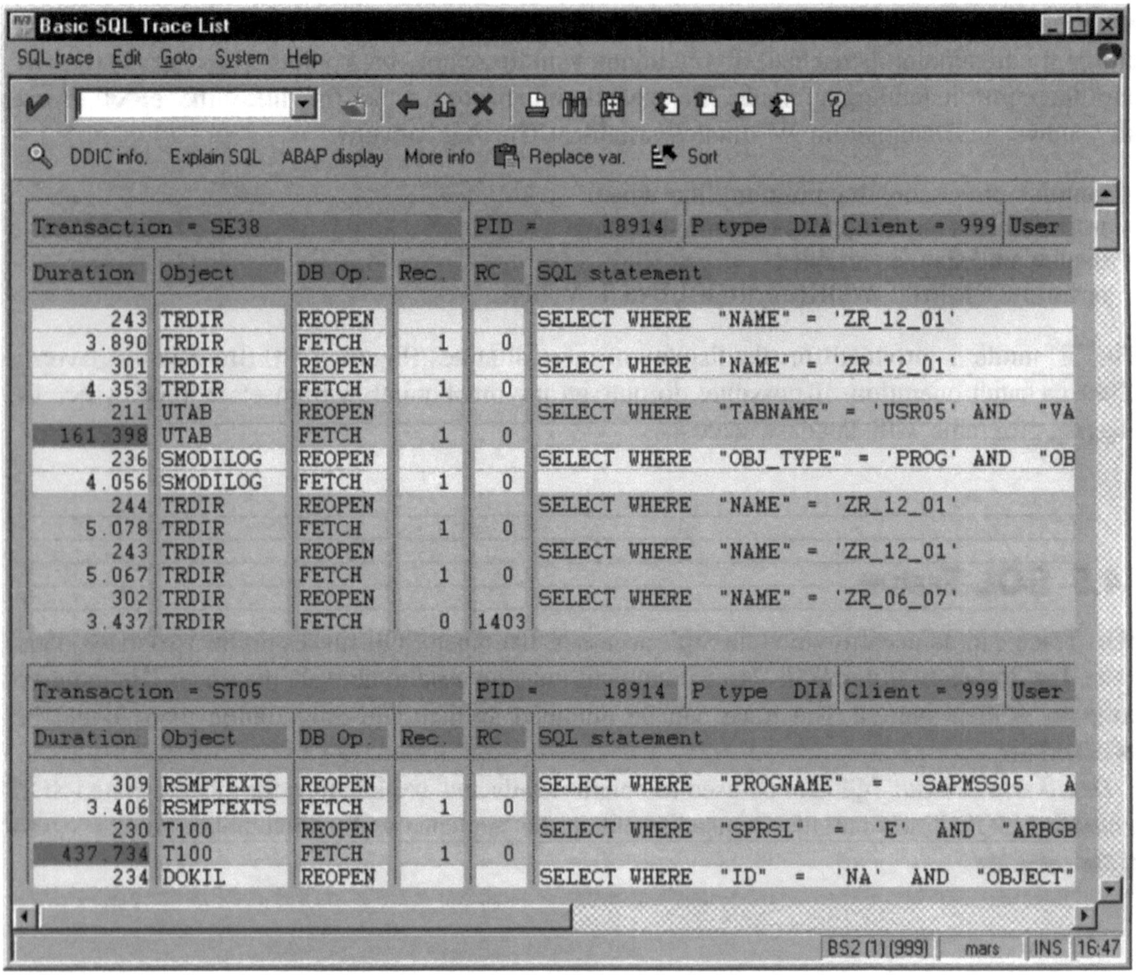

Figure 14.9: Result of the SQL Trace from program ZR-06-02

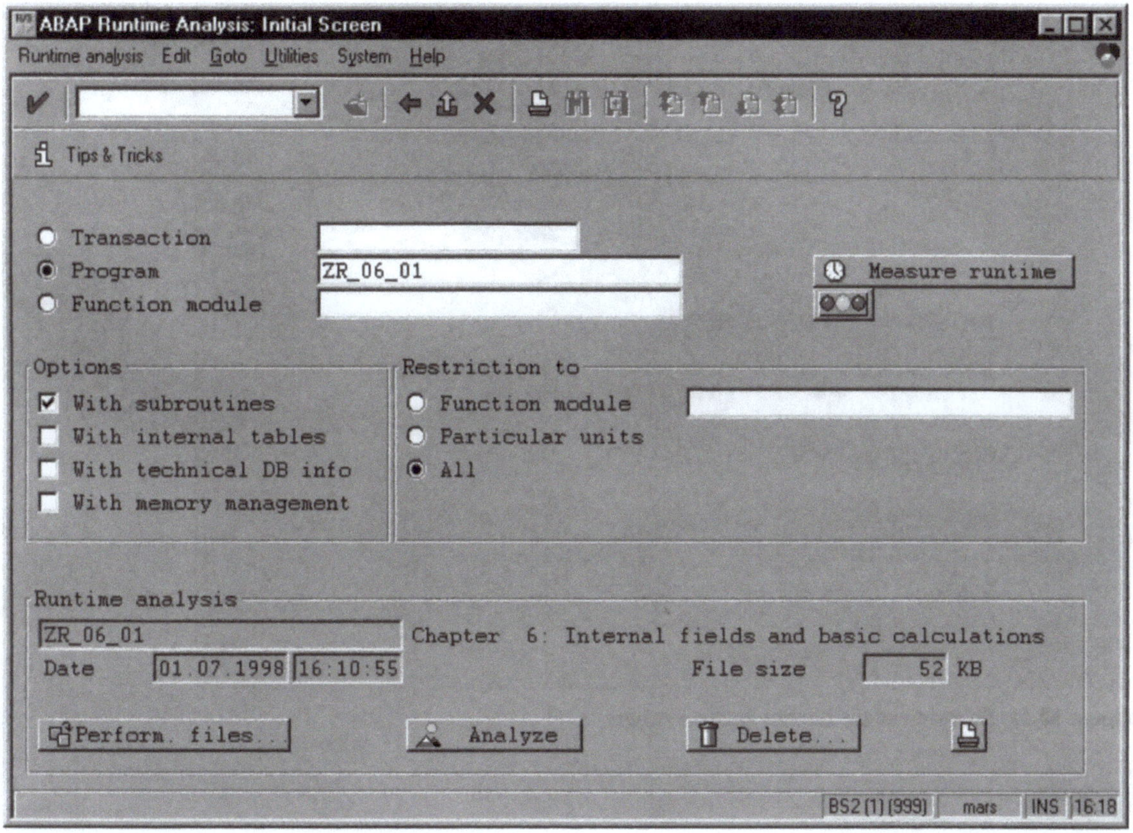

Figure 14.10: Entry into the runtime analysis

Figure 14.11 shows the analysis of the results. You receive a general distribution of the program runtime resulting from ABAP, database and system. Further steps provide more detailed information. It is also possible to display an invocation tree of those tables that have been used.

At this point, particular notice should be made on the tips and tricks integrated in the runtime analysis that can be started with the pushbutton in Figure 14.10. Efficient and less-efficient solutions for typical ABAP problems are compared here. The runtime measurements for both variants provide a very good indication of the various tuning capabilities.

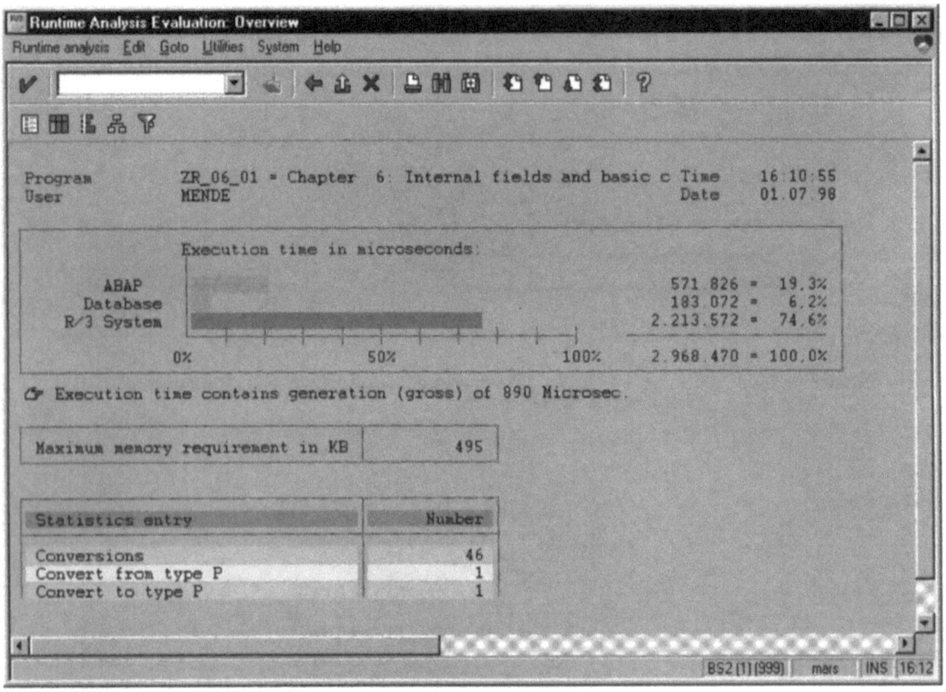

Figure 14.11: Overview of the runtime analysis results

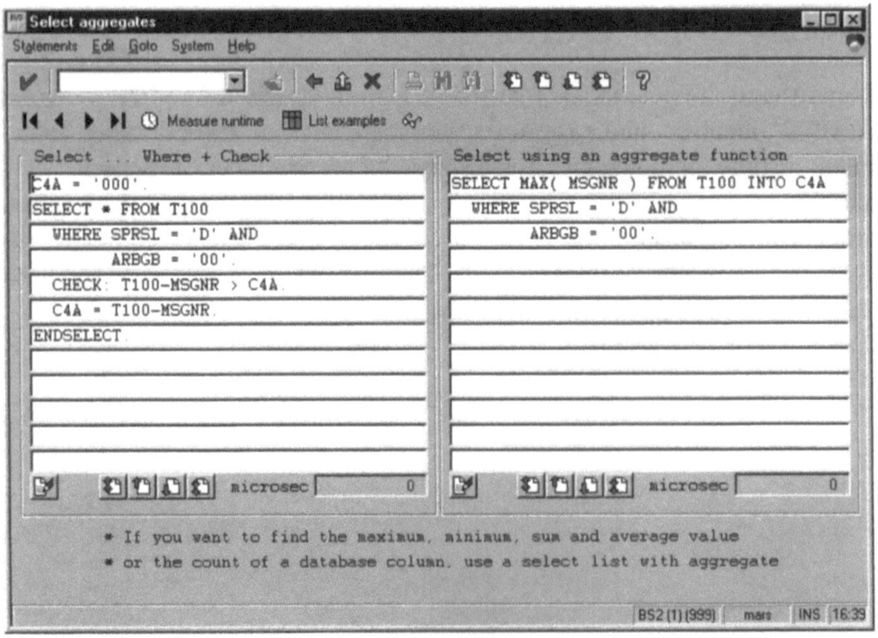

Figure 14.12: Runtime measurements within tips and tricks

Appendix

A Important System Fields from the SYST Structure

The system fields are grouped according to application and sorted alphabetically within the application. The system fields used most often are emphasized.

System Field	Type	Length	Meaning
Internal tables			
SY-TABIX	INT4	10	Runtime: Current line of an internal table
SY-TFILL	INT4	10	Current number of entries in internal table
SY-TLENG	INT4	10	Line width of an internal table
SY-TMAXL	INT4	10	Maximum number of entries in internal table
SY-TNAME	CHAR	30	Name of internal table after an access
SY-TOCCU	INT4	10	OCCURS parameter for internal tables
SY-TPAGI	INT4	10	Flag indicating roll-out of internal table
SY-TTABC	INT4	10	Number of line last read in an internal table
SY-TTABI	INT4	10	Offset of internal table in the roll area
Program			
SY-CPROG	CHAR	8	Runtime: Main program
SY-DBNAM	CHAR	2	Logical database for executable ABAP programs
SY-FDPOS	INT4	10	Location of a found string
SY-FMKEY	CHAR	3	Current function code menu
SY-INDEX	INT4	10	Number of loop passes
SY-LDBPG	CHAR	8	Program: ABAP database program for SY-DB
SY-MACDB	CHAR	4	Program: ABAP database program for SY-DB
SY-REPID	CHAR	8	Program: Name of ABAP program
SY-SUBRC	INT4	10	Return value after specific ABAP/4 state
SY-SUBTY	RAW	1	ABAP: Call type for SUBMIT
SY-TCODE	CHAR	4	Session: Current transaction code
SY-TITLE	CHAR	70	Title of ABAP program
SY-UCOMM	CHAR	70	Interact.: Command field function entry
SY-XCODE	CHAR	70	Extended command field

System Field	Type	Length	Meaning
Lists			
SY-COLNO	INT4	10	Current column during list creation
SY-CPAGE	INT4	10	Current page number
SY-CUCOL	INT4	10	Cursor position (column)
SY-CUROW	INT4	10	Cursor position (line)
SY-LILLI	INT4	10	Number of current list line
SY-LINCT	INT4	10	Number of list lines
SY-LINNO	INT4	10	Current line for list creation
SY-LINSZ	INT4	10	Current line for list creation
SY-LISEL	CHAR	255	Interact.: Selected line
SY-LISTI	INT4	10	Number of current list line
SY-LSIND	INT4	10	Number of secondary list
SY-LSTAT	CHAR	16	Interact.: Status information for each list
SY-PAGCT	INT4	10	Do not use this field any more
SY-PAGNO	INT4	10	Runtime: Current page in list
SY-STACO	INT4	10	Interact.: List displayed from column
SY-STARO	INT4	10	Interact.: Page displayed from line
SY-WTITL	CHAR	1	Standard page header indicator
Window			
SY-SCOLS	INT4	10	Standard page header indicator
SY-SROWS	INT4	10	Lines on screen
SY-WILLI	INT4	10	Number of current window line
SY-WINCO	INT4	10	Cursor position in window (column)
SY-WINDI	INT4	10	Index of current window line
SY-WINRO	INT4	10	Cursor position in window (line)
SY-WINSL	CHAR	79	Interact.: Selected window line
SY-WINX1	INT4	10	Window coordinate (column left)
SY-WINX2	INT4	10	Window coordinate (column right)
SY-WINY1	INT4	10	Window coordinate (line left)
SY-WINY2	INT4	10	Window coordinate (line right)
SY-Dynpro			
SY-DYNGR	CHAR	4	Screen group of current screen
SY-DYNNR	CHAR	4	Number of current screen
SY-LOOPC	INT4	10	Number of LOOP lines at screen step loop
SY-STEPL	INT4	10	Number of LOOP line at screen step

Print			
SY-CALLR	CHAR	8	Print: ID for print dialog function
SY-PAART	CHAR	16	Print: Format
SY-PDEST	CHAR	4	Print: Output device
SY-PEXPI	NUMC	1	PRINT: Spool retention period
SY-PLIST	CHAR	12	Print: Name of spool request (list name)
SY-PRABT	CHAR	12	Print: Department on cover sheet
SY-PRBIG	CHAR	1	Print: Selection cover sheet
SY-PRCOP	NUMC	3	Print: Number of copies
SY-PRDSN	CHAR	6	Print: Name of spool dataset
SY-PRIMM	CHAR	1	PRINT: Print immediately
SY-PRNEW	CHAR	1	PRINT: New spool request (list)
SY-PRREC	CHAR	12	Print: Recipient
SY-PRREL	CHAR	1	PRINT: Delete after printing
SY-PRTXT	CHAR	68	Print: Text for cover sheet
SY-RTITL	CHAR	70	Print: Report title of print program
Date, time			
SY-DAYST	CHAR	1	Is 'daylight saving time' active?
SY-FDAYW	INT1	3	Factory calendar weekday
SY-TSTLO	NUMC	14	User's timestamp
SY-TZONE	INT4	10	Time difference from Greenwich Mean Time
SY-ZONLO	CHAR	6	User's timezone
Currency/rate			
SY-CCURS	DEC	9	Rate specification/result field (CURRENCY CONVERT)
SY-CCURT	DEC	9	Table rate from currency conversion
SY-CDATE	DATS	8	Date of rate from currency conversion
SY-CTABL	CHAR	4	Exchange rate table from currency conversion
SY-CTYPE	CHAR	1	Exchange rate type 'M','B','G' from CURRENCY CONV.
SY-WAERS	CUKY	5	T001: Company code currency after reading
System			
SY-APPLI	RAW	2	SAP applications
SY-BATCH	CHAR	1	Batch active (X)
SY-BINPT	CHAR	1	Batch-input active (X)
SY-CALLD	CHAR	1	Call-mode active (X)
SY-DATUM	DATS	8	SYSTEM: Current date
SY-DBSYS	CHAR	10	System: Database system
SY-DCSYS	CHAR	4	System: Dialog system
SY-HOST	CHAR	8	Host

SY-LANGU	LANG	1	Language key from SAP logon
SY-MANDT	CLNT	3	Client number from SAP logon
SY-MODNO	CHAR	1	Number of alternative sessions
SY-OPSYS	CHAR	10	System: Operating system
SY-SAPRL	CHAR	4	System: SAP release
SY-SYSID	CHAR	8	System: SAP system ID
SY-UNAME	CHAR	12	Session: SAP user from SAP logon
SY-UZEIT	TIMS	6	SYSTEM: Time
Batch			
SY-BATZD	CHAR	1	Background SUBMIT: Daily
SY-BATZM	CHAR	1	Background SUBMIT: Monthly
SY-BATZO	CHAR	1	Background SUBMIT: One-off
SY-BATZS	CHAR	1	Background SUBMIT: Immediately
SY-BATZW	CHAR	1	Background SUBMIT: Weekly
SY-BREP4	CHAR	4	Background SUBMIT: Root name of request
SY-BSPLD	CHAR	1	Background SUBMIT: List output to spool
SY-PREFX	CHAR	3	ABAP prefix for background jobs
Runtime			
SY-ABCDE	CHAR	26	Constant: Alphabet (A,B,C,...)
SY-DATAR	CHAR	1	Flag: Data received
SY-DSNAM	CHAR	8	Runtime: Name of dataset for spool output
SY-PFKEY	CHAR	8	Runtime: Current PF key status
SY-SPONO	NUMC	5	Runtime: Spool number for list output
SY-SPONR	NUMC	5	Runtime: Spool number from TRANSFER statement
SY-TFDSN	CHAR	8	Runtime: Dataset for data extracts
Messages			
SY-MSGID	CHAR	2	Message-ID
SY-MSGLI	CHAR	60	Interact.: Message line (line 23)
SY-MSGNO	NUMC	3	Message-Number
SY-MSGTY	CHAR	1	Message-Type (E, I, W, ...)
SY-MSGV1	CHAR	50	Message variable
SY-MSGV2	CHAR	50	Message variable
SY-MSGV3	CHAR	50	Message variable
SY-MSGV4	CHAR	50	Message variable

B Important Transaction Codes

The following table contains important transaction codes. These codes can be used in the following manner to invoke transactions:

- Start the transactions using the command field with one of the prefixes
  /n invoke transaction in the same mode
  /o invoke transaction in a new mode
  /h invoke transaction in debug mode
- Start the transaction from an area menu
- Start the transaction from a program using
  START TRANSACTION
  CALL TRANSACTION

Code	Functionality
S00	Short message
SA38	ABAP Reporting
SA39	SA38 for Parameter Transaction
SAR	Maintain Transaction Codes
SAR0	Display Standard Reporting Tree
SCC0	Client Copy
SD11	Data Modeler
SDMO	Dynamic Menu (old)
SDW0	ABAP/4 Development WB Initial Screen
SE01	Transport Organizer
SE09	Workbench Organizer
SE11	ABAP/4 Dictionary Maintenance
SE12	ABAP/4 Dictionary Display
SE13	Maintain Technical Settings (Tables)
SE14	Utilities for Dictionary Tables
SE15	ABAP/4 Repository Information System
SE16	Data Browser
SE17	General Table Display
SE30	ABAP Runtime Analysis
SE36	ABAP/4: Logical Databases
SE37	ABAP/4: Function Modules
SE38	ABAP/4: Editor
SE39	Split-screen Editor: Program Compare
SE41	Menu Painter
SE43	Maintain Area Menu

Code	Functionality
SE51	Screen Painter
SE80	Repository Browser
SE86	ABAP/4 Repository Information System
SEU	Repository Browser
SM02	System Messages
SM04	User Overview
SM12	Display and Delete Locks
SM21	System Log
SM30	Call View Maintenance
SM31	Table Maintenance
SM35	Batch Input Monitoring
SM36	Define Background Job
SM37	Background Job Overview
SM50	Work Process Overview
SM64	Release of an Event
SM65	Background Processing Analysis Tool
SM66	System-wide Work Process Overview
SM67	Job Scheduling
SM68	Job Administration
SO00	SAPoffice: Short message
SU01	User Maintenance
SU02	Maintain Authorization Profiles
SU03	Maintain Authorizations

C Programs

The listed programs are described in the indicated chapters. The list created for each report is also described. The table data in Appendix D can be used to check the listings. The programs are grouped according to level of difficulty: *easy*, *medium* and *difficult*.

Program	Chapter	Description	Level
ZI_00_01		Download source code with log	medium
ZR_06_01	6	Internal fields and basic calculations	easy
ZR_06_02	6	Internal fields and functions	easy
ZR_06_03	6	Date arithmetic	easy
ZR_06_04	6	Output statements	easy
ZR_06_05	6	IF-Statement	easy
ZR_06_06	6	String operators	easy
ZR_06_07	6	Logical operators	easy
ZR_06_08	6	CASE statement	easy
ZR_06_09	6	DO loop	easy
ZR_06_10	6	WHILE loop	easy
ZR_06_11	6	Structures defined with INCLUDE STRUCTURE	easy
ZR_06_12	6	Structures defined with LIKE	easy
ZR_06_13	6	Internal tables: LOOP and WHILE	easy
ZR_06_14	6	Internal tables: APPEND	easy
ZR_06_15	6	Internal tables: MODIFY and DELETE	easy
ZR_06_16	6	Complex data types	medium
ZR_06_17	6	Field symbols	easy
ZR_06_21	6	Selection of partners with ZIP-code like 9%	easy
ZR_06_22	6	Select all accounts into an internal table	easy
ZR_06_23	6	Combined SELECTs and view	medium
ZR_06_24	6	COMMIT WORK and ROLLBACK WORK	easy
ZR_06_25	6	Dynamic select	medium
ZR_06_26	6	Native SQL with subselect to DB/2	medium
ZR_06_27	6	Native SQL to DB/2	easy
ZR_07_01	7	Event control in reports	easy
ZR_07_02	7	Details lists	medium
ZR_07_03	7	Control break with ON CHANGE OF	medium
ZR_07_04	7	Control break with AT NEW	medium

Program	Chapter	Description	Level
ZR_08_01	8	Macro definitions for program generation	easy
ZR_08_02	8	Form with table parameters	easy
ZR_08_03	8	Forms with complex parameters	medium
ZR_08_04	8	Recursive calculation of faculties	medium
ZR_08_05	8	Recursive path search inside a net	difficult
ZR_08_06	8	Call of a reports with SUBMIT	medium
ZR_08_07	8	EXPORT TO MEMORY and SET PARAMETER	easy
ZR_08_08	8	IMPORT FROM MEMORY and GET PARAMETER	easy
ZR_08_09	8	Report on ZDF logic database	medium
ZM_09_01	9	Screen elements in dialog programs	easy
ZM_09_02	9	Calculator	medium
ZM_09_03	9	Dialog for document entry	difficult
ZR_09_04	9	Two table controls on one screen	difficult
ZR_10_01	10	Creating and starting a batch job	medium
ZR_10_02	10	Reading a job log	medium
ZR_11_01	11	Read a file from the workstation, output to appl. server	easy
ZR_11_02	11	Download of a report with line numbers	medium
ZR_11_03	11	Split lines into single fields	medium
ZR_11_04	11	Generating a logical file interface	difficult
ZR_11_05	11	Buffered reading of a control table	difficult
ZR_11_06	11	Processing data with ZLF logical file interface	medium
ZR_12_01	12	Create batch input folders from a file	medium
ZR_12_02	12	Batch input using CALL TRANSACTION	medium
ZR_13_01	13	RFC call between two R/3 systems	medium
ZR_13_02	13	ABAP as OLE client on an EXCEL server	medium
ZR_13_03	13	ABAP as OLE client with WinWord	medium

D Sample Tables

ZPOSTK Table

Field	Key	Type/ Length	Data Element	Domain	Significance
MANDT	X	CLNT 3	MANDT	MANDT	Client
PSTKY	X	NUMC 3	PSTKY_DE	PSTKY _DO	Posting key

ZPOSTKYT Table

Field	Key	Type/Len.	Data Element	Domain	Significance
MANDT	X	CLNT 3	MANDT	MANDT	Client
SPRAS	X	LONG1	SPRAS	SPRAS	Language key
PSTKY	X	NUMC 3	PSTKY_DE	PSTKY_DO	Posting key
PSTKYT		CHAR 20	PSTKYT_DE	PSTKYT_DO	Posting key text

MANDT	LANGU	PSTKY	PSTKYT
101	E	1	Part benefits
101	E	2	Prepayment
101	E	3	Manual posting
101	E	4	Delay interest
101	E	5	Payment on account
101	E	6	Illness
101	E	7	Back-payment
101	E	8	Net premium
101	E	9	Refund

ZPARTNER Table

Field	Key	Type/ Length	Data Element	Domain	Significance
MANDT	X	CLNT 3	MANDT	MANDT	Client
PARTNO R	X	NUMC 8	ZPARTNO DE	PARTNO DO	Partner number
SNAME		CHAR 15	ZSNAME DE	CHAR15	Second name
FNAME		CHAR 15	ZFNAME DE	CHAR15	First name
TITLE		CHAR 10	ZTITLE DE	CHAR10	Title
SEX		CHAR 1	ZSEX DE	ZSEX DE	Sex
STREET		CHAR 30	ZSTREET DE	STREET DO	Street
TOWN		CHAR 16	ZTOWN DE	CHAR16	Town
ZIP		CHAR 5	ZZIP DE	CHAR5	ZIP-code

MANDT	PARTNO	LNAME	FNAME	TITLE	SEX	STREET	TOWN	ZIP-CODE
101	1000	Stone	Sharon	Mrs.	F	P.O. Box 4123	Hollywood	90028
101	1001	Stone	Paul	Mr. Dr.	M	P.O. Box 4123	Hollywood	90028
101	1002	Black	Frank	Mr.	M	6000 Uni Parkway	San Bernadino	92407
101	1003	Black	Jane	Mrs. Dr.	F	6000 Uni Parkway	San Bernadino	92407
101	1004	Huesing	Wanda	Mrs.	F	5550 Carpenteria Avenue	Carpenteria	93013
101	1005	Wolf	Peter	Mr.	M	2229 East University Drive	Pheonix	85034
101	1006	Wolf	Mary-Ann	Mrs. Dr.	F	2229 East University Drive	Phoenix	85034
101	1007	Smith	John	Mr.	M	1105 Santa Barbara Street	Santa Barbara	90028
101	1008	Hernandez	Miguel	Mr. Dr.	M	732 Union	Romeoville	60441
101	1009	Hernandez	Maria	Mrs.	F	733 Union	Romeoville	60441
101	1010	Li	Anh	Mrs.	F	P.O. Box 5422	Hattisburg	39406

ZPRODUCT Table

Field	Key	Type/ Length	Data Element	Domain	Significance
MANDT	X	CLNT 3	MANDT	MANDT	Client
PRODNO	X	NUMC 8	ZPRODNO DE	ZPRODNR DO	Product number
PRODGRP		CHAR 5	ZPRODGRP DE	ZPRODGR DO	Product group
PRODTXT		CHAR 20	ZPRODTXT_DE	CHAR20	Product text

MANDT	PRODNO	PRODGRP	PRODTXT
101	2000	PI	Third-party insurance
101	2001	PI	Third-party insurance
101	2002	PI	Car third-party insurance
101	2003	PI	Car third-party insurance
101	2004	PI	Car fully-comprehensive insurance
101	2005	PI	Car fully-comprehensive insurance
101	2006	PI	Car fully-comprehensive insurance
101	2007	PI	Passenger insurance
101	2008	LI	Life insurance
101	2009	LI	Life insurance
101	2010	LI	Term life insurance
101	2011	LI	Pension plan
101	2012	LI	Pension plan
101	2013	LI	Group insurance

ZCONTRACT Table

Field	Key	Type/ Length	Data Ele-ment	Domain	Significance
MANDT	X	CLNT 3	MANDT	MANDT	Client
CONTNO	X	NUMC 8	ZCONTNO_DE	ZCONTNO_DO	Contract number
PARTNO		NUMC 8	ZPARTNO_DE	ZPARTNO_DO	Partner number
PRODNO		NUMC 8	ZPRODNO_DO	ZPRODNO_DO	Product number
ACCNO		NUMC 8	ZACCNO_DO	ZACCNO_DO	Account number
STARTDAT		DATS 8	ZSTARTDAT_DE	DATE	Starting date of contract
ENDDAT		DATS 8	ZENDDAT_DE	DATE	End date of contract
BASAM		CURR 13	ZBASAM_DE	CURRV13	Basic amount
CURRKY		CUKY 5	CURRKY_DE	WAERS	Currency key
OFFERV_		CHAR 1	ZOFFERV_DE	XFELD	Offer validity

MANDT	CONTNO	PARTNR	PRODNO	ACCNO	STARTDAT	ENDDAT	BASAM	CUURKY	OFFERV
101	3000	1001	2001	4001	19960723	20060712	1200	USD	
101	3001	1002	2002	4002	19960723	20060712	1450	USD	X
101	3002	1003	2003	4003	19960723	20060712	1700	USD	
101	3003	1004	2004	4004	19960723	20060712	1950	USD	
101	3004	1001	2005	4005	19960723	20060712	2200	USD	
101	3005	1001	2006	4001	19960723	20060712	2450	USD	
101	3006	1005	2002	4007	19960723	20060712	2700	USD	
101	3007	1006	2004	4008	19960723	20060712	2950	USD	
101	3008	1007	2003	4009	19960723	20060712	3200	USD	
101	3009	1008	2001	4010	19960723	20060712	3450	USD	
101	3010	1009	2005	4012	19960723	20060712	3700	USD	
101	3011	1010	2705	4130	19960723	20060712	3950	USD	
101	3012	1001	2006	4014	19960723	20060712	4200	USD	
101	3013	1010	2004	4010	19960723	20060712	4450	USD	X
101	3014	1005	2000	4002	19960723	20060712	4700	USD	
101	3015	1008	2001	4003	19960723	20060712	4950	USD	
101	3016	1001	2002	4004	19960723	20060712	5200	USD	
101	3017	1009	2005	4005	19960723	20060712	5450	USD	X

ZACCOUNT Table

Field	Key	Type/ Length	Data Element	Domain	Significance
MANDT	X	CLNT 3	MANDT	MANDT	Client
ACCNO	X	NUMC 8	ZACCNO_DE	ZACCNO_DO	Account number
ACCTP		CHAR 1	ZACCTP_DE	YKONTNO_DO	Account type
BLOCK		CHAR 1	ZBLOCK_DE	XFELD	Account blocked

MANDT	ACCNO	ACCTP	BLOCK
101	4000	P	
101	4001	P	
101	4002	P	
101	4003	P	X
101	4004	K	
101	4005	P	
101	4006	P	X
101	4007	K	
101	4008	P	
101	4009	P	
101	4010	P	
101	4011	P	
101	4012	P	

ZDOCHD Table

Field	Key	Type/ Length	Data Element	Domain	Significance
MANDT	X	CLNT 3	MANDT	MANDT	Client
DOCNO	X	NUMC 8	ZDOCNO_DE	ZDOCNO_DE	Document number
CCODE		CHAR 4	BUKRS	BUKRS	Company code
CONTNO		NUMC 8	ZCONTNO_DE	EZCONTNO_DO	Contract number
ACCNO		NUMC 8	ZACCNO_DE	EYKONTNR_DO	Account number
DOCTYPE		CHAR 5	ZDOCTYP_DE	ZDOCTYP_DO	Document type
CURRKY		CUKY 5	CURRKY	WAERS	Currency key
PSTDAT		DATS 8	ZPSTDAT_DE	DATE	Posting date
DOCTXT		CHAR 20	ZDOCTXT_DE	ECHAR20	Document text

MAND	DOCN	CCODE	CONTNO	ACCNO	DOCTY	CURRKY	PSTDAT	BELTXT
DOCT	5000	1	3001	4001	EB	USD	19960824	Doctext01
101	5001	1	3001	4001	EB	USD	19960824	Doctext02
101	5002	1	3002	4001	ER	USD	19960824	Doctext03
101	5003	1	3003	4002	EB	USD	19960824	Doctext04
101	5004	1	3003	4002	EB	USD	19960824	Doctext05
101	5005	1	3004	4003	EB	USD	19960824	Doctext06
101	5006	1	3007	4004	FB	USD	19960824	Doctext07
101	5007	1	3007	4011	EB	USD	19960824	Doctext08
101	5008	1	3007	4012	EB	USD	19960824	Doctext09
101	5009	1	3006	4003	EB	USD	19960824	Doctext10
101	5010	1	3003	4008	FB	USD	19960824	Doctext11
101	5011	1	3005	4010	EB	USD	19960824	Doctext12
101	5012	1	3005	4010	EB	USD	19960824	Doctext13
101	5013	1	3005	4005	EB	USD	19960824	Doctext14
101	5014	1	3005	4005	EB	USD	19960824	Doctext15
101	5015	1	3006	4001	ER	USD	19960824	Doctext16
101	5016	1	3010	4007	FB	USD	19960824	Doctext17
101	5017	1	3011	4007	ER	USD	19960824	Doctext18
101	5018	1	3012	4007	EB	USD	19960824	Doctext19

ZDOCITEM Table

Field	Key	Type/Len	Data Ele-	Domain	Significance
MANDT	X	CLNT 3	MANDT	MANDT	Client
DOCNO	X	NUMC 8	ZDOCNO_DE	ZDOCNO_DO	Document number
ITEMNO	X	NUMC 3	ZITEMNO_DE	NUMC3	Item number
PSTKY		NUMC 3	ZPSTKY_DE	ZPSTKY_DO	Posting key
AMOUNT		CURR 13	ZAMOUNT_DE	CURRV13	Amount
ENDDAT		DATS 8	ZENDDAT_DE	DATE	End date
ITEMTXT		CHAR 20	ZITEMTXT_DE	CHAR20	Item text

MANDT	BELNR	POSNR	BUGRD	WRBTR	FAEDAT	POSTXT
101	5006	2	6	50	19970415	Itemtext025
101	5007	1	7	2950	19970515	Itemtext026
101	5007	2	2	100	19970515	Itemtext027
101	5008	1	3	2950	19970615	Itemtext028
101	5009	1	5	2700	19970801	Itemtext029
101	5009	2	5	100	19970801	Itemtext030
101	5010	1	1	1950	19970201	Itemtext031
101	5011	1	9	2450	19970720	Itemtext032
101	5011	2	4	200	19970720	Itemtext033
101	5011	3	6	10	19970720	Itemtext034
101	5012	1	7	2450	19970820	Itemtext035
101	5012	2	7	50	19970820	Itemtext036
101	5013	1	2	2450	19970301	Itemtext037
101	5014	1	1	2450	19970301	Itemtext038
101	5014	2	9	50	19970301	Itemtext039
101	5015	1	3	2700	19970525	Itemtext040
101	5016	1	2	3700	19970513	Itemtext041
101	5016	2	5	60	19970513	Itemtext042
101	5017	1	5	3950	19970606	Itemtext043
101	5018	1	7	4200	19970201	Itemtext044

E Diskette Contents

The diskette for the book contains the TRANSP and UPLOAD directories.

TRANSP Directory

All development objects (domains, data elements, tables, matchcodes, logical databases, message classes, programs, etc.) used in the examples for this book have been assigned to the ZABP development class. The TRANSP directory contains all the files needed for a transport of the YABP development class into (unknown) R/3-system DUM (Dummy). The following steps must be performed:

- First use FTP (WinFTP) to copy the following files in binary mode to the R/3 transport directory "/usr/sap/trans" (UNIX) or "drive\USR\SAP\TRANS" (Windows NT):
  - D900172.BV1 to /usr/sap/trans/data (correspondingly for Windows NT)
  - R900172.BV1 to /usr/sap/trans/data (correspondingly for Windows NT)
  - K900172.BV1 to /usr/sap/trans/cofiles (correspondingly for Windows NT)

  In UNIX, all file names must be stored in uppercase and <sid>adm as owner.
- The order with the name "BV1K900172" then must be placed in the import buffer of the customer system:
  - Login as <sid>adm
  - cd /usr/sap/trans/bin
  - tp addtobuffer BV1K900172 <SID>

  Then start the import with the following command:
  - tp import BV1K900172 <SID> client=<targetclient> U1

  Because the "DUM" SID was exported, the U1 *unconditional mode* is significant.

UPLOAD Directory

The UPLOAD directory contains all source code for the sample programs of the book (reports, includes, module pools, procedures, function modules). The *Upload* command can be used to load *individual* source code into the Workbench editor. The procedure is particularly suitable for those reports that do not access the tables of the ZABP development class, e.g., for the ZR_11_04 report to generate logical file interfaces.

The ZLF.XLS Excel folder also contains all sample tables. The ErstelleAsciiDatei() Excel macro, also contained in this folder, can be used to write these sample tables into a text file ZLF.TXT. The ZR_11_06 report can import this file into the system once the tables have been created.

Bibliography

Buck-Emden, Rüdiger; Galimov, Jürgen:
SAP R/3 System – A Client Server Technology
Addison-Wesley, 1996

Hanusch, Thomas; Matzke, Bernd; Perez, Mario:
SAP R/3 On The Internet
Addison-Wesley, 1998

Keller, Gerhard; Teufel,Thomas:
SAP R/3 Process Oriented Implementation
Iterative Process Prototyping
Addison-Wesley, 1997

Kretschmer, Rüdiger; Weiss, Wolfgang:
SAP R/3 Development with ABAP/4
Sybex, 1996

Matzke, Bernd:
ABAP/4. The Programming Language of SAP´s System R/3
Addison-Wesley, 1996

Will, Liane; Hienger, Christiane; Straßenburg, Frank; Himmer, Rocco:
SAP R/3 – Administration
Addison-Wesley, 1997

Index

P

R

S

T

U

V

W

MIX
Papier aus verantwortungsvollen Quellen
Paper from responsible sources
FSC® C105338

If you have any concerns about our products,
you can contact us on
ProductSafety@springernature.com

In case Publisher is established outside the EU,
the EU authorized representative is:
Springer Nature Customer Service Center GmbH
Europaplatz 3, 69115 Heidelberg, Germany

Printed by Libri Plureos GmbH
in Hamburg, Germany